Matins with the Fathers:
Patristic Commentaries for the Office of Matins

Athanasius Schneider

Matins with the Fathers: Patristic Commentaries for the Office of Matins

BENEDICTUS BOOKS
Manchester, NH

BENEDICTUS
BOOKS

Benedictus Books
Box 5284, Manchester, NH 03108
1-800-888-9344

www.PrayBenedictus.com

ISBN 979-8-88911-542-7

eBook ISBN 979-8-88911-543-4

Library of Congress Control Number: 2025937480

First printing

CONTENTS

Introduction 3

Tempus Adventus...7

Tempus Nativitatis 30

Tempus Post Epiphaniam 34

Tempus Septuagesimae.. 75

Tempus Quadregesimae 91

Tempus Paschale 101

Tempore Post Pentecosten.. 132

Adnotationes Biographicae Auctorum 358

Matins with the Fathers:
Patristic Commentaries for the Office of Matins

INTRODUCTION

THE Fathers of the Church are the privileged witnesses of Sacred Tradition and authoritative teachers of the Catholic Faith. They lived, taught, and remained faithful to the Catholic Faith within the communion of the Church in a holy, wise, and constant manner; and gave their lives for Jesus Christ either through a courageous confession of faith, as confessors, or through martyrdom.[1] "In the flow of living Tradition that continues from the beginning of Christianity over the centuries up to our present time, they occupy an entirely special place which makes them stand out compared with other protagonists of the history of the Church. They laid down the first basic structures of the Church together with the doctrinal and pastoral positions that remain valid for all times."[2] Well known is the phrase of St. John Henry Newman: "The Fathers made me a Catholic."[3]

The Fathers of the Church were primarily commentators on Sacred Scripture. "They are still true teachers for us and superior in many ways to the exegetes of the modern era."[4] The Fathers interpreted Holy Scripture in the only appropriate atmosphere to deal with the Word of God, that is, one of prayer, contemplation, and of fidelity to the Church's teaching, according to the rule of the faith (*regula fidei*) as proposed by the apostolic tradition. "They instructed the Church with what they themselves learned from the Church,"[5] as St. Augustine said, and "what they found in the Church they kept; what they learned they were teaching; what

---

1   See St. Vincent of Lerins, *Commonitorium* 28, 6.

2   Congregation for Catholic Education, *Instruction on the Study of the Fathers of the Church in the Formation of Priests* (November 10, 1989), no. 18.

3   *Difficulties Felt by Anglicans in Catholic Teaching* (London: Burns, Oates, 1872), 376.

4   *Instruction on the Study of the Fathers*, no. 26.

5   *Contra Julianum, Op. imperfectum*, 1, 117.

they received from the fathers they taught the children."[6] The exegesis or biblical interpretation of the Fathers "is entirely centered on the mystery of Christ to whom all the individual truths are referred in a wonderful synthesis. Rather than getting lost in numerous marginal problems, the Fathers embrace the totality of the Christian mystery by following the basic movement of Revelation and of the economy of salvation that goes from God through Christ to the Church, sacrament of union with God and dispenser of divine grace, in order to return to God."[7]

The Roman Breviary lacks Patristic commentaries for the ferial office; an office which could be spiritually and doctrinally enriched by the inestimable treasure of the exegesis of the Fathers. The present collection of Patristic biblical commentaries has therefore been compiled as a help for the spiritual life, as well as an aid in strengthening the Catholic Faith and promoting a living and tender love for the Word of God among the faithful. Indeed, as St. Basil the Great said, the distinctive mark of the faithful consists in "conforming their lives with the same complete certainty to the meaning of the words of Scripture, not daring to remove or add a single thing."[8]

Our Lady is our supreme example of love for the Word of God; both incarnate and living within her in the Person of Our Lord Jesus Christ, and written in the pages of Sacred Scripture, because "the entire Scripture is only one book that speaks of Christ."[9] The Blessed Virgin Mary, in the words of St. Jerome, "had read the sacred Scriptures, knew the prophets, and recalled that the angel Gabriel had said to her the same things that the prophets had foretold. She looked at her newborn child, her only son, lying in the manger and crying. What she saw was, in fact, the Son of God; she compared what she saw with all that she had read and heard."[10]

6   *Ibid.*, 2, 10, 34.
7   *Instruction on the Study of the Fathers*, 27.
8   *Moralia*, Regula 80, 22.
9   St. Augustine, *Enarratio in Psalmum 103*, 4, 1.
10   *Homilia de Nativitate Domini*, 4.

May the intercession of the same Blessed Virgin, Mother of the Word incarnate, graciously accompany all who take up these pages in order to deepen their encounter with the living Word of God through the exegesis of the great Church Fathers.

—January 1st, of the Jubilee Year 2025
✠ *Athanasius Schneider, Auxiliary Bishop of the*
Archdiocese of Saint Mary in Astana

TEMPUS ADVENTUS

INFRA HEBDOMADAM I ADVENTUS

Feria Secunda: Is 1:16–28

S. Joannes Chrysostomus, *Commentarius in sanctum Joannem Apostolum et Evangelistam* (hom. 69, 3)

Cur corpus ornas, dum animam impuritate correptam negliges? Cur non tantam animae quantam corpori curam impendis, cum majorem opporteret? Dic, quaeso, si quis te interroget, quid malueris, an corpus tuum vegetum formosumque esse ac vilibus indutum vestibus, an mutilum, morbosum et auro ornatum, annon optares potius in natura corporis pulchra gaudere forma, quam vestium ambitu? an in corpore sic optares, in anima secus? ac dum illam turpem, deformem, nigram habes, ex aureis ornamentis te fructum percipere putas? Quaenam haec amentia? Ornatum in interiora verte, et torquibus illis animam circumda. Nam quae circum corpus ponuntur, neque ad valetudinem, neque ad formam

Why do you adorn your body, while your soul is neglected, possessed by uncleanness? Why do you not bestow as much thought upon your soul as on your body? You ought to bestow greater. For tell me, if any one asked you which you would choose, that your body should be fresh and of good habit and surpassing in beauty, and wear mean raiment, or having the body deformed and full of diseases, to wear gold and finery; would you not much prefer to have beauty depending on the nature of your person, than on the raiment with which you are clothed? And will you choose this in the case of your body, but the contrary in the case of your soul; and, when you have that ugly and unsightly and black, do you think to gain anything from golden ornaments? What

juvant: non nigrum album reddunt, neque quod turpe est formosum efficiunt. Haec autem si animae circumponas, cito illam pro nigra albam reddes, pro turpi et deformi, pulchram et formosam. Non meus hic sermo est, sed Domini dicentis: "Si fuerint peccata vestra ut coccinum, ut nivem dealbabo" (Is 1:18).

madness is this! Shift this adorning within, put these necklaces about your soul. The things that are put about your body help neither to its health nor to its beauty, for it will not make black white, nor what is ugly either beautiful or good looking. But if you put them about your soul, you shall soon make it white instead of black, instead of ugly and unsightly, you shall make it beautiful and well-favored. The words are not mine, but those of the Lord Himself, Who says, "Though your sins be as scarlet, I will make them white as snow" (Is 1:18).

Feria Tertia: Is 2:1–9
S. Leandrus Hispalensis, *Homilia in laudem ecclesiae*

"Erit in novissimis diebus praeparatus mons domus Domini in vertice montium, et elevabitur super colles, et fluent ad eum omnes gentes, et ibunt populi multi, et dicent: Venite ascendamus ad montem Domini, et ad domum Dei Jacob" (Is 2:1–3). Mons enim Christus est, et domus Dei Jacob, una Ecclesia est ejus, ad quam, et gentium concursum, et populorum pronuntiat confluere conventum. Qui, ut notesceret quae

"In the last days the mountain of the Lord's house will be prepared on the top of the mountains, and it will be raised above the hills, and all nations will flow to it, and many peoples will go and say: Come, let us go up to the mountain of the Lord, and to the house of the God of Jacob" (Is 2:1–3). For the mountain is Christ, and the house of the God of Jacob is His one Church, to which He pronounces the confluence of the nations and the as-

ventura essent genti, vel populo, quae ab unius Ecclesiae communione recidissent, secutus est: "gens enim, et regnum, quod non servierit tibi, peribit" (Is 60:12). Alio denique loco similiter ait: "Ecce gentem, quam nesciebas, vocabis; et gentes, quae non cognoverunt te, ad te current" (Is 55:5). Unus enim est Christus Dominus, cujus est una per totum mundum Ecclesia, sancta possessio; ille igitur caput, et ista corpus, de quibus in principio Genesis dicitur: "Erunt duo in carne una" (Gn 2:24); quod apostolus in Christo intelligit et in Ecclesia. Dum ergo ex omnibus gentibus unam vult Christus habere Ecclesiam, quicunque extraneus est ab ea, licet Christi nomine nuncupetur, Christi tamen corporis compage non continetur.

sembly of the peoples. He followed him in order to know what was to come to the nation, or to the people, who had fallen away from the communion of the one Church: for "the nation and the kingdom that does not serve you will perish" (Is 60:12). Finally, in another place he says in the same way: "Behold, you will call a nation that you did not know; and the nations that did not know you will run to you" (Is 55:5). For Christ the Lord is one, Whose Church, the holy possession, is one throughout the whole world; He therefore is the head, and she is the body, of which it is said at the beginning of Genesis: "They shall be two in one flesh" (Gn 2:24); which the apostle understands in Christ and in the Church. Therefore, while Christ wants the Church to be one of all the nations, whoever is a stranger to it, even though he is called by the name of Christ, is not included in the framework of Christ's body.

Feria Quarta: Is 3:1–11
S. Justinus, *Dialogus cum Tryphone* (cap. 136)

Manifesta ergo res est, si Dominus istis ita irascitur et paucissimos relicturum minatur, alios quosdam adducturum se pollicetur, qui habitaturi sint in monte sancto ejus (cf. Is 65:8–9). Vos enim nec vocantem eum perfertis, nec loquentem auditis, sed et malum fecistis coram Domino. In hoc autem maxime exuberat nequitia vestra, quod etiam oderitis justum, quem occidistis, et eos qui ab eo accepere ut sint id quod sunt, pii, justi et humani. Itaque "Vae animae ipsorum," dicit Dominus, "eo quod consilium ceperunt" (Is 3:9) adversus seipsos dicentes: Tollamus justum, quoniam inutilis est nobis. Neque enim et vos Baali sacrificastis, ut patres vestri, nec in lucis et in excelsis locis bellaria obtulistis militiae caeli; sed non suscepistis Christum Dei. Nam qui hunc ignorat, consilium Dei ignorat, et qui hunc injuria afficit, eumque odit, eum videlicet, a quo missus est, odit et injuria afficit. Et si quis non credit in eum, non credit prophetarum vaticiniis il-

It is plain then that if the Lord thus be angry with them, and threaten to leave very few of them, He promises to bring forth certain others, who shall dwell in His mountain. But these are the persons whom He said He would sow and beget. For you neither suffer Him when He calls you, nor hear Him when He speaks to you, but have done evil in the presence of the Lord. But the highest pitch of your wickedness lies in this, that you hate the Righteous One, and slew Him; and so, treat those who have received from Him all that they are and have, and who are pious, righteous, and humane. Therefore, "Woe unto their soul," says the Lord, "for they have devised an evil counsel" (Is 3:9) against themselves, saying, let us take away the righteous, for he is distasteful to us. For indeed you are not in the habit of sacrificing to Baal, as were your fathers, or of placing cakes in groves and on high places for the host of heaven: but you have not accepted God's Christ. For he who knows not Him, knows not the will of God; and he who insults and hates Him, insults and hates

lum praenuntiantibus et apud omnes praedicantibus.

Him that sent Him. And whoever believes not in Him, believes not the declarations of the prophets, who preached and proclaimed Him to all.

Feria Quinta: Is 4:1–3; 5:1–7
S. Basilius Magnus, *In Hexaemeron* (lib. 5, cap. 6)

"Vinea namque, inquit, factu est dilecto in cornu, in loco pingui" (Is 5:1); et, "vineam plantavi, et sepem circumdedi" (Mt 21:33). Animas humanas plane vineam dicit, quas sepe, mandatorum scilicet tutela et angelorum custodia circumdedit. "Immittet enim angelus Domini in circuitu timentium eum" (Ps 33:8). "Deinde etiam, constitutis in Ecclesia primum apostolis, secundo prophetis, tertio doctoribus" (1 Cor 12:28), quasi valla nobis defixit. Atque antiquorum ac beatorum virorum exemplis in sublime evexit nostram mentem, nec eam prosterni humi, aut conculcatione dignam esse sivit. Defoditur autem anima, cum mundi curis, qua cordibus nostris sunt oneri, se ipsam exuit. Quamobrem qui carneum amorem, aut suum erga divitias studium deposuit, aut qui

"My well beloved, says He, has a vineyard in a very fruitful hill" (Is 5:1), and elsewhere, "I have planted a vineyard and hedged it round about" (Mt 21:33). Evidently, He calls human souls His vine, those souls whom He has surrounded with the authority of His precepts and a guard of angels. "The angel of the Lord encamps round about them that fear him" (Ps 33:8). And further: He has planted for us, so to say, props, "in establishing in His Church apostles, prophets, teachers" (1 Cor 12:28); and raising our thoughts by the example of the blessed in olden times, He has not allowed them to drag on the earth and be crushed under foot. He also asks us to allow ourselves to be dug about; and that is what the soul does when it disembarrasses itself from the cares of the world, which are a weight on our hearts. He, then, who

miserae hujus gloriolae libidinem conspuendam et aspernabilem duxit, is veluti defossus est, ac, terrae affectionis inani pondere excusso, respiravit.

is freed from carnal affections and from the love of riches, and, far from being dazzled by them, disdains and despises this miserable vainglory, is, so to say, dug about and at length breathes, free from the useless weight of earthly thoughts.

Feria Sexta: Is 6:1–10
S. Cyrillus Alexandrinus, *Commentarium in Isaiam* (lib. 1, orat. 4)

Cum vero *Sanctus* ter dicunt, claudunt hymnum in hoc Dominus Sabaoth, in una Deitatis natura sanctam constituentes Triadem. Hoc quidem nos testatum faciunt per hos sanctos Seraphim, qui universam terram majestate ejus plenam dictitant, futura praecinentes, et administratae per Christum dispensationis mysterium praenuntiantes. Priusquam enim Verbum caro factum esset, ille daemon, ille exitialis, ille draco, ille defector orbem terrarum occupabat, et criatura prae Creatore et Conditore adorabatur. At ubi factus est homo unigenitum Dei Verbum, omnis terra majestate ejus repleta est. Illi flectet se omne genu, et illi omnes linguae ac tribus confitebuntur ac illi servient juxta id quod scriptum est.

And when they say the *Sanctus* three times, they conclude the hymn with "Lord of hosts," establishing the holy Triad in one nature of the Godhead. This indeed they attest to us through these holy seraphim, who proclaim the whole earth full of His majesty, foretelling the future, and announcing the mystery of the dispensation accomplished through Christ. For before the Word was made flesh, that demon, that deadly one, that dragon, that traitor held dominion over the world, and the creature was worshiped in place of the Creator and Founder. But when the only begotten Word of God became man, the whole earth was filled with His majesty. To Him every knee shall bow, and to Him all tongues and tribes shall confess, and Him they shall serve, according to what is written.

Sabbato: Is 7:1–6, 10–15
S. Augustinus, *Sermones* (serm. 370, 3)

Intellegite, fratres, quantum desiderium habebant antiqui sancti videndi Christum. Sciebant illum esse venturum, et omnes qui pie vivebant, dicebant: O si hic me inveniat illa nativitas! o si quod credo in Scripturis Dei, videam oculis meis! Et ut noveritis quantum desiderium habebant sancti, qui noverant de Scripturis sanctis virginem parituram, sicut audistis cum Isaias legeretur: "Ecce virgo in utero concipiet, et pariet filium, et vocabitur nomen ejus Emmanuel" (Is 7:14). Emmanuel quid sit, Evangelium nobis aperuit dicens: "quod interpretatur: Nobiscum Deus" (Mt 1:23). Non tibi ergo sit mirum, quaecumque infidelis anima, non tibi videatur impossibile ut virgo pareret, virgo pariens permaneret. Intellege natum Deum, et non miraberis virginis partum.

You must appreciate, brothers, what a tremendous desire possessed the saints of old to see the Christ. They knew He was going to come, and all those who lived devout and blameless lives would say, "Oh, if only that birth may find me still here! Oh, if only I may see with my own eyes what I believe from God's Scriptures!" And to prove to you how great was the desire of the saints who knew from the Holy Scriptures that a virgin was going to give birth, as you heard when Isaias was read: "Behold a virgin shall conceive in the womb, and shall bear a son, and his name shall be called Emmanuel" (Is 7:14). What Emmanuel means the Gospel declares to us, saying, "Which is interpreted, God with us" (Mt 1:23). So do not let it surprise you, unbelieving soul, whoever you are, do not let it strike you as impossible that a virgin should give birth, and in giving birth remain a virgin. Realize that it was God who was born, and you will not be surprised at a virgin giving birth.

INFRA HEBDOMADAM II ADVENTUS
Feria Secunda: Is 13:1–11
S. Ephraem, *In Diatessaron* (cap. 18, 15–17)

Quemadmodum justi et prophetae eum exspectaverunt, putantes eum ipsorum diebus se revelaturum, ita etiam hodie quisque fidelium suo tempore eum suscipere desiderat, quia diem adventus sui non manifestum fecit: idque maxime hanc ob causam, ne quis illum, cujus potestati et dominio numeri et tempora subdita sunt, fato et horae subjectum existimet. Quod ipse definivit, quomodo id esset ei absconditum qui signa adventus sui descripsit? Itaque his verbis signa sua honoravit, ut ex illo die in posterum omnes generationes et saecula existimarent ejus adventum ipsorum tempore futurum esse.

Just as the righteous and the prophets waited for Him, thinking that He would reveal himself in their days, so even today each of the faithful desires to receive Him in his own time, because He did not make the day of His coming manifest: and this especially for this reason, that no one should consider Him, to Whose power and dominion numbers and seasons are subject, subject to fate and time. How could what He Himself defined be hidden from Him Who described the signs of His coming? And so He honored His signs with these words, so that from that day forward all generations and ages would think that His coming would take place in their time.

Feria Tertia: Is 14:1–6, 12–15
S. Ambrosius, *Expositio Psalmi 118* (serm. 16, cap. 15–16)

Qualis enim adversum servulos Dei potest superbus esse, qui adversus Deum se exaltat, et dicit: "In caelum ascendam: super sidera caeli ponam sedem meam: sedebo in monte excelso, super montes altos qui sunt ab Aquilone: ascendam super nubes, et ero similis Altissimo" (Is 14:13–14)? Quid igitur mirum, si gravare homines possit, qui pervicaci spiritu nec Deo cedit? Quomodo mensuram veritatis, et fidem in hominem reservabit, qui sacrilego, impudentique mendacio omnipotenti se Domino adaequandum esse promittit? Quomodo calumniatur singulis, qui totam irritavit terram, concussit reges, posuit universum orbem desertum, et civitates destruxit: eos qui in abductione erant, non solvit? Caveamus ergo ne muros animae nostrae destruat, ne propugnacula nostrae mentis diruat, ne super sidera thronum suum ponat. Ponit super sidera, quando electum decipit, quando justum circumvenit, cujus opera lucent sicut stellae in caelo.

For how can he who exalts himself against God, and says: "I will ascend into heaven: I will set my seat above the stars of heaven: I will sit on a high mountain, on the high mountains that are from the north: I will ascend above the clouds, and I will be like the Most High" (Is 14:13–14) act proudly against the servants of God? What wonder, then, if he who has a stubborn spirit and does not yield to God can burden men? How will he reserve the measure of truth and faith towards man who, with a sacrilegious and shameless falsehood, promises to make himself equal to the Lord? How can he slander individuals, who has disturbed the whole earth, shaken kings, made the whole world desolate, destroyed cities, and did not release those who were in captivity? Let us be careful, then, lest he destroy the walls of our soul, lay waste the fortresses of our mind, or place his throne above the stars. He places it above the stars when he deceives the elect and surrounds the just, whose works shine like stars in the heavens.

Feria Quarta: Is 16:1–8
S. Augustinus, *Enarrationes in Psalmos* (in Ps 109:2–3)

Unicus itaque Filius Dei venturus ad homines, assumpturus hominem, et per id quod sumpsit futurus homo, moriturus, resurrecturus, ascensurus in caelum, sessurus ad dexteram Patris, et impleturus in gentibus quae promisit, et post impletionem promissorum suorum in gentibus etiam hoc impleturus ut veniat, et quod praerogavit, exigat, discernat vasa irae a vasis misericordiae, reddat impiis quod minatus est, justis quod pollicitus est. Hoc ergo totum prophetandum fuit, praenuntiandum fuit, venturum commendandum fuit, ut non subito veniens horreretur, sed creditum exspectaretur.

The only Son of God was to come among men, to take the nature of men, and in this nature to be born as a man. He was to die, to rise again, to ascend into heaven, to sit at the right hand of the Father, and to fulfill His promises among the nations, and after that to come again, to exact now what He had asked for before, to separate those deserving His anger from those deserving His mercy, to execute His threats against the wicked, and to reward the just as He had promised. All this had therefore to be prophesied, foretold, and impressed on us as an event in the future, in order that we might wait for it in faith, not find it a sudden and dreadful reality.

Feria Quinta: Is 19:1–6, 11–13
S. Chromatius Aquilejensis, *Tractatus in Mathaeum* (tr. 6, 1)

Quod autem ad Aegyptum descendit, hoc futurum idem Isaias dudum praenuntiaverat dicendo: "Ecce Dominus sedet super nubem levem et veniet in Aegypto" (Is 19:1). Quo dicto, man-

As to His going down to Egypt, the same Isaias had predicted it long ago when he said, "Behold, the Lord sits upon a light cloud and will come into Egypt" (Is 19:1). By this statement, a manifest sign

ifestum sacramentum dominicae incarnationis ostensum est. Nam quia ipse Dominus "oriens ex alto" (Lk 1:87), "sol justitiae" (Mal 4:2) nuncupatur, non immerito hic venturum eum in "nube levi," id est in corpore sancto, quod nullo peccato potuit praegravari praedixit, per quod majestatis suae lumen velamento corporeae nubis obtexit. Hoseae quoque idipsum ostenditur significare, cum dicit: "Abjectus est rex Israel, propter quod parvulus sit Israel, et ego dilexi eum. Et ex Aegypto vocavi filium meum" (Os 11:1). Post Aegypti olim grave delictum, postque multiplices in eam plagas divinitus irrogatas, Deus Pater omnipotens pietate commotus, Filium suum misit ad Aegyptum, ut quae jamdudum sub Moyse debitas sceleris sui poenas expenderat, nunc suscipiendo Christum, spem salutis acciperet. Quanta Dei misericordia per adventum Filii ejus ostensa est!

of the Lord's Incarnation was revealed. For since the Lord Himself is called "the East from on high" (Lk 1:87) and "the sun of justice" (Mal 4:2), it is not unfitting that he predicted here that He would come on a "light cloud," that is in a holy body, a body incapable of being weighed down by any sin, by which He covered the light of His own majesty with the veil of a bodily cloud. Osee likewise points to this same thing when he says, "The king of Israel has been cast off, for Israel is a child, and I loved Him. And out of Egypt I called My son" (Os 11:1). After the grave transgression of Egypt long ago, and after many blows had been divinely inflicted upon it, God the Father Almighty, moved by godliness, sent His Son to Egypt, so that Egypt, which long ago under Moses had paid out the penalties owed to its wickedness, might now by accepting Christ receive the hope of salvation. How great is God's mercy, revealed through the advent of His Son!

Feria Sexta: Is 24:1–16
S. Gregorius Magnus, *Regula pastoralis* (lib. 2, 7)

A subditis ergo inferiora gerenda sunt, a rectoribus summa cogitanda; ut scilicet oculum, qui praevidendis gressibus praeeminet, cura pulveris non obscuret. Caput namque subjectorum sunt cuncti qui praesunt; et ut recta pedes valeant itinera carpere, haec proculdubio caput debet ex alto providere, ne a provectus sui itinere pedes torpeant, cum curvata rectitudine corporis caput sese ad terram declinat. Qua autem mente animarum praesul honore pastorali inter caeteros utitur, si in terrenis negotiis quae reprehendere in aliis debuit, et ipse versatur? Quod videlicet ex ira justae retributionis per prophetam Dominus minatur, dicens: "Et erit sicut populus, sic sacerdos" (Is 24:2; Os 4:9). Sacerdos quippe est ut populus, quando ea agit is qui spiritali officio fungitur, quae illi nimirum faciunt qui adhuc de studiis carnalibus judicantur.

By the subjects, then, inferior matters are to be transacted, by the rulers the highest thought of; so that no annoyance of dust may darken the eye which is placed aloft for looking forward to the onward steps. For all who preside are the head of their subjects; and, that the feet may be able to take a straight course, the head ought undoubtedly to look forward to it from above, lest the feet linger on their onward journey, the body being bent from its uprightness and the head bowed down to the earth. But with what conscience can the overseer of souls avail himself among other men of his pastoral dignity, while engaged himself in the earthly cares which it was his duty to reprehend in others? And this indeed is what the Lord, in the wrath of just retribution, menaced through the prophet, saying, "And there shall be like people, like priest" (Is 24:2; Os 4:9). For the priest is as the people, when one who bears a spiritual office acts as do others who are still under judgment regarding their carnal pursuits.

Sabbato: Is 25:1–12
S. Cyrillus Alexandrinus, *Commentarius in Isaiam* (lib. 3, tom. 1)

"Et faciet Dominus Sabaoth omnibus gentibus super monte hoc" (Is 25:6). Cum praedixerit Dominum in Sion et in Jerusalem regnaturum, ex hac quasi similitudine rerum sub sensum aspectumque cadentium, mysticum sensum pertexit. Excelsa enim et speciosa Sion, visio autem pacis Jerusalem exponitur. Est autem utrumque hoc vere, Christi Ecclesia: celsa nempe et illustris, et velut in monte posita. Faciet, inquit, Dominus Sabaoth: necque solis Israelitis velut dilectis propter patres et probatis: immo omnibus gentibus, id est, in omni terra sub caelo agentibus. At quid faciet? "Bibent," inquit, "in laetitia, bibent vinum, ungentur unguento in monte hoc" (Is 25:6). Per laetitiam vero videtur hilaritatem in spe, videlicet per Christum subindicare: nam cum Christo regnabimus, et lucrifacientes quae neque cogitatione, neque oratione consequi possumus, omni animi voluptate perfruemur. Per vinum autem mysticam eulogiam et incruenti sacrificii modum significat, quod in sacris ecclesiis consuevimus adimplere.

"And the Lord of hosts will do to all the nations on this mountain" (Is 25:6). When he foretold that the Lord would reign in Sion and in Jerusalem, from this likeness of things falling under the senses and aspects, he reached a mystical meaning. For Sion means high and beautiful, but Jerusalem means vision of peace. But the Church of Christ is truly both: that is, exalted and illustrious, and as it were placed on a mountain. The Lord of hosts will do it, he says, and not only for the Israelites, as loved and approved because of their fathers, but for all nations, that is, those who work in every land under heaven. But what will He do? "They will drink," he says, "in joy, they will drink wine, they will be anointed with ointment on this mountain" (Is 25:6). Joy, indeed, seems to indicate gaiety in hope, that is, through Christ: for we shall reign with Christ, and profiting from what we can obtain neither by thought nor by prayer, we shall enjoy all the pleasure of the soul. But by wine he signifies the mystical blessing and unbloody sacrifice, which we customarily perform in the holy churches.

INFRA HEBDOMADAM III ADVENTUS

Feria Secunda: Is 28:1–7, 16–18

S. Ambrosius, *De officiis ministrorum* (lib. 1, cap. 29)

Fundamentum ergo est justitiae fides; justorum enim corda meditantur fidem: et qui se justus accusat, justitiam supra fidem collocat; nam tunc justitia ejus apparet, si vera fateatur. Denique et Dominus per Isaiam: "Ecce," inquit, "mitto lapidem in fundamentum Sion" (Is 28:18), id est, Christum in fundamenta Ecclesiae. Fides enim omnium, Christus: Ecclesia autem quaedam forma justitiae est. Commune jus omnium: in commune orat, in commune operatur, in commune tentatur. Denique qui se ipsum sibi abnegat; ipse justus, ipse dignus Christo est. Ideo et Paulus fundamentum posuit Christum (cf. 1 Cor 3:11), ut supra eum opera justitiae locaremus; quia fides fundamentum est: in operibus autem aut malis iniquitas, aut bonis justitia est.

The foundation of justice therefore is faith, for the hearts of the just dwell on faith, and the just man that accuses himself builds justice on faith, for his justice becomes plain when he confesses the truth. So the Lord says through Isaias: "Behold, I lay a stone for a foundation in Sion" (Is 28:18). This means Christ as the foundation of the Church. For Christ is the object of faith to all; but the Church is as it were the outward form of justice, she is the common right of all. For all in common she prays, for all in common she works, in the temptations of all she is tried. So he who denies himself is indeed a just man, is indeed worthy of Christ. For this reason, Paul has made Christ to be the foundation, so that we may build upon Him the works of justice (see 1 Cor 3:11), while faith is the foundation. In our works, then, if they are evil, there appears unrighteousness; if they are good, justice.

Feria Tertia: Is 30:18–20, 22–28
S. Joannes Cassianus, *Collationes* (coll. 13, cap. 12)

Advocat etiam nos et invitat cum dicit: "Tota die expandi manus meas ad populum non credentem mihi et contradicentem" (Is 65:2). Et invitatur a nobis cum dicimus ei, "Tota die expandi manus meas ad te" (Ps 87:10). Exspectat nos cum dicitur per prophetam: "Propterea exspectat Dominus, ut misereatur vestri" (Is 30:18), et exspectatur a nobis cum dicimus: "Exspectans exspectavi Dominum, et respexit me" (Ps 39:2). Clamat Jesus, "Si quis sitit, veniat ad me, et bibat" (Jn 7:37). Clamat etiam ad eum Propheta, "Laboravi clamans, raucae factae sunt fauces meae, defecerunt oculi dum spero in Deum meum" (Ps 68:4). Quaerit Dominus dicens: "Quaesivi et non erat vir, vocavi et non erat qui responderet" (Is 66:4). Quaeritur et ipse a sponsa flebiliter conquerente: "In cubili meo in noctibus quaesivi quem dilexit anima mea: quaesivi eum et non inveni; vocavi eum, et non respondit mihi" (Cant 3:1).

He calls and invites us, when He says: All the day long I stretched forth my hands to a disobedient and gainsaying people (Is 65:2). And He is invited by us when we say to Him: "All the day long I have stretched forth my hands unto You." (Ps 87:10) He waits for us, when it is said by the prophet: "Wherefore the Lord waits to have compassion upon us" (Is 30:18) and He is waited for by us, when we say: "I waited patiently for the Lord, and He inclined unto me" (Ps 39:2). Jesus cries: "If any man thirst let him come unto Me and drink" (Jn 7:37). The prophet also cries to Him: "I have labored with crying, my jaws have become hoarse: my eyes have failed, while I hope in my God" (Ps 68:4). The Lord seeks us, when He says: "I sought and there was no man. I called, and there was none to answer" (Is 66:4). And He Himself is sought by the bride who mourns with tears: "I sought on my bed by night Him whom my soul loved: I sought Him and found Him not; I called Him, and He gave me no answer" (Cant 3:1).

Feria Quinta: Is 33:1–6, 14–17
S. Joannes Cassianus, *Collationes* (coll. 11, cap. 13)

Quisquis igitur in hujus fuerit caritatis perfectione fundatus, necesse est ut ad illum sublimiorem caritatis timorem gradu excellentiore conscendat, quem non poenarum terror, nec cupido praemiorum, sed amoris generat magnitudo, quo vel filius indulgentissimum patrem, vel fratrem frater, vel amicum amicus, vel conjugem conjux sollicito reveretur affectu, dum ejus non verbera neque convicia, sed vel tenuem amoris formidat offensam, atque in omnibus non solum actibus, verum etiam verbis attonita semper pietate distenditur, ne erga se quantulumcumque fervor dilectionis illius intepescat. Cujus timoris magnificentiam Isaias unus prophetarum eleganter expressit, "Divitiae," inquiens, "salutis sapientia et scientia: timor Domini ipse thesaurus ejus" (Is 33:6). Non potuit timoris istius dignitatem ac meritum magis evidenter exprimere, quam ut divitias salutis nostrae, quae in vera sapientia Dei scientiaque consistunt, diceret nisi a timore Domini

Whoever then has been established in this perfect love is sure to mount by a higher stage to that still more sublime fear belonging to love, which is the outcome of no dread of punishment or greed of reward, but of the greatest love; whereby a son fears with earnest affection a most indulgent father, or a brother fears his brother, a friend his friend, or a wife her husband, while there is no dread of his blows or reproaches, but only of a slight injury to his love, and while in every word as well as act there is ever care taken by anxious affection lest the warmth of his love should cool in the very slightest degree towards the object of it. And one of the prophets has finely described the grandeur of this fear, saying: "Wisdom and knowledge are the riches of salvation: the fear of the Lord is his treasure" (Is 33:6). He could not describe with greater clearness the worth and value of that fear than by saying that the riches of our salvation, which consist in true wisdom and knowledge of God, can only be preserved by the fear of the Lord.

non posse servari. Ad hunc igitur metum non peccatores, sed sancti propheticis invitantur eloquiis, dicente psalmographo: "Timete Dominum, omnes sancti ejus, quia nihil deest timentibus eum" (Ps 33:10). Qui enim hoc timore Dominum metuit, perfectioni ejus certum est nihil deesse.

To this fear then not sinners but saints are invited by the prophetic word where the psalmist says: "O fear the Lord, all you His saints: for they that fear Him lack nothing" (Ps 33:10). For where a man fears the Lord with this fear it is certain that nothing is lacking to his perfection.

INFRA HEBDOMADAM IV ADVENTUS
Feria Secunda: Is 41:8–16
S. Hieronymus, *Commentaria in Isaiam* (lib. 12, ad cap. 41, vers. 8 et seq.)

"Ego posui te quasi plaustrum triturans novum, habens rostra serrantia" (Is 41:15), hoc significat, quod praedicatio Evangelica conterat adversarias potestates, et spiritualem nequitiam (cf. Eph 6:12) elevantem se contra scientiam Dei (cf. 2 Cor 10:5): quae pro varietate superbiae montes appellantur et colles. Illisque sublatis, et turbinis more dispersis, exsultet Israel atque laetetur in Domino Sancto Israel. Possumus quoque dicere, quod ecclesiasticus vir habens evangelicae praedicationis rostra serrantia in plaustro novo, quod nequaquam operatur in vetustate litterae, sed

"I have placed you as a new thrashing wagon, with teeth like a saw" (Is 41:15), indicates that the preaching of the gospel crushes the adversarial powers and the spiritual forces of wickedness (see Eph 6:12) that raises itself up against the knowledge of God (see 2 Cor 10:5). They are called mountains and hills because of the various kinds of pride; and when these have been removed and scattered like a whirlwind, Israel exults and rejoices in the Lord, the holy one of Israel. We can also say that the man of the Church has teeth like a saw on a new wagon in the preaching of the gospel, because he does not work at all in the old-

in novitate spiritus, conterat incredulorum corda durissima: separans triticum a paleis, et montes collesque comminuens, id est, omnes haereticorum principes, qui comminuti atque contriti, redigantur in pulverem, et nihil esse doceantur, ut qui male fuerant congregati, dividantur in bonum suum.

ness of the letter, but in the newness of the Spirit; he wears away the hardest hearts of unbelievers, separating the wheat from the chaff, and breaking in pieces the mountains and the hills, that is, all the leaders of the heretics. When they have been broken in pieces and crushed, they are reduced to dust and are shown to be nothing, so that those who had been wickedly gathered are divided for their own good.

Feria Tertia: Is 42:1–7, 10–13
Epistula Barnabae (cap. 14, 4–7)

Ipse autem Dominus nos reddidit populum hereditatis, pro nobis passus. Apparuit vero, ut tum illi (Judaei) in peccatis consummarentur, tum nos per heredem testamentum Domini Jesu acciperemus, qui ad hoc paratus erat, ut ipse in terris apparens, praecordia nostra jam a morte assumta et tradita erroris iniquitati redimens e tenebris, verbo suo disponeret in nobis testamentum. Dicit igitur propheta: "Ego Dominus, Deus tuus, vocavi te in justitia et tenebo manum tuam et corroborabo te, et dedi te in testamentum generis, in

The Lord Himself gave [a covenant] to us, that we might be the people of inheritance, since He had suffered for us. And He was manifested, so that they [the Jews] should be made perfect in their sins, and that we, through the heir, should receive the covenant of the Lord Jesus; Who was prepared for this end, that He when appearing, redeeming from darkness our hearts which had been already wasted unto death, and had been given up to the sinfulness of error, He should establish in us the covenant by His Word. Therefore the

lucem gentium, ut aperias oculos caecorum et educas de vinculis illigatos et de domo carceris sedentes in tenebris" (Is 42:6–7). Agnoscite ergo, unde simus redempti. Iterum propheta dicit: "Ecce, posui te in lucem gentium, ut sis in salutem usque ad extremum terrae; haec dicit Dominus redemptor tuus Deus" (Is 49:6–7). Rursus propheta dicit: "Spiritus Domini super me, propter quod unxit me evangelisare humilibus gratiam; misit me sanare contritos corde, praedicare captivis remissionem et caecis visum, nuntiare annum Domini acceptum et diem retributionis, consolari omnes lugentes" (Is 61:1–2).

prophet says, "I the Lord thy God have called thee in righteousness, and I will hold thy hand, and will strengthen thee; and I have given thee to be a covenant for the people, to be a light for the nations, to open the eyes of the blind, and to lead forth from fetters those who have been bound, and out of the prison-house those that are sitting in darkness" (Is 42:6–7). Again the prophet says, "The Spirit of the Lord is upon me, because He has anointed me to preach good tidings to the poor; He has sent me to heal the brokenhearted, to preach deliverance to the captives, and recovery of sight to the blind, to proclaim the acceptable year of the Lord, and the day of recompense, to comfort all that mourn" (Is 62:1–2).

Feria Quarta: Is 51:1–8
S. Justinus, *Dialogus cum Tryphone* (cap. 11)

Neque in alium quemquam speramus (non enim alius est), sed in eum in quem ei vos, Deum Abrahae, et Isaac et Jacob. Speramus autem non per Moysen, neque per legem; sic enim idem ac vos faceremus. Nunc vero legi enim, Trypho, novissimam legem fu-

Nor have we trusted in any other (for there is no other), but in Him in whom you also have trusted, the God of Abraham, and of Isaac, and of Jacob. But we do not trust through Moses or through the law; for then we would do the same as yourselves. But now—for I have

turam et testamentum omnium-firmissimum, quod nunc custodiri ab omnibus decet, quicumque hereditatem Dei consequi volunt. Nam quae in Horeb promulgata lex est, vetus jam et vestra solum est; haec autem omnium prorsus est; lex autem adversus legem posita priorem abrogat; similiter testamentum posterius superiori finem imposuit, ac aeterna nobis et novissima lex Christus datus est, et testamentum fidele, post quod non lex, non praeceptum, non mandatum. An tu ea non legisti, quae dicit Isaias: "Audite me, audite me, populus meus, et reges auscultate mihi; quoniam lex a me exibit et judicium meum in lucem gentium. Appropinquat celeriter justitia mea, et egredietur salutare meum, et in brachium meum gentes sperabunt" (Is 51:4–5).

read, Trypho, that there shall be a final law, and a covenant, the most important of all, which it is now incumbent on all men to observe, as many as are seeking after the inheritance of God. For the Law promulgated on Horeb is now old and belongs to yourselves alone; but this is for all universally. Now, law placed against law has abrogated that which is before it, and a covenant which comes after in like manner has put an end to the previous one; and an eternal and final law—namely, Christ—has been given to us, and the covenant is trustworthy, after which there shall be no law, no commandment, no ordinance. Have you not read this which Isaias says: "Hearken unto Me, hearken unto Me, My people; and, you kings, give ear unto Me: for a law shall go forth from Me, and My judgment shall be for a light to the nations. My righteousness approaches swiftly, and My salvation shall go forth, and nations shall trust in My arm" (Is 51:4–5).

Feria Quinta: Is 64:1–11
S. Joannes Cassianus, *De incarnatione Christi* (lib. 5, cap. 13)

Hoc ergo sacramentum, quod et manifestatum est in carne, et apparuit in mundo, et gentibus praedicatur, multi sanctorum veterum sicut praevidebant in spiritu, ita videre etiam in carne voluerunt. "Amen" enim, inquit Dominus, "dico vobis quia multi prophetae et justi cupierunt videre quae vos vidistis, et non viderunt, et audire quae audistis et non audierunt" (Mt 13:17). Et ideo Isaias propheta, "Utinam," inquit, "Domine, disrumperes caelos, et descenders" (Is 64:1). Sed et David: "Domine, inclina caelos, et descende" (Ps 143:5). Moses quoque: "Ostende," inquit, "mihi teipsum, ut manifeste videam te" (Ex 33:18). Nemo admodum propius quam Moses legem capiens, alloquentem e nubibus Deum, atque ad ipsam admodum praesentiam majestatis accessit. Et quomodo cum nemo propiora quam ille de Deo cerneret, adhuc manifestiora poscebat dicens: "Ostende mihi," inquit, "teipsum, ut manifeste videam te," scilicet quia hoc ille fieri precabatur quod

This mystery then, which was manifested in the flesh and appeared in the world, and was preached to the Gentiles, many of the patriarchs of old longed to see in the flesh, as they foresaw it in the spirit. For "Verily," says the Lord, "I say unto you that many prophets and righteous men have desired to see the things which you see, and have not seen them; and to hear the things which you hear and have not heard them" (Mt 13:17). And so the prophet Isaias says: "O that You, Lord, would rend the heavens and come down" (Is 64:1), and David too: "O Lord, bow the heavens and come down" (Ps 143:5). Moses also says: "Show me Thyself that I may see Thee plainly" (Ex 33:13). No one ever approached nearer to God speaking out of the clouds, and to the very presence of His glory than Moses who received the Law. And if no one ever saw more closely into God than he did, why did he ask for a still clearer vision, saying, "Show me Thyself that I may see Thee plainly"? Simply because he prayed that this might happen

iisdem admodum verbis Apostolus factum esse dicebat, id est, ut palam Dominus manifestaretur in carne, palam appareret mundo, palam assumeretur in gloria (cf. 1 Tm 3:16); et omnia oculis tandem carnalibus sancti cernerent, quae spiritalibus praevidebant.

which the apostle tells us in almost the same words actually did happen; namely, that the Lord might be openly manifested in the flesh, might openly appear to the world, openly be received up in glory; and that at last the saints might with their very bodily eyes see all those things which with spiritual sight they had foreseen.

Feria Sexta: Is 66:5–16
S. Methodius Olympius, *Sermo de Simeone et Anna* (cap. 3)

Quod vero impollutus fuerit ille partus, nec piacularibus hostiis obnoxius, testis est Isaias, diserte universae sub sole terrae denuntians: "Antequam," inquit, "aut parturiens pariat, aut antequam veniat labor pariendi, effugit, et peperit masculum. Quis tale quid audivit? aut qui simile vidit?" (Is 66:7–8). Effugit ergo quae sunt muliebria sanctissima Virgo Mater, antequam etiam pareret: ut nimirum, Spiritu Sancto eam sibi jam ante desponsante et sanctificante, absque virili congressione conciperet. Peperit illa primogenitum, et Patris unigenitum Filium: eum, inquam, qui in superis, unigene, absque matre, ex paterna

That that parturition was not polluted, and stood not in need of expiatory victims, Isaias is our witness, who proclaims distinctly to the whole earth under the sun: "Before she travailed," he says, "she brought forth before her pains came, she escaped and brought forth a man-child. Who has heard such a thing? Who has seen such things?" (Is 66:7–8). The must holy virgin mother, therefore, escaped entirely the manner of women even before she brought forth: doubtless, in order that the Holy Spirit, betrothing her unto Himself, and sanctifying her, she might conceive without intercourse with man. She has brought forth her firstborn Son,

substantia eluxit, virginitatemque naturalis unitatis indivisam inseparabilemque conservavit: quique in terris, nuptiali Virginis thalamo, Adae sibi naturam immobili unione ceu sponsus conjunxit; ac Matris puritatem indivulsam incorruptamque servavit: eum denique, qui in supernis nulla corruptione genitus, ineffabili in hisce inferioribus ratione natus est.

even the only begotten Son of God, Him, I say, Who in the heavens above shone forth as the only begotten, without mother, from out His Father's substance, and preserved the virginity of His natural unity undivided and inseparable; and Who on earth, in the virgin's nuptial chamber, joined to Himself the nature of Adam, like a bridegroom, by an inalienable union, and preserved His mother's purity uncorrupt and uninjured—Him, in short, Who in heaven was begotten without corruption, and on earth brought forth in a manner quite unspeakable.

TEMPUS NATIVITATIS

✣

Die 29 Decembris: Infra Octavam Nativitatis Domini
S. Cyrillus Alexandrinus, *Quod sit Christus* (PG 75, 1287)

Suscipit itaque servi formam, ea quae exininationi annexa sunt sibi asciscens, et similitudinem nostri non aspernatus. Neque enim fieri poterat ut alia ratione servitus cum honore commutaretur, nisi id quod servituti convenit proprium ipsius factum fuisset, ut et ipsius gloria illustraretur. Vincit enim semper id quod praestantius est, et turpitudo ex servitute orta in nobis abolita est. Factus enim nostri similis, qui nobis superior est, et servilem conditionem subiit qui natura est liber. Idcirco etiam in nos dignitas propagata est. Vocati enim sumus et nos filii Dei, et Patrem nobis vindicavimus, qui peculiariter ipsius est. Facta enim etiam ipsius quae hominum propria erant. Proinde cum dicimus eum formam servi accepisse, universum in eo administrationis in carne mysterium continetur.

He receives therefore bondman's form, making His own the results of the emptying and not spurning the likeness to us: for it were not possible otherwise to honor the bond unless that which befits the bond had been made His that it might be made illustrious by the glory that is from Him: for that which excels ever has the pre-eminence and the shame from our bondage was wiped out by us. For He Who is above us has been made as we and the Free by Nature was in the measure of the servants. Hence the dignity has passed unto us too: for we too have been called sons of God and inscribed as our Father Him Who is properly His Father; for our human things have been made His also. Therefore, in saying that He took bondman's form, is the whole mystery of the economy in the flesh.

Die 30 Decembris: Infra Octavam Nativitatis Domini
S. Athanasius, *Epistula ad Adelphium* (cap. 4;6)

Neque enim dedecus Verbo caro attulit, absit! Sed ipsa potius gloriam ab illo accepit. Nec item quia formam servi accepit Filius, qui in forma Dei est (cf. Phil 2:6), diminutus Divinitate est. Sed contra, universae carnis rerumque omnium creatarum liberator ipse fuit. Et vero si Deus misit Filium suum ex muliere genitum, nihil sane dedecoris, sed potius gloriam et gratiam magnam nobis res illa comparavit. Siquidem factus homo est, ut nos in seipso deos efficeret, factus est ex muliere, et genitus est ex Virgine, ut errantem nostri ortum transferret in seipsum, atque jam nos genus sanctum et "divinae consortes naturae" efficeremur, quemadmodum scripsit beatus Petrus (2 Pt 1:4). Nostra autem fides recta est, atque ex doctrina apostólica deducta, necnon cum Novi tum Veteris Testamenti auctoritate confirmata. Noverint igitur nos, cum Dominum in carne adoramus, non rem creatam adorare, sed Creatorem creato induto corpore.

The flesh did not diminish the glory of the Word; far be the thought: on the contrary, it was glorified by Him. Nor, because the Son that was in the form of God took upon Him the form of a servant (cf. Phil 2:6) was He deprived of His Godhead. On the contrary, He is thus become the deliverer of all flesh and of all creation. And if God sent His Son brought forth from a woman, the fact causes us no shame but contrariwise glory and great grace. For He has become man, that He might deify us in Himself, and He has been born of a woman, and begotten of a virgin, in order to transfer to Himself our erring generation, and that we may become henceforth a holy race, and "partakers of the divine nature," as blessed Peter wrote (2 Pt 1:4). Our faith is right and starts from the teaching of the apostles and tradition of the Fathers, being confirmed both by the New Testament and the Old. And let them know that in worshipping the Lord in the flesh we do not worship a creature, but, as we said above, the Creator Who has put on the created body.

Die 31 Decembris: Infra Octavam Nativitatis Domini
S. Amphilochius Iconiensis, *Orationes et Homiliae* (or. 1, cap. 3–4)

O miraculum! Qui non definitur caelis, in praesepi demoratus es ut parvulus, quique brevi sermone universa constituit, muliebribus fovebatur ulnis; ac qui supercaelestibus omnibus virtutibus donavit ut essent, impollutis lactabatur Virginis sacrae uberibus. Quae omnipotens, et faciens mortalem, divinae Providentiae benevolentia? Quod grande astutissimumque stratagema adversus diabolum? Mundus assertus est in libertatem per Virginem, qui per virginem olim sub peccatum corruerat. Virginali partu tot tantaeque invisibilium daemonurn copiae in tartarum praecipites datae sunt. Factus est Dominus conformis servis, ut servi iterum conformes Deo fierent. O Betlehem urbs sanctificata, et communis hereditas hominibus facta! O praesepe, o praesepe comparticeps cherubim, eodemque seraphim honore! Qui enim iis aeternum sedibus divine inequitat (cf. Ps 79:2), nunc in te rursum corporaliter degit. O Maria, o Maria,

O miracle! Thou who art not bound by the heavens, Thou wast kept in a manger like a little child, and Thou who established all things with a brief word, were cherished by women's arms; and Thou who gavest the angels all the virtues that they might be, wast fed by the unpolluted breasts of the sacred Virgin. How great is the benevolence of divine Providence, being omnipotent and becoming mortal! What great and most cunning stratagem against the devil! The world was declared free through the Virgin, who through a virgin had once fallen under sin. At the virgin birth, so many and such great forces of invisible demons were cast headlong into hell. The Lord was made like unto His servants, that His servants might again be made like unto God. O Bethlehem, a sanctified city, and made a common inheritance for men! O manger, O manger, partaking the lot of the cherubim, with the same honor of the seraphim! For He Who is divinely enthroned upon these eternal seats (cf. Ps 79:2), now dwelleth

quae universorum Creatorem habuisti primogenitum!

in thee again bodily. O Mary, O Mary, thou who hadst thy firstborn as the Creator of the universe!

TEMPUS POST EPIPHANIAM

———— ✚ ————

Feria Secunda: 1 Cor 2:1–13
S. Joannes Chrysostomus, *In Epistulam I. ad Corinthios* (hom. 7, cap. 1)

Etenim non erit totum mysterium divinum, cum a te ipso aliquid addideris. Alioquin vero mysterium vocatur, quia non quae videmus, credimus, sed alia videmus, alia credimus. Talis namque est mysteriorum nostrorum natura. Alio igitur modo ego, et alio infidelis circa haec affecti sumus. Audio ego, quod crucifixus sit Chrisus, et ejus erga homines amorem statim admiror; audit ille, et imbecillitatem putat. Audio quod servus factus sit, et providentiam admiror; audit ille et dedecus esse putat. Audio quod mortuus sit, et de potentia ejus obstupesco, quod a morte non superatus sit, imo etiam mortem dissolverit; audit ille, et imbecillitatem suspicatur.

It will not be a mystery, divine and whole in all its parts, when thou addest anything to it of thyself also. And in another sense, too, a mystery is so called; because we do not behold the things which we see, but some things we see and others we believe. For such is the nature of our mysteries. I, for instance, feel differently upon these subjects from an unbeliever. I hear, Christ was crucified; and immediately I admire His loving kindness unto men: the other hears, and esteems it weakness. I hear, He became a servant; and I wonder at His care for us: the other hears, and counts it dishonor. I hear, He died; and am astonished at His might, that being in death He was not holden, but even broke

Cum audit ille resurrectionem, fabulam esse putat; ego vero post acceptas ex rebus ipsis demonstrationes, Dei oeconomiam adoro. Non enim ex visu judico illa quae apparent, sed mentis oculis.

the bands of death: the other hears and surmises it to be helplessness. Hearing of the Resurrection, he say, the thing is a legend; I, aware of the facts which demonstrate it, fall down and worship the dispensation of God. Hearing of a laver, he counts it merely as water: but I behold not simply the thing, which is seen, but the purification of the soul which is by the Spirit.

Feria Tertia: 1 Cor 5:1–11
S. Cyprianus, *De Lapsis* (22–23; 29)

Alta et erecta cervix nec quia cecidit inflexa est. Tumens animus et superbus nec quia victus est fractus est. Irasceris ei qui abs te avertere iram Dei nititur; ei minaris qui pro te Domini misericordiam deprecatur, qui vulnus tuum sentit quod ipse non sentis, qui pro te lacrimas fundit, quas forsitan ipse non fundis. Oneras adhuc crimen et cumulas; et cum sis ipse implacabilis ad antistites et sacerdotes Dei, putas circa te Dominum posse placari? Accipe potius et admitte quae loquimur. Quid surdae aures salutaria praecepta non audiunt quae monemus? quid caeci oculi paenitentiae iter non vident

His stiff and arrogant neck was not bowed even by his fall; his proud and swollen spirit was not quelled even by defeat. Thou ravest against him who is trying to shield thee from the anger of God, thou abusest him who invokes Our Lord's mercy upon thee, who feels thy wound as his own which thou dost not feel thyself, who weeps for thee, who, it seems, weepest not for thy self. Thou art only heaping up and adding to thy guilt, and if thou pursuest the bishops and priests of God so unrelentingly, dost thou think that Our Lord will be moved to relent towards thee? No—hear what we say and take it to heart.

quod ostendimus? quid perculsa et alienata mens remedia vitalia non percipit quae de Scripturis caelestibus et discimus et docemus? Convertamur ad Dominum mente tota; et, paenitentiam criminis veris doloribus exprimentes, Dei misericordiam deprecemur. Illi se anima prosternat, illi maestitia satisfaciat, illi spes omnis incumbat.

Why art thine ears deaf to the rules of salvation that we propose? Why art thine eyes blind to the road of penitence that we point to? Why is thy mind closed and prejudiced in the presence of the life-giving remedies which we learn and proclaim from the Holy Scriptures? Let us turn back to the Lord with our whole heart and, expressing our repentance in deep sorrow, implore God for His mercy. Let our souls bow before Him, let our sorrow be offered to Him in satisfaction, let our hopes all rest in Him.

Feria Quarta: 1 Cor 6:1–18
S. Joannes Chrysostomus, *In Epistulam ad Romanos* (hom. 4, cap. 2–3)

Passiones omnes ignominiose sunt, maxime vero insania erga masculos: etenim anima plus patitur et rubore suffunditur in peccatis, quam corpus in infirmitatibus. Oportebat duos, virum et mulierem, unum esse: nam ait, "Erunt duo in carne una" (Gn 2:24). Hac autem sublata diabolus concupiscentia, et in alium modum derivata, sic sexus a mutuo consortio divisit, et id effecit, ut quod unum erat, duae essent partes, idque contra Dei legem.

All these affections were vile, but chiefly the mad lust after males; for the soul is more the sufferer in sins, and more dishonored, than the body in diseases. It was meet, that the twain should be one, I mean woman and the man. "For the twain," it says, "shall be one flesh" (Gn 2:24). This desire the devil having taken away, and having turned the course thereof into another fashion, he thus sundered the sexes from one another and made the one to become two parts in

In ipsam quoque naturam inique egerunt. Nihil est, nihil utique est hac contumelia irrationabilius et gravius. Si enim de fornicatione loquens Paulus, dicebat: "Omne peccatum, quodcumque fecerit homo, extra corpus est; qui vero fornicatur, in proprium corpus peccat" (1 Cor 6:18); quid dixerimus de hac insania, quas tanto deterior est fornicatione, quanto dici nequit? Undenam haec orta sunt mala? O voluptate, ab eo quod Deum non cognosceretis: cum enim quidam ejus timorem eiecerint, omnia demum bona avolant.

opposition to the law of God. For beside what have been mentioned they also behaved lawlessly against nature itself. For there is not, there surely is not, a more grievous evil than this insolent dealing. For if when discoursing about fornication Paul said, that, "Every sin which a man does is without the body, but he that commits fornication sins against his own body" (1 Cor 6:18); what shall we say of this madness, which is so much worse than fornication as cannot even be expressed? Whence then were these evils born? Of luxury; of not knowing God. For so soon as any have cast out the fear of Him, all that is good straightway goes to ruin.

Feria Quinta: 1 Cor 7:1–14
S. Augustinus, *De sancta virginitate* (cap. 19; 21)

Alii quippe appetendo virginitatem nuptias tamquam adulterium detestandas esse putaverunt; alii vero defendendo connubium excellentiam perpetuae continentiae nihil mereri amplius quam conjugalem pudicitiam voluerunt; quasi vel Susannae bonum, Mariae sit humiliatio; vel Mariae majus bonum, Susannae debeat

Some forsooth by aiming at virginity, have thought marriage hateful even as adultery: but others, by defending marriage, would have the excellence of perpetual continence to deserve nothing more than married chastity; as though either the good of Susanna be the lowering of Mary: or the greater good of Mary ought to be the condemnation of

esse damnatio. Gloriam majoris illius boni esse majorem, quod ejus adipiscendae causa bonum conjugale transcenditur. Non humana sententia, sed divinae Scripturae auctoritate ad tam excellens donum homines exhortandi sunt, non mediocriter neque praetereunter agendum est, ne cuiquam ipsa divina Scriptura in aliquo mentita videatur. Unde enim confidant verum esse, quod scriptum est: "Et qui non dat nuptum melius facit" (1 Cor 7:38); si falsum putant esse, quod juxta superius nihilominus scriptum est: "Et qui dat virginem suam, bene facit" (1 Cor 7:38)? Si autem loquenti Scripturae de nuptiarum bono indubitanter crediderint, eadem caelestis eloquii veracissima auctoritate firmatae ad melius suum ferventi ac fidenti alacritate transcurrent.

Susanna. The glory of that greater good is greater from the fact that, in order to obtain it, the good of married life is surmounted. It is not by human judgment, but by authority of Divine Scripture, that men must be exhorted unto so excellent a gift, we must plead not in a commonplace manner, or merely by the way, that divine Scripture itself seem not to any one in any matter to have lied. For whence can they feel sure that that is true, which is written, "And he, who gives her not in marriage, does better" (1 Cor 7:38): If they think that false, which yet is written close above, "Both he, who gives his virgin, does well" (1 Cor 7:38)? If they shall without all doubt have believed Scripture speaking of the good of marriage, confirmed by the same most true authority of the divine oracle, they will hasten beyond unto their own better part with glowing and confident eagerness.

Feria Sexta: 1 Cor 13:1–13
S. Augustinus, *De Trinitate* (lib. 8, cap. 4, 6)

Et quid est Deum scire nisi eum mente conspicere firmeque percipere? Priusquam valeamus conspicere atque percipere Deum sicut conspici et percipi potest, quod mundis cordibus licet: "Beati enim mundi cordes quia ipsi Deum videbunt" (Mt 5:8), nisi per fidem diligatur, non poterit cor mundari quo ad eum videndum sit aptum et idoneum. Ubi sunt enim illa tria propter quae in animo aedificanda omnium divinorum librorum machinamenta consurgunt, fides, spes, caritas nisi in animo credente quod nondum videt et sperante atque amante quod credit? Amatur ergo et quod ignoratur sed tamen creditur. Nimirum autem cavendum est ne credens animus id quod non videt fingat sibi aliquid quod non est et speret diligatque quod falsum est. Quod si fit, non erit caritas de corde puro et conscientia bona et fide non ficta, qui finis praecepti est sicut idem apostolus dicit (cf. 1 Tm 1:5).

What is it to know God except to behold Him and steadfastly perceive Him with the mind? But before also that we have power to behold and to perceive God, as He can be beheld and perceived, which is permitted to the pure in heart; for "blessed are the pure in heart. for they shall see God" (Mt 5:8); except He is loved by faith, it will not be possible for the heart to be cleansed, in order that it may be apt and meet to see Him. For where are there those three, in order to build up which in the mind the whole apparatus of the divine Scriptures has been raised up, namely faith, hope, and charity, except in a mind believing what it does not yet see, and hoping and loving what it believes? Even He therefore Who is not known, but yet is believed, can be loved. But indisputably we must take care, lest the mind believing that which it does not see, feign to itself something which is not, and hope for and love that which is false. For in that case, it will not be charity out of a pure heart, and of a good conscience, and of faith

unfeigned, which is the end of the commandment, as the same apostle says (cf. 1 Tm 1:5).

Sabbato: 1 Cor 16:1–14
S. Basilius Magnus, *Epistulae* (ep. 25 vel ep. 251 (Evaesenis), 1; 4)

Revera difficile jam inventu ac prorsus rarum, Ecclesia sincera, nihil ex temporum difficultate laesa, sed integram et inoffensam servans apostolicam doctrinam. Nos autem, dilecti fratres, parvi quidem et humiles sumus, semper tamen iidem Dei gratia, nec unquam cum rebus immutati sumus. Fides apud nos, non alia Seleuciae, alia Constantinopoli, alia Zelis, et Lampsaci alia, et Romae alia: nec quae nunc circumfertur, a prioribus diversa, sed una et eadem semper. Quemadmodum enim accepimus a Domino, sic baptizamur; quemadmodum baptizamur, sic credimus; quemadmodum credimus, sic et glorificamus. Circumspicite orbem terrarum, et videte exiguam esse hanc partem, quae morbo laborat; reliquam autem Ecclesiam, quam a terminis usque ad terminos Evangelium suscepit, in sana hac versari et incorrupia doctrina.

Truly nowadays it is hard to find, and extraordinary to see, a Church pure, unharmed by the troubles of the times, preserving the apostolic doctrine in all its integrity and completeness. I, however, brethren beloved, small and insignificant as I am, but remaining ever by God's grace the same, have never changed with the changes of the world. My creed has not varied at Seleucia, at Constantinople, at Zela, at Lampsacus, and at Rome. My present creed is not different from the former; it has remained ever one and the same. As we received from the Lord, so are we baptized; as we are baptized, so we make profession of our faith; as we make profession of our faith, so do we offer our doxology. Look over all the world and see how small the part is which is unsound. All the rest of the Church which has received the gospel, from one end of the world to the other, abides in this sound and unper-

Quorum et nos precamur, ne excidamus communione, partemque vobiscum habeamus in justo Domini nostri Jesu Christi die, cum veniet unicuique nostrum secundum opera sua daturus.

verted doctrine. From their communion I pray that I may never fall, and I pray that I may have part and lot with you in the righteous day of Our Lord Jesus Christ, when He shall come to give to everyone according to his conduct.

INFRA HEBDOMADAM II POST EPIPHANIAM

Feria Secunda: 2 Cor 3:1–13

S. Joannes Chrysostomus, *In Secundam ad Corinthios epistolam commentarius* (hom. 6, cap. 2)

Epistulam Christi eos vocat, ut qui Dei legem inscriptam habeant. Nam quae Deus cum omnibus aliis, tum vobis etiam nota esse volebat, haec in cordibus vestris inscripta sunt. Ut enim Moses lapides et tabulas sculpsit, sic nos quoque animas vestras: ideo ait, "Ministrata a nobis" (2 Cor 3:3). Quantum autem inter Spiritum et atramentum, atque inter lapideas et carnales tabulas interest, tantum etiam inter has et illas esse discriminis: ac proinde inter eos quoque, qui his operam navarunt, et eum, qui illis operam navavit. Ob eamque causam, quia magnifice loquutus fuerat, confestim seipsum carpit, dicenente: "Fiduciam autem talem habemus

He called them an epistle of Christ, as having the Law of God written in them. For what things God wished to declare to all and to you, these are written in your hearts. But it was we who prepared you to receive the writing. For just as Moses hewed the stones and tables, so we, your souls. Whence he says, "Ministered by us" (2 Cor 3:3). Wide as the difference between the Spirit and ink, and a stony table and a fleshy, so wide is that between these and those; consequently, between themselves who ministered, and him who ministered to them. Yet because it was a great thing he had uttered, he therefore quickly checks himself, saying, "And such confidence have we through Christ to

per Christum ad Deum" (2 Cor 3:4); ac rursus totum id Deo adscribit: horum enim nobis Christus causa est, inquit: "Non quod sufficientes simus cogitare aliquid ex nobis tamquam ex nobis" (2 Cor 3:5).

Godward" (2 Cor 3:4). And again, he refers all to God: for it is Christ, says he, Who is the Author of these things to us. "Not that we are sufficient of ourselves to account anything as from ourselves" (2 Cor 3:5).

Feria Tertia: 2 Cor 5:1–4, 6–15
S. Augustinus, *De Civitate Dei* (lib. 14, cap. 3)

Quod si quisquam dicit carnem causam esse in malis moribus quorumcumque vitiorum, eo quod anima carne affecta sic vivit, profecto non universam hominis naturam diligenter advertit. "Quo sumus in hac habitatione, ingemescimus gravati, in quo nolumus exspoliari, sed supervestiri, ut absorbeatur mortale a vita" (2 Cor 5:4). Et adgravamur ergo corruptibili corpore, et ipsius adgravationis causam non naturam substantiamque corporis, sed ejus corruptionem scientes nolumus corpore spoliari, sed ejus inmortalitate vestiri. Corruptio corporis, quae adgravat animam, non peccati primi est causa, sed poena; nec caro corruptibilis animam peccatricem, sed anima peccatrix fecit esse corruptibilem carnem.

If anyone says that the flesh is the cause of all vices and ill conduct, inasmuch as the soul lives wickedly only because it is moved by the flesh, it is certain he has not carefully considered the whole nature of man. "For we that are in this tabernacle do groan, being burdened: not for that we would be unclothed, but clothed upon, that mortality might be swallowed up in life" (2 Cor 5:4). We are then burdened with this corruptible body; but knowing that the cause of this burdensomeness is not the nature and substance of the body, but its corruption, we do not desire to be deprived of the body, but to be clothed with its immortality. For the corruption of the body, which weighs down the soul, is not the cause but the punishment of the first sin; and it was not the

Ex qua corruptione carnis licet existant quaedam incitamenta vitiorum et ipsa desideria vitiosa, non tamen omnia vitae iniquae vitia tribuenda sunt carni, ne ab his omnibus purgemus diabolum, qui non habet carnem.

corruptible flesh that made the soul sinful, but the sinful soul that made the flesh corruptible. And though from this corruption of the flesh there arise certain incitements to vice, and indeed vicious desires, yet we must not attribute to the flesh all the vices of a wicked life, in case we thereby clear the devil of all these, for he has no flesh.

Feria Quarta: 2 Cor 7:1–10
S. Augustinus, *De civitate Dei* (lib. 14, cap. 8)

Ipsa quoque tristitia, pro qua Stoici nihil in animo sapientis inveniri posse putaverunt, reperitur in bono et maxime apud nostros. Nam laudat Apostolus Corinthios, quod contristati fuerint secundum Deum (cf. 2 Cor 7:10–11). Quae enim secundum Deum est tristitia, paenitentiam in salutem impaenitendam operatur; mundi autem tristitia mortem operatur. Ecce enim idipsum secundum Deum contristari, quantam perfecit in vobis industriam (cf. 2 Cor 7:8–11). Ac per hoc possunt Stoici pro suis partibus respondere, ad hoc videri utilem esse tristitiam, ut peccasse paeniteat; in animo autem sapi-

Sorrow itself, too, which the Stoics would not allow to be represented in the mind of the wise man, is used in a good sense, and especially in our writings. For the apostle praises the Corinthians because they had a godly sorrow (cf. 2 Cor 7:10–11). For godly sorrow works repentance to salvation not to be repented of, but the sorrow of the world works death. For, behold, this selfsame thing that you sorrowed after a godly sort, what carefulness it wrought in you! (cf. 2 Cor 7:8–11). Consequently the Stoics may defend themselves by replying, that sorrow is indeed useful for repentance of sin, but that this can have no place in the mind

entis ideo esse non posse, quia nec peccatum in eum cadit, cujus paenitentia contristetur, nec ullum aliud malum, quod perpetiendo et sentiendo sit tristis. Cives sanctae civitatis Dei in hujus vitae peregrinatione secundum Deum viventes metuunt cupiuntque, dolent gaudentque, et quia rectus est amor eorum, istas omnes affectiones rectas habent. Metuunt peccare, cupiunt perseverare; dolent in peccatis, gaudent in operibus bonis.

of the wise man, inasmuch as no sin attaches to him of which he could sorrowfully repent, nor any other evil the endurance or experience of which could make him sorrowful. The citizens of the holy city of God, who live according to God in the pilgrimage of this life, both fear and desire, and grieve and rejoice. And because their love is rightly placed, all these affections of theirs are right. they fear to sin, they desire to persevere; they grieve in sin, they rejoice in good works.

Feria Quinta: 2 Cor 10:1–12
S. Hilarius Pictaviensis, *De Trinitate* (lib. 12, cap. 20)

Aequum est humanas doctrinas non tam diffugere, quam refellere; et simpliciores, ne ab his spolientur, et obstruere et instruere. Oportet eos, qui Christum praedicant mundo, irreligiosis mundi imperfectisque doctrinis per scientiam sapientis omnipotentiae contraire, secundum illud beati Apostoli dictum: "Nostra enim arma non sunt carnalia, sed potentia Deo, ad destructionem munitionum, rationes destruentia, et omnem altitudinem elevatam adversus cognitionem Dei"

We should not flee from the doctrines of men, but rather overthrow them; and we must restrain and instruct the simple-minded lest they be spoiled by these teachers. For since God can do all things, and in His wisdom can do all things wisely, for neither is His purpose unarmed with power nor His power unguided by purpose, it behooves those who proclaim Christ to the world, to face the irreverent and faulty doctrines of the world with the knowledge imparted by that wise Omnipotence, according to the saying of the

(2 Cor 10:4–5). Fidem non nudam Apostolus atque inopem rationis reliquit: quae quamvis potissima ad salutem sit, tamen nisi per doctrinam instruatur, habebit quidem inter adversa tutum refugiendi recessum, non etiam retinebit constantem obnitendi securitatem. Contundendae sunt ergo insolentes adversum Deum disputationes, et destruenda rationum fallacium munimenta, et elevata ad impietatem ingenia conterenda, nec carnalibus armis, sed spiritalibus; nec terrena doctrina, sed caelesti sapientia: ut quanta rerum divinarum humanarumque discretio est, tanta ultra terrena studia ratio caelestis excedat.

blessed apostle: "For our weapons are not carnal but powerful for God, for the casting down of strongholds, casting down reasonings and every high thing which is exalted against the knowledge of God" (2 Cor 10:4–5). The apostle did not leave us a Faith which was bare and devoid of reason; for although a bare faith may be most mighty to salvation, nevertheless, unless it is trained by teaching, while it will have indeed a secure retreat to withdraw to in the midst of foes, it will yet be unable to maintain a safe and strong position for resistance. Therefore, we must beat down the insolent arguments which are raised against God, and destroy the fastnesses of fallacious reasoning, and crush cunning intellects which hit themselves up to impiety, with weapons not carnal but spiritual, not with earthly learning but with heavenly wisdom.

Feria Sexta: 2 Cor 12:1–11
S. Augustinus, *Enarrationes in Psalmos* (In Ps 97:5)

"Si bona percepimus de manu Domini, mala non sustinebimus?" (Jb 1:11). O sonum fortem! o sonum dulcem! Quem non dormientem excitet sonus iste? quem

"Shall we receive good at the hand of God, and shall we not receive evil?" (Jb 1:11). O courageous, O sweet sound! Whom will not that sound awake from sleep? Whom will not

non excitet praesumptio in Deo, ut adversus diabolum securus procedat in praelium; non suis viribus obtenturus, sed illius qui probat? Quia ipse etiam tundit; non enim faceret malleus de seipso. De ipso malleo in manu Dei posito, id est in potestate Dei, tunduntur ductiles tubae, ut resonent laudes Dei. Videte quemadmodum (audeo dicere, fratres mei,) de isto malleo etiam Apostolus tundebatur: "In magnitudine," inquit, "revelationum ne extollar, datus est mihi stimulus carnis meae angelus satanae, qui me colaphizet" (12 Cor 12:7). Ecce tunditur; videamus quemadmodum sonet: "Propter quod," inquit, "ter Dominum rogavi, ut auferret eum a me; et dixit mihi, Sufficit tibi gratia mea; nam virtus in infirmitate perficitur" (12 Cor 12:8–9). Ego tubam, inquit ille fabricator, perficere volo; non perficiam nisi tundam: "in infirmitate virtus perficitur." Et audi jam ipsam tubam ductilem bene sonantem: "Quando infirmor, tunc potens sum" (2 Cor 12:10).

confidence in God awake, to march to battle fearlessly against the devil; not to struggle with his own strength, but His Who proves him? For He it is Who hammers, for the hammer could not do so of itself. By means of this hammer placed in the hand of God, that is, in His power, the ductile trumpets are beaten out, that they may re-echo His praises. See how (I dare so speak, my brethren) even the apostle was beaten with this very hammer: "Lest I should be exalted," he says, above measure through the abundance of the revelations, there was given to me a thorn in the flesh, the messenger of Satan, to buffet me" (12 Cor 12:7). Behold he is under the hammer: let us hear how he speaks of it: "For this thing," he says, "I besought the Lord thrice, that it might depart from me. And He said unto me, My grace is sufficient for thee: for My strength is made perfect in weakness" (12 Cor 12:8–9). I, says His Maker, wish to make this trumpet perfect; I cannot do so unless I hammer it; "In weakness is strength made perfect." Hear now the ductile trumpet itself sounding as it should; "When I am weak, then am I strong" (2 Cor 12:10).

Sabbato: 2 Cor 13:1–13
S. Joannes Chrysostomus, *In Epistulam II ad Corinthios*
(hom. 29, cap. 5)

Sicut enim ille dives est, non qui multis rebus, sed qui nulla re indiget: sic clarus ille, non qui gloriae cupiditate aestuat, sed qui eam contenmit: umbra enim gloriae est haec gloria. Nemo enim picto pane conspecto, etiamsi millies fame teneatur, picturam attinget. Ne tu quoque umbras consecteris: gloriae enim umbra hoc est, non gloria. Quod denique is, qui eam habet aut habere expetit, hinc appellatus, pudore suffunditur. Unde igitur haec cupiditas? inquies; et quo pacto exsistit hic affectus? Ab animi imbecillitate; neque enim dumtaxat accusare opus est, sed etiam corrigere; ab imperfecta mente, a puerili sententia. Quocirca pueritiam deponamus ac viros nos praebeamus, atque ubique, hoc est, in opibus, in voluptate, in deliciis, in gloria, in potentia, veritatem, ac non umbras sequamur. Umbras enim sequi hominis est insania laborantis.

For as he is rich, not who is in need of many things, but who is in need of nothing; so, he is glorious, not who loves glory, but who despises it; for this glory is but a shadow of glory. No one having seen a loaf painted, though he should be pressed with hunger ever so much, will attack the picture. Neither then do thou pursue these shadows, for this is a shadow of glory, not glory. And he who has it or covets it are ashamed to be called by its name. "Whence then is this desire," says one, "and how is the passion engendered?" By littleness of soul, for one ought not only to accuse it, but also to correct it, by an imperfect mind, by a childish judgment. Let us then cease to be children and let us become men: and let us everywhere pursue the reality, not the shadows, both in wealth, and in pleasure, and in luxury, and in glory, and in power; and this disease will cease, and many others also. For to pursue shadows is a madman's part.

INFRA HEBDOMADAM III POST EPIPHANIAM
Feria Secunda: Gal 3:1–14
S. Augustinus, *Expositio epistolae ad Galatas* (cap. 20-21)

Deinde adhibet exemplum patris Abraham. "Benedicentur in te omnes Gentes" (Gal 3:8), imitatione utique fidei ejus, qua justificatus est, etiam ante sacramentum circumcisionis, quod ad fidei signaculum accepit, et ante omnem servitutem legis, quae multo post data est. Non itaque ex fide vivit, quisquis praesentia, quae videntur, vel cupit vel timet, quia fides Dei ad invisibilia pertinet, quae post dabantur. Nam est ista quaedam in operibus legis justitia, quando sine suo praemio relicta non est, ut qui fecerit ea vivet in eis. Unde et ad Romanos dicit: "Si enim Abraham ex operibus justificatus est, habet gloriam, sed non ad Deum" (Rom 4:2). Qui omnino non justificatur, nec illa servat, quae temporale habent praemium, nec illa quae aeternum, qui autem in operibus legis justificatur non apud Deum justificatur, quia temporalem inde exspectat visibilemque mercedem.

Then he cites the example of our father Abraham. "For in you shall all nations be blessed" (Gal 3:8), that is, in imitation of his faith, by which he was justified even before the sacrament of circumcision, which he received as a seal of faith before all slavery to the Law, which was given much later. And so, whoever desires or fears present, visible things does not live by faith, for faith in God refers to invisible things that will be given hereafter. For there is a kind of righteousness by works of the law that is not without its reward, such that whoever does them shall live by them. In this regard he also says to the Romans: "For if Abraham was justified by works, he has something to boast about, but not before God" (Rom 4:2). One who is not justified at all observes neither the things that have a temporal reward nor the things that have an eternal reward. On the other hand, one who is justified by works of the Law is not justified before God, because he expects from them temporal and visible compensation.

Feria Tertia: Gal 5:1–17
S. Hieronymus, *Commentaria in Epistulam ad Galatas* (lib. III, vers. 13)

De servitute legali ad Evangelii libertatem vocatos (quibus superius dicitur: "State, et nolite rursum iugo servitutis haerere": Gal 5:1) etiam nunc moneri, ut leve Christi iugum et delectabilia Evangelii praecepta sectantes, nequaquam putent sibi licere, ut hac ipsa libertate vivendi, in occasione carnis utantur: scilicet ut juxta carnem vivant. Dicat quispiam: Si cessavi, o Paule, esse sub Lege, et de servitute ad libertatem vocatus sum: ergo debeo ita vivere ut convenit libertati, nec aliquibus praeceptis teneri, sed quodcumque placuerit, et voluntas suggesserit, hoc facere implere, sectari. Ad quod respondit Apostolus: "Vocatos quidem nos esse in spiritus libertatem: sed ita, ut libertas ipsa carni non serviat" (Gal 5:13). Nec putemus quia nobis omnia licent, omnia expedire: quin potius quia servi legis esse cessavimus, facti liberi, magis per charitatem nobis invicem serviamus, ut laciniosae legis praecepta, uno dilectionis capitulo concludantur.

Those called from slavery to the Law to freedom in the gospel—those to whom it was said above, "Stand firm and do not let yourselves be burdened again by a yoke of slavery" (Gal 5:1)—are being warned now not to think by any means that they can use this freedom as a license to indulge in the flesh. Someone may say: So, Paul, if I am no longer under the Law and have been called from slavery to freedom, then I must live in a way that does justice to this freedom and not be bound by any commandments. Whatever tickles my fancy and whatever desire suggests to me, that I must do, that I must fulfill, that I must chase after. The apostle's response is that we are indeed "called to freedom of the Spirit, provided that it does not entail slavery to the flesh" (Gal 5:13). We should not think that everything is expedient just because everything is permissible. Rather, because we have ceased to be slaves to the Law and have been made free, let us serve one another in love more so that the convoluted precepts of the Law may be collected under the one rubric of love.

Feria Quarta: Eph 1:1–14
S. Joannes Chrysostomus, *In Epistulam ad Ephesios commentarius* (hom. 1, cap. 4)

Quando maxime erant perituri, tunc salvi fuerunt. Ἀνακεφαλαιώσθαι, inquit. Quid est ἀνακεφαλαιώσθαι? Conjungere. Caeterum studeamus quam proxime accedere ad ipsam veritatem. Nam a nobis quidem, ut etiam in more est positum, dicitur ἀνακεφαλαίωσις, quae prolixe dicta sunt in breve contrahere. Nam hoc quoque ita habet: quae enim longo tempore dispensabantur in ipso ἀνακεφαλαιώσατο, hoc est, in summam redegit. Verbum enim consummans, et in justitia abbrevians, et illa comprehendit, et alia addidit. Hoc est, ἀνακεφαλαίωσις et reductio in summam. Est et aliud quod significatur. Quodnam hoc? Unum omnibus posuit caput, nempe Christum secundum carnem, et angelis et hominibus: hoc est, et angelis unum dedit principium, et hominibus: his quidem id quod est secundum carnem, illis autem illis autem secundum spiritum, Deum Verbum. Ita enim fiet unitas, ita accurata et perfecta fuerit

At that time when they were on the very point of perishing, then they were rescued. Ἀνακεφαλαιώσθαι (He might sum up), he says. What is the meaning of ἀνακεφαλαιώσθαι (sum up)? It is to knit together. Let us, however, endeavor to get near the exact import. With ourselves then, in common conversation, the word ἀνακεφαλαίωσις means the summing into a brief compass things spoken at length, the concise account of matters described in detail. And it has this meaning. For Christ has gathered up in Himself the dispensations carried on through a lengthened period, that is to say, He has cut them short. He both comprehended former dispensations and added others beside. This is the meaning of ἀνακεφαλαίωσις and summing up. It has also another signification; and of what nature is this? He has set over all one and the same Head, that is, Christ according to the flesh, alike over angels and men. That is to say, He has given to angels and men one and the same government; to

conjunctio, quando omnia redacta fuerint sub unum caput.

the one the Word of God according to the flesh, to the other the Word of God according to the Spirit. For thus will a union be effected, thus will a close bond be effected, if one and all can be brought under one and the same Head.

Feria Quinta: Eph 4:1–15
S. Leo Magnus, *Sermones* (In Nativitate Domini IV, serm. 24, cap. 6)

Magnum praesidium est fides integra, fides vera, in qua nec augeri ab ullo quidquam, nec minui potest: quia nisi una est, fides non est, dicente Apostolo: "Unus Dominus, una fides, unum baptisma; unus Deus et Pater omnium, qui super omnes, et per omnia, et in omnibus nobis" (Eph 4:5). Huic unitati, dilectissimi, inconcussis mentibus inhaerete, et in hac "omnem sectamini sanctitatem" (Heb 12:14). In hac praeceptis Domini deservite, quia "sine fide impossibile est placere Deo" (Heb 11:6), et nihil sine illa sanctum, nihil castum est, nihil vivum: "justus enim ex fide vivit" (Hb 2:4); quam qui diabolo decipiente perdiderit, vivens mortuus est, quia sicut per fidem justitia, ita etiam per fidem veram vita obtinetur aeterna.

A mighty bulwark is a sound faith, a true faith, to which nothing has to be added or taken away: because unless it is one, it is no faith, as the apostle says, "One Lord, one faith, one baptism, one God and Father of all, who is above all, and through all, and in us all" (Eph 4:5–6). Cling to this unity, dearly beloved, with minds unshaken, and in it "follow after all holiness" (Heb 12:14), in it carry out the Lord's commands, because "without faith it is impossible to please God" (Heb 11:6), and without it nothing is holy, nothing is chaste, nothing alive: "For the just lives by faith" (Hb 2:4), and he who by the devil's deception loses it, is dead though living, because as righteousness is gained by faith, so too by a true faith is eternal life gained.

Feria Sexta: Eph 5:1–14
S. Augustinus, *De Baptismo contra Donatistas* (lib. 4, cap. 18)

Constituamus alium fornicatorem, immundum, luxuriosum, avarum, vel etiam apertius idolis deditum, veneficum, discordiosum, contentiosum, aemulum, animosum, seditiosum, invidum, ebriosum, comisatorem, sed catholicum: numquid propter hoc solum quod catholicus est regnum Dei possidebit, agens talia de quibus sic concludit Apostolus: "Quae praedico vobis, sicut praedixi, quoniam qui talia agunt, regnum Dei non possidebunt" (Gal 5:21)? Si hoc dicimus, nos ipsos seducimus. Nam sermo Dei non nos seducit, qui nec tacet, nec parcit, nec ulla adulatione nos decipit. Ideo quippe et alibi dicit: "Hoc enim scitote cognoscentes, quoniam omnis fornicator, aut immundus, aut avarus, quod est idolorum servitus, non habet hereditatem in regno Christi et Dei: nemo vos seducat inanibus verbis" (Eph 5:5–6). Non est ergo quod de sermone Dei conqueramur. Dicit omnino, et aperte ac libere dicit, eos qui male vivunt, ad regnum Dei non pertinere.

Let us suppose another, a fornicator, unclean, lascivious, covetous, or even more openly given to idolatry, a student of witchcraft, a lover of strife and contention, envious, hot-tempered, seditious, jealous, drunken, and a reveler, but a Catholic; can it be that for this sole merit, that he is a Catholic, he will inherit the Kingdom of God, though his deeds are of the kind of which the apostle thus concludes: "Of the which I tell you before, as I have also told you in time past, that they which do such things shall not inherit the Kingdom of God" (Gal 5:21)? If we say this, we lead ourselves astray. For the Word of God does not lead us astray, which is neither silent, nor lenient, nor deceptive through any flattery. Indeed, it speaks to the same effect elsewhere: "For this you know, that no whoremonger, nor unclean person, nor covetous man, which is an idolater, has any inheritance in the kingdom of Christ and of God. Let no man deceive you with vain words" (Eph 5:5–6). We have no reason, therefore, to complain of

the Word of God. It certainly says, and says openly and freely, that those who live a wicked life have no part in the Kingdom of God.

Sabbato: Eph 6:1–13
S. Athanasius, *Vita Sancti Antonii* (cap. 21–22)

Hostes habemus formidandos et callidos, malignos scilicet daemones, et adversis illos colluctatio nobis est, ut ait Apostolus: "Non adversus carnem et sanguinem; sed adversus principatis et potestates, mundi rectores tenebrarum harum, adversus spiritualia nequitiae in caelestibus" (Eph 6:12). Magna illorum turba in aere nobis proximo est, neque procul nobis sunt, magna quoque inter illos est discrepantia. Quod vero jam necessarie nobis incumbit, est nosse eorum adversum nos calliditates. Primum itaque hoc nosse debemus daemones appellari daemones, non quod tales fuerint conditi: nihil enim mali condidit Deus: sed boni etiam ipsi facti sunt; lapsi vero a caelesti sapientia, post in terra volulati. Invidiaque in nos Christianos ardentes, nihil non movent, ut caelorum nobis aditum intercludant, ne eo

For we have terrible and crafty foes—the evil spirits—and against them we wrestle, as the apostle said, "Not against flesh and blood, but against the principalities and against the powers, against the world rulers of this darkness, against the spiritual hosts of wickedness in the heavenly places" (Eph 6:12). Great is their number in the air around us, and they are not far from us. Now there are great distinctions among them. But at this time, it is pressing and necessary for us only to know their wiles against ourselves. First, therefore, we must know this: that the demons have not been created like what we mean when we call them by that name; for God made nothing evil, but even they have been made good; having fallen, however, from the heavenly wisdom, since then they have been groveling on earth. On the one hand they deceived the

nos ascendamus unde lapsi illi sunt. Quapropter multa oratione, multa exercitatione opus est, ut accepta quis per Spiritum discretionis gratia, quae illos spectant possit agnoscere: quinam scilicet illorum minus nequam, quinam nequiores sint: quo studio singuli eorum teneantur: qua quisque ratione prosternatur et eiiciatur.

Greeks with their displays, while out of envy of us Christians they move all things in their desire to hinder us from entry into the heavens; in order that we should not ascend there from whence they fell. Thus, there is need of much prayer and of discipline, that when a man has received through the Spirit the gift of discerning spirits, he may have power to recognize their characteristics: which of them are less and which more evil; of what nature is the special pursuit of each, and how each of them is overthrown and cast out.

INFRA HEBDOMADAM IV POST EPIPHANIAM

Feria Secunda: Phil 4:1–10

S. Augustinus, *De bono viduitatis* (cap. 22)

"De cetero, fratres, quaecumque sunt vera, quaecumque sancta, quaecumque justa, quaecumque casta, quaecumque carissima, quaecumque bonae famae, si qua virtus, si qua laus, haec cogitate: quae et didicistis et accepistis et audistis et vidistis in me" (Phil 4:8). Cernis, quemadmodum illorum duorum, id est bonae vitae et bonae famae vel, quod brevius dicitur, virtutis et laudis, unum

"For the rest, brethren, whatsoever things are true, whatsoever things are holy, whatsoever things are just, whatsoever things are pure, whatsoever things are most dear, whatsoever things are of good report; if any virtue, if any praise, these things think on, which you have both learned, and received, and heard, and seen in me" (Phil 4:8). But of these two, that is, of a good life, and a good report, or as

propter se ipsum sapientissime [Apostolus] retinebat, alterum propter alios misericordissime providebat. Sed quoniam quantalibet humana cautela suspiciones malevolentissimas non potest omni ex parte vitare, ubi pro existimatione nostra quidquid recte possumus fecerimus, si aliqui de nobis vel mala fingendo vel male credendo famam nostram decolorare conantur, adsit conscientiae solacium planeque etiam gaudium, quod merces nostra "magna est in caelis" (Mt 5:11–12), etiam cum dicunt homines mala multa de nobis, pie tamen justeque viventibus.

is said more shortly, of virtue and praise, the one for his own sake he [the apostle] most wisely kept, the other for the sake of others he most mercifully provided. But, forasmuch as human caution, how great soever, cannot on every side avoid most malevolent suspicions, when for our good report we shall have done whatever we rightly can, if any, either by falsely pretending evil things of us, or from believing evil of us, endeavor to stain our fair fame, let there be present the solace of conscience, and clearly also the joy, in that our "reward is great in heaven" (Mt 5:11–12), even when men say many evil things of us, and we yet live godly and righteously.

Feria Tertia: Col 1:1–18
S. Athanasius, *Expositio fidei* (cap. 2–3)

Nec vero sentimus creatum et factum, aut ex nihilo esse rerum omnium creatorem Deum, Dei Filium, ex exsistente exsistentem, ex solo solum, cui ab aeternitate ex Patre par gloria et virtus simul ingenita est: "nam qui videt Filium, videt et Patrem" (Jn 14:9). Nempe omnia per Filium creata sunt: at non ipse res est cre-

We do not regard God the Creator of all, the Son of God, as a creature, or thing made, or as made out of nothing, for He is truly existent from Him Who exists, alone existing from Him Who alone exists, in as much as the like glory and power was eternally and conjointly begotten of the Father. For "He that has seen the Son has seen the Father"

ata, uti his verbis docet Paulus: "Quia in ipso creata sunt omnia, et ipse est ante omnia" (Col 1:16) Non autem dicit eum ante omnia creatum esse, sed esse ante omnia. Hoc igitur verbum, creatum esse, de omnibus quidem dicitur: sed esse ante omnia soli utique Filio congruit. Ille itaque foetus est natura perfectus ex perfecto, ante omnes colles genitus (cf. Prv 8:25), hoc est, ante omnem creaturam ratione et intelligentia praeditam, quemadmodum alibi Paulus eum vocat "primogenitum omnis creaturae" (Col 1:15).

(Jn 14:9). All things to wit were made through the Son; but He Himself is not a creature, as Paul says of the Lord: "In Him were all things created, and He is before all" (Col 1:16). Now He says not, "was created" before all things, but "is" before all things. To be created, namely, is applicable to all things, but "is before all" applies to the Son only. He is then by nature an offspring, perfect from the Perfect, begotten before all the hills (cf. Prv 8:25), that is before every rational and intelligent essence, as Paul also in another place calls Him "first-born of all creation" (Col 1:15).

Feria Quarta: Col 3:12–25; 4:1–2
S. Joannes Chrysostomus, *In Epistulam ad Colossenses commentarius* (hom. 8, cap. 2)

"Super omnia autem haec caritatem, quae est vinculum perfectionis" (Col 3:14). Hoc est autem quod vult dicere: Illa nihil prosunt; dissolvuntur enim illa omnia; nisi fiant cum caritate: haec omnia illa constringit. Quodcumque bonum dixeris, si ea absit, nihil est, sed diffluit. Et sicut in navi, etiamsi magna sint instrumenta, et non sint quae eam succingant tabulata,

"And above all these things, love, which is the bond of perfection" (Col 3:14). Now, what he wishes to say is this: that there is no profit in these things, for all those things break asunder, except they be done with love; this it is which binds them all together. Whatsoever good thing it be you say, if love be absent, it is nothing, it melts away. And it is as in a ship, even though

nihil prodest; et in domo si non sint contignationes; et in corpore, etiamsi magna sint ossa, non sint autem ligamenta, nihil juvat. Cujusmodicumque enim quispiam bona habeat opera et recta facta, evanescunt omnia, nisi sit caritas. Non dixit, est fastigium, sed quod est majus, "vinculum": hoc enim est magis necessarium, quam illud. Nam fastigium quidem est intentio perfectionis; vinculum autem est complexus et comprehensio eorum quae perfectionem efficiunt, tamquam radix.

her rigging be large, yet if there be no girding ropes, it is of no service; and in a house, if there be no tie beams; and in a body, though the bones be large, if there be no ligaments, they are of no service. For whatsoever good deeds any man may have, all vanish away unless there is love. He said not that it is the summit, but what is greater, "the bond": this is more necessary than that. For the summit indeed is an intention of perfection, but the bond is the embrace and connection of those things that produce perfection; it is, as it were, the root.

Feria Quinta: 1 Thes 1:1–10; 2:1–6
S. Fulgentius Ruspensis, *Epistula ad Gallam viduam* (ep. 2, cap. 35)

Laudari quippe in bonis operibus debes, sed in eo quod operaris, hominum laudes exspectare non debes. Laudet te quidem humana lingua, sed tu laudem a solo Deo desidera. Atque ita fiet ut, dum tu laudem ab hominibus non quaesieris, Deus laudetur in operibus tuis. Cum ergo dicit Dominus ut attendamus ne faciamus justitiam nostram coram hominibus, ut videamur ab eis, et iterum jubet ut lux nostra lu-

For thou oughtest to be praised for thy good works, yet for what thou dost thou must not expect praise from men. Human tongue indeed praises thee, but thou desirest praise from God alone. And it will be so that, while thou sleekest not praise from men, God will be praised in thy works. When, therefore, the Lord says that we should take care not to do our justice before men, that we may be seen by them, and again commands that

ceat coram hominibus, numquid contraria praecepit? Absit; sed sic jubet opera bona fieri, ut non nos ipsos, sed Deum velimus in nostra operatione laudari. Nam et Apostolus in suis operibus gloriam humanam vitabat, sed divinam gloriam quaerebat. Propter quod dicit, Thessalonicensibus scribens: "Neque enim aliquando fuimus in sermone adulationis, sicut scitis; neque in occasione avaritiae, Deus testis est; nec quaerentes ab hominibus gloriam, neque a vobis, neque ab aliis" (1 Thes 2:5).

our light should shine before men, did he command the contrary? It is far away; but in this way he commands good works to be done, so that we would not want ourselves but God to be praised in our work. For even the apostle in his works avoided human glory but sought divine glory. For this reason, he says, writing to the Thessalonians: "For we never came with words of flattery, as you know, nor with a pretext for greed, God is witness. Nor did we seek glory from people, whether from you or from others" (1 Thes 2:5).

Feria Sexta: 1 Thes 4:1–12
S. Cyprianus, *De zelo et livore* (cap. 14–15)

Obterenda sunt, fratres dilectissimi, vitia et peccata carnalia, et terreni corporis infesta labes spiritali vigore calcanda, ne, dum iterum ad veteris hominis conversationem revolvimur, lethalibus laqueis implicemur, Apostolo hoc idem providenter et salubriter praemonente: "Itaque," inquit, fratres, "non secundum carnem vivamus: si enim secundum carnem vixeritis, incipietis mori: si autem spiritu opera carnis mortificaveri-

Vices and carnal sins must be trampled down, beloved brethren, and the corrupting plague of the earthly body must be trodden under foot with spiritual vigor, lest, while we are turned back again to the conversation of the old man, we be entangled in deadly snares, even as the apostle, with foresight and wholesomeness, forewarned us of this very thing, and said: "Therefore," brethren, "let us not live after the flesh; for if you live after the

tis, vivetis. Quotquot enim Spiritu Dei aguntur, hi filii Dei sunt" (Rom 8:12–14). Si filii Dei sumus, si templa ejus esse jam coepimus, si, accepto Spiritu sancto, sancte et spiritaliter vivimus, si de terris oculos ad caelum sustulimus, si ad superna et divina plenum Deo et Christo pectus ereximus, non nisi quae sunt Deo et Christo digna faciamus. Hoc est enim mutasse quod fueras et coepisse esse quod non eras, ut in te divina nativitas luceat, ut ad Patrem Deum deifica disciplina respondeat, ut honore et laude vivendi Deus in homine clarescat.

flesh, you shall begin to die; but if you, through the Spirit, mortify the deeds of the flesh, you shall live. For as many as are led by the Spirit of God they are the sons of God" (Rom 8:12–14). If we are the sons of God, if we are already beginning to be His temples, if, having received the Holy Spirit, we are living holily and spiritually, if we have raised our eyes from earth to heaven, if we have lifted our hearts, filled with God and Christ, to things above and divine, let us do nothing but what is worthy of God and Christ. For this is to change what thou hadst been, and to begin to be what thou wert not, that the divine birth might shine forth in thee, that the godly discipline might respond to God, the Father, that in the honor and praise of living, God may be glorified in man.

Sabbato: 2 Thes 1:1–11; 2:1–4
S. Basilius Magnus, *Epistula Alexandrinis* (cap. 1–2)

Christianorum nomen habeant et ipsi persecutores. Ad has autem cogitationes illa etiam accessit: Num Dominus Ecclesias suas reliquit? num novissima hora est, et defectio per haec ingreditur,

Our persecutors too bear the name of Christians. To my reflections has been added this thought too; Can the Lord have wholly abandoned His Churches? Has the last hour come, and is the falling away thus

ut "reveletur tandem iniquus ille, filius perditionis qui adversatur, et effertur adversus omnem qui dicitur Deus aut numen" (2 Thes 2:4)? Sed tamen sive temporaria est ista tentatio, ferte illam, boni Christi athletae: sive etiam res summo interitui traditae sunt, animo ne concidamus ob praesentia. Etenim, si creatura omnis dissolvetur, et transmutabitur mundi hujus figura, quod mirum est nos quoque, qui rerum creatarum pars sumus, communibus malis affici, ac tradi afflictionibus, quas pro virium nostrarum modulo infligit nobis justus Judex, "non tentari nos sinens supra id quod possumus, sed dans una cum tentatione exitum, ut perferre possimus" (1 Cor 10:13)?

coming upon us, "that now the lawless one may be revealed, the son of perdition who opposes and exalts himself above all that is called God and is worshipped" (2 Thes 2:4)? But if the temptation is for a season, bear it, you noble athletes of Christ. If the world is being delivered to complete, and final destruction, let us not lose heart for the present, but let us await the revelation from heaven, and the manifestation of our great God and Savior Jesus Christ. If all creation is to be dissolved, and the fashion of this world transformed, why should we be surprised that we, who are apart of creation, should feel the general woe, and be delivered to afflictions which our just God inflicts on us according to the measure of our strength, "not letting us be tempted above that we are able, but with the temptation giving us a way to escape that we may be able to bear it" (1 Cor 10:13)?

INFRA HEBDOMADAM V POST EPIPHANIAM
Feria Secunda: 1 Tm 3:1–16; 4:1
S. Irenaeus, *Adversus haereses* (lib. 5, cap. 20, 1–2)

Eorum autem qui ab Ecclesia sunt semita, circumiens mundum universum, quippe firmam habens ab Apostolis traditionem, et videre nobis donans omnium unam et eandem esse fidem, omnibus unum et eundem Deum Patrem praecipientibus, et eandem dispositionem incarnationis Filii Dei credentibus, et eandem donationem Spiritus scientibus, et eadem meditantibus praecepta, et eandem figuram ejus quae est erga Ecclesiam ordinationis custodientibus, et eundem exspectantibus adventum Domini, et eandem salutem totius hominis, id est animae et corporis, sustinentibus. Et Ecclesiae quidem praedicatio vera et firma, apud quam una et eadem salutis via in universo mundo ostenditur. Ubique enim Ecclesia praedicat veritatem: et haec est ἑπνάμυξος lucerna Christi bajulans lumen. Confugere [oportet] autem ad Ecclesiam, et in ejus sinu educari, et dominicis Scripturis

The path of those belonging to the Church circumscribes the whole world, as possessing the sure tradition from the apostles, and gives unto us to see that the faith of all is one and the same, since all receive one and the same God the Father, and believe in the same dispensation regarding the Incarnation of the Son of God, and are cognizant of the same gift of the Spirit, and are conversant with the same commandments, and preserve the same form of ecclesiastical constitution, and expect the same advent of the Lord, and await the same salvation of the complete man, that is, of the soul and body. And undoubtedly the preaching of the Church is true and steadfast, in which one and the same way of salvation is shown throughout the whole world. For the Church preaches the truth everywhere, and she is the seven-branched candlestick which bears the light of Christ. It behooves us, therefore, to flee to the Church, and be brought up in her bosom, and be nourished with the

enutriri. Plantata est enim Ecclesia Paradisus in hoc mundo.

Lord's Scriptures. For the Church has been planted as a garden (paradise) in this world.

Feria Tertia: 2 Tm 1:1–13
S. Vincentius Lerinensis, Commonitorium (I, cap. 23–24)

Si novitia veteribus, extranea domesticis, et profana sacratis admisceri coeperint, proserpat hic mos in universum necesse est ut nihil posthac apud Ecclesiam relinquatur intactum, nihil illibatum, nihil integrum, nihil immaculatum, sed sit ibidem deinceps impiorum ac turpium errorum lupanar ubi erat antea castae et incorruptae sacrarium veritatis. "Profanas," inquit, "vocum novitates" (2 Tm 2:16). Vocum, id est, dogmatum, rerum, sententiarum novitates, quae sunt vetustati atque antiquitati contrariae: quae si recipiantur, necesse est ut fides beatorum patrum, aut tota, aut certe magna ex parte violetur; necesse est ut omnes omnium aetatum fideles, omnes sancti omnes casti, continentes, virgines, omnes clerici, levitae et sacerdotes, tanta confessorum millia, tanti martyrum exercitus, tanta urbium, tanta populorum celebritas et multitudo, tot insulae,

If what is new begins to be mingled with what is old, foreign with domestic, profane with sacred, the custom will of necessity creep on universally, till at last the Church will have nothing left untampered with, nothing unadulterated, nothing sound, nothing pure; but where formerly there was a sanctuary of chaste and undefiled truth, thenceforward there will be a brothel of impious and base errors. May God's mercy avert this wickedness from the minds of His servants; be it rather the frenzy of the ungodly. "Profane novelties of words" (2 Tm 2 :16). That is, of doctrines, subjects, opinions, such as are contrary to antiquity and the faith of the olden time. Which if they be received, it follows necessarily that the Faith of the blessed Fathers is violated either in whole, or at all events in great part; it follows necessarily that all the faithful of all ages, all the saints, the chaste, the continent,

provinciae, reges, gentes, regna, nationes, totus postremo jam pene terrarum orbis, per catholicam fidem Christo capiti incorporatus, tanto seculorum tractu ignorasse, errasse, blasphemasse, nesciisse quid crederet, pronuntietur.

the virgins, all the clergy, deacons and priests, so many thousands of confessors, so vast an army of martyrs, such multitudes of cities and of peoples, so many islands, provinces, kings, tribes, kingdoms, nations, in a word, almost the whole earth, incorporated in Christ the Head, through the Catholic Faith, have been ignorant for so long a tract of time, have been mistaken, have blasphemed, have not known what to believe, what to confess.

Feria Quarta: 2 Tm 3:1–13
S. Augustinus, *De Civitate Dei* (lib. 18, cap. 51)

Videns autem diabolus templa daemonum deseri et in nomen liberantis Mediatoris currere genus humanum, haereticos movit, qui sub vocabulo Christiano doctrinae resisterent Christianae, quasi possent indifferenter sine ulla correptione haberi in civitate Dei, sicut civitas confusionis indifferenter habuit philosophos inter se diversa et adversa sentientes. Nam et id, quod ait idem doctor, "Quicumque volunt in Christo pie vivere, persecutionem patiuntur," (2 Tm 3:12) nullis putandum est deesse posse

The devil, seeing the temples of the demons deserted, and the human race running to the name of the liberating Mediator, has moved the heretics under the Christian name to resist the Christian doctrine, as if they could be kept in the city of God indifferently without any correction, just as the city of confusion indifferently held the philosophers who were of diverse and adverse opinions. For it is not to be thought that what the same teacher says can at any time fail. "Whoever will live piously in Christ shall suffer persecution" (2 Tm 3:12). Because even

temporibus. Multi sunt intus, qui corda pie viventium suis perditis moribus cruciant; quoniam per eos blasphematur Christianum et catholicum nomen; quod quanto est carius eis, qui volunt pie vivere in Christo, tanto magis dolent, quod per malos intus positos fit, ut minus, quam piorum mentes desiderant, diligatur. Ipsi quoque haeretici, cum cogitantur habere nomen et sacramenta Christiana et scripturas et professionem, magnum dolorem faciunt in cordibus piorum. His atque hujus modi pravis moribus et erroribus hominum persecutionem patiuntur, qui volunt in Christo pie vivere, etiam nullo infestante neque vexante corpus illorum.

when those who are without do not rage, and thus there seems to be, and really is, tranquility, which brings very much consolation, especially to the weak, yet there are not wanting, yea, there are many within who by their abandoned manners torment the hearts of those who live piously, since by them the Christian and Catholic name is blasphemed; and the dearer that name is to those who will live piously in Christ, the more do they grieve that through the wicked, who have a place within, it comes to be less loved than pious minds desire. The heretics themselves also, since they are thought to have the Christian name and sacraments, Scriptures, and profession, cause great grief in the hearts of the pious. By these and similar depraved manners and errors of men, those who will live piously in Christ suffer persecution, even when no one molests or vexes their body.

Feria Quinta: Ti 1:1–15
S. Hilarius, De Trinitate (lib. 8, cap. 1)

Beatus apostolus Paulus formam constituendi Episcopi fingens, et plane novum Ecclesiae hominem praeceptis suis condens,

The blessed apostle Paul in laying down the form for appointing a bishop and creating by his instructions an entirely new type of mem-

hanc veluti summam consummatarum in eo virtutum esse docuit dicens: "Obtinentem secundum doctrinam fidei verbum, ut potens sit exhortari ad doctrinam sanam, et contradicentes revincere. Sunt enim multi et non subditi, vaniloqui et seductores" (Ti 1:9–10). Non statim boni atque utilis sacerdotis est, aut tantummodo innocenter agere, aut tantummodo scienter praedicare: cum et innocens sibi tantum proficiat, nisi doctus sit; et doctus sine doctrinae sit auctoritate, nisi innocens sit. Non enim apostolicus sermo probitatis honestatisque praeceptis hominem tantum saeculo conformat ad vitam, neque rursum per doctrinae scientiam scribam Synagogae instituit ad legem: sed perfectum Ecclesiae principem perfectis maximarum virtutum bonis instituit, ut et vita ejus ornetur docendo, et doctrina vivendo. Contradicendum itaque est, et impietati insolenti, et insolentiae vaniloquae, et vaniloquio seducenti: et contradicendum per doctrinae sanitatem, per fidei veritatem,

ber of the Church, has taught us in the following words the sum total of all the virtues perfected in him: "Holding fast the word according to the doctrine of faith that he may be able to exhort to sound doctrine and to convict gainsayers. For there are many unruly men, vain talkers and deceivers" (Ti 1:9–10). For in this way he points out that the essentials of orderliness and morals are only profitable for good service in the priesthood if at the same time the qualities needful for knowing how to teach and preserve the Faith are not lacking, for a man is not straightway made a good and useful priest by a merely innocent life or by a mere knowledge of preaching. For an innocent minister is profitable to himself alone unless he be instructed also; while he that is instructed has nothing to support his teaching unless he be innocent. For the words of the apostle do not merely fit a man for his life in this world by precepts of honesty and uprightness, nor on the other hand do they educate in expertness of teaching a mere scribe of the Synagogue for the expounding of the Law: but the apostle is training a

per verborum sinceritatem; ut et sinceritas veritatis sit, et veritas sanitatis.

leader of the Church, perfected by the perfect accomplishment of the greatest virtues, so that his life may be adorned by his teaching, and his teaching by his life. Hence, we must utter our voice against arrogant wickedness and boastful arrogance and seductive boastfulness—yes, we must speak against such things through the soundness of our doctrine, the truth of our Faith, the sincerity of our preaching, so that we may have the purity of truth and the truth of sound doctrine.

Feria Sexta: Ti 2:15; 3:1–11
S. Augustinus, *Contra duas Epistolas Pelagianorum* (lib. 3, cap. 3, 5)

Numquid non per lavacrum sanctum regenerati (cf. Ti 3:5), adoptati, redempti sumus? Et tamen restat regeneratio, adoptio, redemptio, quam in fine venturam nunc patienter exspectare debemus, ut tunc filii saeculi hujus ex nulla parte jam simus. Si a me quispiam quaesierit, utrum per baptismum salvi facti fuerimus, negare non potero dicente Apostolo: "Salvos nos fecit per lavacrum regenerationis et renovationis Spiritus Sancti" (Ti 3:5). Sed si quaesierit, utrum per idem

Have we not been regenerated, adopted, and redeemed by the holy washing (cf. Ti 3:5)? And yet there remains a regeneration, an adoption, a redemption, which we ought now patiently to be waiting for as to come in the end, that we may then be in no degree any longer children of this world. For if anyone should ask of me whether we have been saved by baptism, I shall not be able to deny it, since the apostle says, "He saved us by the washing of regeneration and renewing of the Holy Ghost" (Ti

lavacrum omni prorsus modo jam nos fecerit salvos respondebo: Non ita est. Item quippe idem dicit Apostolus: "Spe enim salvi facti sumus. Spes autem quae videtur non est spes: quod enim videt quis, quid et sperat? Si autem quod non videmus speramus, per patientiam expectamus" (Rom 8:24–25). Salus ergo hominis in baptismate facta est, quia dimissum est quod peccati a parentibus traxit vel quidquid etiam proprie ante baptismum ipse peccavit; salus vero ejus tanta post erit, ut peccare omnino non possit.

3:5). But if he should ask whether by the same washing He has already absolutely in every way saved us, I shall answer: it is not so. Because the same apostle also says, "For we are saved by hope; but hope that is seen is not hope: for what a man sees, why does he yet hope for? But if we hope for that we see not, we with patience wait for it" (Rom 8:24–25). Therefore the salvation of man is effected in baptism, because whatever sin he has derived from his parents is remitted, or whatever, moreover, he himself has sinned on his own account before baptism; but his salvation will hereafter be such that he cannot sin at all.

Sabbato: Phlm 1–19
S. Hieronymus, *Commentaria in Epistulam ad Philemonem* (ad vers. 14)

Potuit itaque et apostolus Paulus absque voluntate Philemonis, Onesimum sibi in ministerium retinere. Sed si hoc sine voluntate Philemonis fecisset: bonum quidem erat, sed non voluntarium. Quod autem non erat voluntarium, alio genere arguebatur non esse bonum. Nihil quippe bonum dici potest, nisi quod ultroneum est. Ex quo Apostoli consideranda

Even the apostle Paul was able to detain Onesimus with himself for ministry without the free consent of Philemon. But if he had done this without the free consent of Philemon, it would have been a "good" to be sure, but not a "freely willed." For nothing can be called "good" except what is voluntary. The reason the apostle's prudence needs to be considered is because

prudentia est: qui idcirco fugitivum servum remittit ad dominum, ut prosit domino suo: qui prodesse non poterat, si domino teneretur absente. Superior ergo quaestio ita solvitur: Potuit Deus hominem sine voluntate ejus facere bonum. Porro si hoc fecisset, non erat bonum voluntarium, sed necessitatis. Quod autem necessitate bonum est, non est bonum, et alio genere malum arguitur. Igitur proprio arbitrio nos relinquens, magis ad suam imaginem et similitudinem fecit. Similem autem Deo esse absolute bonum est.

he sends back a runaway slave to the master in order to benefit his own master; one who was not able to benefit, if he was held back from his absent master. The question posed higher up, therefore, is resolved as follows: God could have made man good without free will. Moreover, if he had done this, "good" would not have been "freely willed" but "of necessity." But what is good by necessity is not good and is exposed as evil in another respect. Therefore, by leaving us to personal choice, He made [us] rather in His own image and likeness. But to be like God is good absolutely.

INFRA HEBDOMADAM VI POST EPIPHANIAM

Feria Secunda: Heb 3:1–8, 12–16

S. Ephraem Syrus, *Commentarii in Epistulas D. Pauli* (Epistula ad Hebraeos, cap. 3)

Et ipse Jesus Christus fidelis fuit ei (cf. Heb 3:2), qui pontificem fecit illum, non in sanctis sanctorum, sed in omnibus, quae sunt in caelo, et in terra: "sicut fidelis fuit Moyses" (Heb 3:2) in omni ingressu in sancta sanctorum interiora. Verum eo quod dixerit, sicut Moyses, ne putetis, eum tamquam Moysem esse (Heb 3:3). Similiter

And Jesus Christ Himself was faithful to Him (cf. Heb 3:2), Who made Him pontiff, not in the Holy of Holies, but in all things that are in heaven and on earth: just "as Moses was faithful" (Heb 3:2) in every entry into the interior of the Holy of Holies. True to what He said, like Moses, do not think that He is like Moses (Heb 3:3). Similarly,

amplior est honor Domini et Filii prae Moyse servo; Omnis namque domus fabricata ab homine fabricatur: qui autem Movsen creavit, et omnia perfecit, Deus est (cf. Heb 3:4). Et Moyses quidem fidelis fuit, sed tamquam minister, tamquam famulus namque fidelis erat in toto domo, ut testimonio esset verborum, quos inibi dicebantur (cf. Heb 3:5). Christus vero non sicut Moyses servus fidelis est, sed tamquam Filius fidelis fuit, non supra tabernaculum internum, sed supra animas hominum; "nos enim domus ejus" sumus (Heb 3:6), si in fiducia sua dumtaxat firmi stemus, et non confundamur in gloria spei ejus; ea enim est passio ejus.

the honor of the Lord and the Son is greater than that of the servant Moses. For every house that is built is built by man: but He that created Moses, and finished all things, is God (cf. Heb 3:4). And Moses was indeed faithful, but as a minister, as a servant, for he was faithful in the whole house, that he might be a witness to the words which were said there (cf. Heb 3:5). But Christ is not like Moses a faithful servant, but like a faithful Son, He was not above the internal tabernacle, but above the souls of men, for "we are His house" (Heb 3:6), if we stand firm in His trust, and are not confounded in the glory of His hope; for His glory is His Passion.

Feria Tertia: Heb 4:1–12

S. Augustinus, *Enarrationes in Psalmos* (in ps. 149, 12)

"Sermo ergo Dei, gladius bis acutus" (Heb 4:12). Unde bis acutus? Dicit de temporalibus, dicit de aeternis. In utroque probat quod dicit, et eum quem ferit, separat a mundo. Nonne ipse est gladius, de quo Dominus dicit: "Non veni pacem mittere in terram, sed gladium" (Mt 10:34)?

By "swords sharpened on both sides," we understand the Word of the Lord (Heb 4:12). How is it two-edged? It speaks of things temporal, it speaks also of things eternal. In both cases it proves what it says, and him whom it strikes, it severs from the world. Is not this the sword whereof the Lord said, "I am not come to send peace

Attende quomodo venit disjungere, quomodo venit separare. Disjungit sanctos, disjungit impios, separat a te quod te impedit. Filius vult servire Deo, pater non vult: venit gladius, venit sermo Dei; dividit filium a patre. Filia vult, mater non vult; gladio dividuntur ab invicem. Nurus vult, socrus non vult; veniat gladius bis acutus, afferat promissionem vitae praesentis et futurae, consolationem temporalium, aeternorum perfruitionem. Ecce gladius ex utraque parte acutus, promittens temporalia et aeterna. Utilis tibi erit gladius bis acutus. Utiliter te ille separat.

upon earth, but a sword" (Mt 10:34)? Observe how He came to divide, how He came to sever. He divides the saints, He divides the ungodly, He severs from thee that which hinders thee. The son wills to serve God, the father wills not: the sword comes, the Word of God comes, and severs the son from the father. The daughter wills to serve God, the mother will not; they are divided from each other by the sword. The daughter-in-law wants to serve God, the mother-in-law does not want it; let the double-edged sword come, bring the promise of the present and future life, the consolation of the temporal, the fruition of the eternal. Behold a sword sharpened on both sides, promising temporal and eternal things. A double-edged sword will be useful to thee. He separates thee usefully.

Feria Quarta: Heb 6:1–10

S. Ambrosius, *De paenitentia* (lib. 2, cap. 2, 7; 1–12)

Quia de remittenda praedicavit paenitentia, debuit et de iis qui iterandum putant baptismum, non silere: et prius sollicitudinem nobis auferri oportuit, ut sciremus etiam post baptismum, si qui pec-

Inasmuch, then, as the apostle spoke of remitting penance, he could not be silent as to those who thought that baptism was to be repeated. And it was right first of all to remove our anxiety, and to let us

carent, donari eis posse peccatum. De baptismate autem dictum verba ipsa declarant, quibus significavit impossibile esse lapsos renovari in paenitentiam (cf. Heb 6:4). Potens est Deus quando vult donare nobis peccata, etiam quae putamus non posse concedi. Et ideo quod nobis impossibile impetratu videtur, Deo donare possibile est. Nam et impossibile videbatur, ut peccatum ablueret aqua: denique Naaman Syrus lepram suam mundari per aquam posse non credidit. Sed quod impossibile erat, fecit Deus esse possibile, qui tantam nobis donavit gratiam (cf. 4 Kgs 5:11). Similiter impossibile videbatur per paenitentiam peccata dimitti: concessit hoc Christus apostolis suis, quod ab apostolis ad sacerdotum officia transmissum est (cf. Jn 20:22). Factum est igitur possibile quod impossibile videbatur. Sed tamen de baptismo dictum, ne quis iteraret, vera ratione persuadet.

know that even after baptism, if any sinned their sins could be forgiven them. And that the apostle was speaking of baptism is evident from the very words in which it is stated that it is impossible to renew unto repentance those who were fallen (cf. Heb 6:4). God is able whenever He wills to forgive us our sins, even those which we think cannot be forgiven. And so it is possible for God to give us that which it seems to us impossible to obtain. For it seemed impossible that water should wash away sin, and Naaman the Syrian thought that his leprosy could not be cleansed by water (cf. 4 Kgs 5:11). But that which was impossible God made to be possible, Who gave us so great grace. In like manner it seemed impossible that sins should be forgiven through repentance, but Christ gave this power to His apostles, which has been transmitted to the priestly office (cf. Jn 20:22). That, then, has become possible which was impossible. But, by a true reasoning, he convinces us that the reiteration by any one of the sacrament of baptism is not permitted.

Feria Quinta: Heb 7:1–12
S. Ambrosius, *De fide* (lib. 3, cap. 11)

Christus idem ergo sacerdos, idem et hostia: et sacerdotium tamen, et sacrificium humanae conditionis officium est; nam et agnus ad immolandum ductus est, et "sacerdos est secundum ordinem Melchisedech" (Ps 109:4). Nemo igitur ubi ordinem cernit humanae conditionis, ibi jus divinitatis asserat. Nam et illum Melchisedech per quem Abraham hostias suas obtulit (cf. Gn 14:18), non angelum utique secundum Judaica ludibria intelligit Ecclesia, sed virum sanctum, ac sacerdotem Dei, qui typum gerens Domini, et sine Patre, et sine matre, et sine generationis enarratione, et sine initio, et sine fine describitur; ut ostenderet sempiternum Filium Dei in hunc mundum esse venturum. Ergo illum Melchisedech in Christi typo sacerdotem Dei accepimus: sed illum in typo, hunc in veritate: typus autem umbra est veritatis: illum in nomine unius civitatis, hunc regem in reconciliatione totius mundi.

Christ is priest and victim; the priesthood and sacrifice are, however, exercised under the conditions of humanity, for He was led as a lamb to the slaughter, and He is a "priest after the order of Melchisedech" (Ps 109:4). Let no man, therefore, when he beholds an order of human establishment, contend that in it resides the claim of divinity; for even that Melchisedech, by whose office Abraham offered sacrifice (cf. Gn 14:18), the Church does certainly not hold to be an angel (as some Jewish triflers do), but a holy man and priest of God, who, prefiguring Our Lord, is described as without father or mother, without history of his descent, without beginning and without end, in order to show beforehand the coming into this world of the eternal Son of God. This Melchisedech, then, have we received as a priest of God made upon the model of Christ, but the one we regard as the type, the other as the original. Now a type is a shadow of the truth, and we have accepted the royalty of the one in the name of a single city, but that of the other as shown in the reconciliation of the whole world.

Feria Sexta: Heb 11:1–10
S. Joannes Damascenus, *Expositio accurata fidei orthodoxae* (lib. 4, cap. 10-11

Fides porro duplex est, "Est enim fides ex auditu" (Rom 10:17). Scripturas namque Sacras audiendo, Spiritus Sancti doctrinae credimus. Atque haec fides per omnia illa, quae a Christo statuta sunt, perficitur opere videlicet credentis, pietatem colens, et ejus qui nos instauravit, praeceptis obsequens. Nam qui secundum Ecclesiae catholicae traditionem non credit, vel per flagitiosa opera cum diabolo communicat, hic infidelis est. Rursus: "Fides est sperandarum substantia rerum, argumentum non apparentium" (Heb 11:1), vel est spes minime dubia nec ambigua, qua confidimus fore, ut quae nobis divinitus promissa sunt, et quae postulamus, adipiscamur. Ac prior quidem, nostrae voluntatis est; altera autem inter Spiritus dona censenda est. Qui vero fide veluti manu ductus, Deum bonum et omnipotentem, et verum, et sapientem, et justum cogitat, omnia plana et aequabilia, viamque rectam inveniet. Nam fieri non potest ut quis sine fide salutem consequa-

Faith is twofold. "For faith comes by hearing" (Rom 10:17). For by hearing the divine Scriptures we believe in the teaching of the Holy Spirit. The same is perfected by all the things enjoined by Christ, believing in work, cultivating piety, and doing the commands of Him Who restored us. For he that believes not according to the Tradition of the Catholic Church, or who has intercourse with the devil through strange works, is an unbeliever. But again, "Faith is the substance of things hoped for, the evidence of things not seen" (Heb 11:1), or undoubting and unambiguous hope alike of what God has promised us and of the good issue of our prayers. The first, therefore, belongs to our will, while the second is of the gifts of the Spirit. But if anyone, under the guidance of faith, should consider the divine goodness and omnipotence and truth and wisdom and justice, he will find all things smooth and even, and the way straight. For it is impossible for anyone to attain salvation without faith.

tur. Fides porro est assensus omni curiosa inquisitione vacans.

Further, faith is an assent free from all meddlesome inquisitiveness.

Sabbato: Heb 13:1–12
S. Alexander Alexandrinus, *Epistula encyclica* (cap. 4)

Quomodo absimilis substantiae Patris fuerit, qui est imago perfecta splendorque Patris, quique ait: "Qui videt me videt et Patrem" (Jn 14:9)? Quo pacto Verbum seu Ratio et Sapientia Dei Filius est, fuit tempus quo non esset? Perinde est enim ac si dicerent: Deum aliquando flatione et sapientia caruisse. Qui item verti mutarive potest, qui ait per se quidem ipse: "Ego in Patre et Pater in me" (Jn 14:10), et "Ego et Pater unum sumus" (Jn 10:30), per prophetam vero: "Videte me, quia ego sum et non mutor" (Mal 3:6). Nam etsi ad Patrem dictum illud referri queat, aptius tamen de Filio jam dicitur, quia cum factus homo sit, nequaquam mutatus est; sed ut ait Apostolus: "Jesus Christus heri et hodie ipse et in saecula" (Heb 13:8). Quis induxit illos ut dicerent, propter nos illum factum esse, licet Paulus dicat: "Propter quem omnia, et per quem omnia" (Heb 2:10).

How is He unlike to the substance of the Father, Who is the perfect image and brightness of the Father, and Who says, "He that hath seen Me hath seen the Father" (Jn 14:9)? And how, if the Son is the Word or Wisdom and Reason of God, was there a time when He was not? It is all one as if they said that there was a time when God was without speech and wisdom. How, also, can He be changeable and mutable, Who says indeed by Himself: "I am in the Father, and the Father in Me" (Jn 14:10), and "I and My Father are one" (Jn 10:30); and by the prophet, "I am the Lord, I change not" (Mal 3:6). For even though one saying may refer to the Father Himself, yet it would now be more aptly spoken of the Word, because when He became man, He changed not; but, as says the apostle, "Jesus Christ, the same yesterday, today, and forever" (Heb 13:8). Who has induced them to say, that for our sakes He was made; whereas Paul says, "For Whom are all things, and by Whom are all things." (Heb 2:10).

TEMPUS SEPTUAGESIMAE

INFRA HEBDOMADAM SEPTUAGESIMAE

Feria Secunda: Gn 1:27–31; 2:1–10
S. Augustinus, *De Civitate Dei* (lib. 22, cap. 30)

"Et requievit Deus die septimo ab omnibus operibus suis, quae fecit, et benedixit Deus diem septimum et sanctificavit eum, quia in eo requievit ab omnibus operibus suis, quae inchoavit Deus facere" (Gn 2:2–3). Dies enim septimus etiam nos ipsi erimus, quando ejus fuerimus benedictione et sanctificatione pleni atque refecti. Ibi vacantes videbimus quoniam ipse est Deus; quod nobis nos ipsi esse voluimus, quando ab illo cecidimus, audientes a seductore: "Eritis sicut dii" (Gn 3:5) et recedentes a vero Deo, quo faciente dii essemus ejus participatione, non desertione. Quid enim sine illo fecimus, nisi quod in ira ejus defecimus? A quo refecti et gratia majore perfecti vacabimus in

"And God rested on the seventh day from all His works which He had made. And God blessed the seventh day and sanctified it; because that in it He had rested from all His work which God began to make" (Gn 2:2–3). For we shall ourselves be the seventh day, when we shall be filled and replenished with God's blessing and sanctification. There shall we be still, and know that He is God; that He is that which we ourselves aspired to be when we fell away from Him, and listened to the voice of the seducer, "You shall be as gods" (Gn 3:5), and so abandoned God, who would have made us as gods, not by deserting Him, but by participating in Him. For without Him what have we accomplished, save

aeternum, videntes quia ipse est Deus, quo pleni erimus quando ipse erit omnia in omnibus.

to perish in His anger? But when we are restored by Him, and perfected with greater grace, we shall have eternal leisure to see that He is God, for we shall be full of Him when He shall be all in all.

Feria Tertia: Gn 2:15–24
S. Augustinus, *De Civitate Dei* (lib. 22, cap. 17)

Ut enim in exordio generis humani de latere viri dormientis costa detracta femina fieret, Christum et ecclesiam tali facto jam tunc prophetari oportebat. Sopor quippe ille viri mors erat Christi, cujus exanimis in cruce pendentis latus lancea perforatum est atque inde sanguis et aqua defluxit; quae sacramenta esse novimus, quibus aedificatur ecclesia. Nam hoc etiam verbo scriptura usa est, ubi non legitur "formavit" aut "finxit," sed: "Aedificavit eam in mulierem" (Gn 2:22); unde et apostolus aedificationem dicit corporis Christi (cf. Eph 4:12), quod est ecclesia. Creatura est ergo Dei femina sicut vir; sed ut de viro fieret, unitas commendata; ut autem illo modo fieret, Christus, ut dictum est, et ecclesia figurata est. Qui ergo ut-

For at the beginning of the human race the woman was made of a rib taken from the side of the man while he slept; for it seemed fit that even then Christ and His Church should be foreshadowed in this event. For that sleep of the man was the death of Christ, whose side, as He hung lifeless upon the Cross, was pierced with a spear, and there flowed from it blood and water, and these we know to be the sacraments by which the Church is built up. For Scripture used this very word, not saying He "formed" or "framed," but "built her up into a woman" (Gn 2:22); whence also the apostle speaks of the edification of the body of Christ (cf. Eph 4:12), which is the Church. The woman, therefore, is a creature of God even as the man; but by her creation from man unity is commended; and

rumque sexum instituit, utrumque restituet.

the manner of her creation prefigured, as has been said, Christ and the Church. He, then, Who created both sexes, will restore both.

Feria Quarta: Gn 3:1–20
S. Augustinus, *Enchiridion* (25–27)

Mortis supplicium Dominus homini comminatus fuerat, si peccaret: sic eum munerans libero arbitrio, ut tamen regeret imperio, terreret exitio: atque in paradisi felicitate, tamquam in umbra vitae, unde justitia custodita in meliora conscenderet, collocavit. Hinc post peccatum exsul effectus, stirpem quoque suam, quam peccando in se tamquam in radice vitiaverat, poena mortis et damnatione obstrinxit: ut quidquid prolis ex illo, et simul damnata, per quam peccaverat, conjuge, per carnalem concupiscentiam, in qua inobedientiae poena similis retributa est, nasceretur, traheret originale peccatum, quo traheretur per errores doloresque diversos ad illud extremum cum desertoribus angelis, vitiatoribus et possessoribus et consortibus suis, sine fine supplicium.

God had threatened him with this punishment of death if he should sin, leaving him indeed to the freedom of his own will, but yet commanding his obedience under pain of death; and He placed him amid the happiness of Eden, as it were in a protected nook of life, with the intention that, if he preserved his righteousness, he should thence ascend to a better place. Thence, after his sin, he was driven into exile, and by his sin the whole race of which he was the root was corrupted in him, and thereby subjected to the penalty of death. And so it happens that all descended from him, and from the woman who had led him into sin, and was condemned at the same time with him—being the offspring of carnal lust on which the same punishment of disobedience was visited—were tainted with the Original Sin, and were by it drawn through various errors and

sufferings into that last and endless punishment which they suffer in common with the fallen angels, their corrupters and masters, and the partakers of their doom.

Feria Quinta: Gn 4:1–16
S. Ephraem Syri, *Commentarius in Librum Primum Pentateuchi* (Gn 3:2–4:7, lect. III, 2–4)

Attulit autem Abel cum delectu, Cain autem sine delectu. "Abel elegit et attulit de primogenitis et de pinguioribus" (Gn 4:4); Cain autem si spicas attulisset, et si cum spicis fructus inventos tempore spicarum attulisset, etiam si minor fuisset oblatio ejus quam fratris sui, si non eum negligentia attulisset eam, sicut oblatio fratris sui accepta fuisset, quia laete obtulisset: unus ex agnis gregis sui et alter ex fructibus terrae suae obtulissent. Quia despectam habuit Cain primam oblationem a se oblatam, noluit Deus accipere illam ab eo, ut doceret eum quomodo offerenda esset. Rejicit igitur Deus oblationem ejus propter id quod fecerat et propter id quod facturus erat. Accepta est igitur oblatio Abel propter delectum Abel, rejectaque est etiam

Abel was very discriminate in his choice of offerings, whereas Cain showed no such discrimination. "Abel selected and offered the choicest of his first born and of his fat ones" (Gn 4:4); while Cain either offered young grains or certain fruits that are found at the same time as the young grains. Even if his offering had been smaller than that of his brother, it would have been as acceptable as the offering of his brother, had he not brought it with such negligence, because his brother gladly had offered it. They made their offerings alternately; one offered a lamb of his flock, the other the fruits of the earth. But because Cain had taken such little regard for the first offering that he offered, God refused to accept it in order to teach Cain how he was to make an offering. Thus, God de-

oblatio Cain propter despectum ejus. Non parvitas oblationis ejus causa fuit cur repulsus esset ille, sed propter deformitatem suam et improbitatem non acceptus est.

spised Cain's offering not only because of what he had done, but also because of what he was about to do. Abel's offering was accepted, therefore, because of his discrimination whereas that of Cain was despised because of his negligence. It was not the smallness of his offering that caused him to be rejected, but because of his deformity and dishonesty it was not accepted.

Feria Sexta: Gn 4:17–26; 5:1–5
S. Augustinus, *De Civitate Dei* (lib. 15, cap. 15, 17)

Cum itaque istae duae series generationum, una de Seth, altera de Cain, has duas, de quibus agimus, distinctis ordinibus insinuent civitates, unam caelestem in terris peregrinantem, alteram terrenam terrenis tamquam sola sint gaudiis inhiantem vel inhaerentem. Noluit enim Spiritus Dei in terrenae civitatis generationibus tempora notare ante diluvium, sed in caelestis maluit, tamquam essent memoria digniores. Cum ergo esset Adam utriusque generis pater, id est et cujus series ad terrenam, et cujus series ad caelestem pertinet ciuitatem, occiso Abel atque in ejus interfectione commendato

These two series of generations accordingly, the one of Cain, the other of Seth, represent the two cities in their distinctive ranks, the one the heavenly city, which sojourns on earth, the other the earthly, which gapes after earthly joys, and grovels in them as if they were the only joys. But though eight generations, including Adam, are registered before the flood, no man of Cain's line has his age recorded at which the son who succeeded him was begotten. For the Spirit of God refused to mark the times before the flood in the generations of the earthly city, but preferred to do so in the heavenly line, as if it were

mirabili sacramento facti sunt duo patres singulorum generum, Cain et Seth, in quorum filiis, quos commemorari oportebat, duarum istarum civitatum in genere mortalium evidentius indicia clarere coeperunt. Cain quippe genuit Enoch, in cujus nomine condidit civitatem, terrenam scilicet, non peregrinantem in hoc mundo, sed in ejus temporali pace ac felicitate quiescentem.

more worthy of being remembered. Since, then, Adam was the father of both lines—the father, that is to say, both of the line which belonged to the earthly, and of that which belonged to the heavenly city—when Abel was slain, and by his death exhibited a marvelous mystery, there were henceforth two lines proceeding from two fathers, Cain and Seth, and in those sons of theirs, whom it behooved to register, the tokens of these two cities began to appear more distinctly. For Cain begot Enoch, in whose name he built a city, an earthly one, which was not from home in this world, but rested satisfied with its temporal peace and happiness.

Feria Sabbato: Gn 5:15–31
S. Cyprianus, *De mortalitate* (cap. 23–24)

Invenimus et Enoch translatum esse, qui Deo placuit, sicut in Genesi testatur et loquitur Scriptura divina: "Et placuit Enoch Deo, et non est inventus postmodum, quia Deus illum transtulit" (Gn 5:24). Hoc fuit placuisse in conspectu Dei, de hoc contagio saeculi meruisse transferi. Sed et per Salomonem docet Spiritus

We find that Enoch also was translated, who pleased God, as in Genesis the Holy Scripture bears witness, and says, "And Enoch pleased God; and afterwards he was not found, because God translated him" (Gn 5:24). To have been pleasing in the sight of God was thus to have merited to be translated from this contagion of the

sanctus eos qui Deo placeant maturius istinc eximi et citius liberari, ne, dum in isto mundo diutius immorantur, mundi contactibus polluantur. "Raptus est," inquit, "ne malitia mutaret intellectum illius" (Ws 4:11). Placita enim erat Deo anima ejus. Propter hoc properavit abducere eum de media iniquitate. Ejus est in mundo diu velle remanere quem mundus oblectat, quem saeculum blandiens atque decipiens illecebris terrenae voluptatis invitat. Porro, cum mundus oderit Christianum, quid amas eum qui te odit, et non magis sequeris Christum, qui te et redemit et diligit?

world. And moreover, also, the Holy Spirit teaches by Solomon, that they who please God are more early taken hence, and are more quickly set free, lest while they are delaying longer in this world they should be polluted with the contagions of the world. "He was taken away," says he, "lest wickedness should change his understanding" (Ws 4:11). For his soul was pleasing to God; wherefore hasted He to take him away from the midst of wickedness. It is for him to wish to remain long in the world whom the world delights, whom this life, flattering and deceiving, invites by the enticements of earthly pleasure. Again, since the world hates the Christian, why dost thou love that which hates thee?

INFRA HEBDOMADAM SEXAGESIMAE
Feria Secunda: Gn 7:1–5, 10–14, 17
S. Maximus Taurinensis, *Sermones* (serm. 50, cap. 2)

Pro misericordia plane videmus illud fuisse diluvium quo, veluti baptismo quodam, totius mundi facies est innovata: scilicet ut qui perditorum hominum scelere sordebat ad crimina, beati Noe habitatione floreret ad gratiam; et qui

By mercy, we plainly see that it was a flood by which, as if by a kind of baptism, the face of the whole world was renewed: that is to say, so that he who was polluted with crimes through the wickedness of lost men might flourish in grace

iniquitatis erat prostibulum tunc, modo fieret domicilium sanctitatis. Diluvium, inquam, illud hujus nostri fuit similitudo baptismatis. Hoc enim tunc gestum est quod nunc agitur: hoc est, ut, exuberantibus aquarum fontibus, periclitarentur vitia, et justitia sola regnaret; mergerentur in profundum peccata, sanctitas vicina caelo portaretur. Tunc enim, sicut dixi, hoc agebatur quod nunc agitur in Ecclesia Christi. Nam sicut Noe aqua, submersis omnibus vitiis, peccatorum adulta ferebatur, ita baptismatis fonte caelo vicina portatur Ecclesia, et deletis omnibus superstitionibus idolorum, fides regnat in terris, quae de Salvatoris arca procedit. Ad similitudinem diluvii, tamquam in naufragio saeculi, sola ad instar arcae illius in altum cum suis virtutibus elevatur Ecclesia.

by the habitation of blessed Noe; and that he who had been a den of iniquity should become the abode of holiness. I say that the flood was a similitude of our baptism. For what was done then is being done now: that is, that, by as the fountains of waters burst forth, vices might be destroyed, and justice alone might reign; sins would sink into the depths, sanctity would be brought near to heaven. For then, as I have said, this was done which is now being done in the Church of Christ. For just as Noe was carried by water full of sins, while all the vices were destroyed, so the Church is carried by the baptismal font close to heaven, while all the superstitions of idols are destroyed, and faith reigns on earth, which proceeds from the ark of the Savior. In the likeness of the flood, as in the shipwreck of the age, the Church alone, like that ark, is lifted up high with its virtues.

Feria Tertia: Gn 8:1–13
S. Beda Venerabilis, Homiliae (lib. 1, hom. 11)

Emisit post eum columbam; a illa venit ad eum vespere, portans ramum olivae virentibus foliis, in ore suo. Animadvertitis credo, fratres, et me loquentem vestro intellectu praevenitis, ramum olivae virentibus foliis gratiam esse Spiritus Sancti vitae verbis abundantiam: de cujus plenitudine super Christum requiescente, psalmus ait: "Unxit te Deus, Deus tuus, oleo laetitiae, prae consortibus tuis" (Ps 44:8). De cujus dono consortibus Christi dato loquitur Joannes: "Vos unctionem habetis a sancto, et nostis omnia" (1 Jn 2:20). Et pulcherrima comparatione umbra veritatis concinit. Ramum olivae columba corporalis ablutam diluvii aquis detulit in arcam, Spiritus Sanctus in specie columbae corporalis baptizatum aqua Jordanis descendit in Dominum. Nos quoque Christi et Ecclesiae membra, quos non solum homines qui erant in arca cum Noe, sed et animantia quae arca continebat, et ipsa quoque ligna ex quibus

After [the raven] he sent a dove, and it came to him in the evening, carrying in its mouth an olive branch with green leaves. You are paying attention, I believe, brothers, and with your intellect you anticipate me as I speak—the olive branch with green leaves is the grace of the Holy Spirit, rich in the words of life, the fullness of which rests upon Christ, as the psalm says, "God, your God, has anointed you with the oil of gladness above your fellows" (Ps 44:8). Concerning this gift given to Christ's fellows, John speaks: "You have the anointing from the holy one, and you know all things" (1 Jn 2:20). And by a most beautiful conjunction, the figure agrees with the fulfillment—a corporeal dove brought the olive branch to the ark which was washed by the waters of the flood; the Holy Spirit descended in the form of a corporeal dove upon the Lord when He was baptized in the waters of the Jordan. Not only the human beings who were in the ark with Noe, but also the living things which the ark contained, and also

eadem facta est arca, figurant post acceptum undae regenerationis lavacrum.

the very wood from which the ark was made, prefigure us members of Christ and of the Church after our reception of the washing of the waters of regeneration.

Feria Quarta: Gn 8:15–22; 9:1–6
S. Ambrosius, *De Noe et arca* (cap. 22, 80)

"Recogitans non adjiciam maledicere terram propter opera hominum; quia permanet cor hominis diligenter super mala a juventute" (Gn 8:21). Non ergo adhuc percuteret omnem terram, sicut fecit, omnibus diebus terrae. Etsi vindicaverat in hominum genus; tamen cognoverat quia vindicta legis ad timorem proficit, et cognitionem doctrinae, magis quam ad naturae commutationem, quae corrigi in aliquibus potest, in omnibus mutari non potest. Vindicavit ergo Dominus, ut timeremus: pepercit, ut reservaremur. Et vindicavit semel ad exemplum timoris, pepercit in reliquum, ne dominaretur semper amaritudo peccati. Pietatem suam circa universitatem hominum voluit declarare, et tamen securitatem et negligentiam quamdam mentibus humanis afferre non debuit, in paucos vin-

"The Lord God reconsidered and said: I will not again curse the earth on account of the works of men, because the heart of man remains firmly fixed on evils from his youth" (Gn 8:21). It will not thus add that He would strike all flesh, as He had done, for all the days of the earth. Even if He punished the race of men again, still He knew that punishment leads more to fear of the law and the knowledge of discipline than to the transformation of nature, which can be corrected in some aspects but cannot be changed in all. Thus, the Lord punished them so that we might fear, but He spared us that we might be preserved, and at one point He punished us as an example to inspire fear; in the future He will spare us, so that bitter sin not be restrained only through subjugation. He wants to declare His own mercy towards all of humanity, yet He also should not im-

dicat, plures reservat. Deinde cum dicit: "Non adjiciam," ostendit quod allevet magis aerumnas hominum quam ingravet, sciens quod penitus peccata hominum auferri non queant.

part to human hearts any laxity and negligence. Hence when it says: "I will not again," it shows that He alleviates the troubles of people rather than weighing them down, knowing that the sins in people cannot be entirely removed.

Feria Quinta: Gn 9:12–15, 20–29
S. Joannes Chrysostomus, *Homiliae in Genesim* (in cap. 9, hom. 28, 3)

"Hoc signum testamenti mei quod posui inter me, et inter omnem carnem quae est super terram" (Gn 9:12). Accepisti, inquit, signum id quod dedi inter me et omnem carnem quae est super terram. Ad hoc respice, et ipse bonam spem habeto, et omnes qui post te futuri sunt hinc consolationem accipiant: et aspectus signi fiduciam eis praestet, quod numquam talis tempestas terram invasura sit. Nam quamvis peccata hominum crescant, ego tamen quae promisi adimplebo, et numquam talem indignationem in omnes exhibebo. Vidistis quam ingens sit Domini bonitas? vidistis quantum ad nostram vilitatem verbis se demittat? vidistis ejus erga nos providentiae magnitudinem? vidistis promittentis lib-

"This is the sign of the covenant I made between Me and all creatures that are upon the earth" (Gn 9:12). Thou didst recognize, He is saying, the sign I gave of agreement between me and every creature living on the earth. Worry thy head no longer, nor upset thy thinking; instead, fix thy gaze on this and allow thyself the luxury of firm hope; let all those coming after thee enjoy comfort from this sign, and let sight of it provide the basis for confidence that never again will such an awful deluge destroy the world. I mean, even if people's sins are intensified, nevertheless I will keep these promises I have made. Do you see the excess of His goodness? Do you see the extent of His considerateness? Do you see the degree of His care? Do you see His promise of generosity? After all, He did not

eralitatem? Non enim beneficium suum usque ad duas, vel tres, vel decem generationes extendit, sed promisit quamdiu subsistet mundus extendendum: ut ex utroque emendatiores reddamur, et ex eo quod illi propter multitudinem peccatorum tali poena puniti sunt, et ex eo quod ille per ineffabilem misericordiam suam, nos tanta promissione dignatus est. Nam cordatos beneficia magis quam poenae alliciunt ad mandata servanda.

simply extend His kindness to two or three or even ten generations; instead, He promised it would last as long as the duration of the universe so that we might be the wiser for each instance, both the fact that they suffered such terrible punishment for the enormity of their sins and also the fact that we were accorded such marvelous promise owing to His ineffable love. People of sense, you see, are drawn to obedience of commands rather by kindnesses than by punishments.

Feria Sexta: Gn 10:1–6; 11:1–8
S. Augustinus, *In Joannis Evangelium tractatus* (tr. 6, cap. 10, 2)

Aliquando enim et linguae per superbiam discordaverunt, et tunc sunt factae linguae ex una multae. Post diluvium enim superbi quidam homines, velut adversus Deum se munire conantes, quasi aliquid esset excelsum Deo, aut aliquid tutum superbiae, erexerunt turrim; quasi ne diluvio, si postea fieret, delerentur. Audierant enim et recensuerant quia omnis iniquitas erat deleta diluvio: ab iniquitate temperare nolebant; altitudinem turris contra diluvium requirebant; aedificaverunt turrim

Once the tongues became discordant through pride, and then of one became many tongues. For after the flood certain proud men, as if endeavoring to fortify themselves against God, as if anything were high for God, or anything could give security to pride, raised a tower, apparently that they might not be destroyed by a flood, should there come one thereafter. For they had heard and considered that all iniquity was swept away by a flood; to abstain from iniquity they would not; they sought the height

excelsam. Vidit Deus superbiam ipsorum, et hunc errorem illis immitti fecit, ut non se cognoscerent loquentes; et factae sunt diversae linguae per superbiam (cf. Gn 11:1–9). Si superbia fecit diversitates linguarum, humilitas Christi congregavit diversitates linguarum. Jam quod illa turris dissociaverat, Ecclesia colligit. De una lingua factae sunt multae; noli mirari, superbia hoc fecit: de multis linguis fit una; noli mirari, caritas hoc fecit.

of a tower as a defense against a flood; they built a lofty tower. God saw their pride, and frustrated their purpose by causing that they should not understand one another's speech, and thus tongues became diverse through pride (cf. Gn 11:1–9). If pride caused diversities of tongues, Christ's humility has united these diversities in one. The Church is now bringing together what that tower had sundered. Of one tongue there were made many; marvel not: this was the doing of pride. Of many tongues there is made one; marvel not: this was the doing of charity.

Feria Sabbato: Gn 11:10–23
S. Augustinus, *De Civitate Dei* (lib. 16, cap. 10, 2)

Tenenda est igitur series generationum ab ipso Sem, ut ipsa ostendat post diluvium civitatem Dei, sicut eam series generationum ab illo, qui est appellatus Seth, ostendebat ante diluvium. Propter hoc ergo scriptura divina cum terrenam civitatem in Babylone, hoc est in confusione, monstrasset, ad patriarcham Sem recapitulando revertitur et orditur inde generationes usque ad

It is necessary, therefore, to preserve the series of generations descending from Sem, for the sake of exhibiting the city of God after the flood as before the flood it was exhibited in the series of generations descending from Seth. And therefore does divine Scripture, after exhibiting the earthly city as Babylon or confusion, revert to the patriarch Sem, and recapitulate the generations from him to Abraham, spec-

Abraham, commemorato etiam numero annorum, quanto quisque ad hanc seriem pertinentem filium genuisset quantoque vixisset. Quid enim aliud intellegendum est terram esse divisam nisi diversitate linguarum? Omissis igitur ceteris filiis Sem ad hanc rem non pertinentibus illi conectuntur in ordine generationum, per quos possit ad Abraham perveniri; sicut illi conectebantur ante diluvium, per quos perveniretur ad Noe generationibus, quae propagatae sunt ex illo Adam filio, qui est appellatus Seth. Sic ergo incipit generationum ista contextio: Et hae generationes Sem.

ifying besides, the year in which each father begot the son that belonged to this line, and how long he lived. For what can we understand by the division of the earth, if not the diversity of languages? And, therefore, omitting the other sons of Sem, who are not concerned in this matter, Scripture gives the genealogy of those by whom the line runs on to Abraham, as before the flood those are given who carried on the line to Noe from Seth. Thus begins this interweaving of generations: and these are the generations of Sem.

INFRA HEBDOMADAM QUINQUAGESIMAE

Feria Secunda: Gn 13:1–16

S. Joannes Chrysostomus, *Homiliae in Genesin* (in cap. 13, hom. 33, 2)

Vide quomodo hic neque prosperitate, neque divitiarum affluentia remissior vel negligentior factus est: sed iterum contendit ad eum locum, ubi prius fuerat, priusquam in Aegyptum concederet. Cogita, obsecro, quantum erat quietis et tranquillitatis amator, et in divino cultu quam sedulus. "Ad eum enim locum," inquit, "acces-

Notice how he had not become less resolute or devoted under the influence of great prosperity or the abundance of wealth, but rather he pressed on once more to that place where he had formerly been before going down into Egypt. Consider, I ask thee, how he was a lover of peace and quiet, and was constantly attentive to divine worship. The

sit, in quo prius altare aedificaverat, et in quo nomen Domini invocaverat" (Gn 13:3). Ecce jam multis antea saeculis implevit hoc quod postea a David dictum est: "Elegi abjectus esse in domo Dei mei magis quam habitare in tabernaculis peccatorum" (Ps 83:11). Solitudo enim propter invocationem nominis Dei gratior ei erat, quam civitates. Sciebat enim, sciebat utique, civitatis magnitudinem non ex aedificiorum pulchritudine, neque ex civium multitudine constare: sed ex inhabitantium virtute, propter quam ipsa solitudo civitatibus dignior fuit, quae virtute justi ornabatur, et orbe toto fulgidior erat.

text says, remember, that "He went down to that place where he had previously built the altar; by calling on the name of God" (Gn 13:3). He already right from the very beginning fulfilled in anticipation that saying of David, "I would rather be of no account in the house of my God than take up residence in sinners' dwellings" (Ps 83:11). In other words, solitude turned out to be preferred by him for invoking the name of God, instead of the cities. After all, he well knew that cities' greatness is not constituted by beauty of buildings nor by multitude of inhabitants, but by the virtue of the residents—hence too the desert proved to be more desirable than the cities, adorned as it was by the just man's virtue and thus a more resplendent vision than the whole world.

Feria Tertia: Gn 14:8–20
S. Cyprianus, *Epistulae* (63, 4)

In sacerdote Melchisedech sacrificii Dominici sacramentum praefiguratum videmus, secundum quod Scriptura divina testatur et dicit: "Et Melchisedeh, rex Salem, protulit panem et vinum" (Gn 14:18). Fuit autem sacerdos

In the priest Melchisedech we see prefigured the sacrament of the sacrifice of the Lord, according to what divine Scripture testifies, and says, "And Melchisedech, king of Salem, brought forth bread and wine" (Gn 14:18). Now

Dei summi, et benedixit Abraham. Quod autem Melchisedech typum Christi portaret, declarat in psalmis Spiritus Sanctus ex persona Patris ad Filium dicens: "Ante luciferum genui te. Tu es sacerdos in aeternum secundum ordinem Melchisedech" (Ps 109:4–5). Qui ordo utique hic est de sacrificio illo veniens et inde descendens, quod Melchisedech sacerdos Dei summi fuit, quod panem et vinum obtulit, quod Abraham benedixit. Nam quis magis sacerdos Dei summi quam Dominus noster Jesus Christus, qui sacrificium Deo Patri obtulit, et obtulit hoc idem quod Melchisedech obtulerat, id est panem et vinum, suum scilicet corpus et sanguinem?

he was a priest of the most high God, and blessed Abraham. And that Melchisedech bore a type of Christ, the Holy Spirit Declares in the psalms, saying from the person of the Father to the Son: "Before the morning star I begot You; You are a priest forever, after the order of Melchisedech" (Ps 109:4–5), which order is assuredly this coming from that sacrifice and thence descending; that Melchisedech was a priest of the most high God; that he offered wine and bread; that he blessed Abraham. For who is more a priest of the most high God than Our Lord Jesus Christ, Who offered a sacrifice to God the Father, and offered that very same thing which Melchisedech had offered, that is, bread and wine, to wit, His Body and Blood?

TEMPUS QUADREGESIMAE

Feria III Majoris Hebdomadae
S. Hieronymus, *Commentaria in Jeremiam* (lib. 2, ad cap. 11:18ff.)

"Ego quasi agnus mansuetus, qui portatur ad victimam, et non cognovi quia super me cogitaverunt consilia" (Jer 11:19). Omnium Ecclesiarum iste est consensus, ut sub persona Jeremiae, a Christo haec dici intelligant, quod ei Pater monstraverit, quomodo eum oporteat loqui, et ostenderit illi studia Judaeorum, et ipse, "quasi agnus ductus ad victimam, non aperuerit os suum" (Is 53:7), et non cognoverit, subauditur peccatum; juxta illud quod ab apostolo dicitur: "Qui cum non cognovisset peccatum, pro nobis peccatum factus est" (2 Cor 5:21), et dixerint: "Mittamus lignum in panem ejus" (Jer 11:19), crucem videlicet in corpus Salvatoris. Ipse est enim qui ait: "Ego sum panis, qui de caelo descendi" (Jn 6:51), et eradicemus, sive "conter-

"I was as a meek lamb, that is carried to be a victim: and I knew not that they had devised counsels against me" (Jer 11:19). This is the consensus of all the churches, that they understand these things to be said referring to Christ under the person of Jeremias, that the Father showed Him how He ought to speak, and showed Him the designs of the Jews, "and He, like a lamb led to the sacrifice, did not open His mouth" (Is 53:7), and "He knew not," that is to say sin, according to what is said by the apostle: "He who knew no sin became sin for us" (2 Cor 5:21), and they said: "Let us put wood into his bread" (Jer 11:19), that is, a Cross into the body of the Savior. For He is the one Who says: "I am the bread that came down from heaven" (Jn 6:51). And let us eradicate Him, even

amus eum de terra viventium" (Jer 11:19). "Videam ultionem tuam ex eis" (Jer 11:20), eorum videlicet, qui in scelere perseverant, et non eorum, qui convertuntur ad paenitentiam. De illis ait in cruce: "Pater, ignosce illis, quod enim faciunt nesciunt" (Lk 23:34). Revelatque Patri et aperit causam suam: quia nullo suo merito, sed scelere populi crucifixus est.

"We will crush him from the earth of the living" (Jer 11:19). "Let me see your vengeance on them" (Jer 11:20), that is, on those who persist in crime, and not on those who turn to repentance. He said of them on the Cross: "Father, forgive them, for they know not what they do" (Lk 23:34). And He reveals to the Father and discloses His cause: that He was crucified by no fault of His own, but by the crime of the people.

Feria IV Majoris Hebdomadae
S. Augustinus, *Sermo Guelferbytanus* 3 (PLS 2, 545–546)

Passio Domini et salvatoris nostri Jesu Christi fiducia gloriae est, et doctrina patientiae. Quid enim non sibi de Dei gratia promittant corda fidelium, pro quibus Dei Filius unicus et Patri coaeternus parum fuit ut homo ex homine nasceretur, nisi etiam manibus hominum, quos creavit, moreretur ipse ab eis? Magnum est quod futurum a Domino promittitur nobis; sed multo est majus quod recolimus jam factum esse pro nobis. Ubi erant aut quid erant, quando pro impiis mortuus est Christus? Quis dubitet eum donaturum sanctis vitam suam, qui

The Passion of Our Lord and Savior Jesus Christ is the confidence of glory and the teaching of patience. For what can the hearts of the faithful not hope for from the grace of God, for whom the only begotten Son of God, coeternal with the Father, considered it little to be born as man from man, unless He Himself died at the hands of those men whom He Himself created? Great indeed is what the Lord promises us for the future, but far greater is what we remember has already been done for us. Where were they, or what were they, when Christ died for the ungodly? Who doubts that

eisdem donavit adhuc mortem suam? Quid cunctatur humana fragilitas credere futurum esse, ut vivant homines aliquando cum Deo? Multo incredibilius jam factum est, quod mortuus est propter homines Deus. Mirum proinde nobiscum egit mutua participatione commercium: nostrum erat, unde mortuus est; illius erit, unde vivamus. Non solum ergo erubescere non debemus de morte Domini Dei nostri, verum etiam maxime in ea fidere maximeque gloriari.

He will give His life to the saints, Who already gave His death for them? Why does human frailty hesitate to believe that men will one day live with God? Something much more incredible has already happened: God died for the sake of men. He therefore dealth a wonderful exchange with us by mutual participation: ours was what caused His death; His shall be what brings us life. Not only, therefore, should we not be ashamed of the death of the Lord our God, but we should also trust and glory in it most highly.

Feria VI in Parasceve
Lect. IV: S. Melito Sardianus, *Homilia in Pascha* (nn. 65–71: SCh 123, 94–100)

Ipse enim adductus est ut agnus et occisus ut ovis, veluti ab Aegypto nos a mundi cultu redemit et servavit nos de servitute diaboli quasi de manu Pharaonis; et consignavit animas nostras proprio Spiritu, et membra corporis nostri suo sanguine. Hic est qui confusione mortem induit et diabolum in planctu constituit, sicut Moyses Pharaonem. Hic est qui iniquitatem percussit et injustitiam, sicut Moyses Aegyptum steril-

He was led forth like a lamb; He was slaughtered like a sheep. He ransomed us from our servitude to the world, as He had ransomed Israel from the land of Egypt; He freed us from our slavery to the devil, as He had freed Israel from the hand of Pharaoh. He sealed our souls with His own Spirit, and the members of our body with His own Blood. He is the One Who covered death with shame and cast the devil into mourning, as Moses cast Pha-

itate damnavit. Hic est qui nos eripuit de servitute ad libertatem, de tenebris ad lucem, de morte ad vitam, a tyrannide in regnum perpetuum, et fecit nos sacerdotium novum et populum electum, aeternum. Hic est Pascha salutis nostrae. Hic est agnus sine voce; hic est agnus occisus; hic est natus ex Maria pulchra agna; hic est qui de grege assumptus et ad mactationem tractus et vespere immolatus et nocte sepultus est; qui super lignum non fractus, et subter terram non solutus est; qui resurrexit a mortuis et de inferiore sepulcro hominem resuscitavit.

raoh into mourning. He is the One Who smote sin and robbed iniquity of offspring, as Moses robbed the Egyptians of their offspring. He is the One Who brought us out of slavery into freedom, out of darkness into light, out of death into life, out of tyranny into an eternal kingdom; Who made us a new priesthood, a people chosen to be His own forever. He is the Passover that is our salvation. He is the mute lamb, the slain lamb, the lamb born of Mary, the fair ewe. He was seized from the flock, dragged off to be slaughtered, sacrificed in the evening, and buried at night. On the tree no bone of His was broken; in the earth His Body knew no decay. He is the One Who rose from the dead, and Who raised man from the depths of the tomb.

Lect. V: S. Joannes Chrysostomus, *Catecheses* (cat. 3, cap. 13–19)

Vis et aliam hujus sanguinis scrutari virtutem? Volo unde primum cucurrit inspicias et de quo fonte manavit. De ipsa primum cruce processit, latus illud dominicum initium fuit. Mortuo enim, ait, Jesu et adhuc in cruce pendente, approximat miles, latus lancea

Dost thou wish to learn from another source as well the strength of this Blood? Look whence it first flowed and where it had its source! It flowed down from the Cross, from the Master's side. St. John says that, when Christ was dead but still on the Cross, the soldier

percussit et exinde aqua fluxit et sanguis. Unum baptismatis symbolum, aliud sacramenti. Latus miles aperuit et templi sancti parietem patefecit et ego thesaurum praeclarum inveni et fulgentes divitias me gratulor reperire. Sic et de illo agno factum est. Judaei ovem occiderunt et ego fructum de sacrificio cognovi. De latere sanguis et aqua. Nolo tam facile, auditor, transeas tanti secreta mysterii. Restat enim mihi mystica atque secretalis oratio. Dixi baptismatis symbolum et mysteriorum aquam illam et sanguinem demonstrari. Ex his enim sancta fundata est Ecclesia, per "lavacri regenerationem et renovationem Spiritus Sancti" (Ti 3:5), per baptisma, inquam, et mysteria quae ex latere videntur esse prolata. Ex latere igitur suo Christus aedificavit Ecclesiam, sicut de latere Adam ejus conjux Eva prolata est (cf. Gn 2:23).

came and pierced His side with a lance, and straightway there came out water and blood. The one was a symbol of baptism, and the other of the mysteries. It was the soldier, then, who opened Christ's side and dug through the rampart of the holy temple, but I am the one who has found the treasure and gotten the wealth. So it was with the lamb. The Jews sacrificed the victim, but I reaped the reward of salvation which came from their sacrifice. Do not pass this mystery by without a thought. For I have still another mystical explanation to give. I said that there was a symbol of baptism and the mysteries in that blood and water. It is from both of these that the Church is sprung through "the bath of regeneration and renewal by the Holy Ghost" (Ti 3:5), through baptism and the mysteries. But the symbols of baptism and the mysteries come from the side of Christ. It is from His side, therefore, that Christ formed His Church, just as He formed Eve from the side of Adam (cf. Gn 2:23).

Lect. VI: S. Athanasius, *Oratio de Incarnatione Verbi* (cap. 25, 1–3)

Si quis vero ex nostris non contendendi sed discendi studio quaerat, cur non aliam quam crucis mortem toleraverit: audiat etiam iste, idcirco hoc mortis genus Dominum pertulisse, quia nulla alia nobis conducebat. Nam si ideo venit ut maledictionem, in quam incideramus, portaret, quomodo aliter factus fuisset maledictio, nisi maledictionis mortem suscepisset? Ea autem crux est, nam scriptum est: "Maledictus qui pendet in ligno" (Dt 21:23; Gal 3:13). Deinde, si mors Domini pretium est omnium, ejusque morte "medius paries maceriae solvitur" (Eph 2:14), ac fit vocatio gentium, quomodo nos convocasset, nisi fuisset crucifixus? siquidem in sola cruce extensis manibus mori quis potest. Quocirca id mortis genus Dominum pati et manus extendere decuit, ut altera veterem populum, altera gentes attraheret, ac utrosque in seipso conjungeret. Id quippe et ipse dixit significans qua morte omnes esset redempturus: "Cum exaltatus fuero, omnes traham ad meipsum" (Jn 12:32).

But if any of our own people also inquire, not from love of debate, but from love of learning, why He suffered death in none other way save on the Cross, let him also be told that no other way than this was good for us, and that it was well that the Lord suffered this for our sakes. If He came Himself to bear the curse laid upon us, how else could He have become a curse, unless He received the death set for a curse? And that is the Cross. For this is exactly what is written: "Cursed is he that hangs on a tree" (Dt 21:23; Gal 3:13). Again, if the Lord's death is the ransom of all, and by His death "the middle wall of partition is broken down" (Eph 2:14), and the calling of the nations is brought about, how would He have called us to Him, had He not been crucified? For it is only on the cross that a man dies with his hands spread out. Whence it was fitting for the Lord to bear this also and to spread out His hands, that with the one He might draw the ancient people, and with the other those from the Gentiles, and unite both in Himself. For this is what

He Himself has said, signifying by what manner of death He was to ransom all: "I, when I am lifted up," He says, "shall draw all men unto Me" (Jn 12:32).

Sabbato Sancto

Lect. IV: *Ex antiqua Homilia in sancto et magno Sabbato* (PG 43, 439, 451, 462–463)

Quid istud rei est? Hodie silentium magnum in terra; silentium magnum, et solitudo deinceps; silentium magnum, quoniam Rex dormit; "terra timuit et quievit" (Ps 75:9), quoniam Deus in carne obdormivit, et a saeculo dormientes excitavit. Deus in carne mortuus est, et infernum concitavit. Profecto primum parentem tamquam perditam ovem quaesitum vadit. Omnino in tenebris et in umbra mortis sedentes invisere vult; omnino captivum Adam, unaque captivam Evam, ex doloribus solutum vadit Deus illiusque Filius. Ingressus est Dominus ad eos, victricia arma crucis tenens. Quem ubi vidit Adam primus parens, prae stupore pectus verberans, exclamavit ad omnes dixitque: Dominus meus cum omnibus. Et respondens Christus

What is happening? Today there is a great silence over the earth, a great silence, and stillness, a great silence because the King sleeps; "The earth was in terror and was still" (Ps 75:9), because God slept in the flesh and raised up those who were sleeping from the ages. God has died in the flesh, and the underworld has trembled. Truly He goes to seek out our first parent like a lost sheep; He wishes to visit those who sit in darkness and in the shadow of death. He goes to free the prisoner Adam and his fellow-prisoner Eve from their pains, He Who is God, and Adam's son. The Lord goes in to them holding His victorious weapon, His Cross. When Adam, the first created man, sees Him, he strikes his breast in terror and calls out to all: My Lord be with you all. And Christ in reply

dicit Adamo: Et cum spiritu tuo. Et apprehensa manu excitat, dicens: Expergiscere, qui dormis, et surge a mortuis, et illucescet tibi Christus.

says to Adam: And with your spirit. And grasping his hand He raises him up, saying: Awake, O sleeper, and arise from the dead, and Christ shall give you light.

Lect. V:

Exite; et qui in tenebris: Illuminamini; et sopitis: Resurgite. Tibi praecipio: Expergiscere, qui dormis: etenim non ideo te feci, ut in inferno contineare vinctus. Surge a mortuis; ego sum vita mortuorum. Surge, opus manuum mearum; surge, effigies mea, quae ad imaginem meam facta es. Surge, exeamus hinc; tu enim in me, et ego in te, una et indivisa sumus persona. Propter te ego Deus tuus, factus sum filius tuus; propter Dominus, servilem tuam speciem sumpsi; propter te, qui sum supra caelos, veni in terram, et subtus terram; propter te hominem "factus sum tamquam homo sine adjutorio, inter mortuos liber" (Ps 87:5–6); propter te, qui ex horto egressus es, ex horto Judaeis traditus, et in horto crucifixus sum. Aspice faciei meae sputa, quae quidem propter te suscepi, ut te in prisitinum illud spiraculum restituerem. Aspice mearum

Come forth, and those in darkness: Have light, and those who sleep: Rise. I command thee: Awake, sleeper, I have not made thee to be held a prisoner in the underworld. Arise from the dead; I am the life of the dead. Arise, O man, work of My hands, arise, thou who wert fashioned in My image. Rise, let us go hence; for thou in Me and I in thee, together we are one undivided person. For thee, I thy God became thy son; for thee, I the Master took on thy form; that of slave; for thee, I Who am above the heavens came on earth and under the earth; for thee, man, "I became as a man without help, free among the dead" (Ps 87:5–6); for thee, who left a garden, I was handed over to Jews from a garden and crucified in a garden. Look at the spittle on My face, which I received because of thee, in order to restore thee to that first divine inbreathing at cre-

maxillarum alapas, quas sustinui, ut tuam corruptam speciem reformarem, ad imaginem meam. Aspice mei tergi flagellationem, quam suscepi, ut dispergerem peccatorum tuorum onus, quod tergo tuo impositum est. Aspice clavis bene ad lignum affixas manus meas, propter te, qui manum tuam ad lignum male quondam extenderas.

ation. See the blows on My cheeks, which I accepted in order to refashion thy distorted form to My own image. See the scourging of My back, which I accepted in order to disperse the load of thy sins which was laid upon your back. See My hands nailed to the tree for a good purpose, for thee, who stretched out thy hand to the tree for an evil one.

Lect. VI:

Dormivi in cruce, et romphaea penetravit meum latus, propter te, qui in paradiso obdormisti, et Evam ex latere protulisti. Meum latus sanavit dolorem lateris. Meus somnus educet te ex inferni somno. Mea romphaea romphaeam coercuit, quae contra te vertebatur. "Surge, eamus hinc" (Jn 14:31). Eduxit te hostis ex terra paradisi; ego vero te non amplius in paradiso, sed in caelesti throno colloco. Prohibuit te a ligno typico vitae; verum ecce ego, qui vita sum, tibi sum conjunctus. Constitui cherubim, qui famuli in morem custodirent te; facio ut cherubim, pro eo ac Deum decet, adorent te. Cherubicus thronus apparatus est, geruli prompti et

I slept on the Cross and a spear pierced My side, for thee, who slept in paradise and brought forth Eve from thy side. My side healed the pain of thy side; My sleep will release thee from thy sleep in hell; My sword has checked the sword which was turned against thee. But "arise, let us go hence" (Jn 14:31). The enemy brought thee out of the land of paradise; I will reinstate thee, no longer in paradise, but on the throne of heaven. I denied thee the tree of life, which was a figure, but now I Myself am united to thee, I Who am life. I posted the cherubim to guard thee as they would slaves; now I make the cherubim worship thee as they would God. The cherubim throne has

parati, thalamus constructus est, parati cibi, aeterna tabernacula et mansiones adornatae, thesauri bonorum aperti sunt, regnumque caelorum ante saecula paratum est.

been prepared, the bearers are ready and waiting, the bridal chamber is in order, the food is provided, the everlasting houses and rooms are in readiness; the treasures of good things have been opened; the Kingdom of heaven has been prepared before the ages.

TEMPUS PASCHALE

Feria Secunda: Acts 1:1–26
S. Bedae Venerabilis, *Expositio super Acta Apostolorum*
(lib. 1, cap. 16)

In undenario numero Petrus apostolus remanere metuit. Omne enim peccatum undenarium est, quia dum perverse agit, praecepta Decalogi transit. Unde quia nulla nostra justitia per se innocens est, tabernaculum quod arcam Domini continebat intus undecim velis cilicinis desuper obvelabatur. Numerumque apostolorum duodenarium redintegrat, ut per duas septenarii partes (ter enim quaterni decus dipondium) gratiam quam verbo praedicabant, et cum numero servarent, et qui mundo quadriformi fidem sanctae Trinitatis praedicaturi erant, Domino dicente: "Ite, docete omnes gentes, baptizantes eos in nomine Patris, et Filii, et Spiritus sancti" (Mt 28:19), jam operis perfectionem numeri quoque sacramento

The apostle Peter was apprehensive about continuing with the number eleven [of apostles], for every sin is an eleven, because when one does wicked things, he goes beyond the commandments of the Decalogue. Hence, because no righteousness of ours is innocent of itself, the tabernacle which contained the Lord's ark was covered from above by eleven veils of goats' hair. Peter restored the number of apostles to twelve, so that through two parts of six each (for three times four is twelve) they might preserve by an eternal number the grace which they were preaching by word, and so that those who were to preach the Faith of the Holy Trinity to the four parts of the world—in line with the Lord's saying, "Go, teach all nations, baptizing them in

firmarent. Iuxta altiorem autem intellectum, damnum Ecclesiae quod in falsis fratribus patitur, hactenus ex parte maxima perdurat incorrectum. At cum in fine mundi populus Judaeorum qui Dominum crucifixit reconciliandus Ecclesiae creditur, velut quinquagesimo die propinquante, apostolorum est summa restituta.

the name of the Father and of the Son and of the Holy Spirit" (Mt 28:19)—might already certify the perfection of the work by the sacramental sign of their number as well. According to a deeper sense, however, the evil which the Church suffers in false brethren remains so far uncorrected for the most part. But since at the end of the world it is believed that the Jewish people who crucified the Lord are to be reconciled to the Church, as the fiftieth day drew nigh the full number of apostles was restored.

Feria Tertia: Acts 2:1–31

S. Augustinus, *In Evangelium Joannis tractatus* (tr. 6, cap. 3)

Cum mitteret Spiritum Sanctum, duobus modis eum ostendit visibiliter; per columbam, et per ignem: per columbam, super Dominum baptizatum; per ignem, super discipulos congregatos. Cum enim ascendisset Dominus in caelum post resurrectionem, peractus cum discipulis suis quadraginta diebus, impleto die Pentecostes, misit eis Spiritum Sanctum, sicut promiserat. Hac vidimus columbam super Dominum, hac linguas divisas super discipulos congrega-

When He sent the Holy Spirit, He manifested Him visibly in two ways—by a dove and by fire: by a dove upon the Lord when He was baptized, by fire upon the disciples when they were gathered together. For when the Lord had ascended into heaven after His Resurrection, having spent forty days with His disciples, and the day of Pentecost being fully come, He sent unto them the Holy Ghost as He had promised. He [Stephen] held fast to the unity of the dove. Here we

tos: ibi simplicitas, hic fervor ostenditur. Inhaeserat [Stephanus] unitati columbae. Prior enim illud fecerat magister, super quem descendit columba; qui pendens in cruce ait: "Pater, ignosce illis, quia nesciunt quid faciunt" (Lk 23:34). Ergo ne Spiritu sanctificati dolum habeant, in columba demonstratum est: ne simplicitas frigida remaneat, in igne demonstratum est. "Linguae," inquit, "divisae velut ignis, qui et insedit super unumquemque eorum" (Acts 2:3). Distant inter se linguae, sed linguarum distantia non sunt schismata. In linguis divisis noli dissipationem timere, unitatem cognosce in columba.

have seen a dove descending upon the Lord; there, cloven tongues upon the assembled disciples: in the former, simplicity is shown; in the latter, fervency. For his Master, upon whom the dove descended, had done the same thing before him; Who, while hanging on the Cross, said, "Father, forgive them, for they know not what they do" (Lk 23:34). Wherefore by the dove it is shown that they who are sanctified by the Spirit should be without guile; and that their simplicity should not continue cold is shown us by the fire. Nor let it trouble you that the tongues were divided; for tongues are diverse, therefore the appearance was that of cloven tongues. "Cloven tongues," it says, "as of fire, and it sat upon each of them" (Acts 2:3). There is a diversity of tongues, but the diversity of tongues does not imply schisms. Be not afraid of separation in the cloven tongues; in the dove recognize unity.

Feria Quarta: Acts 3:1–16
S. Joannes Cassianus, *De incarnatione Christi* (lib. 7, cap. 19)

Petrus enim apostolus claudo illi qui sedebat ad speciosam portam templi, "In nomine," inquit, "Jesu Christi surge, ambula" (Acts 3:6). Et iterum in civitate Joppe, ad eum qui ab annis octo paralyticus jacebat in lecto: "Aenea, sanet te," inquit, "Dominus Jesus Christus; surge et sterne tibi" (Acts 9:34). Siquidem nulli umquam apostolorum post Domini resurrectionem vel daemonem vel ullam infirmitatem obstitisse agnovimus. Hi qui potestatem a Deo acceperunt, numquam potestate ipsa ut sua usi sunt, sed potestatem ipsam ad eum a quo acceperant retulerunt: quia nec potestas ipsa vim ullam umquam habere potuit, nisi per nomen ipsius qui dedit. Ideoque et apostoli et omnes ministri Dei nihil in suo umquam, sed in Christi nomine atque invocatione fecerunt; quia potestas ipsa inde accipiebat virtutem, unde habebat exordium; et dari per ministros nequaquam poterat, nisi ab auctore venisset.

The apostle Peter says to that lame man who was sitting at the beautiful gate of the Temple: "In the name of Jesus Christ arise and walk" (Acts 3:6). And again in the city of Joppe to the man who had been lying on his bed paralysed for eight years he says, "Aeneas, may the Lord Jesus Christ heal thee: arise and make thy bed for thyself" (Acts 9:34). We never heard of any devil or infirmity able to resist any of the apostles since the Lord's Resurrection. How then did the Spirit make Him to be feared, Who made others to be feared? Or was He in Himself weak, Whose faith even through the instrumentality of others reigned over all things? Finally, those men who received power from God, never used that power as if it were their own: but referred the power to Him from Whom they received it: for the power itself could never have any force except through the name of Him Who gave it. And so, both the apostles and all the servants of God never did anything in their own name, but in the name and invo-

cation of Christ: for the power itself derived its force from the same source as its origin, and could not be given through the instrumentality of the ministers, unless it had come from the Author.

Feria Quinta: Acts 5:1–16
S. Hieronymus, *Epistulae Ad Demetriadem* (ep. 130, cap. 14)

Consideremus, quam sapienter sapientia sit locuta: "Vende quae habes." Cui ista praecipiuntur? Nempe illi, cui dictum est: "Si vis esse perfectus." Non partem bonorum tuorum vende: sed omnia. Cumque vendideris, quid sequitur? "Et da pauperibus" (Mt 19:21). Non divitibus, non propinquis, non ad luxuriam, sed ad necessitatem. In Actis Apostolorum (4:34), quando Domini nostri adhuc calebat cruor, et fervebat recens in credentibus fides, vendebant omnes possessiones suas, et pretia earum ad Apostolorum deferebant pedes, ut ostenderent pecunias esse calcandas: dabaturque singulis, prout cuique opus erat (cf. Acts 4:34–35). Ananias et Sapphira dispensatores timidi, imo corde duplici, et ideo condemnati, quia post votum ob-

Let us consider how wisely Wisdom has spoken. "Sell that thou hast." To whom is the command given? Why, to him to whom it was said, "If thou wilt be perfect." Sell not a part of thy goods but all that thou hast. And when thou have sold them, what then? "Give to the poor" (Mt 19:21). Not to the rich, not to thy kinsfolk, not to minister to self-indulgence; but to relieve need. We read in the Acts of the Apostles (4:34) how, while the Blood of the Lord was still warm and believers were in the fervor of their first faith, they all sold their possessions and laid the price of them at the apostles' feet (to show that money ought to be trampled underfoot) and distribution was made unto every man according as he had need (cf. Acts 4:34–35). But Ananias and Sapphira proved timid stewards, and what is more, deceit-

tulerunt quasi sua et non ejus, cui semel ea voverant: partemque sibi alienae substantiae reservaverunt, metuentes famem, quam vera fides non timet, praesentem meruere vindictam: non crudelitate sententiae, sed correptionis exemplo. Denique et apostolus Petrus nequaquam imprecatur eis mortem, ut stultus Porphyrius calumniatur; sed Dei judicium prophetico spiritu annuntiat, ut poena duorum hominum sit doctrina multorum.

ful ones; they brought, therefore, on themselves condemnation. For having made a vow they offered their money to God as if it were their own and not His to Whom they had vowed it; and keeping back for their own use a part of that which belonged to another, through fear of famine which true faith never fears, they drew down on themselves suddenly the avenging stroke, which was meant not in cruelty towards them but as a warning to others. In fact, the apostle Peter by no means called down death upon them as Porphyry foolishly says. He merely announced God's judgment by the spirit of prophecy, that the doom of two persons might be a lesson to many.

Feria Sexta: Acts 8:9–24

S. Augustinus, *In Evangelium Joannis tractatus* (tr. 11, cap. 9, 1–2)

Quia et per malos verum praedicabatur, et per malorum ora Christus praedicabatur; si quos isti sui similes baptizabant, mali malos baptizabant: si quos isti baptizabant tales, quales admonet Dominus cum dicit, "Quae dicunt facite; quae autem faciunt, facere nolite" (Mt 23:3), mali bonos baptizabant. Boni malos baptizabant,

Through evil men the truth was preached, and by the mouths of evil men Christ was preached. If these men baptized any persons like themselves, evil men baptized evil men: if they baptized such as the Lord admonishes, when He says, "Whatsoever they bid you, do; but do not ye after their works" (Mt 23:3), they were evil men that

quomodo a Philippo sancto Simon Magus baptizatus est (cf. Acts 8:13). Nota sunt ergo ista quatuor genera, fratres mei. Ecce iterum ea repeto, tenete illa, numerate illa, advertite illa; cavete quae mala sunt, tenete quae bona sunt. Per bonos boni nascuntur, cum per sanctos sancti baptizantur: per malos mali, cum et qui baptizant et qui baptizantur, inique et impie vivunt: per malos boni, cum mali sunt qui baptizant; et boni qui baptizantur: per bonos mali, cum boni sunt qui baptizant, et mali qui baptizantur.

were baptizing good. Good men baptized evil men, as Simon the sorcerer was baptized by Philip, a holy man (cf. Acts 8:13). Therefore these four sorts, my brethren, are known. See, I repeat them again, hold them, count them, think upon them; guard against what is evil; keep what is good. Good men are born of good, when holy men are baptized by holy; evil men are born of evil, when both they that baptize and they that are baptized live unrighteously and ungodly; good men are born of evil, when they are evil that baptize, and they good that are baptized; evil men are born of good, when they are good that baptize, and they evil that are baptized.

Sabbato: Acts 10:1–17, 34–41
S. Bedae Venerabilis, *Expositio super Acta Apostolorum* (cap. 10, 11–12)

Quatuor initiis submitti de caelo in terram. Quatuor initia, quibus linteum dependebat, quatuor plagas orbis terrarum designant, quibus extenditur Ecclesia. Ipsa est enim civitas Dei nostri in monte sancto ejus, dilatans exsultationes universae terrae. Possunt etiam quatuor initiis evangelistae figurari, per quos Ecclesia caelesti

Lowered by its four corners from heaven to earth. The four corners from which the linen sheet hangs down designate the four regions of the world to which the Church extends, for she is the city of our God upon His holy mountain, spreading sounds of joy to every land. Also, the four corners may be figures of the evangelists, through whom the

munere imbuitur atque sublimatur. "Surge, Petre, occide, et Manduca" (Acts 10:13). Surge, inquit, ad evangelizandum praeparare. Occide in gentibus quod fuerant, et fac quod es. Praecipit ergo ut nationes per incredulitatem ante foris positae, interfecta praeterita vita, societati Ecclesiae, quam significat Petrus, inserantur. Hoc autem factum est per ter. Quia per quatuor partes orbis terrarum mysterium sanctae Trinitatis a duodecim apostolis praedicandum erat, ideo quatuor lineae tertia vice de caelo demissae sunt. Et statim receptum est vas in caelum. Post trinam submissionem linteum caelo recipitur, quia post hujus saeculi conversationem, qua per fidem et baptismum mundata peregrinatur Ecclesia, caelestis inhabitatio felix et aeterna sequitur.

Church is nourished and exalted with heavenly gifts. "Arise, Peter, kill and eat" (Acts 10:13). Arise, it says, to make ready to preach the gospel. Kill what the Gentiles were, and make them what you are. Therefore it commanded that the nations, formerly excluded due to their lack of belief, should, once their former life had been put to death, be incorporated within the society of the Church, which Peter represents. Now, this happened three times. Because the mystery of the Holy Trinity was to be preached by the twelve apostles throughout the four parts of the world, therefore four lines were sent down from heaven the third time. And immediately the vessel was taken up into heaven. After the threefold lowering, the linen sheet is taken up to heaven, since after the affairs of this world—through which the Church, cleansed by faith and baptism, sojourns—there follows a happy and everlasting heavenly dwelling.

INFRA HEBDOMADAM II POST OCTAVAM PASCHAE

Feria Secunda: Acts 15:5–29

S. Cyrillus Hierosolymitanus, *Catecheses* (cat. 17, cap. 29)

Idem Spiritus Sanctus, qui ex consensu Patris et Filii Novum Testamentum in Ecclesia catholica excitavit, liberavit nos ab difficilibus ad ferendum legis oneribus. Iis dico quae mundum et immundum, cibosque spectant; a sabbatis et noviluniis, et cirfcumcisione, aspersionibus, et sacrificiis. Quae pro ratione temporis data, umbram habebant futurorum bonorum (cf. Heb 10:1); accedente autem veritate merito subtracta sunt. Cum enim, propter excitatam Antiochiae quaestionem, ab iis, qui ajebant necessarium esse circumcidi et Moysis consuetudines observare, missi essent Paulus et Barnabas. Apostoli qui isthic in Hierosolymis erant, ab universo legis et figurarum instructu, per conscriptam epistolam orbem totum liberaverunt. Neque vero sibi ipsis tantae molis rei auctoritatem tribuere, sed epistola scripto data ita confitentur: "Visum est enim Spiritui Sancto et nobis, ne quidam amplius vobis imponeremus oneris,

This Holy Spirit, Who in unison with Father and Son has established the New Covenant in the Catholic Church, has set us free from the burdens of the Law grievous to be borne—those I mean, concerning things common and unclean, and meats, and Sabbaths, and new moons, and circumcision, and sprinklings, and sacrifices; which were given for a season, and had a shadow of the good things to come (cf. Heb 10:1), but which, when the truth had come, were rightly withdrawn. For when Paul and Barnabas were sent to the apostles, because of the question moved at Antioch by them who said that it was necessary to be circumcised and to keep the customs of Moses, the Apostles who were here at Jerusalem by a written injunction set free the whole world from all the legal and typical observances; yet they attributed not to themselves the full authority in so great a matter, but send an injunction in writing, and acknowledge this: "For it has seemed good unto the Holy Ghost and to us, to

quam haec necessaria; videlicet ut abstineatis ab iis quae sunt idolis immolata, et a sanguine, et suffocato et fornicatione" (Acts 15:28–29). Per ea quae scripserunt, hoc aperte indicantes, quod tametsi por homines apostolos illud scriptum erat, tamen ex Spiritu Sancto praeceptum esset ad totum orbem pertinens.

lay upon you no greater burden than these necessary things; that you abstain from things sacrificed to idols, and from blood, and from things strangled, and from fornication" (Acts 15:28–29); showing evidently by what they wrote, that though the writing was by the hands of human apostles, yet the decree is universal from the Holy Ghost.

Feria Tertia: Acts 17:22–18:4
S. Augustinus, *De Trinitate* (lib. 15, cap. 12, 16)

Deus est, et quidem "non longe positus ab unoquoque nostrum," sicut apostolus dicit adjungens: "In illo enim vivimus et movemur et sumus" (Acts 17:28). Quod si secundum corpus diceret, etiam de isto corporeo mundo posset intellegi. Nam et in illo secundum corpus vivimus et movemur et sumus. Unde secundum mentem quae facta est ad ejus imaginem debet hoc accipi excellentiore quodam eodemque non visibili sed intellegibili modo. Non tamen omnes cum illo sunt eo modo quo ei dictum est: "Ego semper tecum" (Ps 72:23), nec ipse cum omnibus eo modo quo dicimus: Dominus vobiscum. Magna itaque hominis

And indeed, "He is not far from anyone of us," as the apostle says, and then adds: "In him we live and move and have our being" (Acts 17:28). If this were said with regard to the body, it could also be understood of this corporeal world, for we also live and move and have our being in Him according to the body. Therefore, it must be understood in a more excellent and, at the same time, invisible and intelligible way, namely, with respect to the mind that has been made to His image. Yet not all are with Him in that way in which it was said to Him: "I will always be with thee" (Ps 72:23). Nor is He Himself with all things in that way in which we say: The Lord be

miseria est cum illo non esse sine quo non potest esse. In quo enim est procul dubio sine illo non est, et tamen si ejus non meminit eumque non intellegit neque diligit, cum illo non est.

with you. The great wretchedness of man, therefore, is not to be with Him without Whom he cannot be. For undoubtedly, he is not without Him in Whom he is, and yet if he does not remember Him, and does not understand Him, nor love Him, he is not with Him.

Feria Quarta: Acts 20:17–38
S. Joannes Chrysostomus, *Commentarius in Acta Apostolorum* (hom. 44, cap. 2)

Duo praecepit. Igitur neque alios corrigere solum habet quidpiam lucri. "Timeo" enim, inquit, "ne aliis praedicans, ipse reprobus efficiar" (1 Cor 9:27); neque sui solius curam habere. Nam qui seipsum amat, quae sua sunt tantum quaerit, et similis est ei, qui talentum defodit. Haec dicit, non quod pretiosior sit nostra salus quam gregis; sed quia, si nobis ipsis attendamus, tunc et grex lucrum habet. "In quo vos Spiritus Sanctus posuit episcopos, ut pasceretis Ecclesiam Dei" (Acts 20:28). Spiritu ordinationem habetis, inquit: id enim sibi vult illud, "Posuit." Una haec est necessitas: deinde, "ut pascatis Ecclesiam Dei." Ecce et secunda: et tertia, "Quam acqui-

He enjoins them two things. Neither success in bringing others right of itself is any gain—for, "I fear," he says, "lest by any means, when I have preached to others, I myself should be a castaway" (1 Cor 9:27); nor the being diligent for oneself alone. For such one is selfish, and seeks his own good only, and is like to him who buried his talent. This he says, not because our own salvation is more precious than that of the flock, but because, when we take heed to ourselves, then the flock also is a gainer. "In which the Holy Ghost hath made you overseers, to feed the Church of God" (Acts 20:28). See, it is from the Spirit you have your ordination. This is one constraint: then he says, "To feed

sivit sanguine suo" inquit. Multum ostendit, dum dicit pretiosam rem; nec de parvis rebus esse periculum, siquidem Dominus pro Ecclesia neque sanguini suo pepercit, nos autem fratrum salutem contemnimus.

the Church of the Lord." Lo! another obligation: the Church is the Lord's. And a third: "which He has purchased with His own Blood." It shows how precious the concern is; that the peril is about no small matters, seeing that even His own Blood He spared not, but we despise the salvation of our brethren.

Feria Quinta: Acts 24:10–27
S. Joannes Chrysostomus, *Commentarius in Acta Apostolorum* (hom. 50, cap. 2)

"Credens," inquit, "omnibus, quae in lege sunt" (Acts 24:14). Hoc dixit, ostendens nullum hominem, qui credat resurrectionem futuram, talia facturum esse; quam et illi exspectant. Non dixit de his, quod credant iis quae in prophetis scripta sunt (neque enim credebant); sed hic omnibus credebat, non illi. Tanta dixit, et nusquam Christi meminit. Hic autem ut dixit, "Credens," etiam ea, quae Christum spectabant, complectitur; sed interim in resurrectionis sermone moratur, quod dogma ipsis commune erat, et omnem seditionis suspicionem aufert. "Eleemosynas," inquit, "et oblationes facturus in gentem meam,

"Believing all things which are written in the Law" (Acts 24:14). Now a man who believed a resurrection, would never have done such things, which (resurrection) they themselves also await. He does not say it of them, that they believe all things written in the prophets: it was he that believed them all, not they. He said so much, and never mentions Christ. Yet here, by saying, "Believing," he does introduce what relates to Christ; for the present he dwells on the subject of the resurrection, which doctrine was common to them also, and removed the suspicion of any sedition. And for the cause of his going up, "I came," he says, "to bring alms to my

veni, idque per annos plures" (Acts 24:17). Quomodo ergo turbasset eos, quibus eleemosynam daturus tantum iter susceperat? Ita confidebat se mundum esse a crimine, ut etiam provocet eos. Et non eos solum, qui ab Asia erant, verum etiam eos, qui ex Jerusalem accusatores non rejicit. Etenim ideo ab initio aegre ferebant, quod resurrectionem praedicaret. Et bene sic faciebat: hoc enim ostenso, facile et Christum et resurrectionem ejus inducebat.

nation and offerings" (Acts 24:17). How then should he have troubled those, for the bringing offerings to whom he had come so long a journey? He was so confident that he was clean from crime that he even challenged them. And not only those who were from Asia, but also those who did not reject the accusers from Jerusalem. For in fact, it was on this account they were sore troubled from the first, because he preached the Resurrection. This being proved, the things relating to Christ also were easily introduced, that He was risen.

Feria Sexta: Acts 25:1–12
S. Joannes Chrysostomus, *Commentarius in Acta Apostolorum* (hom. 51, cap. 4)

Modo nobis ipsis non insidiemur, nemo nobis insidiari poterit; imo insidiantur quidem, sed nihil nocent, sed maxime prosunt. Itaque penes nos est, et malo affici et non affici. Ecce testificor et magna tubaque clariore voce dico, et si liceret ex alto loco clamare, non recusarem: Christianum non posse a quovis homine in terra habitante laedi. Et quid dico, homine? Ne ipse quidem daemon,

So long as we do not make ill designs against ourselves, no one will be able to have ill designs against us: or rather, people may do this, but they do us no hurt; nay, even benefit us in the highest degree: for it rests with ourselves, whether we shall suffer evil, or not suffer evil. Lo! I testify, and proclaim with a loud voice, more piercing even than the sound of a trumpet—and were it possible to ascend on high and

vel tyrannus, vel diabolus potest, nisi se ipse laedat. Si ergo quis nobis malum inferre velit, incassum tentabit. Sicut enim Angelum nullus in terra homo laedat, sic nec homo hominem. Sed neque ipse alium laedere poterit, donec bonus erit. Ergo Angelus quidam est et Deo similis. Talis enim et Deus est; sed ille natura, hic proposito. Neque ergo laedi, neque laedere potest. Illa quippe natura nec damnum accipit, nec infert: nam hoc aliud damnum esset. Etenim non alio nos ipsos modo laedimus, quam alios laedendo, et maxima peccata nostra ex damno nobis importato fiunt. Ideo ergo Christianus laedi nequit, quo laedere non possit.

cry aloud, I would not shrink from doing it — him that is a Christian, none of all the human beings that inhabit the earth will have power to hurt. And why do I say, O man? Not even the evil spirit himself, the tyrant, the devil, can do this, unless the man injure himself; be what it may that anyone works, in vain he works it. For even as no human being could hurt an angel, if he were on earth, so neither can one human being hurt another human being. But neither again will he himself be able to hurt another, so long as he is good. Therefore, he is a kind of an angel and similar to God. For such is God; but God is good by nature, man is good by purpose. God's nature neither receives nor inflicts damage: for this would be another damage. Indeed, we do not harm ourselves in any other way than by harming others, and our greatest sins are caused by the harm inflicted on us. Therefore, as long as a Christian does not inflict harm on others, he cannot be harmed.

Sabbato: Acts 28:16–31
S. Joannes Chrysostomus, *Commentarius in Acta Apostolorum*
(hom. 55, cap. 3)

Viden' quomodo omnia praevideat sacrum illud et divinum caput, ille qui animam habet omnia simul complectentem, qui primas partes occupat, Paulus? cujus solum nomen scientibus sufficit ad animam excitandam, ad vigilantiam, ad somnum excutiendum omnem. Excepit illum Roma vinctum, ex marino itinere littus tangentem, a naufragio servatum, et liberata est a naufragio erroris. Sicut enim rex post navalem pugnam et victoriam, in splendidam illam regiamque urbem ingressus est. De his scribens, dicebat: "Veniam" et vobiscum quiescam "in plenitudine benedictionis evangelii" (Rom 15:29). Jam prope erat ut coronam acciperet: excepit illum Roma vinctum, viditque coronatum et proclamatum. Illic "vobiscum quiescam" (Rom 15:32) inquit. Isthuc vado, ministraturus in Jerusalem. Hoc autem initium cursus iterum erat, et tropaea tropaeis addebat, inexpugnabilis cum esset.

Dost thou mark how he did not foresee everything—that sacred and divine head, the man higher than the heavens, that had a soul able to grasp all at once, the holder of the first place—Paul? The man whose very name, to them that know him, suffices for rousing of the soul, for vigilance, for shaking off all sleep! Rome received him bound, coming up from the sea, saved from a shipwreck—and was saved from the shipwreck of error. Like an emperor that has fought a naval battle and overcome, he entered into that most imperial city. Of this he says, "I will come" and rest together with you "in the fullness of the blessing of the gospel" (Rom 15:29). He was nearer now to his crown. Rome received him bound and saw him crowned and proclaimed conqueror. There he had said, "I will rest together with you" (Rom 15:32), but this was the beginning of a course once more, and he added trophies to trophies, a man not to be overcome.

INFRA HEBDOMADAM III POST OCTAVAM PASCHAE

Feria Secunda: Apoc 2:1–17

S. Caesarius Arelatensis, *Expositio de Apocalypsi sancti Joannis* (hom. 2)

Fratres carissimi, in candelabro, de quo cum Apocalypsis legeretur audistis, populus intelligitur. Quod autem ait, "Movebo candelabrum tuum" (Apoc 2:5); hoc est, dispergam populum pro peccatis. "Et pugnabo cum eis in gladio oris mei" (Apoc 2:16): id est, proferam praecepta mea, per quae arguantur peccata vel crimina sua. Quod vero dixit, "Facies ejus sicut sol lucet in virtute sua" (Apoc 1:16): et de adventu vel praesentia Christi, quia per faciem quisque manifestatur atque cognoscitur; et de Ecclesia potest hoc accipi, cui istam claritatem Christus promisit, de qua dicit, "Tunc fulgebunt justi sicut sot in regno Patris eorum" (Mt 13:43). "Stellam matutinam" (Apoc 2:28) primam resurrectionem dicit, quae per gratiam baptismi fit. Stella matutina noctem fugat, et lucem annuntiat, id est, peccatum tollit et gratam tribuit: si tamen accepta gratia bona opera sequantur. Sicut enim magnam arborem virere et fruc-

Beloved brethren, in the candlestick, of which you heard when the Apocalypse was read, is meant the people. But what He said, "I will move your candlestick" (Apoc 2:5); that is, I will scatter the people for their sins. "And I will fight with them with the sword of My mouth" (Apoc 2:16): that is, I will bring forth My precepts, by which they will be accused of their sins or crimes. What he actually said, "His face is like the sun shining in its power" (Apoc 1:16): and about the coming or presence of Christ, because everyone is manifested and known by His face; and this can be referred to the Church, to whom Christ promised this brightness, of which He says, "Then shall the righteous shine as the sun in the Kingdom of their Father" (Mt 13:43). He calls "the morning star" (Apoc 2:28) the first resurrection, which takes place through the grace of baptism. The morning star dispels the night and announces the light, that is, it takes away sin

tum non reddere nihil prodest; sic nihil prodest christianum dici, et christiana opera non habere.

and gives grace: if, however, grace is received, good works follow. For just as a great tree grows and does not bear fruit, it is of no use; so it is of no use to be called a Christian, and not to have Christian works.

Feria Tertia: Apoc 4:1–11
S. Victorinus Petavionensis, *Scholia in Apocalypsin Joannis*
(ex capite 4, ad vers. 8)

"Alas senas" (Apoc 4:8) Testimonia sunt Veteris Testamenti librorum. Ideo viginti et quatuor totidem faciunt, quot sunt seniores super tribunalia sedentes. Sed sicut animal volare non potest nisi pennas habeat, sic, nec praedicatio Novi Testamenti fidem habet, nisi habeat Veteris Testamenti praenuntiata testimonia, per quae tollitur a terra et volat. Semper enim, quod ante dictum est, et postea factum invenitur, illud fidem facit indubitabilem. Rursum et alae si non haereant animalibus, vitam unde trahant, non habent. Nisi enim quae praedixerunt prophetae, in Christo essent consummata, inanis erat praedicatio eorum. Haec enim tenet Ecclesia catholica quae et antea predicata, et postea consummata sunt. Et

"Six wings" (Apoc 4:8). They are the testimonies of the books of the Old Testament. Therefore they are twenty-four in all, which is also the same number of elders on the judgment seats. But just as a creature cannot fly without having wings, so neither does the preaching of the New Testament have credibility unless it is supported by the foretold testimonies of the Old Testament, through which it is lifted from earth and flies. For whenever that which was previously spoken is later fulfilled, it renders faith indubitable. Again, if wings do not adhere to animals, there is no source from which to draw life. For unless the prophecies of the prophets were fulfilled in Christ, their preaching will have been in vain. The Catholic Church holds fast to that which was foretold

volat quippe et merito tollitur a terra vivum animal. Haereticis autem qui testimonio prophetico non utuntur, adsunt et eis animalia, sed non volant, quia sunt terrena. Judaeis autem qui non accipiunt Novi Testamenti praedicationem, adsunt alae, sed non volant, id est inanem vaticinationem hominibus afferunt, facta dictis non conferentes.

and later accomplished. And thus the living creature both flies and is justly lifted up from the earth. Heretics, who do not use the testimony of the prophets, also have creatures, but they do not fly, for they are earthly. As for the Jews, who do not accept the preaching of the New Testament, they possess wings, but they do not fly; that is, they bring a worthless prophecy to men, not confirming their words by deeds.

Feria Quarta: Apoc 5:1–14
S. Victorinus Petavionensis, *Scholia in Apocalypsin Joannis*
(ex capite 5, ad vers. 8 -9)

"Viginti quatuor seniores et quatuor animalia citharas et phialas habentes, et cantantes canticum novum" (Apoc 5:8–9). Conjuncta Veteris Testamenti praedicatio cum novo, populum christianum significat cantantem canticum novum, id est confessionem suam publice conferentem. Novum est, filium Dei hominem fieri. Novum est, cum corpore in caelos ascendere. Novum est, remissionem peccatorum hominibus dare. Novum, sancto Spiritu signari homines. Novum est, sacerdotium accipere sacrae observationis, et

"Twenty-four elders and four animals, having harps and bowls, singing a new song" (Apoc 5:8–9). The combination of the preaching of the Old Testament with the New signifies the Christian people singing a new song, that is, publicly declaring their confession. It is new that the Son of God becomes man. It is new that He ascends into heaven with His body. It is new that He grants unto men remission of sins. It is new that men are sealed with the Holy Ghost. It is new to receive a priesthood of sacred observance and to expect a Kingdom

regnum exspectare immensae re- promissionis. Cithara et chorda in ligno extensa significat carnem Christi passionis ligno conjunctam. Phiala confessionem, et novi sacerdotii propaginem. Angelorum autem multorum, immo omnium laus, omnium salus est, et testimonium universae creationis Domino nostro referentium gratulationem liberationis hominum de clade mortis. Resignatio sigillorum, ut diximus, apertio est Veteris Testamenti, et praedicatorum praenuntiatio in novissimo tempore futurorum; quae licet scriptura prophetica per singula sigilla dicat, omnibus tamen simul, apertis sigillis, ordinem suum habet praedicatio.

of immeasurable promise. The harp and string stretched upon wood signify the Body of Christ joined to the wood of His Passion. The bowl signifies confession and the propagation of a new priesthood. The praise of many angels, indeed of all, represents the salvation of all, and the testimony of all creation, giving thanks to Our Lord for freeing man from the calamity of death. The unsealing of the seals is, as we have said, the opening of the Old Testament, and the preachers' proclamation of what is to come in the end times. Although prophectic Scripture speaks of individual events through each seal, when all the seals are open together, the foretelling has its order.

Feria Quinta: Apoc 15:1–16:6
S. Beda Venerabilis, *Explanatio Apocalypsis* (lib. 3, cap. 15)

"Et unum ex quatuor animalibus dedit septem angelis septem phialas" (Apoc 15:7). Istae sunt phialae quas cum odoribus ferunt animalia et seniores, qui sunt Ecclesia, qui et septem angeli. Eaedem quippe phialae, et suavitatem supplicationum et iram suppliciorum continere dicuntur,

"And one of the four living creatures gave to the seven angels seven golden bowls" (Apoc 15:7). These are the bowls which are carried with their odors by the living creatures and the elders, who are the Church, and who are also the seven angels. The same bowls are said to contain both the sweetness of sup-

cum a sanctis pro regni Dei adventu funduntur, quando judicia Dei non jam occulta sicut abyssus, sed aperta ut phialae, justis latura salutem, impiis vero praedicuntur inferre perniciem. "Et impletum est templum fumo" (Apoc 15:8). Praedicatura gentibus Ecclesia, prius ipsa caritatis igne calescens, fumum piae confessionis emittit, gratias Deo super inenarrabili dono ejus agens. "Et nemo poterat introire in templum" (Apoc 15:8). Nemo potest Ecclesiae membris incorporari, nisi qui mysteria fidei audiens discit a praedicatoribus, quia Jesus constitutus est a Deo judex vivorum et mortuorum. Quod si fumum abdita judiciorum Dei interpretaris arcana, mortalibus haec impenetrabilia manent et clausa, donec, finitis praesentis saeculi plagis, "adveniat Dominus, qui et illuminet et abscondita tenebrarum" (1 Cor 4:5), et manifestet quantum vel utilitatis ad probandam Ecclesiae fidem, vel justitiae ad excaecandos Judaeos qui caritatem veritatis non receperunt, ut salvi fierent, adventus conferat Antichristi.

plications, and the wrath of punishments. For they are poured forth by the saints before the advent of the Kingdom of God, when the judgments of God, which are now no longer secret as the abyss, but open as the bowls, are announced as being salvation to the righteous, but destruction to the ungodly. "And the temple was filled with smoke" (Apoc 15:8). The Church, when it is to preach to the nations, is first influenced itself with the fire of love, and sends forth the smoke of pious confession, while it gives thanks to God for His unspeakable gift. "And no man was able to enter into the Temple" (Apoc 15:8). No one is able to be incorporated among the members of the Church, but he who hears the mysteries of faith from the preachers and learns that Jesus is constituted by God the Judge both of the living and the dead. But if thou shalt interpret the smoke to be the secret judgment of God, these remain impenetrable, and closed to mortal men until, after the plagues of the present age are ended, "the Lord come, Who is both to bring to light even the hidden things of darkness" (1 Cor

4:5), and make manifest how much the coming of antichrist confers which is either of utility in proving the Faith of the Church, or of judgment in blinding the eyes of the Jews, who received not the love of the truth, that they might be saved.

Feria Sexta: Apoc 19:1–16
S. Beda Venerabilis, *Explanatio Apocalypsis* (lib. 3, cap. 19)

"Post haec audivi quasi vocem magnam tubarum multarum in caelo dicentium: Alleluia" (Apoc 19:1). Haec nunc ex parte dicit Ecclesia; tunc autem perfecte cum discessio facta fuerit, et cum apertius vindicata. "Quae corrupit terram in prostitutione sua" (Apoc 19:2). Duo meretricis facta commemorat, quae se videlicet malis corruperit, et bonos persecuta sit, quibus duobus cuncta reor pravorum crimina comprehendit. "Et iterum dixerunt: Alleluia" (Apoc 19:3). Ecclesia Dominum super judiciis ejus indesinenti affectu collaudat. Alleluia enim dicitur Laudate Dominum. Denique psalmi qui principium habent Laudate Dominum, apud Hebraeos ab alleluia incipiunt. "Et fumus ejus ascendit in saecula sae-

"After these things I heard as it were the voice of many people in heaven, saying: Alleluia" (Apoc 19:1). These things the Church now says in part but will say perfectly when the separation has taken place, and when it has been more openly avenged. "Which corrupted the earth with her fornication" (Apoc 19:2). He relates two actions of the harlot, namely, that she corrupted herself with the bad, and persecuted the good; and in these two, I suppose, he comprehends all the crimes of the wicked. "And again they said: Alleluia" (Apoc 19:3). The Church extols the Lord for His judgments with unceasing love. For Alleluia signifies, Praise ye the Lord. Lastly, the psalms which have for the beginning Praise ye the Lord, begin in the Hebrew with Alleluia. "And

culorum" (Apoc 19:3). Ascendit dixit, non ascendet. Semper autem in perditionem vadit Babylon, et jam crematur in parte, sicut Jerusalem transit in paradisum, Domino manifestante in paupere et divite. "Et viginti quatuor seniores ceciderunt, et quatuor animalia adoraverunt Deum" (Apoc 19:4). Non labiorum tantum officio, sed summae dulcedine devotionis Ecclesia Deum veneratur.

her smoke rises up for ever and ever" (Apoc 19:3). Rises up, he says, not will rise up. But Babylon always goes into perdition, and is in part already burning, while Jerusalem passes into paradise, as the Lord manifests in the poor man and the rich. "And the four and twenty ancients, and the four living creatures fell down and adored God" (Apoc 19:4). The Church worships God, not with the service of the lips alone, but with the sweetness of the highest devotion.

Sabbato: Apoc 22:1–21
S. Hieronymus, *Tractatus in Librum Psalmorum* (tr. de Ps 1)

Et ecce, inquit, vidi thronum positum, et agnum unum, et arborem, inquit, secundum flumen, et ex utraque parte ripae ipsam arborem (cf. Apoc 22:1–3; 4:2): hoc est, ex ista parte erat, et ex illa parte erat. Et habebat, inquit, fructus ipsa arbor, et in anno mensibus singulis duodecim fructus adferebat. Et habebat, inquit, folia, et folia ejus erant ad sanitatem gentium (cf. Apoc 22:2). Vidi, inquit, thronum positum unum. Licet enim credamus in Patrem et Filium et Spiritum Sanctum, et Trinitas sit,

Behold, I saw a throne set up, and one Lamb and a tree alongside a river, and on both sides of the river was that tree (cf. Apoc 22:1–3; 4:2). This means that the tree was both on this side and on that side of the river. And this tree, he says, bore fruit and was yielding its twelve fruits for the year according to each month. And it had leaves, too, and the leaves for the healing of the nations (cf. Apoc 22:2). I saw, he says, a single throne set up. We believe in the Father, and the Son, and the Holy Spirit, that is true,

tamen regnum unum est. Vidi, inquit, thronum positum unum. Et vidi, inquit, in conspectu throni stantem unum agnum (cf. Apoc 5:6). De assumptione corporis dicitur Salvatoris. "Ecce agnus Dei, ecce qui tollit peccata mundi" (Jn 1:29). Et egrediebatur, inquit, fons de subtus medio throni (cf. Apoc 22:1). Videtis igitur quoniam de medio throni fons egreditur gratiarum. Tamen non egreditur fons ille de throno, nisi agnus in contra steterit: nisi enim crediderimus incorporationem Christi, non accipimus istas gratias. Unus fluvius egreditur de throno Dei, hoc est gratia Spiritus Sancti; et ista gratia Spiritus Sancti in Sanctis Scripturis est, hoc est in isto fluvio Scripturarum. Tamen iste fluvius duas ripas habet, et Vetus et Novum Testamentum; et in utraque parte arbor plantata Christus est.

and that they are a Trinity; nevertheless, the kingship is one. I saw a single throne set up, and I saw a single lamb standing in the presence of the throne (cf. Apoc 5:6) This refers to the Incarnation of the Savior. Scripture says: "Behold the lamb of God, Who takes away the sin of the world!" (Jn 1:29) And there was a fountain of water coming forth from beneath the middle of the throne (cf. Apoc 22:1). Notice that it is from the midst of the throne that there issues forth a river of graces. That river does not issue forth from the throne unless the lamb is standing before it, for unless we believe in the Incarnation of Christ, we do not receive those graces. One river comes forth from the throne of God—the grace of the Holy Spirit—and this grace of the Holy Spirit is found in the river of the Sacred Scriptures. This river, moreover, has two banks, the Old Testament and the New Testament, and the tree planted on both sides is Christ.

INFRA HEBDOMADAM IV POST OCTAVAM PASCHAE
Feria Secunda: Jas 1:17–27
S. Augustinus, *Sermones* (serm. 179, cap. 7–9).

"Estote, fratres mei, factores verbi, et non auditores tantum, fallentes vosmetipsos" (Jas 1:22); non Deum, non eum qui praedicat. Ego enim, vel quisquis vobis praedicat verbum, cor vestrum non videt; quid agatis intus in cogitationibus vestris, judicare non potest. Quia homo non potest, intuetur Deus, cui cor humanum non potest occultari. Ipse videt quo studio audias, quid cogites, quid teneas, quantum proficias de supplementis suis, quam instanter ores, quemadmodum depreceris Deum ex eo quod non habes, quomodo gratias agas ex eo quod habes; ille novit qui exacturus est. Nolite ergo, fratres mei, fallere vosmetipsos, quia venistis studiose ad audiendum verbum, si non facitis quod auditis deficiendo. Cogitate si pulchrum est audire, quanto magis facere. Si non audis, auditum negligis, nihil aedificas. Si audis et non facis, ruinam aedificas. Malum est ergo non audire; malum est audire et non facere; restat audire et facere.

"So, my dear brothers, be doers of the Word, and not hearers only, deceiving yourselves" (Jas 1:22), not God, not the one Who is preaching. I, after all, or anyone else who preaches the Word to you, cannot see your hearts; what you are doing inside, in your thoughts, we cannot see. Man cannot do it, but God is looking, since the human heart cannot be concealed from Him. He can see with what eagerness thou listenest, what thou thinkest, what thou graspest, how much thou profitest from what He supplies thee with, how urgently thou prayest, how thou beggest God for what thou hast not, how thou thankest Him for what thou art; He knows all this, because He is going to demand His due. So, my brothers, do not deceive yourselves, just because you come eagerly to hear the Word, if you fail to do what you hear. Just think; if it is lovely to hear, how much more so to do. If thou dost not hear it at all, if thou neglectest the matter of hearing, then thou art building nothing. If thou hear and

dost not, then thou art building a ruin. It is bad not to hear; it is bad to hear and not do; the only thing left is to hear and to do.

Feria Tertia: Jas 2:1–13
S. Augustinus, *Epistulae* (*Ad Hieronymum*, ep. 167, cap. 19)

Lex itaque libertatis, lex caritatis est de qua dicit: "Si tamen legem perficitis regalem secundum Scripturas, Diliges proximum tuum sicut teipsum, bene facitis" (Jas 2:8). "Si autem personas accipitis, peccatum operamini, redarguti a lege tamquam transgressors" (Jas 2:9). "Sic loquimini, inquit, et sic facite, sicut per legem libertatis incipientes judicari" (Jas 2:12). Et quoniam quid paulo ante dixerit, novit, quoniam in multis offendimus omnes, suggerit dominicam tamquam quotidianam quotidianis, etsi levioribus, tamen vulneribus medicinam. "Judicium enim," inquit, "sine misericordia illi qui non facit misericordiam" (Jas 2:13). Hinc enim et Dominus: "Dimittite, inquit, et dimittetur vobis ; date, et dabitur vobis" (Lk 6:37–38). "Superexsultat autem misericordia judicio" (Jas 2:13): non dictum

The law of liberty, therefore, the law of love, is that of which he says: "If you fulfill the royal law according to the Scripture, you shall love your neighbor as yourself, you do well: but if you have respect to persons, you commit sin, and are convinced of the law as transgressors" (Jas 2:8–9). "So speak ye, and so do, as they that shall be judged by the law of liberty" (Jas 2:12). And as he knew by experience what he had said a little before, in many things we offend all, he suggests a sovereign remedy, to be applied, as it were day by day, to those less serious but real wounds which the soul suffers day by day, for he says: "He shall have judgment without mercy that has showed no mercy" (Jas 2:13). For with the same purpose the Lord says: "Forgive, and you shall be forgiven: give, and it shall be given unto you" (Lk 6:37–38). "But mercy rejoices over judgment" (Jas 2:13): it is not said that

est, Vincit misericordia judicium, non enim est adversa judicio; sed, superexsultat, quia plures per misericordiam colliguntur, sed qui misericordiam praestiterunt. "Beati enim misericordes, quia ipsis miserebitur Deus" (Mt 5:7).

mercy prevails over judgment, for it is not an adversary of judgment, but it rejoices over judgment, because a greater number are gathered in by mercy; but they are those who have shown mercy, for, "Blessed are the merciful, for God shall have mercy on them" (Mt 5:7).

Feria Quarta: Jas 2:14–26
S. Beda Venerabilis, *Super epistolas Catholicas* (*Super divi Jacobi Epistulam*, cap. 2)

"Fides si non habeat opera, mortua est in semetipsa" (Jas 2:26). Mortua est enim in semetipsa sine operibus caritatis, quibus reviviscat et animetur. Neque huic sententiae contrarium est quod Dominus ait: "Qui crediderit et baptizatus fuerit, salvus erit" (Mk 16:16). Subintelligendum namque ibi est quod tantummodo vere credat, qui exercet operando quod credit. Et quia fides et caritas ab invicem separari nequeunt. Credere vera esse quae loquitur, multi et mali possunt. Credunt enim esse vera, et nolunt ea facere, quia ad operandum pigri sunt. Credere autem ipsum esse Deum, hoc et daemones potuerunt. Credere vero in Deum, soli novere qui

"Faith, if it does not have works, is dead in itself" (Jas 2:26). Faith observed in name only does not save, for it is dead in itself if it is not made alive by works of charity, by which it may be made to come to life. Nor is that contrary to this statement which the Lord uttered, "He who believes and is baptized will be saved" (Mk 16:16). For it must be understood there that only he truly believes who carries out indeed what he believes. Faith and charity cannot be separated from one another. Many, even the wicked, are able to believe that the things he speaks are true; they believe that they are true and do not wish to make them their own because they are too lazy to do anything about them. Even the

diligunt Deum, qui non solo nomine sunt Christiani, sed et factis et vita. Quia sine dilectione fides inanis.

demons were able to believe, however, that He is God. But they alone know how to believe in God who love God, who are Christians not only in name but also in action and in the way of life, because without love faith is empty.

Feria Quinta: Jas 3:1–10
S. Augustinus, *De natura et gratia* (cap. 16)

"Linguam autem nullus hominum domare potest. Inquietum malum, plena veneno mortifero" (Jas 3:8), utique nocentiore quam bestiarum est atque serpentium; nam illud carnem interficit,hoc vero animam; "Os enim quod mentitur, occidit animam" (Ws 1:11). Non ergo quasi id esset facilius quam mansuefactio bestiarum, sanctus Jacobus illam sententiam pronuntiavit aut ea voce voluit pronuntiari, sed potius ostendens quantum sit in homine linguae malum, ut a nullo homine domari possit, cum ab hominibus domentur et bestiae. Neque hoc ideo dixit, ut hujus in nos mali dominationem per neglegentiam permanere patiamur, sed ut ad domandam linguam divinae gratiae poscamus auxilium. Non

"But the tongue can no man tame, an unruly evil, full of deadly poison" (Jas 3:8), such, of course, as is more noxious than that of beasts and creeping things. For while the one destroys the flesh, the other kills the soul. For, "the mouth that belies slays the soul" (Ws 1:11). It is not, therefore, as if this is an easier achievement than the taming of beasts that St. James pronounced the statement before us, or would have others utter it; but he rather aims at showing what a great evil in man his tongue is—so great, indeed, that it cannot be tamed by any man, although even beasts are tameable by human beings. And he said this, not with a view to our permitting, through our neglect, the continuance of so great an evil to ourselves, but in order that we might be induced to re-

enim ait: Linguam nullus domare potest, sed nullus hominum, ut, cum domatur, Dei misericordia, Dei adjutorio, Dei gratia fieri fateamur. Itaque praecepto facere commonemur, quod conantes et nostris viribus non valentes adjutorium divinum precemur.

quest the help of divine grace for the taming of the tongue. For he does not say: none can tame the tongue; but no man; in order that, when it is tamed, we may acknowledge it to be effected by the mercy of God, the help of God, the grace of God. Thus, we are warned by the precept to do this—namely, to make the attempt, and, failing in our own strength, to pray for the help of God.

Feria Sexta: Jas 4:1–15
S. Beda Venerabilis, *Super epistolas Catholicas* (*Super divi Jacobi Epistulam*, cap. 4)

Sed ne illos putares solos inimicos esse Dei, qui eum aperte blasphemant, qui fidem ejus persequuntur in sanctis, et eos iniquo judicio condemnant, ostendit et eos esse Dei inimicos, qui, sub fide et confessione nominis Christi, mundi illecebris et amori deserviunt, qui, nomine tenus fideles, rebus terrenis caelestia proponunt. Quod et sequenti versiculo instantius inculcat subdens: "Quicunque ergo voluerit amicus esse saeculi hujus, inimicus Dei constituitur" (Jas 4:4). Ergo inimici sunt Dei omnes amatores

That thou mightest not consider enemies of God only those who openly blaspheme Him, who persecute the saints for their faith in Him, and condemn them by unjust judgments, he shows that they are also enemies of God who after faith and confession of His name become slaves to the delights and love of the world, who are faithful in name only and prefer earthly to heavenly things. He also insists more urgently upon this in the following verse, appending, "Whoever, therefore, wishes to be a friend of this world is an enemy of God"

mundi, omnes inquisitores nugarum, omnes qui pertinent ad eos de quibus dicitur: "Quoniam ecce inimici tui, Domine, peribunt" (Ps 91:10). Intrent ecclesias, non intrent ecclesias, inimici Dei sunt. Ad tempus possunt florere sicut fenum, sed ubi ardor judicii apparuerit, peribunt, et decor vultus eorum decidet. Maiorem gratiam Dominus dat quam amicitia mundi, quia haec terrena bona ad tempus, et ea cum dolore amittenda tribuit, ille gaudium largitur aeternum.

(Jas 4:4). Therefore, all lovers of the world, all seekers after trifles, are enemies of God; all belong to those of whom it is said, "Look, how Thy enemies, O Lord, will perish" (Ps 91:10). They may enter the churches, they may not enter the churches, they are enemies of God. For a time they are able to flourish as grass, but when the heat of judgment appears they will perish and the loveliness of their countenance will vanish. The Lord gives greater grace than does the friendship of the world, because this grants earthly goods for a time and things that are to be lost with sorrow; He bestows the eternal joy of life.

Sabbato: Jas 5:1–16

S. Athanasius, *Epistulae Heortasticae* (ep 3, cap. 5; anno 331)

Et sive tempora serena sint sive molesta, ipsi (fideles verique servi Domini) quidem gratias laudationesque Deo extollunt; nullaque temporalium vicissitudinum ratione habita. Deum temporum dominum adorant. Primus quidem ille Jobus omnium constantissimus qui in rerum abundantia versatus fuerat, ita censebat; dum angeretur, tolerabat; dura crucia-

The faithful and true servants of the Lord, knowing that the Lord loves the thankful, never cease to praise Him, ever giving thanks unto the Lord. And whether the time is one of ease or of affliction, they offer up praise to God with thanksgiving, regarding not these things of time, but worshipping the Lord, the God of times. Thus, of old time, Job, who possessed fortitude above all men,

retur, gratias agebat (cf. Jb 1:21). Si nos itaque hujusmodi homines imitabimur, nullum nobis elabetur tempus, quo gratias non agamus. Et nunc quidem potissime cum tempus tribulationum est, quas haeretici adversus nos concitarunt, gratias agere Domino debemus, verba sanctorum usurpantes: "Haec omnia venerunt super nos, nec obliti sumus te" (Ps 43:18). Ita et nos, fratres mei dilecti, cum a verbo Dei dicendo impedimur, tunc id vehementius praedicare debemus, et canere com tribulamur; ut digni simus contemptum atque aerumnam pro veritate pati. Omnino cum damnis afficimur, tunc gratiae a nobis dicendae sunt.

thought of these things when in prosperity; and when in adversity, he patiently endured, and when he suffered, gave thanks (cf. Jb 1:21). Let us, being followers of such men, pass no season without thanksgiving; but especially now, when the time is one of tribulation, which the heretics excite against us, will we praise the Lord; uttering the words of the saints; "All these things have come upon us, yet have we not forgotten Thee" (Ps 43:18). So we, my beloved brethren, though hindered that we should not speak the word of the Lord, will the more proclaim it; and being afflicted, we will sing psalms,that we are accounted worthy to be despised, and to labour anxiously for the truth. Yea, moreover, being grievously vexed, we will give thanks.

INFRA HEBDOMADAM V POST OCTAVAM PASCHAE

Feria Tertia: 1 Pt 4:1–17

S. Beda Venerabilis, *Super epistolas Catholicas: In Primam Epistulam Petri* (cap. 4)

Duo sunt judicia Dei per Scripturas insinuata: unum occultum, alterum manifestum. Occultum judicium est poena, qua nunc unusquisque hominum aut exercetur ad purgationem, aut admonetur ad

There are two judgments of God recorded by the Scriptures, one hidden, the other manifest. The hidden judgment is the punishment by which every human being is either now being tried that

conversionem, aut, si contempserit vocationem et disciplinam Dei, excaecatur ad damnationem. Judicium autem manifestum est, quo venturus est Dominus judicare vivos et mortuos. Nunc autem dicitur esse tempus in quo "incipiat judicium de domo Domini" (1 Pt 4:17), id est, de Ecclesia, quae per exercitium praesentium afflictionum ad futura gaudia praeparatur. Namque reprobi tanto securiores nunc et sine ullo vindictae verbere vitam transitoriam ducunt, quanto eis in futuro nihil nisi vindicta restat, juxta illud beati Job: "Ducunt in bonis dies suos, et in puncto ad inferna descendunt" (Jb 21:13). Si autem primum a nobis, quis finis illorum? Hinc colligitur districtus Judex quanta illic feriat districtione quos reprobat, si hic sic cruciat quos amat.

he may be chastened, or cautioned, that he may be converted, or if he despises the call and discipline of God, blinded for condemnation. The manifest judgment, however, is when the Lord will come to judge the living and the dead. But it is said that "now is the time for judgment to begin from the Lord's house" (1 Pt 4:17), that is, from the Church, which is being prepared for future joys by being faced with present afflictions. Yet the condemned are leading their transition life now much more securely and without any infliction of chastisement as is proportionate to the chastisement that awaits them in the future, according to the saying of blessed Job, "They spend their days in good things and in a moment they go down to the lower world" (Jb 21:13). But if it begins first with us, what will be the end of those who do not believe the gospel of God? From this is gathered with what severity the strict Judge will deal with those whom He condemns, if here He so torments those whom He loves.

TEMPORE POST PENTECOSTEN

Feria Secunda: 1 Kgs 1:1–11
S. Joannes Chrysostomus, *In Epistulam ad Ephesios commentarius* (cap. 6, hom. 24, 3)

Vis discere vigiliam animae? Vade ad Annam, et audi verba ejus: "Adonai, Eloi Sabaoth" (1 Kgs 1:11). Nos viros pudore suffundat haec mulier; nos pudeat qui pro regno supplicamus et oscilamus, quod ea oret pro filio et fundat lacrimas. "Et stetit," inquit, "coram Domino," et quod dicit? "Adonai Domine, Eloi Sabaoth." Id est autem, si interpreteris, Domine Deus virtutum seu exercituum. Linguam praecurrebant lacrimae; his sperabat se Deum esse flexuram. Ubi sunt lacrimae, omnino etiam illic est afflictio: ubi autem est afflictio, illic quoque est multa philosophia et attentio. "Si audiens," inquit, "exaudias orationem ancillae tuae, et dederis mihi

Wouldst thou understand what watchfulness in prayer is? Go to Anna, hearken to her very words, "Adonai, Eloi Sabaoth" (1 Kgs 1:11). Let us be ashamed, us that are men, at the example of this woman; let us be ashamed, that are suing and gasping for a kingdom, at her, praying and weeping for a little child. "And she stood," it says, "before the Lord"; and what are her words? "Adonai, Lord, Eloi Sabaoth!" and this is, being interpreted, O Lord, the God of Hosts. Her tears went before her tongue; by these she hoped to prevail with God to bend to her request. Where tears are, there is always affliction also: where affliction is, there is great wisdom and heedfulness.

filium, dabo ipsum Domino toto tempore" (1 Kgs 1:11). Non dixit, anno uno, aut duobus, sicut nos; nec dixit si dederis mihi filium, do pecunias; sed, ipsum donum reddo integrum, primogenitum, orationis filium. Haec filia est Abrahae. Ille autem rogatus eum dedit; ipsa vero dedit etiam ante petitionem.

"If Thou wilt indeed," she continues, "look on the affliction of your handmaid, and will give to your handmaid a man child, then will I give him unto the Lord all the days of his life" (1 Kgs 1:11). She said not, for one year, or, for two, as we do — nor said she, if Thou wilt give me a child, I will give Thee money; but, I give back to Thee the very gift itself entire, my firstborn, the son of my prayer. Truly here was a daughter of Abraham. He gave when it was demanded of him. She offers even before it is demanded.

Feria Tertia: 1 Kgs 1:12–28
S. Cyprianus, *De oratione Dominica* (cap. 5–6)

Quod Anna, in primo Regnorum libro, Ecclesiae typum portans, custodit et servat; quae Dominum non clamosa petitione, sed tacite et modeste intra ipsas pectoris latebras precabatur. Loquebatur prece occulta, sed manifesta fide; loquebatur, non voce, sed corde, quia sic Deum sciebat audire: et impetravit efficaciter quod petiit, quia fideliter postulavit. Declarat Scriptura divina quae dicit: "Loquebatur in corde suo, et labia ejus movebantur, et vox ejus non au-

This Anna in the first book of Kings, who was a type of the Church, maintains and observes, in that she prayed to God not with clamorous petition, but silently and modestly, within the very recesses of her heart. She spoke with hidden prayer, but with manifest faith. She spoke not with her voice, but with her heart, because she knew that thus God hears; and she effectually obtained what she sought, because she asked it with belief. Divine Scripture asserts this, when it says, "She spoke in her

diebatur; et exaudivit eam Deus" (1 Kgs 1:13). Item legimus in Psalmis: "Dicite in cordibus et in stratis vestris, et transpungimini" (Ps 4:5). Adorans autem, fratres dilectissimi, nec illud ignoret quemadmodum in templo cum Pharisaeo publicanus oraverit, non allevatis in caelum impudenter oculis, nec manibus insolenter erectis, sed pectus suum pulsans, et peccata intus inclusa contestans, divinae misericordiae implorabat auxilium.

heart, and her lips moved, and her voice was not heard; and God did hear her" (1 Kgs 1:13). We read also in the psalms, "Speak in your hearts, and in your beds, and be pierced" (Ps 4:5). And let not the worshipper, beloved brethren, be ignorant in what manner the publican prayed with the Pharisee in the Temple. Not with eyes lifted up boldly to heaven, nor with hands proudly raised; but beating his breast, and testifying to the sins shut up within, he implored the help of the divine mercy.

Feria Quarta: 1 Kgs 2:12–21
S. Hieronymus, *Adversus Jovinianum* (lib. 1, cap. 35)

Heli pontifex, qui corripuerat quidem filios; sed quia non abiecerat delinquentes, retrorsum cecidit, et mortuus est, antequam lucerna Dei exstingueretur (cf. 1 Kgs 2 et 4). Cernis igitur, quod episcopus, presbyter, et diaconus non ideo sint beati, quia episcopi, vel presbyteri sint, aut diaconi, sed si virtutes habuerint nominum suorum et officiorum. Alioqui si diaconus sanctior episcopo suo fuerit, non ex eo quod inferior gradu est, apud Christum deterior erit. Aut Stephanus diaconus, qui

Heli the priest, who had indeed rebuked his sons, but because he had not put away the offenders, fell backwards and died before the lamp of God went out (cf. 1 Kgs 2 and 4). Thou seest then that the blessedness of a bishop, priest, or deacon, does not lie in the fact that they are bishops, priests, or deacons, but in their having the virtues which their names and offices imply. Otherwise, if a deacon be holier than his bishop, his lower grade will not give him a worse standing with Christ. If it were so,

primus martyrio coronatus est, minor futurus est in regno caelorum multis episcopis, et Timotheo ac Tito, quos ut subjicere non audeo, ita nec anteponere (Acts 6 et 7). In hoc campo et praelio, quo contra daemones dimicamus, non quaeruntur nomina, sed opera; et gloriosior ille sub vero imperatore Christo, non qui nobilior, sed qui fortior est.

Stephen the deacon, the first to wear the martyr's crown, would be less in the Kingdom of heaven than many bishops, and than Timothy and Titus, whom I venture to make neither inferior nor yet superior to him (cf. Acts 6 and 7). In this camp and in this battle, in which we contend against devils, not names but deeds are needed: and under the true commander, Christ, not the man who has the highest title has the greatest fame, but he who is the bravest warrior.

Feria Sexta: 1 Kgs 2:27–36
S. Augustinus, *De civitate Dei* (lib. 17, cap. 5, 3)

Proprie autem ad hujus domum Heli, cui haec dicebantur, quod sequitur pertinet: "Et omnis qui superaverit domus tuae, decidet in gladio virorum. Et hoc tibi signum, quod veniet super duos filios tuos hos, Ophni et Phinees: uno die morientur ambo" (3 Kgs 2:30, 27–28, 31–33). Hoc ergo signum factum est mutandi sacerdotii de domo hujus, quo signo significatum est mutandum sacerdotium domus Aaron. Mors quippe filiorum hujus significavit mortem non hominum, sed ipsius sacer-

What follows belongs properly to the house of Heli, to whom these things were said: "And every one of your houses that is left shall fall by the sword of men. And this shall be a sign unto you that shall come upon these your two sons, Hophni and Phinehas; in one day they shall die both of them" (3 Kgs 2:30, 27–28, 31–33). This, therefore, is made a sign of the change of the priesthood from this man's house, by which it is signified that the priesthood of Aaron's house is to be changed. For the death of this man's sons signi-

dotii de filiis Aaron. Quod autem sequitur, ad illum jam pertinet sacerdotem, cujus figuram gessit huic succedendo Samuel. Proinde quae sequuntur, de Christo Jesu Novi Testamenti vero sacerdote dicuntur: "Et suscitabo mihi sacerdotem fidelem, qui omnia quae in corde meo et quae in anima mea faciat; et aedificabo ei domum fidelem" (1 Kgs 2:35). Ipsa est aeterna et superna Jerusalem. Quod autem ait: Coram Christo meo transibit, de ipsa domo utique intellegendum est, non de illo sacerdote, qui est Christus ipse mediator atque salvator.

fied the death not of the men, but of the priesthood itself of the sons of Aaron. But what follows pertains to that Priest whom Samuel typified by succeeding this one. Therefore, the things which follow are said of Christ Jesus, the true Priest of the New Testament: "And I will raise Me up a faithful Priest that shall do according to all that is in Mine heart and in My soul; and I will build Him a sure house" (1 Kgs 2:35). The same is the eternal Jerusalem above. But what He says, He shall walk before My Christ, is to be understood entirely of the house itself, not of the priest, Who is Christ Himself, the Mediator and Savior.

Sabbato: 1 Kgs 3:1–12, 15–20
S. Joannis Cassiani, *Collationes* (coll. 2, cap. 13–14)

Absque ullo confusionis operimento omnia debent senioribus revelari, atque ab eis vel remedia vulnerum, vel exempla conversationis ac vitae fiducialiter sumi; in quibus parem opem et similem experiemur effectum, si nihil penitus affectare nostro judicio ac praesumptione tentemus. Denique in tantum placita Deo haec sententia comprobatur, ut

Without any cloak of shame everything should be disclosed to the elders, and remedies for wounds be faithfully received from them together with examples of life and conversation: from which we shall find like help and the same sort of result, if we try to do nothing at all on our own responsibility and judgment. Lastly so far has this opinion been shown to be pleasing to God that

etiam in Scripturis sanctis hanc eamdem institutionem non otiose reperiamus insertam, ita ut puerum Samuelem judicio praelatum suo nollet per semetipsum divini colloquii disciplina Dominus erudire, sed recurrere semel et iterum pateretur ad senem; et quem sua vocatione dignissimum judicarat, senioris mallet institutione formari, ut scilicet et illius qui ad divinum ministerium vocabatur probaretur humilitas, et junioribus forma subjectionis hujus proponeretur exemplo (cf. 1 Kgs 3).

we see that this system not without reason finds a place in Holy Scripture, so that the Lord would not of Himself instruct by the method of a divine colloquy the lad Samuel, when chosen for judgment, but suffered him to run once or twice to the old man, and willed that one whom He was calling to converse with Him should be taught even by one who had offended God, as he was an old man, and preferred that he whom He had deemed worthy to be called by Him should be trained by the elder in order to test the humility of him who was called to a divine office, and to set an example to the younger men by the manner of his subjection (cf. 1 Kgs 3).

INFRA HEBDOMADAM III POST PENTECOSTEN

Feria Secunda: 1 Kgs 10:17–27

S. Joannes Chrysostomus, *De sacerdotio* (lib. 4, cap. 1)

An cum honore sibi per Deum tradito mule usus esset, potuit his verbis eximi ab ira ejus, qui se in regem constituerat? Si in illa humilitate permansissem, haec offendicula facile declinassem; nam cum ex vulgarium et ignobilium essem numero, ad hoc opus missus sum quam fuissem: neque

When he made a bad use of the honor which had been given him by God, were those words of his able to rescue him from the wrath of Him Who had made him king? Had I remained in my low estate I should easily have escaped all these stumbling blocks, for were I one of the obscure multitude, I should never

mihi bellum contra Amalecitas Deus commisisset; quo mihi non commisso in peccatum hujusmodi numquam incidissem. Verum haec omnia ad defensionem infirma sunt; nec infirma modo, sed periculosa, quae Dei magis iram accendant. Eum enim, qui meritis majorem dignitatem accepit, non oportet ad peccatorum excusationem honoris magnitudinem ostendere, sed ad majorem in virtute profectum uti magno illo Dei erga se studio. Ille vero quia meliorem nactus dignitatem, ideo peccare sibi licitum esse existimabat, nihil aliud, quam Dei clementiam peccatorum suorum causam facere conatus est.

have been sent forth on this expedition, nor would God have committed to my hands the war against the Amalekites, and if I had not had it committed to me, I should not have sinned this sin. But all such arguments are weak as excuses, and not only weak, but perilous, inasmuch as they rather kindle the wrath of God. For he who has been promoted to great honor by God, must not advance the greatness of his honor as an excuse for his errors, but should make God's special favor towards him the motive for further improvement; whereas he who thinks himself at liberty to sin because he has obtained some uncommon dignity, what does he but study to show that the loving kindness of God is the cause of his personal transgression.

Feria Tertia: 1 Kgs 12:1–14
S. Irenaeus Lugdunensis, *Adversus haereses* (lib. 4, cap. 26, 4–5)

Quemadmodum Samuel tot annis judicans populum, et sine ulla elatione ducatum gerens super Israel, in fine purgabat se, dicens: "Ego conversatus sum in conspectu vestro a prima aetate mea usque nunc: respondete mihi in conspectu mei, et in conspectu

Samuel, who judged the people so many years, and bore rule over Israel without any pride, in the end cleared himself, saying, "I have walked before you from my childhood even unto this day: answer me in the sight of God, and before His anointed; speak out against me, and I will restore it

Christi ejus. Dicite adversus me, et reddam vobis" (1 Kgs 12:3). Testificatus est Dominus, dicens: "Testis Dominus, et testis Christus ejus in die hac. Et dixerunt ei: Testis" (1 Kgs 12:5). Tales presbyteros nutrit Ecclesia, de quibus et propheta ait: "Et dabo principes tuos in pace, et episcopos tuos in justitia" (Is 60:17). De quibus et Dominus dicebat: "Qui igitur erit fidelis actor, bonus, et sapiens quem praeponit Dominus super familiam suam, ad danda eis cibaria in tempore?" (Mt 24:43). Hi enim et eam quae est in unum Deum, qui omnia fecit, fidem nostram custodiunt: et eam quae est in Filium Dei, dilectionem adaugent, qui tantas dispositiones propter nos fecit, et Scripturas sine periculo nobis exponunt, neque Deum blasphemantes, neque patriarchas exhonorantes, neque prophetas contemnentes.

to you" (1 Kgs 12:3). He called the Lord to witness, saying, "The Lord is witness, and His Anointed is witness this day, that you have not found ought in my hand. And they said to him, He is witness" (1 Kgs 12:5). Such presbyters nourish the Church, of whom also the prophet says: "I will give your rulers in peace, and your bishops in righteousness" (Is 60:17). Of whom also did the Lord declare, "Who then shall be a faithful steward, good and wise, whom the Lord sets over His household, to give them their meat in due season?" (Mt 24:43) For these also preserve this faith of ours in one God Who created all things; and they increase that love we have for the Son of God, Who accomplished such marvelous dispensations for our sake: and they expound the Scriptures to us without danger, neither blaspheming God, nor dishonoring the patriarchs, nor despising the prophets.

Feria Quarta: 1 Kgs 13:1–14

Constitutiones Apostolicae (lib. 8, cap. 46)

Si quis autem ultra sibi traditum officium progredi nitebatur, morte luebat poenas (cf. Nm 4). Hoc vero praecipue demonatravit

But if any one strove to advance beyond the office handed down to him, he was punished by death (cf. Nm 4). Saul's example does show

id, quod Sauli contigit, qui cum existimasset se absque propheta et pontifice Samuele sacrificare posse, ad se peccatum et maledictum nunquam abiiciendum attraxit; neque prophetam movit ac flexit, quod ab ipso Saul in regem unctus fuisset (cf. 1 Kgs 13:13). Hoc etiam evidentiori operatione demonastravit Deus per ea quae Oziae acciderunt, de cujus praevaricatione exegit poenas absque mora; et qui contra pontificatum insanierat, regno quoque pulsus est (cf. 2 Par 26). Ceterum quae sub nobis acta sint, forsitan non ignoratis. Scitis enim omnino episcopos, presbyteros et diaconos a nobis prece ac manuum impositione nominatos esse, qui differentia nominum differentiam quoque rerum ostendant. Non enim qui volebat, apud nos implebat manum, sicut in falso et adulterino vitularum sacerdotio, tempore Jeroboami (cf. 3 Kgs 13:33); sed qui vocabatur a Deo. Nam si nulla lex posita esset, nec ulla ordinum differentia; suffecisset, cuncta per unum nomen perfici.

this most plainly, who, thinking he might offer sacrifice without the prophet and high priest Samuel, drew upon himself a sin and a curse without remedy. Nor did even his having anointed him king discourage the prophet (cf. 1 Kgs 13:13). But God showed the same by a more visible effect in the case of Ozias, when He without delay exacted the punishment due to this transgression, and he that madly coveted after the high priesthood was rejected from his kingdom also (cf. 2 Par 26). As to those things that have happened among us, you yourselves are not ignorant of them. For you know undoubtedly that those that are by us named bishops, and presbyters, and deacons, were made by prayer, and by the laying on of hands; and that by the difference of their names is showed the difference of their employments. For not every one that will is ordained, as the case was in that spurious and counterfeit priesthood of the calves under Jeroboam (cf. 1 Kgs 13:33); but he only who is called of God. For if there were no rule or distinction of orders, it would suffice to perform all the offices under one name.

Feria Quinta: 1 Kgs 14:6–20
S. Beda Venerabilis, *Allegorica expositio in Samuelem* (lib. 2, cap. 6)

Jonathan autem columbae donum, vel columbae dedit, vel Domini donum interpretatur: significans eos, qui omne quidquid habent virtutis, spiritui gratiae tribuunt, atque ab eo se accepisse confitentur. Et Saul in Machmas et in monte Bethel, id est, in humilitate et in monte domus Dei: Jonathan autem in Gabaath Benjamin, hoc est in colle filii dexterae cum suis quoque militibus, mansisse referunt. Quia et reprobi nonnunquam, quamvis sinistra vel instabili mente virtutes spirituales exercere vel etiam docere videntur, soli autem columbina simplicitate praediti, ad regnum sublime Christi, qui est in dextera Dei, pertinere probantur. Sed et hoc quod duo millia cum Saul, mille autem cum Jonathan fuerunt, profecto docet, quia quantum perfectiores, tanto sunt quique pauciores. Vel certe duo millia sunt in humilitate et in monte domus Dei, puritate fidei devoti, et spei sublimitate provecti: mille autem in colle Filii dexterae cari-

But Jonathan interprets the gift of the dove, or gave the dove, or the gift of the Lord: signifying those who, whatever they have of virtue, ascribe to the spirit of grace, and confess that they have received it from Him. They report that Saul remained in Machmas and on Mount Bethel, that is, in humility and on the mountain of the house of God. And Jonathan remained in Gabaath Benjamin, that is, in the hill of the sons of the right hand, with his soldiers also. Because even the reprobate sometimes, although they seem to practice or even teach spiritual virtues with an evil or unstable mind, but only those endowed with the simplicity of a dove, are proved to belong to the sublime Kingdom of Christ, Who is at the right hand of God. But the fact that there were two thousand with Saul, and a thousand with Jonathan, surely teaches us that the more perfect they are, the fewer there are. Or at least two thousand are in humility and on the mountain of the house of God, devoted to the purity of faith, and exalted in the sublimity

tatis, quae nunquam excidit, perfectione gloriosi.

of hope; and there are a thousand on the hill of the Son of the right hand of charity, which never ends, glorious in perfection.

Feria Sexta: 1 Kgs 15:1–11
Constitutiones Apostolicae (lib. 2, cap. 10)

Quod episcopus, qui temere parcit peccatori, culpa non careat. Ad ista autem, qui animum non adverterit, debenti poenas inconsiderate ignoscet, sicut Saul Agago (cf. 1 Kgs 15:9), et Heli liberis suis (cf. 1 Kgs 2:29), ignorantibus Dominum. Hic ergo tum dignitatem suam, tum Dei Ecclesiam sua in paroecia sitam maculat: quocirca coram Deo et hominibus sanctis injustus est, utpote auctor scandali multis, recens baptizatis et catechumenis, itemque utriusque sexus adolescentibus, eumque vae manet, et mola asinaria in collo, et profundus gurges cui obnoxius est (cf. Mt 18:6–7). Nam qui cernent principem suum adeo in judicando negligentem ac iniquum, vacillare incipient, atque eodem vitio occupati, cogentur una cum eo perire; sicut populus cum Jeroboamo, et cum Core (cf. 3 Kgs 12) sceleris socii interiere.

That a bishop who by wrong judgment spares an offender is himself guilty. But he who does not consider these things, will, contrary to justice, spare him who deserves punishment as Saul spared Agag (cf. 1 Kgs 15:9), and Eli his sons (cf. 1 Kgs 2:29), who knew not the Lord. Such a one profanes his own dignity, and that Church of God which is in his parish. Such a one is esteemed unjust before God and holy men, as affording occasion of scandal to many of the newly baptized, and to the catechumens; as also to the youth of both sexes, to whom a woe belongs, add a millstone about his neck, and drowning, on account of his guilt (cf. Mt 18:6–7). For, observing what a person their governor is, through his wickedness and neglect of justice they will grow skeptical, and, indulging the same disease, will be compelled to perish with him; as

was the case of the people joining with Jeroboam, and those which were in the conspiracy with Core (cf. 3 Kgs 12).

Sabbato: 1 Kgs 16:1–11
Commentarii in librum 1 Regum (lib. 6, cap. 3, 2), S. Gregorio Magno attributi

Quid est, quod cornu oleo implere praecipitur, nisi quia talis in sancta Ecclesia pastor eligendus est, qui non argui velut transgressor debeat, sed ad exemplum aliorum miris laudibus commendari? Cornu namque telum animalium est. Auctoritas autem et increpatio summi antistitis quid sunt aliud, nisi tela? Cornu quippe feriunt, quando peccatoribus per increpationem acumina conjunguntur. Ferire etenim cornu, est peccatores acute redarguere. Cornu oleo impletur, quando praedicatoris sublimitas non habet asperitatem minarum, sed blandimenta favorum. Vel cornu oleo impletur, quando electo pastori simul datur et sublimatus culminis, et virtus unctionis, quando et sublimis gradus ascenditur, sed qui ad alta sustollitur, meritorum ubertate repletur. Cornu ergo

What is the reason that it is commanded to fill the horn with oil, except because such a pastor is to be chosen in the holy Church, who should not be blamed as a transgressor, but should be commended as an example to others with wonderful praise? For the horn is the weapon of animals. But what are the authority and rebuke of the supreme Shepherd but weapons? For they strike with the horn, when they are united to sinners by the sharp rebuke. For to blow the horn is to rebuke sinners sharply. The horn is filled with oil, when the exaltation of the preacher has not the harshness of threats, but the sweetness of benevolence. Or the horn is filled with oil, when the chosen shepherd is given at the same time the sublimity of the summit, and the power of anointing, when he ascends to lofty degrees; but

pleno sacerdotes unguntur, qui ad summum gradum perveniunt cum plenitudine gratiarum. Quia vero oleo ignis accenditur, oleum doctoris amor est cordis. In quo ignis accenditur, quia in pinguedine oris virtus et gratia ardet Spiritus Sancti.

he who is raised to a high place is filled with an abundance of merits. Priests are therefore anointed with a full horn, who reach the highest degree with a fullness of grace. Because the fire is kindled with oil, the oil of the teacher is the love of the heart. In him the fire is kindled, because in the fruitfulness of the mouth burns the power and grace of the Holy Spirit.

INFRA HEBDOMADAM IV POST PENTECOSTEN
Feria Secunda: 1 Kgs 17:25–26, 31–36
S. Caesarius Arelatensis, *Sermones* (serm. 121, cap. 3)

Veniente autem David, unus ex fratribus ejus increpavit eum, dicens: "quare dimisisti pauculas oves illas, et venisti ad praelium?" (1 Kgs 17:28). Frater isto senior, qui David typum Domini gerentem per malitiam increpavit, significavit populum Judaeorum, qui per invidiam Christo Domino, qui pro salute humani generis venerat, detraxerunt, et multis frequenter injuriis adfecerunt. "Quare," inquit, "dimisisti oves illas, et venisti ad praelium?" Quasi non tibi videtur per os ejus saluti hominum invidens diabolus loqui? tamquam si diceret Christo: "Quare dimis-

When David came, one of his brothers rebuked him saying: "Why didst thou leave those few sheep, and camest to the battle?" (1 Kgs 17:28). This elder brother, maliciously chiding David who typified Our Lord, signified the Jewish people who jealously slandered Christ the Lord even though He had come for the salvation of the human race, for they frequently chastised Him with many insults. "Why didst thou leave the sheep, and camest to the battle?" Does it not seem to you as though through his lips the devil is speaking in envy of the salvation of men? It is as though he

isti nonaginta et novem oves quae non erraverunt, et venisti ut unam requireres quae perierat" (Mt 18:12), et eam de manu spiritalis Goliae, id est, de potestate diaboli per crucis baculum liberatam ad ovile proprium revocares? Malo quidem et superbo animo, sed tamen verum dicebat: quia Jesus, sicut jam dictum est, dimissurus erat nonaginta et novem oves, ut quaereret unam, et ad ovile proprium, id est, ad angelorum consortium revocaret.

said to Christ: "Why did you leave the ninety-nine sheep who had strayed and come looking for the one which was lost" (Mt 18:12), in order that you might call him back to your sheepfold, after freeing him with the staff of the Cross from the hand of the spiritual Goliath, that is, from the power of the devil? Why didst thou leave those few sheep? He spoke the truth, although in a wicked and haughty spirit. Jesus intended to leave the ninety-nine sheep, as was already said, in order to seek the one, and to bring it back to His sheepfold, that is, to the company of the angels.

Feria Tertia: 1 Kgs 17:38–51
S. Maximus Taurinensis, *Homiliae de diversis* (classis 4, hom. 85, cap. 3)

Cum enim sanctus David non operiretur galea, non praecingeretur gladio, non lancea uteretur; occidit autem illum non telo ferreo, sed gladio spiritali. Quamvis enim inermis oculis hominum videretur, satis tamen erat gratia Divinitatis armatus. Verum ipse spiritalis gladius non fuit gladius; non enim gladio Golias, sed lapide prostratus occubuit. Legimus in Scripturis lapidis vocabulo Christum

For holy David, when he was not covered with a helmet, was not girded with a sword, nor using a lance, yet slew Goliath not with an iron weapon, but with a spiritual sword. For although he appeared unarmed to the eyes of men, yet he was sufficiently armed with the grace of Divinity. However, the spiritual sword itself was not a sword, for Goliath was not slain by the sword but struck down by a stone. We read in

figuraliter designari. Igitur cum lapide Golias percutitur, Christi virtute prosternitur. Et in qua tandem corporis parte prosternitur? In fronte scilicet; gentilis est sacrilegus homo, ibi percutitur a Christo, ubi deerat Christus; et ibi ei infertur mortis exitium, ubi signum salutis non invenitur. Atque ideo ibi percutitur, ubi nudus a Dei gratia reperitur. Nam et David armorum indumentis sese ante praecinxerat; sed cum esset in iis gravis et impeditus, ita ut ambulare vix posset, eadem sine cunctatione proiecit. Simul et illud nos docuit quod non in armis tantum speranda victoria est, sed in nomine Salvatoris oranda.

the Scriptures that Christ is figuratively designated by the term stone. Therefore, when Goliath is struck with a stone, he is struck down by the power of Christ. And in what part of the body is he overthrown? In the forehead, of course. The Gentile is a sacrilegious man, and there he is struck by Christ, where Christ was absent; and there he meets his mortal end where no sign of salvation is found. And therefore he is struck there, where he is found naked of the grace of God. For David, too, had previously girded himself with armor, but when he found it heavy and encumbering, so that he could scarcely walk, he threw them out without hesitation. At the same time, he taught us that victory is not to be hoped for in arms alone, but in praying in the name of the Savior.

Feria Quarta: 1 Kgs 18:6–17
S. Joannes Chrysostomus, *In Epistulam secundam ad Corinthios* (hom. 24, cap. 4)

Ea enim invidiae natura est: norat se ab eo servatum, malebatque perire, quam eum, a quo salutem accepisset, florentem conspicere. Quid hoc affectu gravius esse queat? Non aberrarit, qui diaboli

For such is the nature of envy; he knew that he was saved, yet he would rather have perished than see him that saved him had in honor. What can be more grievous than this passion? One cannot err

foetum eam dixerit: atque in ea quidem inanis gloriae fructus, imo etiam radix est: haec enim duo vitia sese mutuo struere solent. Sic nempe tunc quoque livore afficiebatur Saul, quod dixissent, "Percussit David decem millia" (1 Kgs 18:7). Quo quid stultius fingi possit? Quid enim, quaeso, invidia te afficit? Quod si tibi tam expelenda ea gloria esse videtur, quae ab bominibtis proficiscitur, teque plausus ille, quo quispiam a plurimis excipitur, majorem in modum conturbat; cum eum hujusmodi plausu frui videris, cogitatione ad futurum aevum gloriamque illam transeas: et sicut irruentem feram effugere festinans, in cubiculum ingressus, fores occludis; sic tu nunc quoque ad futuram vitam arcanamque illam gloriam confuge.

in calling it the devil's offspring. And in it is contained the fruit of vainglory, or rather its root also; for both these evils are wont mutually to produce each other. And thus, in truth it was that Saul even thus envied, when they said, "David smote by ten thousands" (1 Kgs 18:7), than which what can be more senseless? For why doest thou envy? Tell me! If the glory that comes of men be so greatly to be coveted in thine account, and if it quite disquiets thee that such and such one is applauded of the many; when thou beholdest him in the enjoyment of that applause, pass over in thy thought to the world to come and the glory which is there. And just as when hurrying to escape the onset of a wild beast, thou enterest into a cabin and shut the doors; so now also flee unto the life to come, and that unspeakable glory.

Feria Quinta: 1 Kgs 19:1–6, 8–10
S. Joannes Chrysostomus, *In Epistulam ad Romanos homiliae* (hom. 28, cap. 2)

Si autem a Spiritu Sancto vacui fuerimus, etiam circa opera claudicabimus: abeunte siquidem illo, spiritus immundus accedit: quod

If we have no works, the Holy Spirit flies away. But if we be deserted by the Spirit, we shall also halt in our works. For when this has

palam est ex Saule. Quid enim, si nos non suffocat perinde atque illum? Sed alio modo praefocat per mala opera. Cithara ergo Davidis opus nobis fuerit, ut divina cantica animae concinamus, et ea quae ad illum pertinent et ea quae ex bonis operibus procedunt. Nam si vel alterum fecerimus, et cantionem audientes, canenti per opera repugnemus, ut tunc Saul faciebat; pharmacum nobis in damnationem erit, et immanior fiet insania. Nam antequam audiamus, timet malignus daemon, ne audientes corrigamur: cum autem audientes iidem ipsi manemus, ipsi metus abscedit. Psallamus canticum per opera, ut peccatum ipso daemone deterius eiiciamus. Nam si linguam canere doceamus, illa canente animam pudebit contraria volentem.

gone, the unclean one comes: this is plain from Saul. For what if he does not choke us as he did him, still he strangles us in some other way by wicked works. We have need then of the harp of David, that we may charm our souls with the divine songs, both these, and those from good actions. Since if we do the one only, and while we listen to the charm, war with the charmer by our actions, as he did of old; the remedy will even turn to judgment to us, and the madness become the more furious. For before we heard, the wicked demon was afraid lest we should hear it and recover. But when after hearing it even, we continue the same as we were, this is the very thing to rid him of his fear. Let us sing then the psalm of good deeds, that we may cast out the sin that is worse than the demon. For if we once teach the tongue to sing, the soul will be ashamed to be devising the opposite of what the tongue sings.

Feria Sexta: 1 Kgs 20:1–7
S. Joannes Chrysostomus, *Homiliae in Epistolam primam ad Corinthios* (hom. 33, cap. 2)

Caritas enim non indecore agit; sed quasi aureis quibusdam alis, omnia delictorum peccata contegit. Sic et Davidem Jonathas amabat, audiensque patrem dicentem, "Fili puellarum ultro venientium, effeminate" (1 Kgs 20:30), non erubescebat, etsi turpitudine plena verba erant. Nam hoc vult significare, Fili meretricularum in viros insanientium, ad praetereuntes accurrentium, enervate, mollis, qui nihil virile habes. Quid igitur, haeccine aegre tulit, et prae pudore se abscondit, et a dilecto recessit? Totum certe contrarium fecit, de amore gloriabatur: etsi ille tunc rex erat, filius vero regis Jonathas, David autem fugitivus. Sed neque sic de amicitia erubuit: cartias enim non indecore agit. Nam hoc in illa mirabile est, quod contumelia affectum, non modo non sinat dolere et morderi, sed etiam ut gaudeat efficiat. Ideoque illo post haec omnia, quasi corona redimitus, sic abiens Davidem complexus est. Neque enim caritas scit quid sit probrum: ideo

Love does nothing unseemly, but as it were with certain golden wings covers up all the offenses of the beloved. Thus also Jonathan loved David; and hearing his father say, "Thou son of damsels that have run away from their homes, thou womanly bred" (1 Kgs 20:30), he was not ashamed, though the words be full of great reproach. For what he means is this: Thou son of mean harlots who are mad after men, who run after the passers-by, thou unnerved and effeminate wretch, who hast nothing of a man. What then? Did he grieve at these things, and hide his face, and turn away from his beloved? Nay, quite the contrary; he displayed his fondness as an ornament. And yet the one was at that time a king, and a king's son, even Jonathan; the other a fugitive and a wanderer, I mean, David. But not even thus was he ashamed of his friendship. For love does not behave itself unseemly. Yea, this is its wonderful quality that not only it suffers not the injured to grieve and feel galled, but

etiam sibi placet in eo, de quo alius erubescit. Pudor enim est nescire amare, et amantem non omne periculum adire omniaque perpeti pro dilectis.

even disposes him to rejoice. Accordingly, he too, of whom we are speaking, after all these things, just as though he had a crown put on him, went away and fell on David's neck. For love knows not what sort of thing shame may be. Therefore, it glories in those things for which another hides his face. Since the shame is, not to know how to love; not, when thou lovest, to incur danger and endure all for the beloved.

Sabbato: 1 Kgs 21:1–9
S. Joannes Chrysostomus, *Homiliae 90 in Matthaeum* (hom. 39, cap. 1)

"Non legistis quid fecerit David, quando esuriit, et qui cumeo erant: quomodo intravit in domum Dei, et panes propositionis comedit, quos non licebat ei edere, neque his qui cum eo erant, nisi solis sacerdotibus?" (1 Kgs 21:6) "aut non legistis in lege quia sabbatis sacerdotes in templo sabbatum violant, et sine crimine sunt"? (Mt 12:3–5). Marcus autem sub Abiathare sacerdote id factum dicit, non repugnantia historiae dicens, sed ostendens illum hominem fuisse, additque ipsum ei panes dedisse (cf. Mk 2:26), simulque magnam affer-

"Have ye not read, says He, what David did in the Temple, when he was a-hungered, himself and all they that were with him? How he entered into the house of God, and did eat the showbread, which was not lawful for him to eat, neither for them which were with him, but only for the priests?" (1 Kgs 21:6). "Do you not know, that in the Temple the priests profane the Sabbath, and are blameless?" (Mt 12:3–5). But Mark says that this happened under Abiathar the priest, not saying the inconsistencies of history, but showing that David was a human being, and adding that the priest himself

ens purgationem, quod sacerdos id permisisset; nec modo permisisset, sed etiam ministrasset. Nec mihi dicas, Davidem fuisse prophetam: nam neque ei licebat, sed penes sacerdotes hoc praerogativa erat: idcirco addidit, Nisi solis sacerdotibus. Etiamsi enim propheta esset, non sacerdos erat; imo etiamsi propheta esset, at non ii qui cum illo erant; nam et illis quoque panem dedit. Quid igitur, inquies, paresne erant illi David? Quid mihi dignitatem memoras, ubi legis transgressio esse putatur, et naturalis instat necessitas? Etenim hac ratione magis illos a crimine purgat, cum is qui major est idipsum fecit.

gave him bread (cf. Mk 2:26), and at the same time bringing a great purification, because the priest had permitted it; not only would he have allowed it, but he would have also ministered to it. For tell me not that David was a prophet, for not even so was it lawful, but the privilege had only the priests': wherefore also He added, but it was allowed for the priests only. For even though he was a prophet, he was not a priest; nay, even if he were a prophet, but not those who were with him; for he also gave them bread. What then, it might be said, were they all equal to David? Why doest thou remind me of dignity, where there seems to be a transgression of the Law, being also a constraint of nature? Yea, and in this way too He has the more entirely acquitted them of the charges, in that he who is greater is found to have done the same.

INFRA HEBDOMADAM V POST PENTECOSTEN

Feria Secunda: 2 Kgs 2:1–11

S. Augustinus, *De cura pro mortuis gerenda* (cap. 9)

Laudantur illi, et a rege David benedicuntur, qui Saulis et Jonathae ossibus aridis sepulturae misericordiam praestiterunt (cf.

Regarding that woeful compassion which I have mentioned, are those praised, and by King David blessed, who to the dry bones of Saul and

2 Kgs 2:5). Quae tandem misericordia praestatur nihil sentientibus? An forte revocandum est ad illam opinionem, quod infernum fluvium insepulti non poterant transmeare (cf. Vergilius, Aen. 6, 326–328)? Absit hoc a fide christiana: alioquin pessime actum est cum tanta martyrum multitudine, quorum non potuerunt corpora sepeliri, et fallaciter eis Veritas dixit: "Nolite timere eos qui corpus occidunt, et postea non habent quid faciant" (Lk 12:4); si eis tanta mala facere potuerunt, quibus impedirentur ad loca exoptata transire. Sed quia hoc sine ulla dubitatione falsissimum est, nec aliquid obest fidelibus negata eorum corporibus sepultura, nec aliquid si exhibeatur infidelibus prodest: cur ergo illi qui Saulem et filium ejus sepelierunt, misericordiam fecisse dicuntur, et ob hoc a rege pio benedicuntur. Et quod sibi exhiberi volunt quando sensuri non sunt, aliis non sentientibus curant exhibere dum ipsi sentiunt?

Jonathan afforded mercy of sepulture (cf. 2 Kgs 2:5). But yet what mercy is that which is afforded to them that have feeling of nothing? Or haply is this to be challenged back to that conceit of an infernal river which men unburied were not able to pass over (cf. Virgil, Aen. 6, 326–328)? Far be this from the faith of Christians: else has it gone most ill with so great a multitude of martyrs, for whom there could be no burying of their bodies, and Truth did cheat them when it said, "Fear not them which kill the body, and after that have no more that they can do" (Lk 12:4). But, because this without all doubt is most false, and it neither any whit hurts the faithful to have their bodies denied sepulture, nor any whit the giving of sepulture unto infidels advantages them; why then are those who buried Saul and his son said to have done mercy, and for this are blessed by that godly king. And what they would have done by them when they shall have no more feeling, that they take care to do by others now having no feeling while themselves have yet feeling?

Feria Tertia: 2 Kgs 3:6–10, 12–21
S. Ambrosius, *De officiis ministrorum* (lib. 2, cap. 7, 33–34)

Ita David sibi gratis officiis plebem obligaverat (cf. 2 Kgs 2:2) primum, ut in discordiis populi exsulare in Hebron mallet, quam in Jerusalem regnare: deinde, ut etiam in hoste positam virtutem diligeret: justitiam etiam his qui arma contra se tulerant aeque ac suis praestandam putaret: denique (cf. 2 Kgs 3) fortissimum adversae partis propugnatorem Abner ducem et inferentem praelia miratus est, et orantem pacis gratiam non aspernatus, honoravit convivio: interemptum insidiis doluit et flevit, prosecutus exsequias honestavit. Non mediocre istud, praesertim in rege, sic obire humilitatis munia, ut communem se exhiberet etiam infimis, alieno periculo cibum non quaerere, potum recusare (cf. 2 Kgs 23:13), peccatum fateri, seque ipsum pro populo offerre morti, ut in se divina indignatio converteretur, cum ferienti angelo offerens se diceret: Ecce sum, ego peccavi, et ego pastor malum feci, et iste grex quid fecit? Fiat manus tua in me.

David had bound the people to himself freely in doing his duty (cf. 2 Kgs 2:2), first, when he during the division among the people preferred to live like an exile at Hebron rather than to reign at Jerusalem; next, when he showed that he loved valour even in an enemy. He had also thought that justice should be shown to those who had borne arms against himself the same as to his own men (cf. 2 Kgs 3). Again, he admired Abner, the bravest champion of the opposing side, while he was their leader and was yet waging war. Nor did he despise him when suing for peace but honored him by a banquet. When killed by treachery, he mourned and wept for him. He followed him and honored his obsequies. It is no small thing, especially in the case of a king, so to perform humble duties as to make oneself like the very lowest. It is noble not to seek for food at another's risk and to refuse a drink of water, to confess a sin, and to offer oneself to death for one's people (cf. 2 Kgs 23:13). This latter David did, so that the di-

vine anger might be turned against himself, when he offered himself to the destroying angel and said: Lo I have sinned: I the shepherd have done wickedly, but this flock, what has it done? Let Thy hand be against me.

Feria Quarta: 2 Kgs 4:5–12; 5:1–7
S. Ambrosius, *De officiis ministrorum* (lib. 2, cap. 7, 35)

Ambulans David in simplicitate, et superborum fugitans, sectator immaculatorum, qui cinerem miscebat alimentis suis, cum peccata propria deploraret, et potum suum temperabat fletibus (cf. Ps 37:14). Merito sic expetitus est ab universo populo, ut venirent ad eum omnes tribus Israel dicentes: "Ecce nos ossa tua et caro tua sumus: heri et nudiustertius cum esset Saul, et regnaret super nos; tu eras qui producebas et inducebas Israel. Et dixit tibi Dominus: Tu pasces populum meum" (2 Kgs 5:1 et seq.). Et quid plura de eo dicam, de quo hujusmodi Dei processit sententia, ut de eo diceret: "inveni David secundum cor meum" (Ps 88:21)? Quis enim in sanctitate cordis et justitia sicut iste ambulavit, ut impleret vol-

David walked in simplicity of heart and fled from the proud. He was a follower of those unspotted from the world, one who mixed ashes with his food when bewailing his sins and mingled his drink with weeping (cf. Ps 37:14). Worthily, then, was he called for by all the people. All the tribes of Israel came to him saying: "Behold, we are thy bone and thy flesh. Also yesterday and the day before when Saul lived, and reigned, thou wast he that led out and brought in Israel. And the Lord said to you, Thou shalt feed My people" (2 Kgs 5:1ff.). And why should I say more about him of whom the Word of the Lord has gone forth to say: "I have found David according to My heart" (Ps 88:21)? Whoever walked in holiness of heart and in justice as he

untatem Dei: propter quem et delinquentibus posteris ejus venia data, et praerogativa est reservata haeredibus (cf. 3 Kgs 11:12–13)?

did, so as to fulfil the will of God; for whose sake pardon was granted to his children when they sinned, and their rights were preserved to his heirs (cf. 3 Kgs 11:12–13)?

Feria Quinta: 2 Kgs 6:1–12
S. Joannes Chrysostomus, *In epistolam ad Galatas commentarius* (cap. 1, 6)

Ubi sunt igitur qui nos ut contentiosos damnant, eo quod cum haereticis habemus dissidium? ubi sunt qui dictitant nullum esse discrimen inter nos et illos, sed ex principatus ambitu proficisci discordiam? Quodque Oza, quoniam arcam alioqui subvertendam fulsit, e vestigio mortuus est (cf. 2 Kgs 6:7), eo quod ministerium ipsi non congruens usurparit? Ergone sabbatum violatum et solus arcae ruiturae contactus ad tantam indignatiotiem Deum provocavit, ut qui haec ausi fuerant, ne minimum quidem veniae sint consequuti. Hic vero qui adoranda ei ineffabilia dogmata corrumpit, excusationem habiturus est et veniam consequetur? Non potest hoc fieri, non potest, inquam. Hoc ipsum igitur est omnium malorum causa, quod ob pusilla non

Where then are those who charge us with being contentious in separating from heretics, and say that there is no real difference between us except what arises from our ambition? And that Ozias, who supported the Ark when on the point of being overturned, was struck suddenly dead (cf. 2 Kgs 6:7), because he had intruded upon an office which did not pertain to him? Wherefore if to transgress the Sabbath, and to touch the falling Ark, drew down the wrath of God so signally as to deprive the offender of even a momentary respite, shall he who corrupts unutterably awful doctrines find excuse and pardon? Assuredly not. A want of zeal in small matters is the cause of all our calamities; and because slight errors escape fitting correction, greater ones creep in. As in the body, a

indignemur. Ob id enim majora scelera subierunt, quod minoribus debita correctio non adhibeatur. Et quemadmodum in corporibus, qui vulnera neglexerunt, febres gignunt et putrefactiones ac mortem denique: itidem et in animis qui pusilla spernunt, majora inducunt.

neglect of wounds generates fever, mortification, and death; so in the soul, slight evils overlooked open the door to graver ones.

Feria Sexta: 2 Kgs 7:4–17
S. Justinus Martyr, *Dialogus cum Tryphone* (cap. 118)

Nathan, cum de eo loqueretur ad Davidem, sic intulit: "Ego ero illi in patrem, et ipse erit mihi in filium; et misericordiam meam non removebo ab eo, sicut feci ab eis qui ante eum erant; et statuam eum in domo mea, et in regno ejus usque in saeculum" (2 Kgs 7:14–15). Hic enim est eximius sacerdos et rex aetenus, Christus, utpote Filius Dei; cujus in secundo adventu ne existimetis lsaiam aut caeteros prophetas dicere, sacrificia sanguinis aut libationum altari imponi, sed vera et spiritalia, laudes et gratiarum actiones. Nec frustra nos in eum credimus, nec ab iis, qui ita docuerunt, decepti sumus; sed et admirabili Dei providentia id contigit, ut vobis,

Nathan likewise, speaking to David about Him, thus continued: "I will be His Father, and He shall be my Son; and my mercy shall I not take away from Him, as I did from them that went before Him; and I will establish Him in My house, and in His Kingdom forever" (2 Kgs 7:14–15). For He is the chosen Priest and eternal King, the Christ, inasmuch as He is the Son of God; and do not suppose that Isaias or the other prophets speak of sacrifices of blood or libations being presented at the altar on His second advent, but of true and spiritual praises and giving of thanks. And we have not in vain believed in Him, and have not been led astray by those who taught us such doctrines; but this

qui Dei amantes et prudentes existimamini, nec estis tamen, prudentiores nos et religiosiores inveniremur per vocationem novi et aeterni Tesiamenti, id est Christi.

has come to pass through the wonderful foreknowledge of God, in order that we, through the calling of the new and eternal covenant, that is, of Christ, might be found more intelligent and God-fearing than yourselves, who are considered to be lovers of God and men of understanding, but are not.

Sabbato: 2 Kgs 11:1–17
S. Gregorius Magnus, *Regula pastoralis* (lib. 1, cap. 3)

Plerumque adversitatis magisterio sub disciplina cor premitur: quod si ad regiminis culmen eruperit, in elationem protinus usu gloriae permutatur. Sic Saul, qui indignum se prius considerans fugerat, mox ut regni gubernacula suscepit, intumuit (cf. 1 Kgs 10:22; 15:17–30); honorari namque coram populo cupiens, dum reprehendi publice noluit, ipsum qui in regnum se unxerat, scidit. Sic David auctoris judicio pene in cunctis actibus placens, mox ut pressurae pondere caruit, in tumorem vulneris erupit (cf. 2 Kgs 11:3 seq.), factusque est in morte viri crudeliter rigidus, qui in appetitu feminae fuit enerviter fluxus; et qui malis ante noverat pie par-

Thus Saul, who had before fled in consideration of his unworthiness, no sooner had assumed the government of the kingdom than he was puffed up (cf. 1 Kgs 10:22; 15:17–30); for, desirous of being honored before the people while unwilling to be publicly blamed, he cut off from himself even him who had anointed him to the kingdom. Thus David, who in the judgment of Him Who chose him was well pleasing to Him in almost all his deeds, as soon as the weight of pressure was removed, broke out into a swelling sore (cf. 2 Kgs 11:3ff.), and, having been as a laxly running one in his appetite for the woman, became as a cruelly hard one in the slaughter of the man; and he who had before known pitifully

cere, in bonorum quoque necem post didicit sine obstaculo retract-ationis anhelare (cf. 2 Kgs 11:15). Prius quippe ferire deprehensum persecutorem noluit, et post cum damno desudantis exercitus etiam devotum militem exstinxit. Quem profecto ab electorum numero culpa longius raperet, nisi hunc ad veniam flagella revocassent.

how to spare the bad learned afterwards, without impediment of hesitation, to pant even for the death of the good (cf. 2 Kgs 11:15). For, indeed, previously he had been unwilling to smite his captured persecutor; and afterwards, with loss to his wearied army, he destroyed even his devoted soldier. And in truth his crime would have snatched him farther away from the number of the elect, had not scourges called him back to pardon.

INFRA HEBDOMADAM VI POST PENTECOSTEN
Feria Secunda: 2 Kgs 13:22–34
S. Hieronymus, *Epistula ad Eustochium* (cap. 12)

Sampson leone fortior, saxo durior et qui unus et nudus mille est persecutus armatos, in Dalilae mollescit amplexibus; David secundum cor domini electus et qui venturum Christum sancto saepe ore cantaverat, postquam deambulans super tectum domus suae Bersabee captus est nuditate, adulterio iunxit homicidium. Ubi et illud breviter adtende, quod nullus sit, etiam in domo, tutus aspectus. Quapropter ad Deum paenitens loquitur: "Tibi soli peccavi et malum coram te feci" (Ps

Samson was braver than a lion and tougher than a rock; alone and unprotected he pursued a thousand armed men; and yet, in Dalila's embrace, his resolution melted away. David was a man after God's own heart, and his lips had often sung of the Holy One, the future Christ; and yet as he walked upon his housetop he was fascinated by Bethsabee's nudity and added murder to adultery. Notice here how, even in his own house, a man cannot use his eyes without danger. Then repenting, he says to the

50:6). Rex enim alium non timebat. Salomon, per quem se cecinit ipsa sapientia, qui disputavit a cedro Libani usque ad hysopum, quae exit per parietem, recessit a domino, quia amator mulierum fuit. Et ne aliquis etiam de sanguinis sibi propinquitate confideret, in inlicitum Thamar sororis Amnon frater exarsit incendium (cf. 2 Kgs 13:22).

Lord: "Against Thee, Thee only, have I sinned and done this evil in Thy sight" (Ps 50:6). Being a king, he feared no one else. So, too, with Solomon. Wisdom used him to sing her praise, and he treated of all plants from the cedar tree that is in Lebanon even unto the hyssop that springs out of the wall; and yet he went back from God because he was a lover of women. And, as if to show that near relationship is no safeguard, Amnon burned with illicit passion for his sister Thamar (cf. 2 Kgs 13:22).

Feria Tertia: 2 Kgs 14:4–7, 10–14, 19–21
S. Joannes Cassianus, *Collationes* (coll. 13, cap. 7)

Propositum namque Dei, quo non ob hoc hominem fecerat ut periret, sed ut in perpetuum viveret, manet immobile. Cujus benignitas cum bonae voluntatis in nobis quantulamcumque scintillam emicuisse perspexerit, vel quam ipse tamquam de dura silice nostri cordis excusserit, confovet eam et exsuscitat, suaque inspiratione confortat, "volens omnes homines salvos fieri, et ad agnitionem veritatis venire" (1 Tm 2:4). "Quia non est, inquit, voluntas ante Patrem vestrum qui

For the purpose of God whereby He made man not to perish but to live forever, stands immovable. And when His goodness sees in us even the very smallest spark of good will shining forth, which He Himself has struck as it were out of the hard flints of our hearts, He fans and fosters it and nurses it with His breath, as "He wills all men to be saved and to come to the knowledge of the truth" (1 Tm 2:4), for as He says, "It is not the will of your Father which is in heaven that one

in caelis est, ut pereat unus ex pusillis istis" (Mt 18:14). Et iterum: Non vult, inquit, Deus perire animam, sed retractat cogitans ne penitus pereat qui abjectus est (cf. 2 Kgs 14:14). Verax namque est et non mentitur Deus, cum obtestatione definiens: "Vivo ego, dicit Dominus Deus, quia nolo mortem impii, sed ut convertatur a via sua et vivat" (Ez 33:11). Qui enim ut pereat unus ex pusillis non habet voluntatem, quomodo sine ingenti sacrilegio putandus est, non universaliter omnes, sed quosdam salvos fieri velle pro omnibus? Ergo quicumque pereunt, contra illius pereunt voluntatem, ita eo contra unumquemque eorum quotidie proclamante: Convertimini a viis vestris pessimis, et "quare moriemini, domus Israel" (Ez 33:11)?

of these little ones should perish" (Mt 18:14), and again it says: Neither will God have a soul to perish, but recalls, meaning that he that is cast off should not altogether perish (cf. 2 Kgs 14:14). For He is true and lies not when He lays down with an oath: "As I live, says the Lord God, for I will not the death of a sinner, but that he should turn from his way and live" (Ez 33:11). For if He wills not that one of His little ones should perish, how can we imagine without grievous blasphemy that He does not generally will all men, but only some instead of all to be saved? Those then who perish, perish against His will, as He testifies against each one of them day by day: turn from your evil ways, and "Why will you die, O house of Israel" (Ez 33:11)?

Feria Quarta: 2 Kgs 15:1–10
S. Augustinus, *Enarrationes in Psalmos* (in Ps 50:15)

Aliquando Deus cui ignoscit in futuro saeculo, corripit eum de peccato in isto saeculo. Nam et ipsi David, cui dictum jam fuerat per prophetam: "Dimissum est peccatum tuum" (2 Kgs 12:13), evenerunt quaedam quae minatus

Sometimes God in this world chastises for his sin him that He pardons in the world to come. For even to David himself, to whom it had been already said by the prophet, "Thy sin is put away" (2 Kgs 12:13), there happened certain

erat Deus propter ipsum peccatum. Nam filius ejus Abessalon adversus eum cruentum bellum gessit, et in multis humilavit patrem suum (cf. 2 Kgs 15:10). Ambulabat ille in dolore, in tribulatione humilationis suae, ita subditus Deo, ut omnia justa ei tribuens confiteretur quod nihil pateretur indigne, habens jam rectum cor cui non displicebat Deus. Injuriosum quemdam et in os sibi dura maledicta iacientem patienter audiebat, ex adversa parte unum ex militibus qui erant cum filio ejus impio. Agnoscens culpam suam, amplexus est poenam suam, quaerens gloriam non suam. Tales sunt omnes recti corde: non hi perversi, qui se rectos putant, et perversum Deum; qui quando aliquid faciunt mali, gaudent; quando aliquid mali patiuntur, blasphemant; insuper positi in tribulatione et flagello, dicunt de corde distorto: Deus, quid tibi feci? Vere quia nihil Deo fecerunt; omnia enim sibi fecerunt.

things which God had threatened for that very sin. For his son Absalom against him waged bloody war, and many ways humbled his father (cf. 2 Kgs 15:10). He was walking in grief, in the tribulation of his humiliation, so resigned to God, that, ascribing to Him all that was just, he confessed that he was suffering nothing undeservedly, having now a heart upright, to which God was not displeasing. A slanderous person and one throwing in his teeth harsh curses he patiently heard, one of the soldiers on the opposite side, that were with his unnatural son (cf. 2 Kgs 16:10). Acknowledging his guilt he embraced his penance, seeking glory not his own. Such are all the upright in heart: not those crooked persons who think themselves upright and God crooked: who when they do any evil thing, rejoice; when they suffer any evil thing, blaspheme; nay, if set in tribulation and scourging, they say from their distorted heart, O God, what have I done to Thee? Truly it is because they have done nothing to God, for they have done all to themselves.

Feria Quinta: 2 Kgs 15:13–20
S. Beda Venerabilis, *Quaestiones super libros Regum* (in librum II, cap. 3)

Illud vero quid significat quod parricida filius Absalon, patrem insequens, primo pater ejus declinans, fugit ante faciem ejus, securus de victoria, quia sciebat impium perire? Quem etiam flevit magno luctu, et deploravit exitum parricidae. Scribitur enim fugisse David a facie bellantis adversum se filii (cf. 2 Kgs 15:14). Et quoniam scriptum est de populo Jerusalem: "Filios enutrivi, et exaltavi, ipsi autem spreverunt me" (Is 1:2): per filium ejus impium significabatur tropice idem populus Judaicus, qui eum tradidit. Absalon autem, sicut quidam interpretantur, intelligitur patris pax: quod mirum in historia videtur, quemadmodum patris pax possit intelligi, qui patrem bello persecutus est. Alii Absalon Judam traditorem accipiunt, quem tanta et tam miranda patientia Christus pertulit tanquam bonum, cum ejus cogitationes non ignoraret, cum adhibuit convivio, in quo corporis et sanguinis sui figuram discipulis commendavit, et tradidit. Quod denique in

But what does that mean, that the parricide son Absalom, pursuing his father, his father declining at first, fled before his face, confident of victory, because he knew that the wicked would perish? He also wept over him with great mourning and lamented the end of the parricide. For it is written that David fled from the face of his son who was fighting against him (cf. 2 Kgs 15:14). And since it is written about the people of Jerusalem: "I nourished their children and exalted them, but they despised me" (Is 1:2): by his wicked son was signified tropically the same Jewish people who betrayed him. But Absalom, as some interpret, is meant the father's peace: which seems strange in history, how the father's peace can be understood, who persecuted his father in war. Others see in Absalom Judas the betrayer, whom Christ endured with so much and so wonderful patience as one would treat a good man, though he was not ignorant of his thoughts, even when used the banquet, in which he commended to

ipsa traditione et osculum accepit: bene intelligitur pacem Christum exhibuisse traditori suo, quamvis ille tam sceleratae cogitationis interno bello vastaretur.

the disciples the figure of His Body and Blood, and delivered it up. Finally, when the Lord delivered to him His Body and Blood, Judas also received the kiss from Him: by this is well understood that Christ showed peace to His betrayer, in spite of the attack by the internal war of such a criminal thought.

Feria Sexta: 2 Kgs 16:5–12
S. Augustinus, *De patientia* (cap. 8–9)

Quamvis autem patientia virtus sit animi, partim tamen ea utitur animus in se ipso, partim vero in corpore suo. In se ipso utitur patientia, quando illaeso et intacto corpore aliquid quod non expediat vel non deceat, facere aut dicere quibuslibet adversitatibus aut foeditatibus rerum seu verborum stimulis incitatur, et patienter mala omnia tolerat, ne ipse mali aliquid opere vel ore committat. Per hanc patientiam sustinemus, etiam dum corpore sani sumus, quod inter hujus saeculi scandala beatitudo nostra differtur. Hac patientia sanctus David conviciantis opprobria toleravit, et cum facile posset ulcisci, non solum non fecit, verum etiam alium pro

Although patience be a virtue of the mind, yet partly the mind exercises it in the mind itself, partly in the body. In itself it exercises patience, when, the body remaining unhurt and untouched, the mind is goaded by any adversities or filthiness of things or words, to do or to say something that is not expedient or not becoming, and patiently bears all evils that it may not itself commit any evil in work or word. By this patience we bear, even while we be sound in body, that in the midst of the offenses of this world our blessedness is deferred: of which is said what I cited a little before, if what we see not we hope for, we do by patience wait for it. By this patience, holy David bore the reviling

se dolentem commotumque com-
pescuit (cf. 2 Kgs 16:5–12); et potestatem regiam magis adhibuit
prohibendo, quam exercendo vindictam. Neque tunc ejus corpus
aliquo morbo affligebatur aut vulnere, sed humilitatis tempus ag-
noscebatur, ac ferebatur voluntas
Dei, propter quam patientissimo
animo amaritudo contumeliae
bibebatur. Hanc patientiam Dominus docuit, quando commotis
zizaniorum permixtione servis, et
volentibus ea colligere, dixit re-
spondisse patremfamilias: "Sinite
utraque crescere usque ad messem" (Mt 13:30). Oportet enim
patienter ferri, quod festinanter
non oportet auferri.

of a railer, and, when he might easily
have avenged himself, not only did it
not, but even refrained another who
was vexed and moved for him; (cf.
2 Kgs 16:5–12) and more put forth
his kingly power by prohibiting than
by exercising vengeance. Nor at that
time was his body afflicted with any
disease or wound, but there was an
acknowledging of a time of humility, and a bearing of the will of God,
for the sake of which there was a
drinking of the bitterness of contu-
mely with most patient mind. This
patience the Lord taught, when, the
servants being moved at the mixing
in of the tares and wishing to gather
them up, He said that the house-
holder answered, "Leave both to
grow until the harvest" (Mt 13:30).
That, namely, must be patience put
up with, which must not be in haste
put away.

Sabbato: 2 Kgs 18:6–12, 14–17

S. Augustinus, *Epistula 185 De Correctione Donatistarum* (cap. 8, 32)

Quis enim nostrum velit non
solum aliquem illorum [Donatis-
tarum] perire, verum etiam aliquid
perdere? Sed si aliter non meruit
pacem habere domus David, nisi
Absalon filius ejus in bello quod

I do not say that one of them [Do-
natists] should perish, but should
even lose any of his possessions?
But if the house of David could not
earn peace on any other terms except
that Absalom his son should have

contra patrem gerebat, fuisset exstinctus, quamvis magna cura mandaverit suis ut eum quantum possent vivum salvumque servarent, ut esset cui paenitenti paternus affectus ignosceret; quid ei restitit, nisi perditum flere, et sui regni pace acquisita suam maestitiam consolari (cf. 2 Kgs 18:5–15, 33; 22:1–51). Sic ergo catholica mater, bellantibus adversus eam quibus aliis quam filiis suis, quia utique ex ipsa magna arbore quae ramorum suorum porrectione toto orbe diffunditur (cf. Is 18:5; Rom 11:17, 19), iste in Africa ramusculus fractus est, cum eos caritate parturiat ut redeant ad radicem sine qua veram vitam habere non possunt; si aliquorum perditione caeteros tam multos colligit, praesertim quia isti, non sicut Absalon casu bellico, sed spontaneo magis interitu pereunt, dolorem materni cordis lenit et sanat tantorum liberatione populorum.

been slain in the war which he was waging against his father, although he had most carefully given strict injunctions to his followers that they should use their utmost endeavors to preserve him alive and safe, that his paternal affection might be able to pardon him on his repentance, what remained for him except to weep for the son that he had lost, and to console himself in his sorrow by reflecting on the acquisition of peace for his kingdom (cf. 2 Kgs 18:5–15, 33; 22:1–51). The same, then, is the case with the Catholic mother (Church); for when war is waged against her by men who are certainly different from sons, since it must be acknowledged that from the great tree, which by the spreading of its branches is extended over all the world, (cf. Is 18:5; Rom 11:17, 19) this little branch in Africa is broken off, while she is willing in her love to give them birth, that they may return to the root, without which they cannot have the true life, at the same time if she collects the remainder in so large a number by the loss of some, she soothes and cures the sorrow of her maternal heart by the thoughts of the deliverance of such mighty nations.

INFRA HEBDOMADAM VII POST PENTECOSTEN
Feria Secunda: 3 Kgs 1:28–35, 38–40
S. Cyrillus Hierosolymitanus, *Catecheses Mystagogicae* (cat. 3, cap. 6–7)

Nosse autem vos oportet chrismatis seu unctionis hujus in Veteri Scriptura symbolum exstare. Quando enim Moyses divinum cum fratre communicavit mandatum, summum eum sacerdotem constituens, ablutum aqua perunxit (cf. Lv 8:1): vocatusque est christus, ab chrismate videlicet seu unctione figarativa. Sic et Salomonem summus pontifex in regem promovens, unxit eum postquam lavisset in Gihon (cf. 3 Kgs 1:39, 45)? At haec in figura contingebant illis: vobis autem non secundum figuram, sed in veritate; siquidem a Spiritu Sancto vere intincti estis. Principium vestrae salutis est Christus; ille enim vere primitiae est (cf. 1 Cor 15:23), vos vero conspersio (cf. 1 Cor 5:7): si autem primitiae sanctae sunt, non dubium quin ad conspersionem transferenda sit sanctitas. Hoc chrisma incontaminatum custodite: de omnibus enim vos docebit, si in vobis manet.

You should know that in the old Scripture there lies the symbol of this chrism. For what time Moses imparted to his brother the command of God, and made him high priest, after bathing in water, he anointed him (cf. Lv 8:1); and Aaron was called Christ or Anointed, evidently from the typical chrism. So also the high priest, in advancing Solomon to the kingdom, anointed him after he had bathed in Gihon (cf. 3 Kgs 1:39, 45)? To them however these things happened in a figure, but to you not in a figure, but in truth, because you were truly anointed by the Holy Ghost. Christ is the beginning of your salvation; for He is truly the first fruit, (cf. 1 Cor 15:23) and you the mass (cf. 1 Cor 5:7); but if the first fruit be holy, it is manifest that its holiness will pass to the mass also. Keep this unspotted: for it shall teach you all things, if it abides in you.

Feria Tertia: 3 Kgs 2:1–9
S. Ephraem Syrus, *In Primum Regnorum qui et Tertius Regum Explanatio* (ad cap. 2)

David finem vitae suae praesentiens (cf. 3 Kgs 2:1) Salomonem pro sua sapientia ac pietate ad tanti imperii gubernationem instituit: Jacob itaque et Moysis exempla recogitans in primis Dei timorem, divinorumque mandatorum observantiam etiam atque etiam eidem inculcat, et praemia ab illo expectare docet amplissima, ac proinde etiam illa, quae patri suo promissa. Bene noverat, sic ut non ipse modo regnum haberet pacatissimum, verum etiam ad suos posteros feliciter transmitteret. Deinde monet, ut publicae tranquillitati prospiciat, pacisque perturbatores coerceat. David expositis Joabi et Semei criminibus eorundem punitionem Salomoni praecipit, modum tamen et qualitatem poenae minime praescribit: "Tu," inquit, "facies juxta sapientiam tuam" (3 Kgs 2:6). David, cum filii sui arbitrio committit praemium rependendum filiis Berzellai Galaaditae (cf. 3 Kgs 2:7) hominis spectatae in Regem fidei et liberalitatis,

David, feeling the end of his life (cf. 3 Kgs 2:1), appointed Solomon for his wisdom and piety to the government of such a great kingdom: therefore, recalling the examples of Jacob and Moses, he first of all emphasizes the fear of God, and respect for the divine commandments, over and over again, and teaches him to wait from Him the most ample rewards, and consequently also that which was promised to his father. He knew well, so that he would not only have a most peaceful kingdom, but also pass it on successfully to his posterity. Then he exhorts him to look after the tranquility of the state, and to check the disturbers of the peace. After exposing the crimes of Joab and Semei, David orders Solomon to punish them, yet he does not at all prescribe the manner and quality of the punishment: "Thou," he says, "do it according to thy wisdom" (3 Kg 2:6). David, when leaving it at the discretion of his son to reward the sons of Berzellai the Galaadite (cf. 3 Kgs 2:7), a man of proven

atque poenam de Joabo et Semei sumendam, facto praevenit, quae Christus de se ipse erat dicturus: "Neque Pater judicat quemquam, sed omme judicium dedit Filio" (Jn 5:22): imo et quae facturus est in supremo mundi die, quo illum credimus venturum bonorum operum remuneratorem et scelerum vindicem.

fidelity and liberality towards the King, and to punish the Joab and Semei, by this his deed he anticipated what Christ Himself was about to say about Himself: "The Father judges no one, but has given all judgment to the Son" (Jn 5:22): yes, and what He is going to do on the last day of the world, when we believe that He will come as the rewarder of good works and the avenger of crimes.

Feria Quarta: 3 Kgs 3:5–13
S. Irenaeus, *Adversus haereses* (lib. 4, cap. 27, 1)

De Salomone, cum perseveraret judicare recte, et sapientiam enarrare, et typum veri templi aedificabat, et glorias exponebat Dei, et adventuram pacem gentibus annuntiabat, et Christi regnum praefigurabat, et loquebatur tria millia parabolarum in adventum Domini, et quinque millia canticorum, hymnum dicens Deo, et eam quae est in conditione sapientiam Dei exponebat psychologice ex omni ligno, et de omni herba, et de volatilibus omnibus, et de quadrupedibus, et de piscibus; et dicebat: "Si vere Deus, quem caeli non capiunt, super ter-

With regard to Solomon, while he continued to judge uprightly, and to declare the wisdom of God, and built the temple as the type of truth, and set forth the glories of God, and announced the peace about to come upon the nations, and prefigured the Kingdom of Christ, and spoke three thousand parables about the Lord's advent, and five thousand songs, singing praise to God, and expounded the wisdom of God in creation, discoursing as to the nature of every tree, every herb, and of all fowls, quadrupeds, and fishes; and he said, "Will God whom the heavens can-

ram habitabit cum hominibus?" (3 Kgs 8:27), et placebat Deo, et omnes eum admirabantur, et omnes reges terrae quaerebant faciem ejus, ut audirent sapientiam ejus, quam dederat illi Deus (cf. 3 Kgs 3:12). Salomon enim servus erat; Christus vero Filius Dei et Dominus Salomonis. Cum igitur sine offensa serviret Deo, et ministraret dispositionibus ejus, tunc glorificabatur.

not contain, really dwell with men upon the earth?" (3 Kings 8:27). And he pleased God and was the admiration of all; and all kings of the earth sought an interview with him that they might hear the wisdom which God had conferred upon him (cf. 3 Kings 3:12). For Solomon was a servant, but Christ is indeed the Son of God, and the Lord of Solomon. While, therefore, he served God without blame, and ministered to His dispensations, then was he glorified.

Feria Quinta: 3 Kgs 4:21–34
S. Augustinus, *Enarrationes in Psalmos* (in Ps 126:2)

Optime igitur etiam hoc egit misericordia Dei et Spiritus ejus, ut quidquid boni per Salomonem dictum est, Deo tribueretur; peccatum autem hominis homini. Quid mirum quia in populo Dei cecidit Salomon? In paradiso non cecidit Adam? Non cecidit de caelo angelus, et diabolus factus est? Ideo docemur in nullo hominum spem esse ponendam. Quia et iste Salomon aedificaverat templum Domino, in typo quidem et in figura futurae Ecclesiae et corporis Domini. Aedificavit sibi templum

The mercy of God and His Spirit, excellently wrought that whatever of good was declared through Solomon, might be attributed unto God, and the man's sin, unto the man. What marvel that Solomon fell among God's people? Did not Adam fall in paradise? Did not an angel fall from heaven, and become the devil? We are thereby taught, that no hope must be placed in any among men. Because this Solomon also had built a Temple for the Lord, indeed in the type and shape of the future Church and the body

verus Salomon Dominus noster Jesus Christus, verus pacificus. Nomen enim Salomonis interpretatur pacificus. Quia ergo ille verus Salomon; Salomon autem ille filius David de muliere Bethsabee, rex Israel, figuram gestabat hujus pacifici, quando templum aedificavit. Omnes currimus, omnes laboramus, omnes aedificamus modo; et ante nos cucurrerunt, laboraverunt, aedificaverunt: sed "nisi Dominus aedificaverit domum, in vanum laboraverunt, aedificantes eam" (Ps 126:1). Nos ergo loquimur foris, ille aedificat intus.

of the Lord. The true Solomon built for himself a temple, Our Lord Jesus Christ, the true peacemaker. For Solomon's name is interpreted as peacemaker, because he is the true Solomon. And Solomon, the son of David by the wife of Bethsabee, the king of Israel, bore the image of this peacemaker when he built the Temple. We all run, we all work, we all build; and they ran before us, they labored, they built: "But unless the Lord had built the house, they labored in vain, building it" (Ps 126:1). We therefore speak without, He builds within.

Feria Sexta: 3 Kgs 5:1–9
S. Beda Venerabilis, *De templo Salomonis* (cap. 2)

Nulli autem dubium, quod Salomon, qui interpretatur pacificus, et ipso nomine, et serenissimo regni sui statu, illum significet, de quo dicit Isaias: "Multiplicabitur ejus imperium, et pacis ejus non erit finis" (Is 9:7). Hiram vero, qui Latine dicitur vivens excelse, credentes ex gentibus et vita simul cum fide gloriosos figuraliter exprimit. Neque aliquid prohibet, quin Hiram, quia rex erat, regalique potentia Salomo-

There is no doubt that Solomon, who is interpreted as the peacemaker, and by his very name, and by the most serene state of his kingdom, signifies Him, of whom Isaias says: "His dominion will be multiplied, and there will be no end to His peace" (Is 9:7). But Hiram, who in Latin is called living on high, figuratively expresses the believers from among the nations and those who are glorious by their life together with faith. Nor does anything

nem in aedificio domus Domini juvabat, conversos ad fidem ipsos rerum dominos typice denuntiet, quorum ope constat Ecclesiam saepius adiutam, nobiliter augmentatam, et contra haereticos, schismaticos, et paganos principalibus erectam esse decretis. Petit ergo Salomon in opere templi auxilium ab Hiram, quia cum veniens in carne Dominus dilectam sibi domum, videlicet Ecclesiam, aedificare disponeret, non de Judaeis tantummodo, verum etiam de gentibus adjutores operis elegit. Misit Hiram Salomoni praecisa de Libano ligna cedrina et abiegna, quae in domum Domini ponerentur, quia conversa gentilitas misit ad Dominum viros quondam in saeculo claros, sed securi dominicae increpationis de monte suae superbiae jam deiectos et humiliatos, qui ad normam evangelicae veritatis instituti, in aedificio Ecclesiae pro suo quoque merito, vel tempore collocantur.

prevent that Hiram, because he was king, and with royal power assisted Solomon in the building of the Lord's house, represented the type of the converted to the Faith and who were also masters of things, by whose help the Church was often aided, increased nobly, and raised against heretics, schismatics, and pagan through principal decrees. Solomon asks, therefore, Hiram for help in the work of the Temple, because when the Lord came in the flesh and determined to build the house He loved, that is to say the Church, He chose not only from the Jews, but also from the Gentiles to help in this work. Hiram sent to Solomon cedar and fir trees cut down from Lebanon, which were to be placed in the house of the Lord, because a converted Gentile sent to the Lord men who had once been famous in the world, but who had already been cast down and humiliated by the ax of the Lord's rebuke from the mountain of their pride, who had been established according to the standard of evangelical truth, were placed in the building of the Church also according to their own merit, or the time.

Sabbato: 3 Kgs 7:51; 8:1–12
S. Beda Venerabilis, *De templo Salomonis* (cap. 25)

Hoc autem argentum, hoc aurum, haec sanctificata vasa Salomon infert in templum, cum Dominus noster peracto universali judicio omnes electos, et doctores videlicet, et caeterorum fidelium coetum in gaudium regni caelestis introducit: reponitque vasa diversi generis argentea sive aurea in thesauris domus Domini, quando eos qui multitudine dulcedinis ejus frui meruerint, abscondit in abdito vultus sui a conturbatione hominum. Et apte multi sunt thesauri, in quibus vasa electionis recondantur, sed una domus Domini in qua iidem sunt facti thesauri, quia et una est Ecclesia, in qua omnes continentur electi, quantumlibet meritis distent: et una est et non diversa patria illa caelestis. Unam ergo domum Domini fecit Salomon, sed multos in ea thesauros ad recipienda vasa diversi generis, una tamen benedictione sanctificata paravit; quae nimirum domus Patris non manufacta aeterna est in caelis, sed multae in ea mansiones, ad recipiendos omnes timentes se ac

And Solomon brings this silver, this gold, and these sanctified vessels into the Temple, when Our Lord, having completed the universal judgment, introduces all the elect, both the teachers and the rest of the assembly of the faithful, into the joy of the heavenly kingdom. He places vessels of different kinds, both silver and gold, in the treasuries of the house of the Lord, when He hides those who have merited to enjoy the abundance of His sweetness in the secret of His presence, away from the disturbances of men. And, fittingly, there are many treasures in which the vessels of choice are kept, but there is one Lord's house in which these treasures were made, because there is one Church in which all the elect are contained, regardless of their difference in merit. And there is one, not different, heavenly fatherland. Therefore Solomon built one house of the Lord, but prepared in it many treasures to receive vessels of different kinds, yet sanctified by one blessing. Indeed, the house of the Father, not made by hand, is

diligentes, quibus Dominus benedixit, pusillis cum majoribus.

eternal in the heavens. it has many mansions in it, to receive all who respect and love Him, Whom the Lord has blessed, both the small and the great.

INFRA HEBDOMADAM VIII POST PENTECOSTEN
Feria Secunda: 3 Kgs 10:1–11
S. Ambrosius, *De officiis ministrorum* (lib. 2, cap. 10)

Justi judicium est, sapientis autem argumentum: in illo censura disceptationis, in hoc calliditas inventionis. Quod si utrumque connectas, erit magna consiliorum salubritas, quae ab universis spectatur admiratione sapientiae et amore justitiae; ut omnes quaerant audire sapientiam ejus viri, in quo utriusque virtutis copula sit: sicut quaerebant omnes reges terrae videre faciem Salomonis, et audire sapientiam ejus; ita ut "et Saba regina veniret ad eum, et tentaret eum in quaestionibus" (3 Kgs 10:2–3). Intellige convivium veri Salomonis, et quae apponuntur in eo convivio, intellige sapienter, et considera in qua terra congregatio nationum audierit famam sapientiae verae atque justitiae, et quibus eum viderit oculis, contemplantibus utique ea quae

Just because it is the judgment of a just man, it is also the conclusion of a wise one: in the one lies the result of the matter in dispute, in the other readiness of invention. And if one connects the two, there will be great soundness in the advice given, which is regarded by all with admiration for the wisdom shown, and with love for its justice. And so all will desire to hear the wisdom of that man in whom those two virtues are found together, as all the kings of the earth desired to see the face of Solomon and to hear his wisdom. Nay, "Even the queen of Saba came to him and tried him with questions" (3 Kgs 10:2–3). Recognize the feast of the true Solomon, and who are set down at that feast; recognize it wisely and think in what land all the nations shall hear the fame of true wisdom and justice, and with what

non videntur. "Quoniam quae videntur, temporalia sunt: quae autem non videntur, aeterna" (2 Cor 4:18). Exempli causa propositus est nobis Salomon, a quo certatim ut audiretur ejus sapientia, postulabatur.

eyes they shall see Him, beholding those things which are not seen. "For the things that are seen are temporal, but the things which are not seen are eternal" (2 Cor 4:18). Solomon is put before us simply for the sake of example, of whom it was eagerly expected that his wisdom should be heard.

Feria Tertia: 3 Kgs 11:1–12
S. Augustinus, *Enarrationes in Psalmos* (in Ps 88:6)

Promisit ex semine ejus in aeternum aliquid; et natus Salomon, factus est tantae sapientiae, ut promissio Dei de semine David in illo putaretur impleta: sed cecidit Salomon, et dedit locum sperando Christo; ut quoniam Deus nec falli posset, nec fallere, quem sciebat casurum, non in eo poneret promissum suum, sed post casum ejus respiceres tu Deum, et flagitares promissum. Ergo, Domine, mentitus es? Non imples quod promisisti? non exhibes quod jurasti? Forte hic dicturus tibi erat Deus: juravi quidem et promisi, sed iste noluit perseverare. Quid ergo? tu, Domine Deus, non praesciebas istum non perseveraturum? Utique scie-

He promised from his seed something for evermore: and, Solomon, born to him, became master of such wisdom, that the promise of God respecting the fruit of David's body was believed to have been fulfilled in him; but Solomon fell, and gave room for hoping for Christ; that since God can neither be deceived nor deceive, He might not make His promise to rest in one who He knew would fall, but you might after the fall of Solomon look back to God, and demand His promise. Hast Thou, O Lord, deceived? Hast Thou failed to fulfil Thy promise? Dost Thou not exhibit what Thou hast sworn? Perhaps God might reply, I swore and promised: but Solomon would not persevere. What

bas. Quare ergo in non persever-
aturo mihi quod aeternum esset
promittebas? Nonne tu dixisti: Si
dereliquerint legem meam, et in
judiciis meis non ambulaverint, et
mandata mea non custodierint, et
testamentum meum profanaver-
int (cf. 3 Kgs 11). Manebit tamen
promissio mea, implebitur juratio
mea? Semel, inquit, juravi, si David mentiar. Exhibe ergo quod
jurasti, redde quod promisisti.
Sublatum est de isto David, ne
exspectaretur in isto David. Ex-
specta ergo quod promisi.

then? Didst not Thou, Lord God,
know beforehand that he would
not persevere? Indeed, Thou knew-
est. Why then didst Thou promise
me what should be eternal in one
who would not persevere? Hast
Thou not answered: But if his children forsake My law, and walk not
in My judgments; if they keep not
My statutes, and profane My testament (cf. 3 Kgs 11). Yet My promise shall remain, and My oath shall
be fulfilled? I have sworn once that
I will not fail David. Show forth
then what Thou hast sworn, give us
what Thou hast promised. The fulfillment is taken from that David,
that it might not be looked for in
that David: wait therefore for what
I have promised.

Feria Quarta: 3 Kgs 11:26–31, 40–43
S. Cyprianus, *De unitate Ecclesiae* (cap. 7)

Possidere non potest indumentum
Christi qui scindit et dividit Ecclesiam Christi. Contra denique
cum, Salomone moriente, regnum
ejus et populus scinderetur, Achias
propheta Jeroboam regi obvius
factus in campo, in duodecim scissuras vestimentum suum discidit
dicens: Sume tibi decem scissuras,

He cannot possess the garment of
Christ who parts and divides the
Church of Christ. On the other
hand, again, when at Solomon's
death his kingdom and people
were divided, Ahias the prophet,
meeting Jeroboam the king in the
field, divided his garment into
twelve sections, saying, Take you

quia haec dicit Dominus: "Ecce scindo regnum de manu Salomonis, et dabo tibi decem sceptra, et duo sceptra erunt ei propter servum meum David et propter Hierusalem civitatem quam elegi ut ponam nomen meum illic" (3 Kgs 11:31–36). Cum duodecim tribus Israel scinderetur, vestimentum suum propheta Achias discidit. At vero, quia Christi populus non potest scindi, tunica ejus per totum textilis et cohaerens divisa a possidentibus non est. Individua, copulata, connexa ostendit populi nostri, qui Christum induimus, concordiam cohaerentem. Sacramento vestis et signo declaravit Ecclesiae unitatem.

ten pieces; for thus says the Lord, "Behold, I will rend the kingdom out of the hand of Solomon, and I will give ten scepters unto you; and two scepters shall be unto him for my servant David's sake, and for Jerusalem, the city which I have chosen to place My name there" (3 Kgs 11:31–36). As the twelve tribes of Israel were divided, the prophet Ahias rent his garment. But because Christ's people cannot be rent, His robe, woven and united throughout, is not divided by those who possess it; undivided, united, connected, it shows the coherent concord of our people who put on Christ. By the sacrament and sign of His garment, He has declared the unity of the Church.

Feria Quinta: 3 Kgs 12:1–8, 13–16
S. Basilius, *Homilia 20 de humilitate* (cap. 1)

Homines etiam ob dignitates quas per suffragia obtinuere, ultra quam natura sinit, efferuntur. Hic certe quasi humanam naturam transcendentes, tantum non ipsis nubibus insidere se arbitrantur, homines subjectos pro scabello ducentes, seque attollentes in ipsos collatae sibi dignitatis aucto-

Men exalt themselves beyond what is due their nature if an exceptional mark of dignity be voted in their favor by the people, thereupon, as though they had risen above human nature, they look upon themselves as well-nigh seated on the very clouds and regard the men beneath them as their footstool. They

res, et adversus eos, quorum opera eximii quidam viri esse videntur, insolescentes. Agunt rem dementiae plenam, cum habeant gloriam somnio debiliorem, circumdenturque splendore nocturnis visis inaniore: qui scilicet populi nutu confletur, et nutu ejusdem dissolvatur. Ejusmodi erat demens ille Salomonis filius, aetate juvenis, mentis prudentia junior, qui cum populo imperium mitius petenti durius comminatus esset, et per minas regnum amisisset, unde regnaturum se augustius sperabat, inde ex dignitale quam habebat, dejectus est (cf. 3 Kgs 12:4). Reddit autem hominem insolentem et manuum vis, et celeritas pedum, et corporis venustas: quae a morbis abolentur, et tempore absumuntur; nec animadvertit quod "omnis caro fenum sit, et omnis gloria hominis, sicut flos feni. Aruit fenum et flos decidit" (Is 40:6–7).

lord it over those who raised them to such honor and exalt themselves over the very ones at whose hands they received their sham distinctions. The position they occupy is entirely out of keeping with reason, for they possess a glory more unsubstantial than a dream. They are surrounded with a splendor more unreal than the phantoms of the night, since it comes into being or is swept away at the nod of the populace. A fool of this sort was that famous son of Solomon, youthful in years and younger still in wisdom, who threatened his people desiring a milder rule with an even harsher one and thereby destroyed his kingdom. By his threat, the very expedient whereby he hoped to be elevated to a more royal state, he was bereft of the dignity already his (cf. 3 Kgs 12:4). Strength of arm, swiftness of foot, and comeliness of body, the spoils of sickness and the plunder of time—also awaken pride in man, unaware as he is that "all flesh is grass and all the glory of man as the flower of the field. The grass is withered, and the flower is fallen (Is 40:6–7).

Feria Sexta: 3 Kgs 14:5–12
Constitutiones Apostolicae (lib. 4, cap. 7)

Quod indignorum hominum oblationes, quandiu ii tales sunt, non modo non placant Deum, sed contra ad indignationem eum provocant. Quin etiam in peccatis versantes, et paenitentiam non agentes, non solum inter orandum non exaudientur, sed insuper Deum irritabunt, illum commonefacientes improbitatis eorum. Evitate igitur hujusmodi subministrationes, tanquam pretium canis, et mercedem meretricis: utraque enim legibus prohibentur (cf. Dn 28:18). Nam nec Elisaeus allata ab Azaele munera accepit, nec Achias a Jeroboamo (cf. 3 Kgs 14:2–3). Quod si Dei prophetae dona impiorum non admisere, aequum est ut neque vos, episcopi, admittatis. Cum etiam Simon Magus, mihi Petro, et Joanni pecuniam offerens, gratiam inaestimabilem conatus est pretio comparare; nos, repulso munere, eum, diris perpetuis constrinximus; quoniam donum Dei non benevolentia erga Numen, sed pecuniae permutatione existimavit possideri. Recu-

The oblations of the unworthy, as long as they remain such, do not only not propitiate God, but on the contrary provoke Him to indignation. Indeed, those who persist in sin and do not repent will not only be unheard when they pray, but will provoke God to anger by reminding Him of their own wickedness. Avoid therefore such offerings, as one would the price of a dog and the hire of a harlot, for both of them are forbidden by the Law (cf. Dn 28:18). For neither did Eliseus receive the presents brought by Hazael, nor Ahias those from Jeroboam (cf. 3 Kgs 14:2–3). If the prophets of God did not accept presents from the impious, it is reasonable, O bishops, that neither should you. When Simon Magus offered money to me, Peter, and to John, trying to purchase invaluable grace, we rejected the offering and bound him with everlasting maledictions, because he thought that God's gift could be possessed through monetary exchange rather than genuine devotion. Refuse therefore offerings brought to the

sate ergo oblationes qua ad altare a male sibi consciis afferuntur.

altar by those who are conscious of their own wickedness.

Sabbato: 3 Kgs 18:21–27
S. Ambrosius, *De officiis ministrorum* (lib. 3, cap. 18)

Notum est ergo hunc esse vere ignem sacrum, qui tunc in typo futurae remissionis peccatorum descendit super sacrificium. Ipse quoque Dominus Jesus quasi ignis inflammabat audientium corda (cf. Lk 12:49), quasi fons refrigerabat; nam ipse in Evangelio suo dicit quod ideo venerit, ut ignem in terras mitteret, et potum sitientibus aquae vivae ministraret (cf. Jn 7:37–38). Eliae quoque tempore descendit ignis, quando provocavit prophetas gentium, ut altare sine igne accenderent. Et cum illi nequissent facere, hostiam suam tertio ipse perfudit aqua, et manabat aqua in circuitu altaris, et exclamavit, et cecidit ignis a Domino de caelo, et consumpsit holocaustum (cf. 3 Kgs 18:38). Hostia illa tu es. Considera tacitus singula. In te descendit vapor Spiritus Sancti, te videtur exurere, cum tua peccata consumit. Denique quod consumptum est sacrificium Moysi tempore, sac-

We know now that this is in truth the sacred fire which then, as a type of the future remission of sins, came down upon the sacrifice. The Lord Jesus, too, like a fire inflamed the hearts of those who heard Him, and like a fount of waters cooled them. For He Himself said in His gospel that He came to send fire on the earth (cf. Lk 12:49) and to supply a draught of living waters to those who thirst (cf. Jn 7:37–38). In the time of Elias, also, fire came down when he challenged the prophets of the heathen to light up the altar without fire. When they could not do so, he poured water thrice over his victim, so that the water ran round about the altar; then he cried out and the fire fell from the Lord from heaven and consumed the burnt offering (cf. 3 Kgs 18:38). Thou art that victim. Contemplate in silence each single point. The breath of the Holy Spirit descends on thee, He seems to burn thee when He consumes thy

rificium pro peccato erat. Unde Moyses ait, sicut in Machabaeorum scriptum est libro (cf. 2 Mc 2:11), eo quod non sit manducatum quod erat pro peccato, consumptum est. Nonne tibi consumi videtur, quando in baptismatis sacramento interit homo totus exterior? Vetus homo noster confixus est cruci, Apostolus clamat (cf. Rom. 6:6).

sins. The sacrifice which was consumed in the time of Moses was a sacrifice for sin, wherefore Moses said, as is written in the book of the Machabees: Because the sacrifice for sin was not to be eaten, it was consumed (cf. 2 Mc 2:11). Does it not seem to be consumed for thee when in the sacrament of baptism the whole outer man perishes? Our old man is crucified, the apostle exclaims (cf. Rom. 6:6).

INFRA HEBDOMADAM IX POST PENTECOSTEN
Feria Secunda: 4 Kgs 2:5–13
S. Beda Venerabilis, *Homiliae* (lib. 2, hom. 9)

Venit Elias ad Jordanem, et exutus palio suo percussit aquas ac divisit (cf. 4 Kgs 2:8). Venit Dominus ad fluvium mortis, quo genus humanum mergi consueverat; et exuens se ad tempus habitu carnis quam assumpserat, mortem moriendo percussit, ac vitae nobis iter resurgendo patefecit. Recte etenim per Jordanem fluxus nostrae mortalitatis ac defectus exprimitur: quia et Jordanis Latine descensus eorum dicitur, et ipse fiuvius in mare mortuum influens laudabiles suas ibi perdit aquas. Transit autem Elias diviso amne per siccum,

Elias came to the Jordan and, taking off his cloak, struck the waters and divided them (cf. 4 Kgs 2:8). The Lord came to the river of death, in which the human race was accustomed to drown; and putting off for a time the habit of flesh which He had assumed, He smote death by dying, and revealed to us the way of life by rising again. Indeed, the flow of our mortality and failure is rightly expressed through the Jordan: for the Jordan is also called their descent in Latin, and the river itself, flowing into the dead sea, loses its praisewor-

transit et Eliseus, quia resurgens a mortuis Salvator fidelibus suis quoque spem resurgendi tribuit. Transito Jordane, Elias dedit optionem Elizeo postulandi quae vollet (cf. 4 Kgs 2:9): et Dominus impleta resurrectionis gloria, plenius discipulorum sensibus inseruit quod et antea promisit; quia quodcumque petieritis in nomine meo, hoc faciam (cf. Jn 15). Petit Elizeus ut fieret spiritus Eliae duplex in se, et edocti a Domino discipuli promissam Spiritus gratiam accipere desiderabant: quam non uni tantum genti Judaeae, quam ipse praesens in carne docuit, sed et cunctis per orbem nationibus praedicare sufficerent.

thy waters there. And Elias passes through the divided stream on dry ground, and Eliseus also passes over, because the Savior, rising from the dead, gives His faithful also the hope of rising again. After crossing the Jordan, Elias gave Eliseus the option of asking what he wanted (cf. 4 Kgs 2:9), and the Lord, filled with the glory of the Resurrection, instilled more fully into the minds of the disciples what He had previously promised; because whatever you ask in My name, I will do it (cf. Jn 15). Eliseus asks that the spirit of Elias may become twofold in him, and the disciples, taught by the Lord, longed to receive the promised grace of the Spirit: which was sufficient to preach not only to one nation of Judea, whom He Himself taught in the flesh, but also to all the nations throughout the world.

Feria Tertia: 4 Kgs 3:6–18

S. Ephraem Syrus, *In Secundum Librum Regnorum qui et Quartus Regum Explanatio* (*Sancti Patris nostri Ephraem Syri opera omnia,* Tomus Primus, Romae 1737, p. 524)

"Et ait: haec dicit Dominus: Fiet hic torrens fossa et fossa. Factum est igitur mane et repleta est terra aquis" (4 Kgs 3:16, 20). Fiet, in-

"Thus saith the Lord: Make the channel of this torrent full of ditches. And it came to pass in the morning, and the country was filled

quit torrens, torrentis videlicet alveus foveae et foveae. Continuo fatiscens humus multiplices passim patefecit sinus ad concipiendas aquas postero mane affluxuras. Allegoria. Canit psaltes et alveus torrentis oppletur aquis, hoc nimirum symbolo praesignanda fuit vox Christi in Cruce quasi in cithara psallentis. Clamavit enim Dominus semel et iterum in Cruce, et clamans voce magna emisit spiritum et continuo centurio gentilis glorificavit Deum. Scilicet postquam Christus in Cruce nostrae salutis canticum novum absolvit, confestim ad gentilem populum ad instar vallis depressum et humilem fluxerunt fontes et torrentes inundaverunt aquarum viventium, id enim ipse ante suam passionem praedixerat. "Qui credit in me, sicut dicit Scriptura, flumina de ventre ejus fluent aquarum viventium" (Jn 7:38), ut juxta prophetae vaticinium, idem qui psallebat in cithara, psalleret in nationibus nomini Domini.

with water" (4 Kgs 3:16, 20). It will become, he says, a torrent, that is to say, a channel of the torrent and pits. Continually the sinking of the ground opened up numerous gulfs here and there to receive the inflowing waters of the following morning. Allegory. He plays the psaltery, and the cistern of the torrent is filled with water. For the Lord cried once and again on the Cross and crying with a loud voice He gave up His spirit, and immediately a hundred Gentiles glorified God. Of course, after Christ completed a new song on the Cross of our salvation, springs and torrents of living waters flowed forth to the Gentile people, low and low like a valley, for this He had foretold before His Passion. "Whoever believes in Me, as the Scripture has said, out of his heart will flow rivers of living water" (Jn 7:38), so that according to the prediction of the prophet, the same one who psalmed on the harp, may psalm in the nations to the name of the Lord.

Feria Quarta: 4 Kgs 4:1–17
S. Caesarius Arelatensis, *Sermones* (serm. 128, cap. 1)

Vidua ergo ista, id est, ecclesia debitum grave contraxerat, non solidorum, sed peccatorum; debitum habebat, et creditorem crudelissimum sustinebat, quia se diabolo multis peccatis obnoxiam fecerat. Sic enim et propheta praedixit: "In peccatis vestris venditi estis, et in sceleribus vestris dimisi matrem vestram" (Is 50:1). Vidua ergo illa pro tam gravi debito captiva quodammodo tenebatur (cf. 4 Kgs 4:1). Captiva erat, quia redemptor nondum advenerat; sed postea quam viduam istam verus redemptor Christus dominus visitavit, ab omnibus debitis liberam fecit. Unde enim vidua illa liberata sit, videamus: unde, nisi de augmento olei? In oleo misericordia intellegitur. Ergo viduae illi ideo debitum creverat, quia oleum misericordiae peccando perdiderat. Considerate, fratres: defecit oleum, et crevit debitum; crevit oleum, et periit debitum. Creverat cupiditas, et perierat caritas; redit caritas, et perit iniquitas. Veniente ergo vero Eliseo Christo Domino, vidua, hoc est, ecclesia per aug-

This widow, that is, the Church, had contracted a heavy debt, not of money, but of sins. She had a debt, and endured a most cruel creditor, because she had exposed himself to the devil with many sins. For thus also the prophet foretold: "For your iniquities you were sold, and for your transgressions your mother was sent away" (Is 50:1). That widow, therefore, was a sense, held captive for such a heavy debt (cf. 4 Kgs 4:1). She was a captive because the Redeemer had not yet come; but after the true Redeemer, Christ the Lord, visited this widow, He freed her from all debts. Let us see whence this widow was freed; whence, except through the increase of oil? Oil is understood as mercy. Therefore, the widow's debt increased because she had lost the oil of mercy by sinning. Consider, brothers: the oil failed and the debt increased; oil increased, and debt disappeared. Greed increased, and charity perished; charity returns, and iniquity perishes. Therefore, with the coming of the true Eliseus, Christ the Lord, the widow, that is,

mentum olei, id est, donum gratiae et misericordiae, vel caritatis pinguedine de peccatorum debito liberatur.

the Church, is freed from the debt of sins by the increase of oil, that is, by the gift of grace and mercy, or by the abundance of charity.

Feria Quinta: 4 Kgs 6:24–33; 7:1
S. Ephraem Syrus, *In Secundum Librum Regnorum qui et Quartus Regum Explanatio* (Sancti Patris nostri Ephraem Syri opera omnia, Tomus Primus, Romae 1737, pp. 535–536)

Atrox et dira fames, quae diu Samaritanos torsit (cf. 4 Kgs 6:25), et insolitos cibos admittere coegit, ostendit panis caelestis inopiam, qua omnes per idem tempus gentes laborabant. Samaria ergo totius generis humani personam, statumque repraesentabat. Porro Elisaei opera calamitas illa demum depulsa est, quia "infirmi accincti sunt robore et, repleti prius, pro panibus se locaverunt" (1 Kgs 2:5), id est gentibus Apostolorum praedicatione salutis scientia communicata est, et exundavit sicut Isaias praedixerat, quasi aquae mare operientes (cf. Is 11:9). Sic enim ratum est ante Deum, "ut famelicus messem stulti comederet et absumerent sitientes divitias ejus" (Jb 5:5). Nam sicut Samaritani convectam in Syrorum castra annonam sibi diripuerunt,

A terrible and terrible famine, which for a long time afflicted the Samaritans (cf. 4 Kgs 6:25), and forced them to accept unusual foods, shows the scarcity of heavenly bread, by which all the nations were suffering at the same time. Samaria therefore represented the person and state of the whole human race. Moreover, the work of Eliseus put an end to that calamity, "because the feeble bind on strength, and those who were hungry have ceased to hunger" (1 Kgs 2:5), that is, the knowledge of salvation was communicated to the nations by the preaching of the apostles, and it overflowed, as Isaias had predicted, like water covering the sea (cf. Is 11:9). For it is right before God that "the hungry eat his harvest, and he takes it even out of thorns, and the thirsty pant

et in subsidium urbis suae secum asportarunt, sic Ecclesia gentium divinos codices in Hebraeorum synagoga repertos sustulit, et ad suae sobolis utilitatem et eruditionem usurpavit.

after his wealth" (Jb 5:5). For just as the Samaritans, brought into the camp of the Syrians, plundered the food for themselves, and carried it away with them for the support of their city, so the Church of the Gentiles took up the divine manuscripts found in the synagogue of the Hebrews, and used them for the benefit and learning of their own children.

Feria Sexta: 4 Kgs 8:1–10
S. Ephraem Syrus, *In Secundum Librum Regnorum qui et Quartus Regum Explanatio* (Sancti Patris nostri Ephraem Syri opera omnia, Tomus Primus, Romae 1737, pp. 545–546)

"Vocavitque rex Joas Joiadam pontificem et sacerdotes, dicens eis: Quare sartatecta non instauratis templi?" (4 Kgs 12:7). Causa, cur rex Joas er Joadas pontifex ad reparandam Dei domum animum appellerent, indicat liber secundus Annalium: "Athalia enim impiissima, et filii ejus, destruxerunt domum Dei, et de universisquae sanctificata fuerant in templo Domini, ornaverunt fanum Baalim" (2 Par 24:7). Cum ergo ejus arbitratu omnia administrarentur, ipsumque regem Ochoziam sibi obsequentem haberet, nihil ab ea

"And king Joas called Joiada the high priest and the priests, saying to them: Why do you not repair the temple?" (4 Kgs 12:7). The second book indicates the reason why King Joas and the priest Joadas urged the repair of God's house. "That wicked woman Athalia and her children have destroyed the house of God, and adorned the temple of Baal with all the things that had been dedicated in the Temple of the Lord" (2 Par 24:7). Because everything was administered by her will, and she had King Ochozias obedient to her, she left nothing undone

praetermissum fuit, quo Judaeos a Divino cultu abstractos ad patriam Sidoniorum religionem traduceret. Quamobrem introducto peregrino cultu veri Dei templum negligitur, multis locis fatiscere coeperat, et facto vitio ruinam minari. Ergo, ut huic malo occurreret rex, auctore pontifice, magnam pecuniam vim a populo libenter subministratam collegit, et sacerdotibus ad destinatum opus delectis tradidit. Sed cum postea animadverteret, ab illis commissum negotium nec cum fide, nec diligentia, quam speraverat tractari, eam curam viris exploratae probitatis detulit, quam et strenue et diligenter gesserunt. Allegoria. Agnosce hic typum Sanctorum, qui scientiae donum a Deo consecuti, ad ejusdem reparandam domum vanis religionibus et variis criminibus labefactam, contulerunt.

by which she might lead the Jews from the worship of the True God to the religion of the Sidonians. Wherefore, with the introduction of alien worship, the Temple of the true God was neglected, and in many places it began to crack, threatening ruin. Therefore, in order to address this evil, the king, under the inspiration of the high priest, collected a large sum of money, willingly supplied by the people, and gave it to the priests chosen for the work intended. But when he afterwards noticed that the task entrusted to them had not been handled with the faith or diligence which he had hoped for, he entrusted this work to men of tested probity, which they carried out with vigor and diligence. Allegory. Recognize here the type of saints who, having received the gift of the knowledge from God, contributed to the reparation of His house undermined by vain religions and by various crimes.

Sabbato: 4 Kgs 9:1–13
S. Rabanus Maurus, *Commentaria in libros Regum* (in librum 4, ad cap. 9)

"Eliseus autem prophetes vocavit unum de filiis prophetarum, et ait illi: Accinge lumbos tuos, et tolle lenticulam olei hanc in manu tu, et vade in Ramothgalaat. Cumque veneris illuc, videbis Jehu filium Josaphat, filii Namsi, et ingressus suscitabis eum de medio fratrum suorum, et introduces in interius cubiculum, tenensque lenticulam olei, fundes super caput, et dices: Haec dicit Dominus: Unxi te regem super Israel" (4 Kgs 9:1–3). Dehinc refertur in historia hac Regum qualiter Jehu Dominus ordinaverit ad exstirpandam domum Achab et sacerdotes Baal interficiendos. Qui et percussit Joram regem Israel, et Ochoziam regem Juda, et Jezabel impiissimam reginam de palatio in Jezrahel praecipitare fecit. Jehu enim typice potest designare gentium principatum, quem Dominus ac Redemptor noster destinavit, ut in sacrilega civitate quae prophetas et ipsum Deum prophetarum occidit, et apostolos ejus persecuta est, judicia exerceret, et aemulati-

"Eliseus the prophet called one of the sons of the prophets and said to him: Gird up thy loins, and take this little bottle of oil in thy hand, and go to Ramoth Galaad. And when thou comest there, thou wilt see Jehu, the son of Josaphat, the son of Namsi, and thou wilt go in and raise him up from among his brothers, and bring him into the inner room, and take a little bottle of oil, pour it on his head, and say: This is what the Lord says: I have anointed thee king over Israel" (4 Kgs 9:1–3). Then, it is related in this history of kings how the Lord ordered Jehu to exterminate the house of Achab and kill the priests of Baal. And he slew Joram, king of Israel, and Ochozias, king of Juda, and caused Jezabel, the most impious queen, to be thrown from the palace into Jezrahel. For Jehu can symbolically designate the dominion of the nations, which Our Lord and Redeemer ordained to execute judgment upon the sacrilegious city that killed the prophets and the very God of the prophets, and persecuted His apostles, and

one justa perimeret, atque sacerdotium vanum, quod post Christi adventum inaniter habuerat, destrueret, templumque subverteret, nec non et impiam Synagogam, quae sanguinem sanctorum semper sitiebat, de regni culmine praecipitaret, ac rectores ipsius interficeret.

Who will exercise judgement and destroy it with a just zeal, as well as abolish the empty priesthood, which after the coming of Christ became vain, and overturn the Temple, and cast down the impious synagogue, which always thirsted for the blood of the saints, from the summit of its kingdom, and kill its rulers.

INFRA HEBDOMADAM X POST PENTECOSTEN

Feria Secunda: 4 Kgs 11:1–7, 9–12

S. Rabanus Maurus, *Commentaria in libros Regum* (in librum 4, ad cap. 10)

"Sed Josaba, filia regis Joram, soror Ochoziae, Joas filium Ochaziae tollens, furata est de medio filiorum regis, qui interficiebantur, et nutricem ejus de triclinio, et abscondit eum a facie Athaliae, ut non interficeretur. Eratque cum ea in domo Domini clam sex annis," (4 Kgs 11:1–3), quia Josaba uxor erat Joadae pontificis. Athalia igitur haec, quae semen David exstinguere moliebatur, et regiam stirpem delere, bene impietatem exprimit Synagogae, quae per nequitiam mentis seminis David, hoc est, Christi insidiatrix erat, et odium contra eum semper in corde gerebat. Quae aliquando

"But Josaba, the daughter of King Joram, the sister of Ochozias, taking Joas the son of Ochazias, stole him away from the midst of the king's sons who were being slain, and his nurse from the dining room, and hid him from the face of Athalia, that he might not be slain. And he was with her hidden in the house of the Lord for six years" (4 Kgs 11:1–3), because Josaba was the wife of Joiada the pontiff. This Athalia, therefore, who sought to extinguish the seed of David and to destroy the royal line, well expresses the impiety of the synagogue, which, through the wickedness of its mind was the plotter against the seed of

regnare videbatur cum legis caeremonias temporaliter observabat. Interpretatur autem Athalia temporalis Domini. Sed Josabae strenuitas interpretatur saturitas Domini, id est, Ecclesiae, in qua verae sunt deliciae. Servatur Joas, qui interpretatur memoria Domini, Christus videlicet, in quo memoria est nominis Domini, ne per crudelitatem saevientis hostis interimatur in cordibus electorum: magisque nutritur in domo Joadae pontificis, qui dilectus Domini sonat, de quo Patris vox ait: "Hic est filius meus dilectus, in quo mihi bene complacui" (Mt 3:17). Cujus domus est sancta Ecclesia, ubi in fide electorum manens quotidie facit "augmentum corporis" sui (Eph. 4:16), donec tempore judicii sceptrum regni et potentiam adversus eos extollat qui eum deprimere cogitabant, et interfectricem sanctorum aeternis deputaverit poenis (cf. Apoc 19).

David, that is, against Christ, and always bore hatred against Him in her heart. The synagogue once seemed to reign when it temporarily observed the ceremonies of the Law. Now, Athalia is interpreted as the temporal dominion of the Lord. But Josaba's vigor is interpreted as the fullness of the Lord, that is, of the Church, in which there are true delights. Joas was preserved, whose name means the memory of the Lord, that is, of Christ, in Whom is the memory of the name of the Lord, lest through the cruelty of the raging enemy the Lord be destroyed in the hearts of the elect. Rather, He is nourished in the house of Joada the pontiff, whose names means the beloved of the Lord, of Whom the voice of the Father said, "This is My beloved Son, in Whom I am well pleased" (Mt 3:17). His house is the holy Church, where, remaining in the faith of the elect, He daily causes "the increase of His body" (Eph 4:16), until at the time of judgment, He lifts up the scepter of His Kingdom and power against those who thought to oppress Him, and consigns the murderer of the saints to eternal punishments (cf. Apoc 19).

Feria Tertia: 4 Kgs 12:1–8
S. Rabanus Maurus, Commentaria in libros Regum (in librum 4, ad cap. 12)

"Dixitque Joas ad sacerdotes: Omnem pecuniam sanctorum, quae allata fuerit in templum Domini a praetereuntibus, quae offertur pro pretio animae, et quam sponte et arbitrio cordis sui inferunt in templum Domini, accipiant illam sacerdotes juxta ordinem suum, et instaurent sartatecta domus, si quid necessarium viderint instauratione" (4 Kgs 12:4–5). Mandat rex noster de doctoribus suis, ut accipiant omnem pecuniam, quae a praetereuntibus offertur in templum Domini pro pretio animae et voto cordis sui, cum quidquid a praetereuntibus justis, scientiae spiritalis vel bonorum exemplorum in thesaurum Domini collatum est, per sacerdotum, hoc est, praedicatorum officia ad instaurationem templi spiritalis conferatur, quatenus ibi quodcumque scissum per errorem vel per vitia invenerint restaurent, ne forte per negligentiam magistrorum depereat multitudo auditorum. Quod autem sequitur: "Igitur usque ad vicesimum tertium annum

"And Joas said to the priests: All the money of the saints which is brought into the temple of the Lord by those who pass by, which is offered for the price of a soul, and which they bring into the temple of the Lord voluntarily and with the will of their heart, let the priests receive it according to their order, let them repair the house wherever any need of repairs is discovered" (4 Kgs 12:4–5). Our king orders His teachers to accept all the money that is offered by passers-by into the Lord's Temple for the price of his soul and the desire of his heart, since whatever has been contributed to the treasury of the Lord by righteous passers-by, of spiritual knowledge or good examples, through the priests, that is, the offices of the preachers, should be assigned to the restoration of the spiritual temple, in so far as they restore whatever there is torn apart by error or by defects, lest perhaps through the negligence of the teachers the multitude of hearers should be lost. And what follows:

regis Joas non instauraverunt sacerdotes sartatecta templi" (4 Kgs 12:6), significat, quod ante adventum Salvatoris licet doctrina legis in gente Judaica fuerit, tamen per doctorum negligentiam in multis corrumpebatur, donec veniret ipse qui legem dedit, et per sanctae Trinitatis fidem Decalogum legis in Moysi et prophetarum scriptis spiritaliter observandum doceret.

"Therefore, until the twenty-third year of King Joas, the priests did not make the repairs of the temple" (4 Kgs 12:6), signifies that before the coming of the Savior, although the teaching of the Law existed in the Jewish nation, it was corrupted in many by the negligence of the teachers, until He Who gave the Law would come and through the faith of the Holy Trinity teach the spiritual observance of the Decalogue of the Law in the writings of Moses and the prophets.

Feria Quarta: 4 Kgs 13:14–21, 24–25
S. Joannes Chrysostomus, *In Sanctum Martyrem Ignatium laudatio* (cap. 5)

Sanctorum enim non modo corpora, sed ipsi loculi et monumenta spirituali gratia conferta sunt. Nam si in Elisaeo id contigit, ut defunctus sepulcrum ejus attingens mortis vincula dissolverit (cf. 4 Kgs 13:21), et ad vitam rursus redierit, multo magis hoc tempore, quo gratia uberior, Spiritus major est vis. Ut si cum fide aliquis arcam attingat, magnam inde virtutem hauriat. Ideo reliquias Sanctorum nobis concessit Deus, volens nos ad eumdem zelum

For not only the bodies of the saints, but the coffins and tombs themselves are filled with spiritual grace. For if in the case of Eliseus it happened that a dead man, touching his tomb, dissolved the bonds of death (cf. 4 Kgs 13:21), and returned to life, much more so at this time, when grace is more abundant and the Spirit's power is greater. So that if someone touches the ark with faith, he will draw great strength from it. For this reason, God granted us the relics of the

per illos adducere, et nobis quasi portum praebere ad formum solatium malorum quae nos assidue corripiunt. Qui enim huc accedit et Sanctum videt, bona haec efficiet stabiliora, et memoria recte factorum ejus animum suum reddet moderatiorem, nec conscientiam suam bonis operibus efferri etque intumescere patietur. Utilis igitur cunctis hic thesaurus est et refugium opportunum, tam iis qui lapsi sunt, ut a tentationibus liberentur, quam iis qui prospere ac feliciter degunt, et diu fruantur bonis; illis qui morbis laborant, ut bonam valetudinem consequantur, illis qui commoda gaudent valetudine, ne in morbum aliquem incurrant. Omni gaudio atque vopultati sacrum hunc locum anteponamus, ut laetitiae et lucri consortes, illic Sanctorum contubernales socii esse valeamus.

saints, wishing to bring us to the same zeal through them, and to provide us with a sort of a harbor of consolation for the evils which constantly afflict us. For whoever approaches and sees the saint, will make these good things more stable, and the memory of his right deeds will make his soul more temperate, and will not allow his conscience to be carried away and puffed up by good works. Therefore, this treasure is useful to all, and a suitable refuge, both for those who have fallen, that they may be freed from temptations, and for those who live prosperously and happily, that they may long enjoy good things; for those who suffer from illness, that they may regain good health, for those who enjoy the comforts of health, that they may not fall into any disease. Let us therefore place this holy place above all joy and desire, that as partakers of joy and gain, we may be able to be companions and fellow citizens of the saints there.

Feria Quinta: 4 Kgs 17:6–9, 13–15, 18–21
S. Joannes Chrysostomus, *Commentarius in sanctum Joannem Apostolum et Evangelistam* (hom. 31, 2)

Non abs re autem fuerit, unde originem habuerint Samaritani narrare. Nam tota illa regio Samaria vocatur. Unde ergo sic appellati sunt? Somor mons ille nominabatur a quodam qui illum possederat (cf. 3 Kgs 16:24), ut dicit Isaias, Et caput Somoron Ephraim (cf. Is 7:9); sed qui illum incolebant non Samaritani, sed Israeliti vocabantur. In decursu vero temporis Deum offenderunt, et Phacee regnante, ascendens Theglath Phalasar, multas cepit urbes, Elam adortus occidit, et Oseae regnum tradidit (cf. 4 Kgs 15:29). Hunc agressus Salmanasar alias cepit urbes et tributarias fecit (cf. 4 Kgs 17:3). Verum Osee primo quidem cessit, deinde vero rebellavit, et ad Aethiopum auxilium confugit (cf. 4 Kgs 17:4). Re cognita, Assyrius exercitum admovit, et capta civitate, gentem illam non ibi amplius habitare permisit, ne iterum deficerent; sed his Babylonem et in Mediam translatis (cf. 4 Kgs 17:5–6), gentes alias variis ex locis eductas in

And it may be worthwhile to the origin of the the Samaritans, since all this country is called Samaria. Whence then did they receive their name? The mountain was called Somor from its owner (cf. 3 Kgs 16:24), as also Isaias says, And the head of Somoron is Ephraim (cf. Is 7:9); but the inhabitants were termed not Samaritans but Israelites. But as time went on, they offended God, and in the reign of Phacee, when Teglathphalasar ascended, he took many cities, attacked Elam, and having slain him, gave the kingdom to Osee (cf. 4 Kgs 15:29). Against him Salmanasar came and took other cities and made them tributaries (cf. 4 Kgs 17:3). At first Osee submitted, but later he rebelled and sought the help of the Ethiopians (cf. 4 Kgs 17:4). When this was known, the Assyrian king gathered an army, and after capturing the city, he did not permit that people to dwell there any longer, lest they fall away again. But he carried them to Babylon and Media (cf. 4 Kgs 17:5–6),

Samariam habitatum misit, ut firmum suum his in locis imperium postea esset, regione fidis incolis tradita. His ita gestis, Deus ut potentiam suam ostenderet, quodque non ob imbecillitatem Judaeos tradidisset, sed propter incolarum peccata, leones in barbaros immisit, qui totam gentem devastabant (cf. 4 Kgs 17:24–25). Haec regi nuntiantur; ille mittit sacerdotem quemdam, qui Dei leges ipsis traderet (cf. 4 Kgs 17:27). Attamen ne sic quidem omnino ab impietate destiterunt sed partim tantum.

and sent other nations from various places to inhabit Samaria, in order to ensure his power over those places, the region being handed over to its new inhabitants. After this, God, desiring to show that He had not given up the Jews through weakness, but because of the sins of those who were given up, sent lions against the foreigners, who ravaged all their nation (cf. 4 Kgs 17:24–25). These things were reported to the king, and he sent a priest to deliver to them the laws of God (cf. 4 Kgs 17:27). Still not even so did they desist wholly from their impiety, but only by halves.

Feria Sexta: 4 Kgs 17:21–27
S. Augustinus, *De civitate Dei* (lib. 17, cap. 23)

In regno Juda pertinente ad Jerusalem etiam regum succedentium temporibus non defuerunt prophetae; sicut Deo placebat eos mittere vel ad praenuntiandum, quod opus erat, vel ad corripiendam peccata praecipiendamque justitiam. Nam et illic, etsi longe minus quam in Israel, tamen exstiterunt reges, qui suis impietatibus Deum graviter offenderent et moderatis flagellis cum populo

In the kingdom of Juda pertaining to Jerusalem prophets were not lacking even in the times of succeeding kings, just as it pleased God to send them, either for the prediction of what was needful, or for correction of sin and instruction in righteousness; for there, too, although far less than in Israel, kings arose who grievously offended God by their impieties, and, along with their people, who were like them, were smit-

simili plecterentur. Piorum sane regum merita ibi non parva laudantur; in Israel autem reges alios magis, alios minus, omnes tamen reprobos legimus. Prius illa pars, quae vocabatur Israel in tribubus decem; postea vero etiam Judas, eversa Jerusalem et templo illo nobilissimo; in quibus terris per annos septuaginta captivum egit otium. Post quos inde dimissa templum, quod eversum fuerat, instauravit; et quamvis plurimi ejus in alienigenarum degerent terris, non habuit tamen deinceps duas regni partes et duos diversos in singulis partibus reges; sed in Jerusalem princeps eorum erat unus, atque ad Dei templum, quod ibi erat, omnes undique, ubicumque essent et undecumque possent, per certa tempora veniebant.

ten with moderate scourges. The no small merits of the pious kings there are praised indeed. But we read that in Israel the kings were, some more, others less, yet all wicked. First, that part of the thirteen tribes called Israel, but afterwards Juda also, when Jerusalem and that most noble Temple was cast down—in which lands it rested seventy years in captivity. Being after that time sent forth thence, they rebuilt the overthrown Temple. And although very many stayed in the lands of the strangers, yet the kingdom no longer had two separate parts, with different kings over each, but in Jerusalem there was one prince over them; and at certain times, from every direction wherever they were, and from whatever place they could, they all came to the Temple of God which was there.

Sabbato: 4 Kgs 18:1–12
S. Augustinus, *Epistola 185 de correctione Donatistarum* (cap. 19)

"Et nunc reges intellegite; erudimini qui judicatis terram. Servite Domino in timore, et exsultate ei cum tremore" (Ps 2:10–11). Quomodo ergo reges Domino serviunt in timore, nisi ea quae contra iussa

"Be wise now, therefore, O you kings; be instructed, you judges of the earth. Serve the Lord with fear and rejoice with trembling" (Ps 2:10–11). How then are kings to serve the Lord with fear, except

Domini fiunt, religiosa severitate prohibendo atque plectendo? Aliter enim servit, quia homo est; aliter, quia etiam rex est: quia homo est enim ei servit vivendo fideliter; quia vero etiam rex est, servit leges justa praecipientes et contraria prohibentes convenienti vigore sanciendo. Sicut servivit Ezechias, lucos et templa idolorum, et illa excelsa quae contra praecepta Dei fuerant constructa destruendo (cf. 4 Kgs 18:4): sicut servivit Josias, talia et ipse faciendo (cf. 4 Kgs 23:4–5): sicut servivit rex Ninivitarum, universam civitatem ad placandum Dominum compellendo (cf. Jon 3:6–9): sicut servivit Darius, idolum frangendum in potestatem Danieli dando, et inimicos ejus leonibus ingerendo (cf. Dn 14:21, 41): sicut servivit Nabuchodonosor, de quo jam diximus, omnes in regno suo positos a blasphemando Deo lege terribili prohibendo (cf. Dn 3:96). In hoc ergo serviunt Domino reges, in quantum sunt reges, cum ea faciunt ad serviendum illi, quae non possunt facere nisi reges.

by preventing and chastising with religious severity all those acts which are done in opposition to the commandments of the Lord? For a man serves God in one way in that he is man, in another way in that he is also king. In that he is man, he serves Him by living faithfully; but in that he is also king, he serves Him by enforcing with suitable rigor such laws as ordain what is righteous and punish what is the reverse. Even as Ezechias served Him, by destroying the groves and the temples of the idols, and the high places which had been built in violation of the commandments of God (cf. 4 Kgs 18:4); or even as Josias served Him, by doing the same things in his turn; (cf. 4 Kgs 23:4–5); or as the king of the Ninevites served Him, by compelling all the men of his city to make satisfaction to the Lord (cf. Jon 3:6–9); or as Darius served Him, by giving the idol into the power of Daniel to be broken, and by casting his enemies into the den of lions (cf. Dn 14:21, 41); or as Nabuchodonosor served Him, of whom I have spoken before, by issuing a terrible law to prevent any of his subjects from

blaspheming God (cf. Dn 3:96). In this way, therefore, kings can serve the Lord, even in so far as they are kings, when they do in His service what they could not do were they not kings.

INFRA HEBDOMADAM XI POST PENTECOSTEN
Feria Quinta: Secunda: 4 Kgs 22:1–13
S. Augustinus, *Contra duas Epistolas Pelagianorum* (lib. 3, cap. 10)

Exceptis quippe librorum veterum sacramentis, quae sola significando ratione praecepta sunt—quamquam et in eis, quoniam spiritaliter intellegenda sunt, recte lex dicitur spiritalis—cetera certe, quae ad pietatem bonosque mores pertinentia non ad aliquam significationem ulla interpretatione referenda, sed prorsus ut sunt dicta facienda sunt, profecto illam Dei legem non solum illi tunc populo, verum etiam nunc nobis ad instituendam recte vitam necessariam nemo dubitaverit. Si enim Christus nobis abstulit illud gravissimum multarum observationum iugum, ne carnaliter circumcidamur, ne pecorum victimas immolemus, ne sabbato septeno dierum volumine redeunte ab operibus etiam necessariis quies-

With the exception of the sacraments of the old books, which were only enjoined for the sake of their significance (although in them also, since they are to be spiritually understood, the Law is rightly called spiritual), the other matters certainly which pertain to piety and to good living must not be referred by any interpretation to some significancy, but are to be done absolutely as they are spoken. Assuredly no one will doubt that that Law of God was necessary not alone for that people at that time, but also is now necessary for us for the right ordering of our life. For if Christ took away from us that very heavy yoke of many observances, so that we are not circumcised according to the flesh, we do not immolate victims of the cattle, we do not rest even from necessary

camus et cetera hujusmodi, sed ea spiritaliter intellecta teneamus remotisque umbris significantibus in rerum ipsarum quae significantur luce vigilemus, numquid propterea dicturi sumus non ad nos pertinere quod scriptum est, ut alienum quodcumque perditum quis invenerit, reddat ei qui perdidit et alia multa similia, quibus pie recteque vivere discitur, maximeque ipsum Decalogum, qui duabus illis lapideis tabulis continetur, excepta sabbati observatione carnali, quae spiritalem sanctificationem quietemque significat? Quis est tam impius, qui dicat ideo se ista legis non custodire praecepta, quia est ipse Christianus nec sub lege, sed sub gratia constitutus.

works on the Sabbath, retaining the seventh in the revolution of the days, and other things of this kind; but keep them as spiritually understood, and, the symbolizing shadows being removed, are watchful in the light of those things which are signified by them; shall we therefore say, that when it is written that whoever finds another man's property of any kind that has been lost, should return it to him who has lost it, it does not pertain to us? And many other like things whereby people learn to live piously and uprightly? And especially the Decalogue itself, which is contained in those two tables of stone, apart from the carnal observance of the Sabbath, which signifies spiritual sanctification and rest? Who is so impious as to say that he does not keep those precepts of the Law because he is a Christian, and is established not under the Law, but under grace?

Feria Tertia: 4 Kgs 23:2–8
S. Augustinus, *Contra Faustum Manichaeum* (lib. 22, cap. 6)

De praeceptis et sacramentis Veteris Testamenti saepe ac multa jam diximus, ut intellegeretur aliud ibi fuisse quod per gratiam

We have repeatedly shown at great length, that the precepts and symbols of the Old Testament contained both what was to be fulfilled

Novi Testamenti faciendo donaretur implendum, aliud quod per veritatem patefactam removendo demonstraretur impletum: cum Dei et proximi dilectione susciperetur Legis perficienda praeceptio, circumcisionis autem atque aliorum illius temporis sacramentorum cessatione ostenderetur Legis persoluta promissio. Praeceptum quippe reos faciebat ad desiderandam salutem, promissum autem figuras celebrabat ad exspectandum Salvatorem: ut per adventum Novi Testamenti illos liberaret gratia donata, illas auferret veritas reddita. Ipsa enim Lex quae per Moysen data est, gratia et veritas per Jesum Christum facta est (cf. Jn 1:17): gratia scilicet, ut data indulgentia peccatorum, quod praeceptum erat ex Dei dono custodiretur, veritas autem, ut ablata observatione umbrarum, quod promissum erat ex Dei fide praesentaretur.

in obedience through the grace bestowed in the New Testament, and what was to be set aside as a proof of its having been fulfilled in the truth now made manifest. For in the love of God and of our neighbor is secured the accomplishment of the precepts of the Law, while the accomplishment of its promises is shown in the abolition of circumcision, and of other typical observances formerly practiced. By the precept men were led, through a sense of guilt to desire salvation; by the promise they were led to find in the typical observances the assurance that the Savior would come. The salvation desired was to be obtained through the grace bestowed on the appearance of the New Testament; and the fulfillment of the expectation rendered the types no longer necessary. The same Law that was given by Moses became grace and truth in Jesus Christ. By the grace in the pardon of sin, the precept is kept in force in the case of those supported by divine help. By the truth the symbolic rites are set aside, that the promise might, in those who trust in the divine faithfulness, be brought to pass.

Feria Quarta: 4 Kgs 23:24–34
S. Hieronymus, *Epistulae* (*Ad Castrutium*, ep. 68, cap. 1)

Quid inter reges Josia sanctius? Aegyptio mucrone interfectus est (cf. 4 Kgs 23:29). Quid Petro, quid Paulo sublimius? Neronianum gladium cruentarunt. Et (ut de hominibus taceam) Dei Filius sustinuit ignominiam crucis: et tu putas beatos, qui felicitate istius saeculi et deliciis perfruuntur? Magna ira est, quando peccantibus non irascitur Deus. Unde et in Ezechiele ad Jerusalem, "Jam," inquit, "non irascar tibi, zelus meus recessit a te" (Ez 16:42). "Quem enim diligit Dominus, corripit" (Prv 3:12); et "castigat omnem filium quem recipit" (Heb 12:6). Non erudit pater, nisi quem amat. Non corripit magister discipulum, nisi eum quem ardentioris cernit ingenii. Medicus si cessaverit curare, desperat. Quod si responderis: quo modo Lazarus recepit mala in vita sua (cf. Lk 16:25), libenter nunc tormenta patiar, ut futura mihi gloria reservetur; "non enim vindicabit Dominus bis in idipsum" (Na 1:9). Job vir sanctus et immaculatus, et justus in genera-

Were any of the kings holier than Josias? Yet he was slain by the sword of the Egyptians (cf. 4 Kgs 23:29). Were there ever loftier saints than Peter and Paul? Yet their blood stained the blade of Nero. And to say no more of men, did not the Son of God endure the shame of the Cross? And yet you fancy those blessed who enjoy in this world happiness and pleasure? God's hottest anger against sinners is when He shows no anger. Wherefore in Ezechiel He says to Jerusalem: "My jealousy will depart from you, and I will be quiet and will be no more angry" (Ez 16:42). "For whom the Lord loves He chastens" (Prv 3:12) and "scourges every son whom He receives" (Heb 12:6). The father does not instruct his son unless he loves him. The master does not correct his disciple unless he sees in him signs of promise. When once the doctor gives over caring for the patient, it is a sign that he despairs. You should answer thus: as Lazarus in his lifetime (cf. Lk 16:25) received evil things so will I now gladly suffer torments that

tioue sua cur tanta perpessus sit ipsius volumine continetur.

future glory may be laid up for me. "For affliction shall not rise up the second time" (Na 1:9). If Job, a man holy and spotless and righteous in his generation, suffered terrible afflictions, his own book explains the reason why.

Feria Quinta: 4 Kgs 23:36–37; 24:1–7
S. Cyprianus, *De oratione Dominica* (cap. 25–26)

In tentationibus nostris nihil malo liceat, nisi potestas inde tribuatur. Probat Scriptura divina quae dicit: Venit Nabuchodonosor rex Babyloniae in Hierusalem, et expugnabat eam, et dedit eam Dominus in manu ejus (4 Kgs 24:11). Datur autem potestas adversus nos malo secundum nostra peccata, sicut scriptum est: Quis dedit in direptionem Jacob et Israel eis qui praedantur illum? nonne Deus cui peccaverunt? et nolebant in viis ejus ambulare neque audire legem ejus, et superduxit super eos iram animationis suae (cf. Is 42:25). Et iterum, Salomone peccante et a praeceptis atque a viis Domini recedente, positum est: "Et excitavit Dominus Satanam ipsi Salomoni" (3 Kgs 11:14). Potestas vero dupliciter adversus nos datur,

In our temptations nothing is permitted to evil unless power is given from Him. This is proved by divine Scripture, which says, Nabuchodonosor king of Babylon came to Jerusalem, and besieged it; and the Lord delivered it into his hand (cf. 4 Kgs 24:11). But power is given to evil against us according to our sins, as it is written, Who gave Jacob for a spoil, and Israel to those who make a prey of Him? Did not the Lord, against whom they sinned, and would not walk in His ways, nor hear His law? And He has brought upon them the anger of His wrath (cf. Is 42:25). And again, when Solomon sinned, and departed from the Lord's commandments and ways, it is recorded, "And the Lord stirred up Satan against Solomon himself" (3 Kgs 11:14). Now power is given against us in

vel ad poenam cum delinquimus, vel ad gloriam cum probamur; sicuti de Job factum videmus, manifestante Deo et dicente: "Ecce omnia quaecumque habet in manus tuas do; sed ipsum cave ne tangas" (Jb 1:12).

two modes: either for punishment when we sin, or for glory when we are proved, as we see was done with respect to Job; as God Himself sets forth, saying, "Behold, all that he has I give unto your hands; but be careful not to touch himself" (Jb 1:12).

Feria Sexta: 4 Kgs 24:8–17
S. Joannes Cassianus, *Collationes* (coll. 5, cap. 12)

Hujus autem rei figura, qua superveniente cenodoxia vitium fornicationis excludi, pulchre satis in Regum libro ac signanter exprimitur, ubi populum Israelem a Nechao rege Aegypti captivatum ascendens Nabuchodonosor rex Assyriorum de finibus Aegypti ad suam transtulit regionem, scilicet non ut eos libertati pristinae et genitali restitueret regioni, sed ad suas abduceret terras, longius asportandos quam fuerant in terra Aegypti captivati (cf. 4 Kgs 23–24). Quae figura in hoc quoque competenter aptabitur: licet enim tolerabilius sit cenodoxiae quam fornicationis vitio deservire, difficilius tamen a cenodoxiae dominatione disceditur. Quodammodo enim longiore itineris spatio captivus abductus laboriosius

The way in which, as we said, the sin of fornication is prevented by an attack of vainglory, there is an excellent and significant figure in the book of Kings, where, when the children of Israel had been taken captive by Nechao, king of Egypt, Nabuchodonosor, king of Assyria, came up and brought them back from the borders of Egypt to their own country, not indeed meaning to restore them to their former liberty and their native land, but meaning to carry them off to his own land and to transport them to a still more distant country than the land of Egypt in which they had been prisoners (cf. 4 Kgs 23–24). And this illustration exactly applies to the case before us. For though there is less harm in yielding to the sin of vainglory than to fornication, yet it

ad genitale solum et libertatem patriam revertetur; meritoque ad eum increpatio illa prophetica dirigitur: Quare inveteratus es in terra aliena? (cf. Bar 3:11). Recte siquidem inveteratus dicitur in terra aliena quisquis a terrenis vitiis non novatur. Superbiae genera sunt duo: primum carnale, secundum spiritale, quod etiam perniciosius est. Illos namque specialius impugnat, quos in quibusdam virtutibus profecisse repererit.

is more difficult to escape from the dominion of vainglory. For somehow or other the prisoner who is carried off to a greater distance, will have more difficulty in returning to his native land and the freedom of his fathers, and the prophet's rebuke will be deservedly aimed at him: Wherefore are you grown old in a strange country? (cf. Bar 3:11). Since a man is rightly said to have grown old in a strange country, if he has not broken up the ground of his faults. Of pride there are two kinds: carnal, and spiritual, which is the worse. For it especially attacks those who are seen to have made progress in some good qualities.

Sabbato: 4 Kgs 24:18–20; 25:1–13
S. Cyrillus Hierosolymitanus, *Catecheses* (cat. 2, cap. 17–19)

Quam de Nabuchodonosore sententiam habes? Quantas ille commeruerat poenas, propter reges interemptos, ob sancta succensa; quod populum in servitutem abegisset, quod vasa sacra in idolorum. templis collocavisset? Numquid non mortes mille pati dignus erat? Nonne audisti regis oculos postquam filios caesos ille conspexerat, eundem excaecasse

What do you think of Nabuchodonosor? Have you not heard out of the Scriptures that he was bloodthirsty, fierce, lion-like in disposition? Have you not heard that he brought out the bones of the kings from their graves into the light? Have you not heard that he carried the people away captive? Have you not heard that he put out the eyes of the king, after he had already seen his children

(cf. 4 Kgs 25:7)? Postea dixit, "Ego Nabuchodonosor oculos meos in caelum levavi, et Altissimo benedixi, et viventem in saecula laudavi et glorificavi" (Dn 4:31). Quando igitur agnovit Altissimum, et grati animi testes ad Deum emisit voces, ad gestorum suprum paenitentiam venit, propriamque imbecillitatem agnovit; tunc illi Deus honorem regni restituit. Qui igitur? Nabuchodonosori, qui tanta perpetraverat, confitenti Deus veniam et regnum dedit; tibi vero paenitenti peccatorum dimissionem et caeleste regnum, si te digne gesseris, non concedet? Benignus est Dominus et ad condonandum promptus, tardus autem ad ulciscendum. Nemo igitur suam ipsius salutem desperet. Petrus apostolorum summus et princeps, coram vili ancillula ter Dominum negavit, sed paenitudine tactus flevit amare: qui fletus intimam et ex corde paeninentiam declarat: atque idcirco non solum negationis hujus veniam accepit, verum etiam apostolicam dignitatem sibi conservatam retinuit.

slain (cf. 4 Kgs 25:7)? Did he not deserve ten thousand deaths? After this, says he, "I, Nabuchodonosor, lifted up my eyes unto heaven, and I blessed the Most High, and to Him that lives forever I gave praise and glory" (Dn 4:31). When, therefore, he recognized the Most High, and sent up these words of thankfulness to God, and repented himself for what he had done, and recognized his own weakness, then God gave back to him the honor of the kingdom. What then? When Nabuchodonosor, after having done such deeds, had made confession, did God give him pardon and the kingdom, and when you repent shall He not give you the remission of sins, and the Kingdom of heaven, if you live a worthy life? The Lord is loving unto man, and swift to pardon, but slow to punish. Let no man therefore despair of his own salvation. Peter, the chiefest and foremost of the apostles, denied the Lord thrice before a little maid: but he repented himself, and wept bitterly. Now weeping shows the repentance of the heart: and therefore he not only received forgiveness for his denial, but also held his apostolic dignity unforfeited.

INFRA HEBDOMADAM I AUGUSTI
Feria Secunda: Prv 3:1–15
S. Augustinus, *De patientia* (cap. 11)

Audiant ergo sancti de Scripturis sanctis praecepta patientiae: "Fili, accedens ad servitutem Dei, sta in justitia et timore, et praepara animam tuam ad tentationem: deprime cor tuum, et sustine; ut crescat in novissimis vita tua. Omne quod tibi supervenerit accipe, et in dolore sustine, et in humilitate tua patientiam habe. Quoniam in igne probatur aurum et argentum, homines vero acceptabiles in camino humiliationis" (Ecclus 2:1–5). Et in loco alio legitur: "Fili, ne deficias in disciplina Domini, neque fatigeris cum ab illo increparis. Quem enim diligit Dominus, corripit; flagellat autem omnem filium quem recipit" (Prv 3:11–12). Quod hic positum est, filium quem recipit; hoc in supra dicto testimonio est, homines receptibiles. Hoc enim justum est, ut qui de pristina felicitate paradisi propter contumacem deliciarum appetentiam dimissi sumus, per humilem molestiarum patientiam recipiamur: fugaces mala faciendo,

Let then the saints hear from holy Scripture the precepts of patience: "My son, when you come to the service of God, stand in righteousness and fear, and prepare your soul for temptation: bring your heart low, and bear up; that in the last end your life may increase. All that shall come upon you receive you, and in pain bear up, and in your humility have patience. For in the fire gold and silver is proved, but acceptable men in the furnace of humiliation" (Ecclus 2:1–5). And in another place we read: "My son, faint not in the discipline of the Lord, neither be wearied when you are chidden of Him. For whom the Lord loves He chastens and scourges every son whom He receives" (Prv 3:11–12). What is here set down, son whom He receives, the same in the above-mentioned testimony is, acceptable men. For this is just, that we who from our first felicity of paradise for contumacious appetence of things to enjoy were dismissed, through humble patience of things that annoy may be re-

reduces mala patiendo; ibi contra justitiam facientes, hic pro justitia patientes. Patientia non venit ex liberi arbitrii viribus, sed ex divino adjutorio.

ceived back: driven away for doing evil, brought back by suffering evil: there against righteousness doing ill, here for righteousness' sake patient of ills.

Feria Tertia: Prv 5:1–13, 20–23
S. Cyrillus Hierosolymitanus, *Catecheses* (cat. 4, cap. 2)

Nam ratio divini cultus ex his duobus constat, piis dogmatibus et actionibus bonis; neque doctrina sine operibus bonis accepta Deo; neque opera recipit Deus a religiosis dogmatibus sejuncta. Quid enim prodest de Deo sentire recte, et turpiter fornicari? quae vero contra utilitas pudicum esse laudabiliter et impie blasphema profari? Pretiosa igitur possessio dogmatum notitia est: cui rei vigilanti mente opus est, quando quidem multi sunt qui per philosophiam et vanam fallaciam (cf. Col 2:8) praedas agunt. Ac gentiles quidem per suaviloquentiam in diversa trahunt: "Mel enim distillat ex labiis mulieris meretrices" (Prv 5:3). Qui vero ex circumcisione sunt, per divinas Scripturas, quas prave falsis interpretamentis torquent accedentes decipiunt (cf. Ti 1:10); a pueritia

The method of godliness consists of these two things, pious doctrines, and virtuous practice: and neither are the doctrines acceptable to God apart from good works, nor does God accept the works which are not perfected with pious doctrines. For what profit is it, to know well the doctrines concerning God, and yet to be a vile fornicator? And again, what profit is it, to be nobly temperate, and an impious blasphemer? A most precious possession therefore is the knowledge of doctrines: there is also need of a wakeful soul, since there are many that make spoil through philosophy and vain deceit (cf. Col 2:8). The Gentiles on the one hand draw men away by their smooth tongue, for "honey drops from a harlot's lips" (Prv 5:3): whereas they of the Circumcision deceive those who come to them by means of the divine Scriptures,

usque ad senectutem commentantes (cf. Is 46:3–4), et in ignoratione rerum consenescentes (cf. 2 Tm 3:7). Haeretici vero, per blandiloquentiam et dicendi suavitatem simplicium corda decipiunt (cf. Rom 16:18), Christi nomine quasi melle, venenata impiorum decretorum jacula contegentes.

which they miserably misinterpret (cf. Ti 1:10); though studying them from childhood to old age (cf. Is 46:3–4), and growing old in ignorance (cf. 2 Tm 3:7). But the children of heretics, by their good words and smooth tongue, deceive the hearts of the innocent (cf. Rom 16:18), disguising with the name of Christ as it were with honey the poisoned arrows of their impious doctrines.

Feria Quarta: Prv 8:1–17
S. Fulgentius Ruspensis, *Epistulae* (ep. 12, cap. 7)

Sapientia in Proverbiis dicit: "Quoniam veritatem meditabuntur fauces meae, abominata vero ante me labia mendacia" (Prv 8:7). Non ergo accipiunt in baptismo salutem, qui non tenent in corde atque ore fidei veritatem. Ac per hoc licet formam pietatis habeant quae constat in sacramento baptismatis, abnegando tamen pietatis virtutem, nec vitam percipiunt, nec salutem. Quid autem talibus restat, nisi damnatio sempiterna quam eis pariet fides non vera, sed ficta? In talibus quippe nec caritas est de corde puro: quia secundum beati Petri sententiam "fide

Wisdom says in Proverbs: "For my mouth will utter truth; wickedness is an abomination to my lips" (Prv 8:7). Therefore, those who do not hold the truth of faith in their hearts and mouths do not receive salvation in baptism. And thus, although they may have the form of piety which is found in the sacrament of baptism, by renouncing the virtue of piety, they neither receive life nor salvation. But what remains for such people, except eternal damnation, which their false and feigned faith will bring upon them? For in such people there is not even charity from a pure heart:

Dominus suorum corda purificat" (Acts 15:9); nec cordis puritas esse potest ubi fides non est: quia nec fides omnino dicenda est, ubi vera non est. Quoniam igitur ubi est caritas de corde puro, ibi fides est non ficta, sed vera, cor autem non fictione fidei, sed veritate purgatur; manifestum est apud haereticos, in quibus non est veritas, sed fictio fidei, caritatem de corde puro nullatenus inveniri. Conscientiam vero bonam quomodo possunt habere, in quibus per incredulitatem habitat princeps ille malitiae?

because according to the assertion of St. Peter, "The Lord purifies the hearts of His faithful by faith" (Acts 15:9); nor can there be purity of heart where there is no faith: because faith cannot truly be called faith where it is not genuine. Therefore, where there is charity from a pure heart, there faith is not feigned, but true, and the heart is not purified by feigned faith, but by truth. It is evident that among heretics, in whom there is no truth, but a fiction of faith, charity from a pure heart is nowhere to be found. But how can they have a good conscience, in whom that prince of wickedness dwells through unbelief?

Feria Quinta: Prv 10:1–16
S. Clemens I Papa, *Epistula I ad Corinthios* (cap. 49)

Qui caritatem in Christo habet, servet Christi mandata. Vinculum caritatis Dei quis potest enarrare? Magnificentiam bonitatis ejus quis, prout oportet, eloqui valet? Altitudo ad quam evehit caritas, inenarrabilis est. Caritas nos Deo agglutinat: "caritas operit multitudinem peccatorum" (Prv 10:12; Jas 5:20; 1 Pt 4:8), "caritas omnia sustinet" (1 Cor 13:4), omnia ae-

Let him who has love in Christ keep the commandments of Christ. Who can describe the bond of the love of God? Who is able to tell the excellence of its beauty, as it ought to be told? The height to which love exalts is unspeakable. Love unites us to God: "Love covers a multitude of sins" (Prv 10:12; Jas 5:20; 1 Pt. 4:8), "Love bears all things" (1 Cor 13:4), is long-suffering in all

quo animo fert; in caritate nihil sordidum, nihil superbum; caritas schisma non habet; caritas seditionem non concitat; caritas omnia facit in concordia; in caritate omnes Dei electi, perfecti sunt facti. Sine caritate nihil acceptum est Deo. In caritate nos assumpsit Dominus; propter caritatem quam erga nos habuit Jesus Christus Dominus noster ex voluntate Dei, sanguinem suum pro nobis tradidit, et carnem pro carne nostra, ut animam pro animabus nostris.

things. There is nothing base, nothing arrogant in love. Love admits of no schisms: love gives rise to no seditions: love does all things in harmony. By love have all the elect of God been made perfect; without love nothing is well-pleasing to God. In love has the Lord accepted us. On account of the love He had towards us, Jesus Christ Our Lord gave His Blood for us by the will of God; His flesh for our flesh, and His soul for our souls.

Feria Sexta: Prv 14:1–16
S. Beda Venerabilis, *Allegorica expositio in Parabolas Salomonis* (lib. 2, cap. 14)

"Sapiens mulier aedificabit domum suam" (Prv 14:1). Et unaquaeque anima fidelis, et Ecclesia per orbem catholica, mansionem sibi in patria caelesti bonis actibus aedificat; at vero reprobi, ea quae bene sunt a bonis ordinata, male vivendo, et etiam aliquando aperte repugnando dissipant. Quare autem stulti sapientum actus lacerent, sequentibus verbis ostenditur, cum dicitur: "Ambulans recto itinere, et timens Deum" (Prv 14:2). Abominatio est enim pec-

"A wise woman builds her house" (Prv 14:1). And every faithful soul, and the Catholic Church throughout the world build for herself a dwelling in the heavenly fatherland by good deeds; but the reprobate destroy those things which the good have ordered well, by living badly, and even sometimes by openly opposing them. The reason why fools tear the actions of the wise, is shown in the following words, when it is said: "He that walks in the right way, fearing the

catori religio. Stultum videtur incredulis, cum fideles propter Dei timorem non tantum abiiciunt timorem, sed et tormenta derident eorum qui occidunt corpus. De quibus adhuc apte subjungitur: "In ore stulti virga superbiae" (Prv 14:3). Quia stulti per vaniloquium humiles quos despiciunt, affligunt; sed iidem humiles spiritu per doctrinam se sapientiae, ne decipiantur, muniunt. "Ubi non sunt boves, praesepe vacuum est" (Prv 14:4). Haerent haec a superioribus. Boves namque doctores catholicos; praesepe, coetuum auditores; segetes, dicit fructus operum bonorum. Ubi autem plurimae operationes apparent virtutum, ibi apertissime claret, quia non haereticus in vanum garrivit, sed pro verbi fruge laboravit ille, qui et ipsum verbum casto ore ruminare, et viam veritatis recto discretionis pede noscet incedere.

Lord" (Prv 14:2). For religion is an abomination to a sinner. It seems foolish to unbelievers when the faithful, for fear of God, not only cast off fear, but also mock the tortures of those who kill the body. Of whom it is fittingly further said: "In the mouth of the fool is a rod of pride" (Prv 14:3). Because fools, by vain talk, afflict the lowly whom they despise; but the same lowly ones in spirit protect themselves by the teaching of wisdom, lest they be deceived. "Where there are no oxen, the crib is empty" (Prv 14:4). These things follow from the previous ones. The oxen are the Catholic teachers; the manger is the audience of the assemblies; the harvest are the fruits of good works. But where the most works of virtue appear, there it is most clearly evident that the heretic did not speak in vain, but labored for the fruit of the word, he who both chews the word with a chaste mouth and knows to walk the way of truth with the right foot of discretion.

Sabbato: Prv 16:1–15
S. Hieronymus, *Contra Pelagianos* (lib. 3, cap. 8)

Salomon loquitur: "Esto confidens in Dominum in toto corde tuo, in tua autem sapientia ne exalteris: in omnibus viis tuis cognosce eum, ut rectas faciat vias tuas" (Prv 3:5–6). Intellige quid loquitur: Nec in sapientia nostra, nec in ullis virtutibus confidendum, sed in solo Domino, a quo gressus hominis diriguntur. Denique praecipitur, ut ostendamus ei vias nostras, et notas esse faciamus, quae non labore proprio, sed illius adjutorio atque clementia rectae fiunt. Unde scriptum est: "Rectam fac in conspectu meo viam tuam," sive ut alia exemplaria habent: "Rectam fac in conspectu tuo viam meam" (Ps 5:9): ut quod tibi rectum est, etiam mihi rectum esse videatur, idem Salomon loquitur, "Devolve super Dominum opera tua, et firmabuntur cogitationes tuae" (Prv 16:3). Tunc enim nostra cogitatio confirmatur, quando omne quod agimus, quasi super stabilem et solidissimam petram, Domini adjutorio devolvimus, eique cuncta reputamus.

Solomon says, "Trust in the Lord with all your heart, and lean not upon your own understanding: in all your ways acknowledge Him, and He shall direct your paths" (Prv 3:5–6). Understand what he says—that we must not trust in our wisdom, but in the Lord alone, by Whom the steps of a man are directed. Lastly, we are bidden to show Him our ways, and make them known, for they are not made straight by our own labour, but by His assistance and mercy. And so it is written, "Make your way right before my face," or as other manuscripts read: "Make my way straight in your sight" (Ps 5:9): so that what is right to you may also seem right to me, Solomon says the same thing: "Commit your works unto the Lord, and your thoughts shall be established" (Prv 16:3). Our thoughts are then established when we commit all we do to the Lord our helper, resting it, as it were, upon the firm and solid rock, and attribute everything to Him.

INFRA HEBDOMADAM II AUGUSTI

Feria Secunda: Eccles 2:1–11
S. Joannes Chrysostomus, *Homliae de statuis ad populum Antiochenum habitae* (hom. 1, cap. 11)

"Fili," inquit, "accedens ad servitium Dei, praepara animam tuam ad tentationem" (Ecclus 2:1). Nemo enim pugnare decernens, absque vulneribus coronam reportare exspectat. Et tu igitur, carissime, cum diabolo totis viribus pugnare aggressus, ne vitam securam et deliciis plenam sequaris. Non enim hic tibi retributiones et promissiones, sed in futuro saeculo omnia praeclara Deus promisit. Cum igitur vel ipse bonum feceris, et contraria receperis, vel alium hoc videris patientem, gaude et laetare: majoris enim tibi retributionis materia est. Ne concidas, neque solvas animi studium, neque segnior fias, sed potius insta cum majori alacritate. Quoniam et apostoli cum praedicabant, etsi flagellarentur, lapidarentur, carceres continue habitarent, non solum post periculorum liberationem, sed et in ipsis periculis cum majore alacritate veritatis praeconium enuntiabant. Quoties igitur frustrati fuerimus, toties

"My son, if thou comest to serve the Lord, prepare thy soul for temptation" (Ecclus 2:1). For surely no one choosing to fight, expects to carry off the crown without wounds! And thou, therefore, who hast undertaken to wage a complete combat with the devil, think not to pursue a life without danger, and full of luxury! God has not pledged to thee His recompense and His promise here; but everything that is splendid for thee in the future life! Be glad and rejoice then, if when thou hast thyself done any good action, thou receive the contrary, or if thou seest another suffering this; inasmuch as this becomes to thee the source of a higher recompense! Do not be downcast: nor give up thy zeal, nor become the more torpid; but rather press onward with more eagerness; since even the apostles, when they preached, although scourged, stoned, and constant inmates of the prisons, did not only after deliverance from dangers, but also in those very dangers, announce with

spiritualis opera aggrediamur: neque dicamus, quare Deus impedimenta permisit? Propter hoc enim permisit, tu studium tuum multo magis demonstres, et multum amorem.

greater forwardness the message of truth. As often then as we are frustrated in spiritual works, so often let us again take them in hand; and let us not say, For what reason did God permit these impediments? For He permitted them to this end, that He might show thine alacrity much more to others, and thy great love.

Feria Tertia: Eccles 3:1–17
S. Hieronymus, *Commentarius in Ecclesiasten* (cap. 3:16–17)

"Et adhuc vidi sub sole locum judicii: ibi impietas; et locum justitiae: ibi iniquitas. in corde meo: Justum et impium judicabit Deus: quia tempus omni voluntati super omne factum ibi" (Eccles 3:16–17). Manifestus est sensus, sed nubilo interpretationis obvolvitur. Sub sole, inquit, isto veritatem et judicium requisivi, et vidi etiam inter judicum ipsa subsellia, non veritatem valere, sed munera. Sive aliter: Arbitratus sum aliquid justitiae in praesenti saeculo geri, et vel pium pro suo nunc merito recipere, vel impium pro suo scelere puniri: et e contrario reperi, quam putabam. Vidi enim et justum multa mala hic perpeti, et impium

"Furthermore, I have observed beneath the sun: in the place of justice there is wickedness, and in the place of righteousness there is wickedness. I mused: God will judge the righteous and the wicked, for there is a time for everything and for every deed, there" (Eccles 3:16–17). The meaning of this is clear but is cloaked by the cloud of interpretation. He says: I sought truth and righteousness under the sun, and I saw that even among the benches of judges truth is not valued, but gifts. Or differently: I thought some kind of justice present in this world and either took the pious man on his own merit or punished the impious for his crimes; and I found the

regnare pro scelere. Postea vero cum corde meo colloquens et reputans, intellexi, non per partes Deum et per singulos nunc judicare, sed in futurum tempus reservare judicium ut omnes pariter judicentur, et secundum voluntatem et opera sua ibi recipiant. Hoc est enim quod ait: Et tempus omni voluntati, et super omne factum ibi (Eccles 3:17), id est, in judicio, quando Dominus coeperit judicare, tunc futura est veritas, nunc injustitia dominatur in mundo. Tale quid et in Sapientia, quae filii Sirach inscribitur, legimus: "Ne dixeris, quid est hoc aut quid est istud? omnia enim tempore suo requirentur" (Ecclus 39:26).

opposite to that which I had been thinking. For I saw a righteous man here suffer much injustice and an impious man made to rule instead of being punished for his crime. But thinking to myself afterwards and considering it carefully I understood that they judge not in respect of God and treating each case one by one, but rather reserve judgement for the future, so that all are judged equally and receive there according to their will and effort. For this is what he says: "And there is a time for everything and for every deed, there" (Eccles 3:17), that is, in judgment when God will have begun to judge, then there will be truth, now injustice prevails in the world. Such as when we read in Wisdom, Sirach wrote: "Lest you say, what is this or what is that? For all things are sought in their own time" (Ecclus 39: 26).

Feria Quarta: Eccles 4:1–13
S. Ambrosius, *De bono mortis* (cap. 7, 28–29)

"Non satiabitur," inquit, "oculus visu, nec auris auditu" (Eccles 1:8). Qui diligit argentum, non satiatur argento. Nullus finis laboris, et nullus est fructus abundantiae. Cupimus quotidie scire nova; et

"The eye is not satisfied with seeing, nor the ear filled with hearing" (Eccles 1:8). He that loves silver shall not be satisfied with silver. There is no end to labor, and there is no fruit of abundance. We want to know new things

quid est ipsa scientia, nisi quotidiani doloris adiectio? Omnia quae sunt jam fuerunt, et nihil sub sole est novum, sed omnia vanitas. Totam vitam odio habui (cf. Eccles 1:10), dixit Ecclesiastes. Qui vitam odio habuit, mortem utique praedicavit. Denique mortuos laudavit magis quam viventes (cf. Eccles 4:2); et illum judicavit beatum, qui in hanc vitam non venit, nec inanem hunc suscepit laborem. Circuivit, inquit, cor meum, ut scirem impii laetitiam, et considerarem, et quaererem sapientiam, et numerum, et ut scirem per imperium laetitiam, et molestiam, et jactationem; et inveni ego eam amariorem, quam mortem (cf. Eccles 6:26): non quia amara sit mors, sed quia impio amara; et tamen amarior vita, quam mors. Gravius est enim ad peccatum vivere, quam in peccato mori; quia impius quamdiu vivit, peccatum auget: si moriatur, peccare desinit. Plerique criminum suorum absolutione laetantur. Si emendaturi sunt, recte: si perseveraturi in eis, stulte; quia longe illis plus damnatio profuisset, ne incrementa facerent peccatorum.

every day; and what is knowledge itself, if not an addiction to daily pain? What has been is what will be, and what has been done is what will be done, and there is nothing new under the sun. I have hated all my life (cf. Eccles 1:10), said Ecclesiastes. He who hated life certainly preached death. Finally, he praised the dead more than the living (cf. Eccles 4:2); and he judged him blessed who did not come into this life, and did not undertake this vain labor. My heart went round, says he, that I might know the joy of the wicked, and consider, and seek wisdom, and number, and that I might know by command joy, and trouble, and boasting; and I found it more bitter than death (cf. Eccles 6:26): not because death is bitter, but because for the wicked death is bitter; and yet life is more bitter than death. For it is more grave to live in order to sin than to die in sin; for as long as the wicked lives, sin increases; if he dies, he ceases to sin. Most of them are happy with the acquittal of their crimes. If they are to be corrected, is it right: if they are to persist in them, it is foolish; because damnation would have benefited them far more, lest they increase their sins.

Feria Quinta: Eccles 5:1–13
S. Joannes Cassianus, *De coenobiorum institutis* (lib. 4, cap. 33)

Non debeat quis facile admitti in monasterio. Sicut namque immensa gloria fideliter servientibus Deo, ac secundum institutionis hujus regulam ei cohaerentibus, repromittitur in futurum: ita poenae gravissimae praeparantur his qui tepide eam negligenterque fuerint exsecuti, et secundum hoc quod professi sunt, vel quod ab hominibus esse creduntur, fructus etiam congruos sanctitatis eidem exhibere neglexerint. "Melius est enim," secundum Scripturam, "non vovere quemquam, quam vovere, et non reddere" (Eccles 5:4); et, "Maledictus qui facit opus Dei negligenter" (Jer 48:10). Ideo igitur a nobis diutissime refutatus es, non quia tuam vel omnium salutem non toto desiderio cupiamus amplecti, et his qui ad Christum cupiunt converti etiam procul occurrere non optemus: sed ne temere recipientes, et nos apud Deum levitatis, et temetipsum reum gravioris supplicii faceremus, si ad praesens facile susceptus, nec pondus

No one should be admitted into a monastery too easily. For as unbounded glory hereafter is promised to those who faithfully serve God and cleave to Him according to the rule of this system; so the severest penalties are in store for those who have carried it out carelessly and coldly, and have failed to show to Him fruits of holiness corresponding to what they professed or what they were believed by men to be. "For it is better," as Scripture says, "that a man should not vow rather than that he should vow and not pay" (Eccles 5:4); and "Cursed is he that does the work of the Lord carelessly" (Jer 48:10) Therefore thou wert for a long while declined by us, not as if we did not desire with all our hearts to secure thy salvation and the salvation of all, nor as if we did not care to go to meet even afar off those who are longing to be converted to Christ; but for fear lest if we received thee rashly we might make ourselves guilty in the sight of God of levity, and make you incur a yet heavier punishment, if, when you had been too easily

professionis hujus intelligens, vel destitutor post haec, vel tepidus exstitisses.

admitted by us without realizing the responsibility of this profession, thou hadst afterwards turned out a deserter or lukewarm.

Feria Sexta: Eccles 6:1–9
S. Gregorius Magnus, *Dialogi* (lib. 4, cap. 4)

"Quid habet amplius sapiens a stulto, et quid pauper, nisi ut pergat illuc ubi est vita" (Eccles 6:8)? Qui igitur dixit: "Nihil habet homo jumentis amplius" (Eccles 3:19), ipse rursum definivit, quia habet aliquid sapiens non solum amplius a jumento, sed etiam ab homine stulto, videlicet ut pergat illuc ubi est vita. Quibus verbis primum indicat quia hic hominum vita non est, quam esse alibi testatur. Habet ergo homo hoc amplius jumentis, quia illa post mortem non vivunt, hic vero tunc vivere inchoat, cum per mortem carnis hanc visibilem vitam consummat. Qui etiam longe inferius dicit: "Quodcumque potest manus tua facere, instanter operare, quia nec opus, nec ratio, nec scientia, nec sapientia erit apud inferos, quo tu properas" (Eccles 9:10). Quomodo ergo unus interitus est hominis et jumenti, et aequa utri-

What has a wise man more than a fool, and what a poor man, but that he may go thither where life is (Eccles 6:8)? He therefore that said: "A man has no more than beasts" (Eccles 3:19): said also with mature deliberation, that a wise man has not only more than a beast, but also more than a foolish man, to wit, that he goes to that place where life is: in which words he does also teach us, that man's life is not in this world, seeing he affirms it to be elsewhere: wherefore man has this more than beasts, because they after death do not live: but he does then begin truly to live, when by mortal death he makes an end of this transitory life: and therefore long after he says: "Whatsoever your hand can do instantly work: because with them in hell whither you go there shall be neither work, nor reason, nor knowledge, nor wisdom" (Eccles 9:10). How then

usque conditio? Aut quomodo nihil habet homo jumentis amplius, cum jumenta post mortem carnis non vivunt; hominum vero spiritus pro malis suis operibus post mortem carnis ad inferos deducti, nec in ipsa morte moriuntur? Sed in utraque tam dispari sententia demonstratur quia concionator verax et illud ex tentatione carnali intulit, et hoc postmodum ex spiritali veritate definivit.

is the death of man and beasts all one, and how is their condition and state alike? Or how has not a man more than beasts, when as they after death live not, and the souls of men, after the death of their bodies, be for their wicked deeds carried to hell, and do not die when they depart this life? But in both these sayings, which seem contrary each to other, it is made manifest that the preacher speaks the truth: the first he mentioned in the meaning of the carnal temptation, and the second he afterwards defined from the spiritual truth.

Sabbato: Eccles 7:1–9, 11–14
S. Joannes Cassianus, *De coenobiorum institutis* (lib. 8, cap. 1)

Irae mortiferum virus de recessibus animae nostrae funditus eruendum est. Hac enim in cordibus nostris insidente, et oculum mentis noxiis tenebris obcaecante, nec judicium rectae discretionis acquirere, nec honestae contemplationis intuitum, nec maturitatem consilii possidere, nec vitae participes, nec justitiae tenaces, sed ne spiritalis quidem ac veri luminis capaces poterimus existere, quia turbatus est, inquit, prae ira oculus

The deadly poison of anger must be utterly rooted out from the inmost comers of our soul. For as long as this remains in our hearts, and blinds with its hurtful darkness the eye of the soul, we can neither acquire right judgment and discretion, nor gain the insight which springs from an honest gaze, or ripeness of counsel, nor can we be partakers of life, or retentive of righteousness, or even have the capacity for spiritual and true light: for, says one, my eye is

meus (cf. Ps 6:8). Nec sapientiae participes effici, tametsi sapientes omnium pronuntiari opinione videamur, quia "ira in sinu insipientium requiescit" (Eccles 7:10). Sed ne vitam quidem immortalitatis consequi poterimus, quamvis prudentes videamur definitione hominum judicari, quia ira perdit etiam prudentes (cf. Prv 15:1). Nec justitiae moderamina perspicaci discretione cordis valebimus obtinere, licet perfecti sanctique cunctorum opinationibus aestimemur, quia "ira viri justitiam Dei non operator" (Jas 1:20). Consilii etiam maturitatem nullatenus valebimus obtinere, quamvis graves et summa scientia praediti videamur, quia vir iracundus agit sine consilio (cf. Prv 15:18).

disturbed by reason of anger (cf. Ps 6:8). Nor can we become partakers of wisdom, even though we are considered wise by universal consent, "for anger rests in the bosom of fools" (Eccles 7:10). Nor can we even attain immortal life, although we are accounted prudent in the opinion of everybody, for anger even slays wise men (cf. Prv 15:1). Nor shall we be able with clear judgment of heart to secure the controlling power of righteousness, even though we are reckoned perfect and holy in the estimation of all men, for "the wrath of man works not the righteousness of God" (Jas 1:20). Nor again can we secure any ripeness of counsel, even though we appear to be weighty, and endowed with the utmost knowledge, because an angry man acts without counsel (cf. Prv 15:18).

INFRA HEBDOMADAM III AUGUSTI

Feria Secunda: Ws 3:1–11; 5:16–21

S. Augustinus, *Sermones* (serm. 298, cap. 3)

Ubi sunt sancti isti, putamus? Ibi ubi bene est. Quid quaeris amplius? Non nosti locum, sed cogita meritum. Ubicumque sunt, cum Deo sunt. "Justorum animae in manu Dei sunt, et non tanget illos

Where are these saints, do you suppose? Where all is well with them. Why inquire any further? You don't know the place but think of what earned it for them. Wherever they are, they are with God. "The souls

tormentum" (Ws 3:1), sed ad locum sine tormento per tormenta transierunt: ad locum latitudinis per angustias pervenerunt. Non ergo timeat laboriosam viam, qui talem desiderat patriam. Tempus, inquit, resolutionis meae instat. "Bonum certamen certavi, cursum consummavi, fidem servavi; de cetero superest mihi corona justitiae" (2 Tm 4:6–8). Merito festinas, merito te immolandum esse laetaris: superest enim tibi corona justitiae. Adhuc imminet amaritudo passionis, sed transit eam passuri cogitatio, et quid ultra sit cogitat; non qua itur, sed quo itur. Et quia cum magno amore cogitatur quo itur, cum magna fortitudine calcatur qua itur.

of the just are in the hand of God, and no torment will touch them" (Wis 3:1). But to the place without torment, they passed through torments; to the wide-open spaces they came through some very tight spots. So, if you are longing for such a home country, you shouldn't be afraid of a difficult and toilsome road. Time, he says, presses for me to cast off. "I have fought the good fight, I have completed the course, I have kept the faith; for the rest there remains for me a crown of justice" (2 Tm 6:4–8). You are right to be in such a hurry, right to rejoice at the prospect of being set apart as a victim; after all, there is awaiting you a crown of justice. The bitterness of suffering is still hanging over him, but his thoughts as he waits to suffer go beyond that, and he thinks of what there is beyond; not of how he is going, but of where he is going. And because he is thinking with great love of where he is going, he treads with great courage the road by which he is going.

Feria Tertia: Ws 6:1–13
S. Augustinus, *Sermones* (serm. 391, cap. 5)

Amare vultis? Amate sapientiam, ambite ut perveniatis ad eam. Ut non vos exhorreat ejus aspectus, in homine vos interiore componite. Sicut lascivi oculi ornamenta corporis, sic illa cordis inquirit. Nec de vestris divitiis haec ornamenta proferatis: quia odit superbos et quasi de suo se jactare cupientes. "Quid autem habes quod non accepisti?" (1 Cor 4:7). Ipsa ergo donat unde illi placeas. Tantum dilige eam, et servabit te; circumda eam, et exaltabit te; honora eam, et amplexabitur te: ut det capiti tuo coronam gratiarum (cf. Prv 4:9). "Clara est et quae numquam marcescet sapientia, et facile invenitur ab his qui diligunt illam" (Ws 6:13). "Non habet amaritudinem conversatio illius" (Ws 8:16). Si amatores estis, hanc amate; si formosi estis, Deo placete; si juvenes estis, diabolum vincite. Daniel ab angelo vir desideriorum appellatus est (cf. Dn 10:11). Quae illa ejus erant desideria, nisi quibus in sapientiae pulchritudinem ardenter inhiabat; quia et in

Do you wish to love? Love wisdom, let attaining her be your ambition. So that the sight of her may not alarm you unduly, bring some order into your inner life. Just as roving, wanton eyes are on the look-out for the embellishments of the body, so is she for those of the heart. And don't imagine you can furnish these embellishments from your own jewel cases, because she hates the proud, and those who are only eager to boast of such things as though they came from themselves. "What, though, do you have that you have not received?" (1 Cor 4:7). So it is she that grants you the means of pleasing her. Only love her, and she will keep you safe; lay siege to her, and she will exalt you; honor her, and she will embrace you, and will place upon your head a wreath of graces (cf. Prv 4:9). "Wisdom is radiant and never fades and is easily found by those who love her" (Ws 6:13). "There is no bitterness in her companionship" (Ws 8:16). If you are lovers, love her; if you are handsome fellows, think of pleasing God; if you are young, overcome

juvenili aetate calcavit lasciviam, et regnum superbiam pressit captivus, et ora leonum clausit inclusus?

the devil. Daniel was called by the angel a man of desires (cf. Dn 10:11). What were those desires of his, but ardent longings for the beauty of wisdom? Because in his youth he had trampled on lust, as a prisoner he had crushed the pride of kings, when shut in close he had shut the mouths of lions?

Feria Quarta: Ws 7:1–14
S. Ambrosius, *Enarrationes in 12 psalmos Davidicos* (in Ps 43, enarr. 93–94)

Cum autem Deus alicubi in tribulatione dilatat; tunc fiet latitudo cordis, sicut arena maris innumerabilis. Quae sit ista latitudo audi dicentem sanctum Salomonem: "Optavi, et datus est mihi sensus: et invocavi, et venit in me spiritus sapientiae" (Ws 7:7). Ut enim acciperet sapientiam a Deo, non divitias, non nobilitatem, non potestatem; sed sapientiam postulavit, et in illa omnia quae etiam non postulavit, invenit. Unde Scriptura dicit quia "talis erat latitudo cordis ejus, sicut arena maris innumerabilis" (3 Kgs 4:29). Unde hanc percipias latitudinem, ait de seipso cognoscens: "In latitudine cordis tui describe eam" (Prv 7:3).

But when God expands somewhere a man in tribulation; then the breadth of the heart will become like the innumerable sand of the sea. What is this breadth, hear St. Solomon saying: "Wherefore I wished, and understanding was given me: and I called upon God, and the spirit of wisdom came upon me" (Ws 7:7). For he might receive wisdom from God, not riches, not nobility, not power; but he asked for wisdom, and in it he found everything that he did not even ask for. Hence the Scripture says that "the breadth of his heart was like the innumerable sand of the sea" (3 Kgs 4:29). Whence you perceive this breadth, he says of

Et ideo qui habet sapientiam, non in occulto teneat eam, non ad momentum; sed canat eam in exitu: ubique quod sentit, cum auctoritate praedicet. Sive tamen afflictatio sit, sive tribulatio, opus est ut nos maneamus in Domino, nec ab eodem recedamus; quoniam praesule Domino et assistente nobis, omne certamen fortiter possumus sustinere. Si autem Dominum negligamus, et longe nos faciamus a Domino, facimus nobis adversarium fortiorem.

himself knowing: "Describe it in the breadth of your heart" (Prv 7:3). And therefore, he that has wisdom, let him not keep it in secret, not for a moment; but he sings it at the exit: wherever he feels, he proclaims with authority. However, whether it be affliction or tribulation, it is necessary that we remain in the Lord, and not depart from Him; because with the help of the Lord and our helper, we can endure every struggle with strength. But if we neglect the Lord, and make ourselves far from the Lord, we make our adversary stronger.

Feria Quinta: Ws 9:13–19; 10:1–9
S. Leo Magnus Papa, *Sermones* (serm. 95, cap. 5)

Terra ergo promissa mitibus, et in possessionem danda mansuetis, caro sanctorum est, quae ob humilitatis meritum felici resurrectione mutabitur et immortalitatis gloria vestietur, in nullo jam spiritui futura contraria, et cum voluntate animi perfectae unitatis habitura consensum. Tunc enim exterior homo interioris hominis erit quieta et intemerata possessio; tunc mens videndo Deo intenta nullis corporeae infirmitatis

To the meek and gentle, to the humble and modest, and to those who are prepared to endure all injuries, the earth is promised for their possession. And this is not to be reckoned a small or cheap inheritance, as if it were distinct from our heavenly dwelling, since it is no other than these who are understood to enter the Kingdom of heaven. For then the outer man will be the peaceful and unblemished possession of the inner man: then

impedietur obstaculis, nec jam dici necesse erit: "Corpus quod corrumpitur aggravat animam, et terrena inhabitatio deprimit sensum multa cogitantem" (Ws 9:15): quoniam habitatori suo non reluctabitur terra, nec immoderatum aliquid contra imperium sui rectoris audebit. Possidebunt enim illam mites pace perpetua, et nihil umquam de eorum jure minuetur, "cum corruptibile hoc induerit incorruptionem, et mortale hoc induerit immortalitatem" (1 Cor 15:53): ut periculum vertatur in praemium, et quod fuit oneri sit honori.

the mind, engrossed in beholding God, will be hampered by no obstacles of human weakness nor will it any more have to be said: "The body which is corrupted, weighs upon the soul, and its earthly house presses down the sense which thinks many things" (Ws 9:15): for the earth will not struggle against its tenant, and will not venture on any insubordination against the rule of its governor. For the meek shall possess it in perpetual peace, and nothing shall be taken from their rights, "when this corruptible shall have put on incorruption, and this mortal shall have put on immortality" (1 Cor 15:53): that their danger may turn into reward, and what was a burden become an honor.

Feria Sexta: Ws 13:1–10
S. Augustinus, *Sermones* (serm. 384, cap. 1)

Qualis sit autem haec gloria futura, et quibus divitiis floreat, quantoque splendore praefulgeat, laudare possumus, explicare non possumus. Quare? Quia legimus: "Nec oculus vidit, nec auris audivit, nec in cor hominis ascendit, quae praeparavit Deus diligentibus se" (1 Cor 2:9). Si igitur tanta

What this future glory will be like, however, how richly it will flourish, with what splendor it will blaze out, while we can sing its praises, we cannot possibly explain. Why not? Because we read, "Eye has not seen, nor era heard, nor has it come up into the heart of man, what things God has prepared for those who

et talia sunt bona aeterna caelestia, quae Dominus omnipotens praeparavit sanctis suis catholicis et fidelibus populis; quid est ipse Deus, qui talia et tanta praeparavit? Quid est, inquam, omnipotens Deus? quid, nisi inaestimabilis, ineffabilis, incomprehensibilis, ultra omnia, extra omnia, praeter omnia? Omnem enim creaturam suam excedit, omnem facturam praeterit, universa praecellit. Si enim quaeras magnitudinem, major est; si pulchritudinem, pulchrior; si dulcedinem, dulcior; si splendorem, fulgidior; si justitiam, justior; si fortitudinem, fortior; si pietatem, clementior. Nulla enim ratio patitur, ut vel factura factori suo aequetur, vel opus artifici comparetur: sicut legitur in propheta: "Qui fecit fortia, fortior est; et qui fecit pulchra, pulchrior illis est" (Ws 13:3–4).

love Him" (1 Cor 2:9). So, if that's what must be said about the eternal good things of heaven, which the almighty Lord has prepared for his holy, Catholic and faithful peoples, what must God Himself be, Who has prepared such great and wonderful things? What, I repeat, must almighty God be like? What but unfathomable, inexpressible, incomprehensible, surpassing all things, beyond all things, apart from all things? He excels, after all, every one of His creatures, He goes far beyond everything He has made, He surpasses the whole universe. I mean, if you are looking for greatness, He is greater; if for beauty, He is more beautiful still; if for delightfulness, He is still more delightful; if for splendor, He is more brilliant; if for justice, He is more just; if for strength, He is stronger; if for fatherly care, He is kinder. Reason, after all, in no way allows us to equate the thing made with its maker, or the work with its craftsman. As we may read in the prophet, "The one who made mighty things is mightier himself; and the one who made beautiful things is more beautiful than they are" (Ws 13:3–4).

Sabbato: Ws 15:1–8
S. Rabanus Maurus, *Commentariorum in Ecclesiasticum libri decem* (lib. 3, cap. 4)

"Tu autem, Deus noster, suavis et verus patiens et in misericordia disponens omnia. Etiam si peccaverimus, tui sumus, scientes magnitudinem tuam. Et si non peccaverimus, scimus quoniam ad te sumus computati" (Ws 15:1–2). Deus noster suavis, quoniam ineffabilis est dilectio. Est verus, quia neminem fallit, et a nemine fallitur. Patiens et in misericordia disponens omnia; propter bonitatem enim suam patienter sustinens nos exspectat converti in melius, nolens quemquam perire, sed omnes salvos esse, et ad agnitionem veritatis pervenire. Qui per prophetam ait: "Nolo mortem peccatoris, sed ut convertatur et vivat" (Ez 33:11). Cujus manum si peccaverimus evadere non possumus, quia ejus creatura sumus. Si autem peccare desierimus et bonis operibus insistimus, certam remunerationem ab illo percipiemus, apud quem omnium bonorum actuum numerus integer servatur. Ipse enim novit omnes, et nullum coram eo latet secretum.

"But Thou, our God, art gracious and true, patient, and ordering all things in mercy. For if we sin, we are Thine, knowing Thy greatness: and if we sin not, we know that we are counted with Thee" (Ws 15:1–2). Our God is sweet, because His love is indescribable. It is true, because it deceives no one, and is deceived by no one. Patient and arranging all things in mercy; for because of His goodness, He patiently endures and waits for us to be converted for the better, not wanting any to perish, but all to be saved, and to come to the knowledge of the truth. He Who said through the prophet: "I do not want the death of the sinner, but that he should be converted and live" (Ez 33:11). We cannot escape from His hand if we have sinned, because we are His creatures. But if we stop sinning and insist on good works, we will receive a sure reward from Him, with Whom the whole number of all good deeds is kept. For He knows all things, and no secret is hidden before Him.

INFRA HEBDOMADAM IV AUGUSTI

Feria Secunda: Ecclus 1:22–40

S. Augustinus, *In Epistulam Joannis ad Parthos tractatus* (tr. 9, cap. 4)

Timor quasi locum praeparat caritati. Cum autem coeperit caritas habitare, pellitur timor qui ei praeparavit locum. Quantum enim illa crescit, ille decrescit; et quantum illa fit interior, timor pellitur foras. Maior caritas, minor timor; minor caritas, major timor. Si autem nullus timor, non est qua intret caritas. Et in hoc saeculo quis nobis nocebit plenis caritate? Videte quomodo exsultet Apostolus de ipsa caritate. "Quis nos, inquit, separabit a caritate Christi? tribulatio? an angustia? an persecutio? an fames? an nuditas? an periculum? an gladius?" (Rom 8:35). Stimulat timor: sed noli timere; intrat caritas quae sanat quod vulnerat timor. Timor Dei sic vulnerat, quomodo medici ferramentum; putredinem tollit, et quasi videtur vulnus augere. Ecce putredo quando erat in corpore, minus erat vulnus, sed periculosum: accedit ferramentum medici; minus dolebat illud vulnus, quam dolet modo cum secatur. Occupet ergo cor tuum timor, ut inducat

Fear, so to say, prepares a place for charity. But when once charity has begun to inhabit, the fear which prepared the place for it is cast out. For in proportion as this increases, that decreases: and the more this comes to be within, is the fear cast out. Greater charity, less fear; less charity, greater fear. But if no fear, there is no way for charity to come in. Even in this world, who shall hurt us, being full of charity? See how the apostle exults concerning this very charity: "Who shall separate us from the charity of Christ? Shall tribulation, or distress, or persecution, or famine, or nakedness, or peril, or sword?" (Rom. 8:35). Fear wounds: but do not be afraid; charity enters, which heals what fear wounds. The fear of God so wounds as does the leech's knife; it takes away the rottenness and seems to make the wound greater. Behold, when the rottenness was in the body, the wound was less, but perilous: then comes the knife; the wound smarted less than it smarts now while the leech is cutting it.

caritatem; succedat cicatrix ferramento medici. Nam si sine timore es, non poteris justificari. Sententia dicta est de Scripturis: Nam "qui sine timore est, non poterit justificari" (Ecclus 1:28). Opus est ergo ut intret timor primo, per quem veniat caritas. Timor medicamentum, caritas sanitas.

Then let fear occupy your heart, that it may bring in charity; let the cicatrice succeed to the leech's knife. For if you be without fear, you cannot be justified. It is a sentence pronounced by the Scriptures: "For he that is without fear, cannot be justified" (Ecclus 1:28). It is necessary then that fear first enter in, and by it charity may come. Fear is the healing operation: charity, the sound condition.

Feria Tertia: Ecclus 2:1–12
S. Leo Magnus Papa, *De quadragesima* (serm. 39, cap. 3–4)

"Fortior est qui in nobis est quam qui adversum nos est" (1 Jn 4:4), et per ipsum validi sumus, in cujus virtute confidimus. Nulla sunt enim, dilectissimi, sine tentationum experimentis opera virtutis, nulla sine probationibus fides, nullum sine hoste certamen, nulla sine congressione victoria. Vita haec nostra in medio insidiarum, in medio praeliorum est. Si nolumus decipi, vigilandum est; si volumus superare, pugnandum est. Et ideo sapientissimus Salomon, "Fili," inquit, "accedens ad servitutem Dei, praepara animam tuam ad tentationem" (Ec-

"Stronger is He that is in us than He that is against us" (1 Jn 4:4), and through Him are we powerful in whose strength we rely. For there are no works of power, dearly beloved, without the trials of temptations, there is no faith without proof, no contest without a foe, no victory without conflict. This life of ours is in the midst of snares, in the midst of battles; if we do not wish to be deceived, we must watch: if we want to overcome, we must fight. And therefore, the most wise Solomon says, "My son, in approaching the service of God prepare your soul for temptation" (Ecclus 2:1). For He

clus 2:1). Vir enim sapientia Dei plenus, sciens studium religionis laborem habere certaminis, cum praevideret pugnae periculum, ante admonuit pugnaturum: ne forte si ad ignorantem tentator accederet, imparatum citius vulneraret. Succinxit lumbos balteo castitatis, calceavit pedes vinculis pacis: quia et discinctus miles cito ab impudicitiae incentore vincitur, et non calceatus facile a serpente mordetur. Scutum fidei ad protectionem totius corporis dedit, capiti galeam salutis imposuit, dexteram gladio, id est verbo veritatis, instruxit: ut spiritalis praeliator non solum sit tutus a vulnere, sed et repugnantem valeat vulnerare.

being a man full of the wisdom of God, and knowing that the pursuit of religion involves laborious struggles, foreseeing too the danger of the fight, forewarned the intending combatant; lest haply, if the tempter came upon him in his ignorance, he might find him unready and wound him unawares. Christ has girted our loins with the belt of chastity, He has shod our feet with the bonds of peace: because the unbelted soldier is quickly vanquished by the suggester of immodesty, and he that is unshod is easily bitten by the serpent. He has given the shield of faith for the protection of our whole body; on our head has He set the helmet of salvation; our right hand has He furnished with a sword, that is with the word of Truth: that the spiritual warrior may not only be safe from wounds, but also may have strength to wound his assailant.

Feria Quarta: Ecclus 3:1–13
S. Joannes Chrysostomus, *In epistolam Secundam ad Timotheum commentarius* (hom. 2, cap. 4)

"Ne glorieris," inquit, "in ignominia patris tui. Neque enim tibi tam gloria est, quem probrum" (Ecclus 3:12). Si de cor-

"Glory not in the dishonor of thy father; for your father's dishonor is no glory unto thee" (Ecclus 3:12). And if this be said of our natural fathers,

poralibus patribus haec dicenda sunt, multo magis de spiritualibus. Reverere, quia quotidie tibi ministrat. Scripturas legi curat, propter le domum ornat, propter te vigilat, propter te precatur, pro te stat Deo supplicans, pro te totus ejus cultus est. Dic mihi, improbus est? Et quid hoc? Num enim qui non improbus est tibi magna bona largitur? Minime: nam secundum fidem tuam totum efficitur. Neque justus tibi proderit, si tu fidelis non sis; neque improbus nocebit, si sis fidelis. Per vaccas in arca operatus est Deus, quando voluit populum salvum facere (cf. 1 Kgs 6:12). Num sacerdotis vita, num virtus ejus tale quid efficit? Non talia sunt ea quae Deus elargitur, ut a sacerdotali virtute perficiantur: totum ex gratia est; hujus (sacerdotis) tantum est os aperire, totum vero Deus operatur; symbolum (ritum) hic (sacerdos) solum implet. Oblatio eadem est, quisquis offerat, sive Paulus, sive Petrus; eadem est, quam Christus dedit discipulis, et quam nunc sacerdotes faciunt: haec illa nihil minor est, quia

much more of our spiritual fathers. Reverence him, in that he every day ministers to thee, causes the Scriptures to be read, sets the house in order for thee, watches for thee, prays for thee, stands imploring God on thy behalf, offers supplications for thee, for thee is all his worship. Reverence all this, think of this, and approach him with pious respect. Say not, he is wicked. What of that? He that is not wicked, does he of himself bestow upon you these great benefits? By no means. Everything works according to thy faith. Not even the righteous man can benefit thee, if thou art unfaithful, nor the unrighteous harm thee, if thou art faithful. God, when He would save His people, wrought for the ark by oxen (cf. 1 Kgs 6:12). Is it the good life or the virtue of the priest that confers so much on you? The gifts which God bestows are not such as to be effects of the virtue of the priest. All is of grace. His part is but to open his mouth, while God works all: the priest only performs a symbol (rite). The offering is the same, any priest offers it, or Paul or Peter offer it. It is the same which Christ gave to His disciples, and which the priests now minister. This

non homines hanc sanctificant, sed is ipse qui illam sanctificavit.

is nowise inferior to that, because it is not men that sanctify this, but the Same Who sanctified it.

Feria Quinta: Ecclus 3:22–34
S. Augustinus, *In evangelium Joannis tractatus* (tr. 53, cap. 7)

"Altiora te ne quaesieris, et fortiora te ne scrutatus fueris" (Ecclus 3:22). Non quia ista negata sunt nobis, cum Deus magister dicat: "Nihil est occultum quod non revelabitur" (Mt 10:26): sed si in quod pervenimus, in eo ambulemus, sicut dicit Apostolus, non solum quod nescimus et scire debemus, sed etiam si quid aliter sapimus, id quoque nobis Deus revelabit (cf. Phil 3:15–16). Pervenimus autem in viam fidei, hanc perseverantissime teneamus: ipsa perducet ad cubiculum regis, "in quo sunt omnes thesauri sapientiae et scientiae absconditi" (Col 2:3). Non enim ipse Dominus Jesus Christus suis illis magnis et praecipue electis discipulis invidebat, quando dicebat: "Multa habeo vobis dicere, sed non potestis illa portare modo" (Jn 16:12). Ambulandum est, proficiendum est, crescendum est, ut sint corda nostra capacia earum rerum quas

"Seek not out the things that are too high for you, neither search the things that are above your strength" (Ecclus 3:22). Not that such things are forbidden us, since the divine Master says, "There is nothing hid that shall not be revealed" (Mt 10:26): but if we walk up to the measure of our present attainments, then, as the apostle tells us, not only what we know not and ought to know, but also if we are minded to know anything else, God will reveal even this unto us (cf. Phil 3:15–16). But if we have reached the pathway of faith, let us keep to it with all constancy: let it be our guide to the chamber of the King, in Whom are hid all the treasures of wisdom and knowledge. (Col. 2:3). For it was in no spirit of grudging that the Lord Jesus Christ Himself acted towards those great and specially chosen disciples of His, when He said, "I have many things to say unto you, but you cannot bear them now" (Jn 16 :12). We must be

capere modo non possumus. Quod si nos ultimus dies proficientes invenerit, ibi discemus quod hic non potuimus.

walking, making progress, and growing, that our hearts may become fit to receive the things which we cannot receive at present. And if the last day shall find us sufficiently advanced, we shall then learn what here we were unable to know.

Feria Sexta: Ecclus 4:1–11
S. Joannes Chrysostomus, *De sacerdotio* (lib. 3, cap. 16)

Viduarum genus tum paupertatis, tum aetatis, tum sexus nomine, immoderata quadam loquendi libertate utitur. Oportet omnia fortiter ferre, neque ob importunas rixas vel absurdas querelas ira commoveri. Illarum enim infelicitas misericordiam potius quam contumeliam meretur. Quamobrem vir quidem sapientissimus, avaritiam superbiamque humanae naturae considerans, gnarus paupertatem hujusmodi esse, ut possit vel generosissimum animum dejicere, eoque deducere ut iisdem in rebus saepius impudenter agat, ne quis petentibus illis irascitur, neu, frequentibus eorum precibus exasperatus, infestus evadat ille, qui opem ferre debet, ut sese mitem et aditu facilem exhibeat, hortatur his verbis: "Inclina pauperi sine

Widows are a class who, both on account of their poverty, their age and natural disposition, indulge in unlimited freedom of speech. Now one should endure all these things in a generous spirit, and not be provoked either by their unreasonable annoyance or their unreasonable complaints. For this class of persons deserve to be pitied for their misfortunes, not to be insulted. On this account the wisest of men, having regard to the avarice and pride of human nature, and considering the nature of poverty and its terrible power to depress even the noblest character, and induce it often to act in these same respects without shame, in order that a man should not be irritated when accused, nor be provoked by continual importunity to become an enemy where he ought to bring aid,

tristitia aurem tuam, et responde illi in mansuetudine pacifica" (Ecclus 4:8); ac missum faciens eum qui exasperat (quid enim jacenti dixeris?) eum alloquitur qui ejus infirmitatem ferre possit, monens, ut vultus blanditie ac verborum mansuetudine etiam ante oblatum donum ipsum erigat. Oportet vero curatorem earum tanta esse aequanimitate, ut non modo indignatione sua dolorem non augeat, sed etiam cohortatione sua moerorem mitiget. Nam quemadmodum qui contumelia afficitur, et si facultatibus abundet, pecuniarum commodum non sentit ob inflictam contumeliae plagam; ita qui blande et leniter compellatur, et cum consolatione donum accipit, gaudet et laetatur, duplexque munus ex largiendi modo consequitur.

instructs him to be affable and accessible to the suppliant, saying, "Incline your ear to a poor man and give him a friendly answer with meekness" (Ecclus 4:8). And passing by the case of one who succeeds in exasperating (for what can one say to him who is overcome?), he addresses the man who is able to bear the other's infirmity, exhorting him before he bestows his gift to correct the suppliant by the gentleness of his countenance and the mildness of his words. One who has the charge of these persons ought to be so long-suffering, as not only not to increase their despondency by his fits of anger, but also to remove their anxiety by his exhortation. For as the man who has been insulted, although he is in the enjoyment of great abundance, does not feel the advantage of his wealth, on account of the blow which he has received from the insult; so on the other hand, the man who has been addressed with kindly words, and for whom the gift has been accompanied with encouragement, exults and rejoices all the more, and the thing given becomes doubled in value through the manner in which it is offered.

Sabbato: Ecclus 4:23–36
S. Augustinus, *Enarrationes in Psalmos* (in Ps 118, enarr. 21, 8)

"Omnis consummationis vidi finem; latum mandatum tuum valde" (Ps 118:96). Omnis autem consummatio mihi videtur hoc loco intellegenda, "usque ad mortem pro veritate certare" (Ecclus 4:33), et pro vero ac summo bono mala omnia tolerare: cujus consummationis finis est excellere in regno Christi, quod non habet finem; et habere ibi sine morte, sine dolore, et cum magno honore vitam, morte hujus vitae ac doloribus et opprobriis acquisitam. Quod autem addidit: "Latum mandatum tuum valde"; non intellego nisi caritatem. Quid enim profuisset quacumque morte imminente, et inter quantacumque tormenta illa martyria confiteri, si caritas in confitente non esset? Audiamus apostolum: "Etsi tradidero, inquit, corpus meum ut ardeam, caritatem autem non habeam, nihil mihi prodest" (1 Cor 13:3). "Caritas autem Dei diffusa est in cordibus nostris per Spiritum sanctum, qui datus est nobis" (Rom 5:5). Latum est ergo mandatum caritatis, mandatum

"I have seen an end of all consummation: but Thy commandment is exceeding broad" (Ps 118:96). For he had entered into the sanctuary of God and had understood the end. Now all consummation appears to me in this place to signify, "the striving even unto death for the truth" (Ecclus 4:33), and the endurance of every evil for the true and chief good: the end of which consummation is to excel in the Kingdom of Christ, which has no end; and there to have without death, without pain, and with great honor, life, acquired by the death of this life, and by sorrows and reproaches. But in what he has added, "Thy commandment is exceeding broad"; I understand only love. For what would it have profited him, whatever death impended over him, in the midst of whatsoever torment, to confess those testimonies, if love were not in the confessor? Let us hear the apostle: "If I give away all I have, and if I deliver up my body to be burned, but have not love, I gain nothing" (1 Cor 13:3).

illud geminum, quo jubetur Deus et proximus diligi. Quid autem latius, quam ut ubi pendeat tota lex et omnes Prophetae (cf. Mt 22:40)?

"God's love has been poured into our hearts through the Holy Spirit who has been given to us" (Rom 5:5). Broad therefore is the commandment of charity, that twofold commandment, whereby we are enjoined to love God and our neighbour. But what is broader than that, on which hang all the Law and the prophets (cf. Mt 22:40)?

INFRA HEBDOMADAM V AUGUSTI

Feria Secunda: Ecclus 7:1–15
S. Fulgentius Ruspensis, *De remissione peccatorum* (lib. 1, cap. 26)

Si qui etiam in Ecclesia catholica sunt, et male vivunt, priusquam istam vitam finiant, festinent ut a mala vita discedant; nec sibi putent ad salutem sufficere catholicum nomen, si Dei non faciant voluntatem. In Proverbiis unusquisque nostrum et timere Dominum jubetur, et a malo discedere. Ibi quippe dicitur: "Time Dominum, et declina ab omni malo, et erit pax corpori tuo, et diligentia ossibus tuis" (Prv 3:7–8). Nam et in libro Ecclesiastico, ne mala faciat unusquisque fidelium sic admonetur: "Noli facere mala, et non apprehendent te. Discede ab iniquo, et discedent

If there are any who are even in the Catholic Church and live evil lives, before they finish this life, let them hasten to give up the evil life, and let them not think that the Catholic name is enough for salvation, if they do not do the will of God. Wherefore also in Proverbs each one of us is commanded both to fear the Lord and to depart from evil. There it is said: "Fear the Lord and turn away from evil. It will be a healing for your flesh and a refreshment for your body" (Prv 3:7–8). And in the book of Ecclesiasticus, each of the faithful is thus warned against doing evil: "Do no evil and evil will never overtake you. Stay away from wrong

mala ab te. Ne semines mala in sulcis injuriae, et non metes illa in septuplum" (Ecclus 7:1–3). In eodem libro rursus ne quisquam peccata peccatis adiiciens de misericordia Dei velit sibi vana cogitatione blandiri, hujuscemodi verbis doctrina salutaris occurrit: "Ne adjicias peccatum super peccatum, et dicas: Miseratio Dei magna est; misericordia enim et ira ab illo, et in peccatores respiciet ira illius" (Ecclus 5:5–7). Et rursus sanctus Job dixit: "Nonne perditio erit iniquo, et alienatio facientibus iniquitatem?" (Jb 31:3). In Proverbiis scriptum est: "Iniquitates suae capient impium; funiculis autem peccatorum suorum unusquisque constringitur. Hic moritur cum indisciplinatis, de multitudine autem vitae suae proiectus est, et perit pro insipientia" (Prv 5:22–23).

and it will turn away from you. Do not sow in the furrows of injustice and you will not reap a sevenfold crop" (Ecclus 7:1–3). Again in the same book, lest anyone, adding sins to sins, wish to comfort himself vainly with the mercy of God, the salutary teaching comes to our attention in words such as these: "Do not be so confident of forgiveness that you add sin to sin. Do not say, His mercy is great for both mercy and wrath are with Him and His anger will rest on sinners" (Ecclus 5:5–7). And again the holy Job says, "Does not calamity befall the unrighteous and disaster, the worker of iniquity?" (Jb 31:3). In Proverbs it is written: "The iniquities of the wicked ensnare them, and they are caught in the toils of their sin. They die for lack of discipline and because of their great folly, they are lost" (Prv 5:22–23).

Feria Tertia: Ecclus 10:1–16

S. Rabanus Maurus, *Commentaria in Ecclesiasticum* (lib. 3, cap. 1)

"Secundum judicem populi, sic et ministri ejus; et qualis rector est civitatis, tales et inhabitantes in ea" (Ecclus 10:2) Civitas enim Christi sancta est Ecclesia, quae

"As the judge of the people is himself, so also are his ministers: and what manner of man the ruler of a city is, such also are they that dwell therein" (Ecclus 10:2). For the holy

ejus vestigia devoto cordis sequitur affectu, et bonorum operum imitatur effectu. Ubi et ministri ejus, hoc est rectores fidelium, et praedicatores sancti, ipsius mandatis sedulo obtemperantes erunt: aliisque similiter facere instanter praecipiunt. Vae ergo terrae, cujus rex est diabolus, semper novarum rerum cupidus; hic judices et principes eos habet, qui amant hujus saeculi voluptates, qui antequam dies mortis adveniat dicunt: "Manducemus et bibamus, eras enim moriemur" (1 Cor 15:32). E contra beata terra Ecclesiae, cujus rex Christus filius ingenuorum, de Abraham, et Isaac, et Jacob, prophetarum quoque et omnium sanctorum stirpe descendens, quibus peccatum non fuit dominatum, et ob id fuerunt liberi; principes quoque ejus sunt apostoli et omnes sancti, qui regem habent filium ingenuorum, nec comedunt mane, nec velociter. Non enim in praesenti saeculo quaerunt voluptatem, sed in tempore suo manducabunt, cum retributionis tempus advenerit.

city of Christ is the Church, which follows His steps with a devoted heart, and imitates them in the performance of good works. Where also His ministers, that is, the leaders of the faithful, and the holy preachers, will be diligently obedient to His commands: and they urgently command others to do the same. Woe therefore to the earth, whose king is the devil, always eager for new things; here are judges and rulers, those who love the pleasures of this world, who say before the day of death comes: "Let us eat and drink, for tomorrow we shall die" (1 Cor 15:32). On the other hand, the blessed land of the Church, whose king is Christ, the son of the pure, Who descends from Abraham, Isaac, and Jacob, from the prophets and all the saints, over Whom sin had no dominion, and for that reason they were free. The Church's leaders, too, are the apostles and all the saints, who have as their king the son of the innocent, and they do not eat in the morning, nor quickly. For they do not seek pleasure in this world, but they will eat it in their time, when the time of retribution has come.

Feria Quarta: Ecclus 13:1–6, 9–22
S. Leo Magnus Papa, *Sermones* (De Quadragesima, serm. 49, 2)

"Angustam esse arduam viam, quae ducit ad vitam" (Mt 7:14): et cum latitudo itineris ad mortem trahentis multis frequentetur agminibus, in salutis semitis paucorum intrantium sunt rara vestigia. Unde autem populosior est via leva, quam dextera, nisi quia ad mundana gaudia et corporalia bona multitudo proclivis est. Et quamvis caducum incertumque sit quod cupitur, libentius tamen suscipitur labor pro desiderio voluptatis, quam pro amore virtutis. Ita cum innumeri sint qui visibilia concupiscant, vix inveniuntur qui temporalibus aeterna praeponant. Magni est ergo operis et laboris, mobilitatem cordis ab omnibus continere peccatis, et cum undique innumerae voluptatum illecebrae blandiantur, ad nulla contagia vigorem animi relaxare. "Quis picem tangit et non inquinatur ab ea?" (Ecclus 13:1). quis non infirmatur in carne? quis non sordescit in pulvere? quis postremo est tantae puritatis, ut iis non polluatur, sine quibus vita non ducitur? Beata igitur mens, quae peregrinatio-

"Narrow and steep is the way that leads to life" (Mt 7:14); and while the breadth of the way that leads to death is crowded with a large company, the steps are few of those that tread the path of safety. And wherefore is the left road more thronged than the right, save that the multitude is prone to worldly joys and carnal goods? And although that which it desires is short-lived and uncertain, yet men endure toil more willingly for the lust of pleasure than for love of virtue. Thus, while those who crave things visible are unnumbered, those who prefer the eternal to the temporal are hardly to be found. A great work and toil it is then to keep our wayward heart from all sin, and, with the numberless allurements of pleasure to ensnare it on all sides, not to let the vigor of the mind give way to any attack. "Who touches pitch, and is not defiled thereby?" (Ecclus 13:1). Who is not weakened by the flesh? Who is not begrimed by the dust? Who, lastly, is of such purity as not to be polluted by those things without which one cannot live? Blessed,

nis suae tempora casta sobrietate transcurrit, et in iis quae necessa est eam ambulare, non remanet: ut hospita magis quam domina terrenorum, nec affectibus desit humanis, et promissionibus sit innixa divinis.

therefore, is the mind that passes the time of its pilgrimage in chaste sobriety and loiters not in the things through which it must walk, so that, as a stranger rather than the possessor of its earthly abode, it may not be wanting in human affections, and yet rest on the divine promises.

Feria Quinta: Ecclus 14:1–17
S. Rabanus Maurus, *Commentaria in Ecclesiasticum* (lib. 3, cap. 14)

"Beatus vir qui non est lapsus verbo ex ore suo, et non est stimulatus in tristitia delicti" (Ecclus 14:1). Beatum dicit eum esse qui verborum suorum cautelam habet, ne forte ea loquatur de quibus postmodum poeniteat: quia qui custodit os suum et linguam suam, custodit ab angustiis animam suam. Huic quippe sententiae concordant verba Jacobi, dicentis: "Si quis in verbo non offendit, hic perfectus est vir" (Jas 3:2). Sed quaeritur quomodo dicit perfectum esse virum, qui in verbo non offendit, cum praemitteret idem apostolus dicens: "In multis offendimus omnes" (Jas 3:2). Ad quod responderi potest quia diversae offensionum sunt species. Aliter namque electi, aliter

"Blessed is the man that hath not slipped by a word out of his mouth and is not pricked with the remorse of sin" (Ecclus 14:1). Blessed, he says, is he who is careful of his words, lest he speak those things of which he afterwards repents: for he that guards his mouth and his tongue, guards his soul from tribulations. Indeed, the words of James agree with this sentence, saying: "If any man offend not in word, the same is a perfect man" (Jas. 3:2). But it is asked how he says that a man is perfect who does not offend in his word, when the apostle foresaw the same thing, saying: "In many things we all offend" (Jas. 3:2). To which we can answer that there are different types of offenses. For in one way the elect offend, in another way the

offendunt reprobi, Salomone testante, qui ait: "Septies enim cadit justus, et resurgit: impii autem corruent in malum" (Prv 24:16). Etsi enim justus per fragilitatem carnis, vel ignorantiam forte offenderit, justus tamen esse non desistit, quia ut quotidiana est hujusmodi et inevitabilis offensio, ita est et quotidiana orationum ac bonorum operum medela, quae offendentem justum, ne in terram proruat, et nuptialem caritatis ac fidei vestem pulvere vitiorum sordidet, ocius erigit.

reprobate offend, as Solomon testifies, who says: "For a just man shall fall seven times and shall rise again: but the wicked shall fall down into evil" (Prv 24:16). For even if the just man offends through weakness of the flesh, or through ignorance, he does not cease to be just. For as this kind of offense is daily and inevitable, so is the daily remedy of prayers and good works, which raises up more quickly the just one who offends, lest he fall to the ground, and soil the nuptial garment of charity and faith with the dust of vices.

Feria Sexta: Ecclus 21:1–16
S. Fulgentius Ruspensis, *De fide* (cap. 3)

Omni homini in hac vita esse potest utilis paenitentia, quam quocunque tempore homo egerit, quamlibet iniquus, quamlibet annosus, si toto corde renuntiaverit peccatis praeteritis, et pro eis in conspectu Dei non solum corporis, sed etiam cordis lacrimas fuderit, et malorum operum maculas bonis operibus diluere curaverit, omnium peccatorum suorum indulgentiam mox habebit. Hoc enim nobis Dominus prophetico promittit eloquio dicens: "Si conversus fueris, et in-

Repentance can be useful to every man in this life, than at any time a man may have done, however wicked, however old, if he renounces his past sins with all his heart, and sheds for them in the sight of God not only the tears of the body, but also the tears of the heart, and if he took care to dilute the stains of bad deeds with good deeds, he will soon have the forgiveness of all his sins. For the Lord promises us this in a prophetic speech, saying: "If thou art converted and groan, thou wilt

gemueris, salvus eris" (Is 30:15). Et alio loco dicitur: "Fili, peccasti; ne adjicias iterum, sed et de praeteritis deprecare, ut tibi dimittantur" (Ecclus 21:1). Nunquam peccanti esset indicta pro peccatis deprecatio, si deprecanti non esset remissio concedenda. Sed etiam paenitentia peccatori tunc prodest, si eam in Ecclesia catholica gerat. In quacunque igitur homo aetate veram peccatorum suorum paenitentiam egerit, et vitam suam Deo illuminante correxerit, non privabitur indulgentiae munere. Verumtamen nullus hominum debet sub spe misericordiae Dei in suis diutius remanere peccatis, cum etiam in ipso corpore nemo velit sub spe futurae salutis diutius aegrotare.

be saved" (Is 30:15). And in another place it is said: "My son, hast thou sinned? do so no more: but for thy former sins also pray that they may be forgiven thee" (Ecclus 21:1). The sinner would never have been told to plead for his sins, if the suppliant had not been granted remission. But even repentance is useful to the sinner, if it is done in the Catholic Church. Therefore, at whatever age a person has done true penance for his sins and corrected his life by God's illumination, he will not be deprived of the gift of forgiveness. Nevertheless, no man ought to remain longer in his sins under the hope of God's mercy, since even in his body no one wants to be sick longer under the hope of future salvation.

Sabbato: Ecclus 32:1–17
S. Gregorius Magnus, *Regula pastoralis* (lib. 2, cap. 6)

Dum praelatus quisque plus se quam decet dejicit, subditorum vitam stringere sub disciplinae vinculo non possit. Teneant ergo rectores exterius quod pro aliorum utilitate suscipiunt; servent interius quod de sua aestimatione pertimescunt. Studeant igitur sine intermissione qui praesunt,

While any superior lowers himself more than is fit, he be unable to restrain the lives of his subordinates under the bond of discipline. Let rulers, then, maintain outwardly what they undertake for the benefit of others: let them retain inwardly what makes them fearful in their estimate of themselves. Therefore,

ut eorum potentia quanto magna exterius cernitur, tanto apud eos interius deprimatur, ne cogitationem vincat, ne in delectationem sui animum rapiat, ne jam sub se mens eam regere non possit, cui se libidine dominandi supponit. Ne enim praesidentis animus ad elationem potestatis suae delectatione rapiatur, recte per quemdam sapientem dicitur: "Ducem te constituerunt, noli extolli, sed esto in illis quasi unus ex illis" (Ecclus 32:1). Hinc etiam Petrus ait: "Non dominantes in clero, sed forma facti gregis" (1 Pt 5:3). Hinc per semetipsam Veritas ad altiora nos virtutum merita provocans, dicit: "Scitis quia principes gentium dominantur eorum, et qui majores sunt, potestatem exercent in eos. Non ita erit inter vos, sed quicunque voluerit inter vos major fieri, sit vester minister; et qui voluerit inter vos primus esse, erit vester servus: sicut Filius hominis non venit ministrari, sed ministrare" (Mt 20:25–28).

let those who preside study without intermission that in proportion as their power is seen to be great externally it be kept down within themselves internally; that it vanquish not their thought; that the heart be not carried away to delight in it; lest the mind become unable to control that which in lust of domination it submits itself to. For, lest the heart of a ruler should be betrayed into elation by delight in personal power, it is rightly said by a certain wise man: "They have made you a leader: lift not up yourself but be among them as one of them" (Ecclus 32:1). Hence also Peter says, "Not as being lords over God's heritage, but being made examples to the flock" (1 Pt 5:3). Hence the Truth in person, provoking us to higher virtuous desert, says, "You know that the princes of the Gentiles exercise dominion over them, and they that are greater exercise authority upon them. It shall not be so among you, but whosoever will be greater among you, let him be your minister; and whosoever will be chief among you, let him be your servant; even as the Son of Man came not to be ministered to, but to minister" (Mt 20:25–28).

INFRA HEBDOMADAM I SEPTEMBRIS
Feria Secunda: Jb 1:13–22
S. Gregorius Magnus, *Moralia in Job* (lib. 2, cap. 16)

Flagella Dei aut non sentire, aut nimis, vitium est. Nonnulli magnae constantiae philosophiam putant, si disciplinae asperitate correpti, ictus verberum doloresque non sentiant. Nonnulli vero tam nimis percussionum flagella sentiunt, ut immoderato dolore commoti, etiam in excessum linguae dilabantur. Non est enim pondus verae virtutis, insensibilitas cordis: quia et valde insana per stuporem membra sunt, quae et incisa dolore nequaquam possunt. Rursus virtutis custodiam deserit, qui dolorem verberum ultra quam necesse est sentit; quia dum nimia afflictione cor tangitur, usque ad impatientiae contumelias excitatur, et qui per flagella corrigere malefacta debuerat, agit ut nequitia per flagellum crescat. Contra insensibilitatem quippe percussorum per prophetam dicitur: "Percussisti eos, nec doluerunt; attrivisti eos, et renuerunt accipere disciplinam" (Jer 5:3). Contra pusillanimitatem percussorum per psalmistam dicitur:

There are some who account it a high degree of philosophical fortitude, if, when corrected by severe discipline, they are insensible to the strokes, and to the pains of those stripes. And there are some who feel to such excess the infliction of the blows, that under the influence of immediate grief, they even fall into excesses of the tongue. The weightiness of true virtue consists not in dullness of heart, as also those limbs are very unhealthy from numbness which cannot feel any pain even when cut. Again, he deserts his guard over virtue, who feels the pain of chastisement beyond what is necessary; for while the heart is affected with excessive sorrow, it is stirred up to the extent of impatient reviling, and he who ought to have amended his misdeeds by means of the stripes, does his part that his wickedness should be increased by the correction. Agreeably to which, against the insensibility in the chastised, the words of the prophet are, "Thou hast stricken them, but they have

"In miseriis non subsistent" (Ps 139:11). In miseriis namque subsisterent, si aequanimiter adversa tolerarent. At postquam mente inter flagella corruunt, quasi inter illatas miserias subsistendi constantiam perdunt. Beatus itaque Job, quia verae philosophiae regulam tenuit, contra utraque mira se aequitatis arte servavit; ut nec dolorem non sentiens, flagella sperneret; nec rursum ultra modum dolorem sentiens, contra judicium flagellantis insaniret. Cunctis enim rebus perditis, cunctis liberis amissis (cf. Jb 1:13–19), "surrexit, scidit vestimenta sua, et tonso capite corruens in terram, adoravit" (Jb 1:20).

not grieved; Thou hast consumed them, but they have refused to receive correction" (Jer 5:3). Against the faintheartedness of the chastened the psalmist hath it, "They will never stand fast in adversity" (Ps 139:11); for they would "stand fast in adversity," if they bore calamities with patience, but so soon as they sink in spirit, when pressed with blows, they as it were lose the firmness of their footing, amidst the miseries inflicted on them. Thus, because blessed Job observed the rule of the true philosophy, he kept himself from either extreme with the evenness of a marvelous skill, that he might not by being insensible to the pain contemn the strokes, nor again, by feeling the pain immoderately, be hurried madly against the visitation of the Striker. For when all his substance was lost, all his children gone (cf. Jb 1:13–19), "he rose up, and rent his mantle, and shaved his head, and fell down upon the ground, and worshipped" (Jb 1:20).

Feria Tertia: Jb 2:1–13
S. Joannes Chrysostomus, *Fragmenta in beatum Job* (cap. 2, 10)

"Si bona suscepimus de manu Domini, mala cur non sustinebimus?" (Jb 2:10). An judicem cogemus, eumdem rerum statum nobis perpetum tribuere? an Dominum docebimus, quemadmodum vita nostra traducenda sit? Ille suorum decretorum potestatem habet, suo arbitratu nostra dispensat: sapiens autem est, et servis suis, quod utile est, largitur. Ne curiosius in Domini judicium inquirendo, tu iis quae ab ejus prudentia dispensantur, solum acquiescito; quidquid tibi dederit, id libenter accipe, in rebus tristibus ostende te non indignum fuisse hilaritate et laetitia qua prius fruebaris. Hac Jobus oratione diaboli incursionem atque impetum repulit, ac propter acceptam cladem, pudorem maximum ei incussit. Ipso oris vultu, contra peccatum summum zelum ostendit, et qui tale improbi daemonis impetum placate et aequanimiter tulit, is adhortationem ad scelus ferre non potuit, ratus scelerata illa quae audierat, acerbiora multo, quam tela quae corpori inhaerebant infixa, et uxorem suam

"If we have received good things at the hand of God, why should we not bear evils?" (Jb 2:10). Shall we compel the judge to grant us the same state of affairs forever? Shall we teach the Lord how our life should proceed? He has the power of His own decrees and disposes of us at His discretion: but He is wise, and bestows on His servants what is useful. Inquiring not more curiously into the Lord's judgment, you must just be content with those things which are dispensed by His prudence; whatever He gives you, accept it gladly, showing in sad things that you were not unworthy of the gaiety and joy which you formerly enjoyed. By this prayer Job repulsed the devil's attack, and because of the defeat he had received, it inculcated into him the greatest reverence. By the very look of his mouth, he showed the highest zeal against sin, and he who took such a wicked attack of the demon with calmness and equanimity, could not bear the incitement to crime, thinking that the crimes about which he had heard were much more bitter than

his verbis objurgavit. Quemadmodum curationem libenti animo admisimus, sic etiam disciplinam moderate feramus: bona, enim dicit, quae delectant, mala vero, tentationes.

the weapons that stuck to the body, and with these words he reprehends his wife. Just as we accept health treatment with a willing heart, so also we should exercise discipline in moderation: for good things, he says, are things that delight, but bad things are temptations.

Feria Quarta: Jb 3:1–16
S. Gregorius Magnus, *Moralia in Job* (lib. 4, cap. 21)

Peccatum quippe peccato adicit qui male gesta etiam defendit; et "noctem solitariam non relinquit" (Jb 3:7) qui culpae suae tenebris etiam patrocinia defensionis adjungit. Hinc est quod primus homo de erroris sui nocte requisitus, eamdem noctem esse solitariam noluit, quia dum requisitione ad paenitentiam vocaretur, ei adminicula excusationis adiunxit dicens: "Mulier, quam dedisti sociam mihi, dedit mihi de ligno et comedi" (Gn 3:12). Scilicet excessus sui vitium in auctorem latenter intorquens, ac si diceret: Tu occasionem delinquendi praebuisti qui mulierem dedisti. Hinc est, quod hujus erroris ramus in humano genere ex illa nunc usque radice protrahitur, ut

He adds sin to sin, who over and above maintains what he has done amiss; and "he does not leave the night alone" (Jb. 3:7), who adds the support of vindication also to the darkness of his fault. It is hence that the first man, when called in question concerning the "night" of his error, would not have the same "night" to be "solitary," in that while by that questioning he was called to repentance, he added the props of self-exculpation, saying, "The woman whom Thou gavest to be with me, she gave me of the tree, and I did eat" (Gn 3:12); that is, covertly turning the fault of his transgression upon his Maker; as if he said, Thou gavest me occasion of transgressing, Who gavest me the woman. It is hence that in the hu-

quod male agitur, adhuc etiam defendatur. Dicat ergo: "Sit nox illa solitaria, nec laude digna" (Jb 3:7). Ac si aperte exoret, dicens: Culpa quam fecimus, sola remaneat, ne dum laudatur et defenditur, in conspectu nos judicis multiplicius astringat. Peccare quidem non debuimus; sed utinam alia non jungentes, vel ea quae fecimus sola deseramus.

man race the branch of this sin is drawn out from that root so far as to this present time, that what is done amiss should be yet further maintained. Let him say then, "Let that light be solitary, and not worthy of any praise" (Jb 3:7). As though he besought in plain words, Let the fault that we have done remain alone, lest while it is praised and upheld, it binds us a hundredfold more in the sight of our Judge. We ought not indeed to have sinned, but would that, by not adding others, we would even leave those by themselves, which we have committed.

Feria Quinta: Jb 4:1–18
S. Gregorius Magnus, *Moralia in Job* (lib. 5, cap. 17)

Sive haeretici quorum amicos beati Job tenere speciem diximus, sive perversi quilibet quam inordinate redarguunt, tam reprehenssibiliter exhortantur. Ait namque: "Quis umquam innocens periit, aut quando recti deleti sunt?" (Jb 4:7). Saepe quippe hic et innocentes pereunt et recti funditus delentur; sed tamen ad aeternam gloriam pereundo servantur. Si enim nullus innocens periret, propheta non diceret: "Justus

Whether it be heretics, of whom we have said that the friends of blessed Job bore an image, or whether any of the forward ones, they are as blamable in their admonitions, as they are immoderate in their condemnation. For he says, "Whoever perished being innocent? or where were the righteous cut off?" (Jb 4:7). Since it often happens that in this life both "the innocent perish," and the righteous are "utterly cut off," yet in perishing they are reserved to

periit et nemo est qui recogitet" (Is 57:1). Si rectos Deus providendo non raperet, nequaquam de justo Sapientia dixisset: Raptus est ne malitia mutaret intellectum ejus (Ws 4:11). Si justos animadversio nulla percuteret, Petrus minime praenuntiaret dicens: "Tempus ut incipiat judicium de domo Dei" (1 Pt 4:17). Illi ergo veraciter recti sunt qui amore supernae patriae ad cuncta praesentis citae adcersa praeparantur. Nam qui pro aeternis bonis mala hic perpeti metuunt, videlicet recti non sunt. Sed Eliphaz vel deleri rectos, vel innocentes hic perire non aestimat quia saepe hi qui non spe caelestis gloriae, sed pro terrena Deo retributione deserviunt, ipsi sibimet fingunt quod quaerunt. Et docere praesumentes, cum terrenam securitatem praedicant, cunctis suis laboribus ostendunt quid amant.

glory eternal. For if none that is innocent perished, the prophet would not say, "The righteous perisheth, and no man layeth it to heart" (Is 57:1). If God did not providentially snatch away the upright, Wisdom would never have said of the just: "He is snatched away lest wickedness should change his understanding" (Wis 4:11). If no visitation ever smote the righteous, Peter would never foretell it, saying, "For the time is come that judgment must begin at the house of God" (1 Pt 4:17). They then are really righteous, who are furnished forth by the love of the country above to meet all the ills of the present life. For all that fear to endure ills here, for the sake of eternal blessings, clearly are not righteous men. But Eliphaz does not take account either that the righteous are cut off, or that the innocent perish here, in that oftentimes they that serve God, not in the hope of heavenly glory, but for an earthly recompense, make a fiction in their own head of that which they are seeking after, and, taking upon themselves to be instructors, in preaching earthly immunity, they shew by all their pains what is the thing they love.

Feria Sexta: Jb 6:1–13
S. Gregorius Magnus, *Moralia in Job* (lib. 7, cap. 14)

"Aut potest aliquis gustare quod gustatum affert mortem?" (Jb 6:6). Durum quippe est appetere quod cruciat, sequi quod vitam fugat. Sed plerumque mens justi ad tantum se virtutis culmen extendit ut et apud se internae rationis arce, praesideat, et quorumdam foris stultitiam tolerando convertat. Quos enim ad fortia trahere nitimur, eorum necesse est ut infirma toleremus quia nec jacentem erigit, nisi qui status sui rectitudinem per compassionem flectit. Cum vero alienae infirmitati compatimur, valentius a nostra roboramur; ut amore futurorum mens ad praesentia adversa se praeparet etcruciatus corporis quos timebat exspectet. Auctis namque desideriis caelestibus angustatur; cumque aetrnae patriae quanta sit dulcedo considerat, pro ea praesentis vitae amaritudines ardenter amat.

"Or can anyone taste that, which by being tasted brings death?" (Jb 6:6). For it is hard to seek after that which torments, to follow that which makes life depart. But very often the life of the righteous stretches itself up to such a height of virtue, that both within it rules in the citadel of interior reason, and without, by bearing with it, brings the folly of some to conversion; for we must needs bear with the weaknesses of those, whom we are striving to draw on to strong things. For neither does any man lift up one that is fallen, save he, who in compassion bends the uprightness of his position. But when we compassionate the weakness of another, we are the more strongly nerved as to our own; so that, from love of the things of futurity, the soul prepares itself to meet the ills of the present time, and looks out for the hurts of the body, which it used to fear. For its heavenly aspirations being enlarged, it is more and more straitened, and when it sees how great is the sweetness of the eternal land, it fervently loves for the sake of that the bitter tastes of the present life.

Sabbato: Jb 7:1–12
S. Gregorius Magnus, *Moralia in Job* (lib. 8, cap. 10)

Quod tamen si ex voce Ecclesiae universalis accipimus, aliquando hanc procul dubio carnis putredine, aliquando autem gravari sordibus pulveris invenimus. Multi quippe in ea sunt qui, dum amori carnis inserviunt, fetore luxuriae computrescunt. Et sunt nonnulli qui a voluptate quidem carnis abstinent sed tamen tota mente in terrenis actibus jacent. Dicat ergo sancta Ecclesia unius membri sui vocibus, dicat quid de utroque genere hominum tolerat: "Induta est caro mea putredine et sordibus pulveris" (Jb 7:5). Ac si aperte insinuet dicens: Sunt plerique qui mihi per fidem membra sunt, sed tamen sana vel munda per actionem non sunt; quia aut victi desideriis turpibus, ad corruptionis putredinem defluunt, aut terrenis actibus dediti, pulvere consperguntur. In illis enim quos lubricas tolero carnem videlicet putrescentem gemo, in istis autem quos terram quaerentes patior quid aliudquam foedatam pulvere porto?

If we take this in the voice of the Holy Church universal, doubtless we find her at one time sunk to the earth by the corruption of the flesh, at another time by the defilement of dust. For she has many in her, who whilst they are devoted to the love of the flesh, turn corrupt with the putrefaction of excess. And there are some that keep indeed from the gratification of the flesh yet grovel with all their heart in earthly practices. So let Holy Church say in the words of one of her members, let her say what she undergoes from either sort of men, "My flesh is clothed with corruption, and the defilements of dust" (Jb 7:5). As if she told in plain words, saying, There are very many that are members of me in faith, yet these are not sound or pure members in practice: in that either being mastered by foul desires, they run out in the rottenness of corruption; or, being devoted to earthly practices, they are besmeared with dust. For in those, whom I must endure, that are full of wantonness, I do plainly lament for the flesh turned corrupt; and in

those, whom I suffer from, that are seeking the earth, what else is this but that I carry it defiled with dust?

INFRA HEBDOMADAM II SEPTEMBRIS

Feria Secunda: Jb 27:1–15
S. Ambrosius, *De Spiritu Sancto* (lib. 2, cap. 7)

Dicit enim alibi sanctus Job: "Vivit Dominus, qui sic me judicat; et omnipotens, qui ad amaritudinem perduxit animam meam: Spiritus autem divinus, qui est in naribus meis" (Jb 27:2–3). Non utique spiritum hic auram vitalem hanc et spiramentum corporeum designavit, sed nares hic interioris sui hominis significat, quibus vitae odorem carpebat aeternae, et gratiam caelestis unguenti geminis quibusdam sensibus hauriebat. Sunt enim nares spiritales, ut legimus, quas habet Sponsa Verbi, cui dicitur: "Et odor naris tuae" (Cant 7:8); et alibi: "Odoratus est Dominus odorem suavitatis" (Gn 8:21). Sunt ergo quaedam interioris membra hominis, cujus manus in actu, aures in auditu, pedes in processu quodam boni operis aestimantur. Itaque ex officiis, veluti quasdam colligimus membrorum figuras; neque enim in interiore

In a certain place holy Job says: "As the Lord lives, Who thus judges me, and the Almighty, Who has brought my soul to bitterness, for the Spirit of God which is in my nostrils" (Jb 27:2–3). He certainly did not here signify by His Spirit the vital breath and bodily breathing passages but signifies the nostrils of the inner man within him, wherewith he gathered in the fragrance of eternal life, and drew in the grace of the heavenly ointment as with a kind of twofold sense. For there are spiritual nostrils, as we read, which the spouse of the Word has, to whom it is said: "And the smell of your nostrils" (Cant 7:8); and in another place: "The Lord smelled a smell of sweetness" (Gn 8:21). There are, then, as it were, inward members of a man, whose hands are considered to be in action, his ears in hearing, his feet in a kind of progress in a good work. And so,

homine secundum carnalia aliquid nos convenit opinari. Et sunt quidam qui corporaliter Deum putant esse formatum, cum legunt aut manum ejus, aut digitum: nec advertunt quod haec non propter formam scripta sint corporis, quia in divinitate nec membra, nec partes sunt: sed propter unitatem divinitatis expressa, ut credamus quia impossibile est a Patre Deo vel Filium, vel Spiritum sanctum separari.

from what is done we gather as it were figures of the members, for it is not suitable for us to imagine anything in the inner man after a fleshly manner. And there are some who suppose that God is fashioned after a bodily manner, when they read of His hand or finger, and they do not observe that these things are written not because of any fashion of a body, since in the Godhead are neither members nor parts, but are expressions of the oneness of the Godhead, that we may believe that it is impossible for either the Son or the Holy Spirit to be separated from God the Father.

Feria Tertia: Jb 28:12–28
S. Augustinus, *Epistulae* (Hieronymo, De sententia Jacobi liber, ep. 167, cap. 11)

Virtus magna sit sapientia: dixit autem ipsa sapientia homini, "Ecce pietas est sapiential" (Jb 28:28). Absit ergo ut dicamus tot ac tantos fideles et pios homines Dei non habere pietatem, quam Graeci εὐσέβειαν vel expressius et plenius θεοσέβειαν vocant: quid autem est pietas, nisi Dei cultus? et unde ille colitur, nisi caritate? Caritas igitur de corde

Wisdom is a great virtue, and wisdom herself has said to man, "Behold the fear of the Lord, that is wisdom" (Jb 28:28). Far be it from us, then, to say that so many and so great believing and pious men have not the fear of the Lord, which the Greeks call εὐσέβεια, or more literally and fully, θεοσέβεια. And what is the fear of the Lord but His worship? And whence is He truly wor-

puro et conscientia bona et fide non ficta, magna et vera virtus est, quia "ipsa est et finis praecepti" (1 Tm 1:5). Huic subservit scientia, cum est utilis; nam sine illa inflat (cf. 1 Cor 8:1): quod vero illa aedificando impleverit, nihil ibi ista inane quod inflet, inveniet. Utilem porro scientiam definiendo monstravit, ubi cum dixisset: "Ecce pietas est sapientia; continuo subiunxit: Abstinere vero a malis, scientia est" (Jb 28:28). Cur ergo non dicimus, qui hanc virtutem habet, habere omnes; cum plenitudo legis sit caritas (cf. Rom 13:10)? An quanto magis est in homine, tanto magis est virtute praeditus.

shipped except from love? Love, then, out of a pure heart, and a good conscience, and faith unfeigned, is the great and true virtue, because "it is the end of the commandment" (1 Tm 1:5). Without love "knowledge puffs up" (1 Cor 8:1), but where love, by edifying, has filled the heart, there knowledge will find nothing empty which it can puff up. He further showed the usefulness of knowledge by defining it; where, after saying: "Behold, piety is wisdom," he immediately added: "But to abstain from evil is knowledge" (Jb 28:28). Why do we not then say that the man who has this virtue has all virtues, since love is the fulfilling of the Law (cf. Rom 13:10)? Is it not true that, the more love exists in a man the more he is endowed with virtue.

Feria Quarta: Jb 31:1–18
S. Gregorius Magnus, *Moralia in Job* (lib. 21, cap. 12)

Beatus Job crimen luxuriae definiens, ait: "Ignis est usque ad perditionem devorans" (Jb 31:12), quia nimirum reatus facinoris non solum usque ad inquinationem maculat, sed usque ad perditionem devorat. Et quia quamlibet

Blessed Job in characterizing the crime of lust says, "It is a fire that consumes to destruction" (Jb 31:12), in this way, that the heinousness of this atrocity not only stains to the length of defilement but devours to the extent of de-

alia fuerint bona opera, si luxuriae scelus non abluitur, immensitate hujus criminis obruuntur, secutus adiunxit: "Et omnia eradicans genimina" (Jb 31:12). Genimina quippe sunt animae operationes bonae. Cui tamen si perverso ordine caro dominatur, igne luxuriae omnia bene prolata concremantur. Nulla quippe ante omnipotentis Dei oculos justitiae pietatisque sunt opera quae corruptionis contagio monstrantur immunda. Quid enim prodest si pie quisquam necessitati compatitur proximi, quando impie semetipsum destruit habitationem Dei? Si ergo per cordis munditiam libidinis flamma non exstinguitur, incassum quaelibet virtutes oriuntur. Ignis quippe terram atque ejus nascentia comedit (cf. Dt 32:22), cum libido carnem, atque per hanc omnia bene acta consumit. Sed solent nonnullos ad humilitatem vitia sternere, atque ad tumorem mentis virtutes elevare.

struction. And because howsoever many other good deeds there may be, if the enormity of lust is not washed out, they are overwhelmed by the immensity of this crime, he added going on, "and rooting out all offsprings" (Jb 31:12). For the offsprings of the soul are good acts. Which soul, nevertheless, if the right order being reversed, the flesh exercises dominion over, all the things that are put forth well are consumed by the fire of lust. For before the eyes of Almighty God the works of righteousness and of pitifulness are none at all, which are shewn to view unclean by the infection of corruptness. For what does it profit, if a man heartily compassionates the need of his neighbour, whilst he heartlessly destroys himself, being the habitation of God? So then if by purity of the heart the flame of lust be not quenched, any virtues whatever spring up in vain. For a fire consumes the earth and her increase (cf. Dt 32:22), when lust consumes the flesh, and all things done well thereby. But some there are whom vices are apt to bring down to humility, and virtues exalt to pride of heart.

Feria Quinta: Jb 38:1–20
S. Gregorius Magnus, *Moralia in Job* (lib. 28, cap. 5)

"Ubi eras quando ponebam fundamenta terrae?" (Jb 38:4). In Scriptura sacra quid aliud fundamenta quam praedicatores accipimus? Quosdum primos Dominus in sancta Ecclesia posuit, tota in eis sequentis fabricae structura surrexit. Unde et sacerdos cum tabernaculum ingreditur duodecim lapides portare in pectore jubetur (cf. Ex 28:21), quia videlicet semetipsum pro nobis sacrificium offerens pontifex noster, dum fortes in ipso exordio praedicatores exhibuit, duodecim lapides sub capite in prima sui corporis parte portavit. Sancti itaque apostoli et pro prima ostensione ornamenti lapides sunt in pectore, et pro prima soliditate aedificii in solo, fundamenta. Unde David propheta cum sanctam Ecclesiam in sublimibus apostolorum mentibus poni aedificarique conspiceret, dixit: "Fundamenta ejus in montibus sanctis" (Ps 86:1). Cum vero in sacro eloquio non fundamenta, sed singulari numero fundamentum dicitur, nullus alius nisi ipse Dominus designatur, per cujus

"Where wast thou, when I was laying the foundations of the earth?" (Jb 38:4). In Holy Scripture what else do we understand by foundations but holy preachers? For since God had placed them first in the Church, the whole structure of the subsequent fabric has risen up upon them. Whence also the priest is ordered, when he enters the tabernacle, to bear twelve stones on his breast (cf. Ex 28:21). Because, namely, our High Priest, in offering Himself a sacrifice for us, when He set forth mighty preachers at the very beginning, carried twelve stones under His head in the front of His body. The holy apostles therefore are stones on the breast, to be displayed as an ornament in front, and foundations in the ground for the first firm basis of the edifice. And hence when David the prophet beheld Holy Church established and built on the lofty minds of the apostles, he says: "Her foundations are on the holy hills" (Ps 86:1) But when in Holy Scripture foundations are not spoken of, but a foundation, in the singular num-

divinitatis potentiam, nutantia infirmitatis nostrae corda solidantur. Ipse quippe fundamentum fundamentorum est, quia et origo est incohantium, et constantia robustorum.

ber, no one is designated, except the Lord Himself, by the power of Whose divinity the tottering hearts of our infirmity are made strong. For He is in truth the foundation of the foundations, because He is the first commencement of beginners, and the constancy of the strong.

Feria Sexta: Jb 40:1–11; 42:1–6
S. Gregorius Magnus, *Moralia in Job* (lib. 32, cap. 5)

"Si habes brachium sicut Deus et si voce simili tonas?" (Jb 40:4). Cum in Deo vox et brachium dicitur, cavendum summopere est, ne quid in eum mens corporeum suspicetur. In antropomorphitarum namque haeresim cadere est, eum qui incircumscripte implet et circumplectitur omnia intra corporalia lineamenta concludere. Sed omnipotens Deus ad sua nos trahens, usque ad nostra se humiliat, atque ut alta insinuet, humilibus condescendit, quatenus parvulorum animus rebus cognitis enutritus, ad inquirenda exsurgat incognita; atque ab eo qui longe super ipsum est quaedam juxta se audiens, quasi quibusdam ad illum passibus moveatur. Unde fit ut per scripturam suam aliquando

"Hast thou an arm like God, and dost thou thunder with a voice like Him?" (Jb 40:4). When a voice and arm are spoken of in God, we must take the greatest care that our mind imagines nothing corporeal in Him. For to confine Him within the lineaments of a body, Who without circumscription fills and embraces all things, is to fall into the heresy of the Anthropomorphites. But Almighty God, in drawing us to His own things, humbles Himself even to ours, and, to teach lofty, condescends to lowly things; in order that the mind of little ones, being nourished with the things it knows, may rise to enquire into those it knows not, and hearing from Him Who is far above it, some truths nigh itself, may move, as it were, some

a corporibus hominum, aliquando a mentibus, aliquando vero ab avibus, aliquando etiam ab insensatis rebus quasdam longe dissimiles in se similitudines trahat. "In scapulis suis obumbrabit tibi" (Ps 90:4). Constat nimirum quod in natura sua nec oculum Deus, nec scapulas habeat, sed quia nos per oculum cernimus, in scapulis vero onera sustinemus. Deus quod omnia videat, oculum habere perhibetur; quod vero nos tolerat, atque eo ipso quo tolerat servat, obumbrare nobis in scapulis dicitur.

steps towards Him. Whence it happens, that in His own Scripture He sometimes from the bodies of men, sometimes from their minds, but sometimes from birds, and sometimes even from insensate objects, applies to Himself some very unlikely resemblances. "He will make a shadow for thee with His shoulders" (Ps 90:4). It is doubtless admitted that God in His own nature has neither eye, nor shoulders; but since we see with our eye, but support burdens on our shoulders, God, because He sees all things, is said to have an eye; but because He carries us, and by carrying preserves us, He is said to make a shadow for us with His shoulders.

Sabbato: Jb 42:7–16
S. Gregorius Magni, *Moralia in Job* (lib. 35, cap. 15)

"Dominus autem benedixit novissimis Job magis quam principio ejus" (Jb 42:12). Haec historice facta credimus, haec mystice facienda speramus. Magis enim novissimis Job quam principio benedicitur, quia quantum ad Israelitici populi susceptionem pertinet, urgente fine praesentis saeculi, dolorem sanctae Eccle-

"The Lord blessed the latter end of Job more than his beginning" (Jb 42:12). We believe that these things have taken place historically, we hope that they are to take place mystically. For the latter end of Job is blessed more than his beginning, because as far as concerns the admission of the People of Israel, when the end of the present

siae Dominus animarurn multiplici collectione consolatur. Tanto quippe locupletius ditabitur, quanto et manifestius innotescit quod ad finem praesentis vitae temporalitas urgetur. Praedicatores namque sanctae Ecclesiae benedictione extremi temporis psalmista ditari conspexerat, cum dicebat: "Adhuc multiplicabuntur in senecta uberi, et bene patientes erunt, ut annuntient" (Ps 91:15–16). In senecta scilicet uberi multiplicantur, quia cum eorum vita differtur, semper ad melius fortitudo producitur, eisque per augmentum temporum crescunt etiam lucra meritorum. Bene autem patientes sunt ut annuntient, quia caelestia praedicantes, tanto robustius adversa tolerant, quanto et per tolerantiam suam animarum commoda locupletius reportant.

world is pressing on, the Lord consoles the pain of Holy Church by a manifold ingathering of souls. For then she will be the more abundantly enriched, the more clearly it becomes known that the temporal condition of the present life is hurrying to its close. For the psalmist had beheld the preachers of Holy Church enriched with the blessing of the latter times, when he said: "They shall still be multiplied in a fruitful old age and shall be well patient to announce" (Ps 91:15–16). They are in truth multiplied in a fruitful old age, because, when their life is prolonged, their strength is ever carried on to a better condition, and the gains of their merits are increased by means of the increase of their age. But they are well patient to announce, because, when preaching heavenly truths, they endure adversities with greater firmness, the more abundantly they bring back benefits for their souls by their very endurance.

INFRA HEBDOMADAM III SEPTEMBRIS
Feria Secunda: Tb 2:1–18
S. Beda Venerabilis, *Allegorica interpretatio in Tobiam* (cap. 2)

Fatigatus est a sepultura, et caecatus (cf. Tb 2:10–11), quia qui infatigabilis in bonis operibus persistit, nunquam fidei luce privatur. Insultabant Tobiae cognati (cf. Tb 2:8, 15), exprobrabat et uxor (cf. Tb 2:22–23), quasi frustra Deo servisset. Quos increpans ille, et instruens, ad Deum se orando convertit. Erant in populo illo quidam qui stulta temeritate ipsius populi miseriis insultarent, quae a felicitate prisca sanctorum patrum, qui apud eos quondam Deo sublimiter serviebant, jam luce distaret. Quos idem populus per doctores quosque et electos suos corrigere sedulus curabat, seseque ad implorandam Dei clementiam pro aeternae vitae perceptione convertebat. Nec ab re debet videri, quae idem Tobias et caecus, et verbum Dei praedicans (cf. Tb 2:11–18), reprobos simul et electos significare dicitur. Nam et Jacob patriarcha, cum angelo, luctans et claudus pariter est factus et benedictus (cf. Gn 32:24–26); in claudicatione vide-

He was tired from the burial, and blinded (cf. Tb 2:10–11), because he who tirelessly perseveres in good works is never deprived of the light of faith. Tobias's relatives insulted him (cf. Tb 2:8, 15), his wife also reproached him (cf. Tb 2:22–23), as if he had served God in vain. Rebuking them, and instructing them, he turned to God in prayer. There were some among that people who, with their foolish rashness, insulted the miseries of their people, which were now far removed from the ancient happiness of the holy fathers, who among them once served God sublimely. The same people, through their teachers and their chosen ones, diligently took care to correct them, and turned themselves to implore the mercy of God for the perception of eternal life. Nor should it be seen from the fact that the same Tobias being blind, preached the Word of God (cf. Tb 2:11–18), signifying thereby both the reprobate and the elect. For the patriarch Jacob, wrestling with the angel, became both lame

licet infideles suae gentis significans, in benedictione fideles.

and blessed (cf. Gn 32:24–26); in the lameness, to wit, signifying the unfaithful of his nation, the faithful in the blessing.

Feria Tertia: Tb 2:19–3:6
S. Augustinus, *Ep. 130 ad Probam* (cap. 25–26)

Molestiae tribulationesque temporales plerumque prosunt, vel ad sanandum tumorem superbiae, vel ad probandam exercendamve patientiam, cui probatae et exercitatae clarior merces uberiorque servatur, vel ad quaecumque flagellanda et abolenda peccata; tamen nos nescientes quid ista prosint, ab omni tribulatione optamus liberari? In his ergo tribulationibus quae possunt et prodesse et nocere, quid oremus, sicut oportet, nescimus: et tamen quia dura, quia molesta, quia contra sensum nostrae infirmitatis sunt, universali humana voluntate, ut a nobis haec auferantur, oramus. Sed hoc devotionis debemus Domino Deo nostro, ut si ea non abstulerit, non ideo nos ab eo neglegi existimemus, sed potius pia patientia malorum, bona speremus ampliora: sic enim virtus in infirmitate perficitur. si aliquid

Vexations and troubles in this world are for the most part profitable either to heal the swelling of pride, or to prove and exercise patience, for which, after such probation and discipline, a greater reward is reserved, or to punish and eradicate some sins; but we, not knowing what beneficial purpose these may serve, desire to be freed from all tribulation? We know not what to pray for as we ought regarding tribulations, which may do us good or harm; and yet, because they are hard and painful, and against the natural feelings of our weak nature, we pray, with a desire which is common to mankind, that they may be removed from us. But we ought to exercise such submission to the will of the Lord our God, that if He does not remove those vexations, we do not suppose ourselves to be neglected by Him, but rather, in patient endurance of

contra quam oramus acciderit, patienter ferendo, et in omnibus gratias agendo, hoc potius oportuisse quod Dei, non quod nostra voluntas habuit, minime dubitare debemus.

evil, hope to be made partakers of greater good, for so His strength is perfected in our weakness. If anything is ordered in a way contrary to our prayer, we ought, patiently bearing the disappointment, and in everything giving thanks to God, to entertain no doubt whatever that it was right that the will of God and not our will should be done.

Feria Quinta: Tb 12:1–17
S. Cyprianus, *De mortalitate* (cap. 10-11)

Tobias, post opera magnifica, post misericordiae suae multa et gloriosa praeconia, caecitatem luminum passus, timens et benedicens in adversis Deum, per ipsam corporis sui cladem crevit ad laudem; quem et ipsum uxor sua depravare tentavit dicens: "Ubi sunt justitiae tuae? Ecce quae pateris" (Tb 2:14). At ille, circa timorem Dei stabilis et firmus, et ad omnem tolerantiam passionis fide religionis armatus, tentationi uxoris invalidae in dolore non cessit, sed magis Deum patientia majore promeruit. Quem postmodum Raphael angelus collaudat et dicit: "Opera Dei revelare et confiteri honorificum est. Nam, quando

Tobias, after his excellent works, after the many and glorious illustrations of his merciful spirit, having suffered the loss of his sight, fearing and blessing God in his adversity, by his very bodily affliction increased in praise; and even him also his wife tried to pervert, saying, "Where are your righteousnesses? Behold what you suffer" (Tb 2:14). But he, steadfast and firm in respect of the fear of God, and armed by the faith of his religion to all endurance of suffering, yielded not to the temptation of his weak wife in his trouble, but rather deserved better from God by his greater patience; and afterwards Raphael the angel praises him, saying, "It is honorable to show forth and to

orabas tu et Sara nurus tua, ego obtuli memoriam orationis vestrae in conspectu claritatis Dei. Et cum sepelires tu mortuos simpliciter, et quia non es cunctatus exsurgere et derelinquere prandium tuum, et abisti et condidisti mortuum, missus sum tentare te, et iterum me misit Deus curare te et Saram nurum tuam. Ego enim sum Raphael unus ex septem Angelis sanctis qui assistimus et conversamur ante claritatem Dei" (Tb 12:11–15). Hanc tolerantiam justi semper habuerunt, hanc Apostoli disciplinam de Domini lege tenuerunt, non mussitare in adversis, sed quaecumque in saeculo accidunt fortiter et patienter accipere.

confess the works of God. For when you prayed, and Sara your daughter-in-law, I did offer the remembrance of your prayer in the presence of the glory of God. And when you buried the dead in singleness of heart, and because you did not delay to rise up and leave your dinner, and went and buried the dead, I was sent to make proof of you. And God again has sent me to heal you and Sara your daughter-in-law. For I am Raphael, one of the seven holy angels, who are present, and go in and out before the glory of God" (Tb 12:11–15). Righteous men have ever possessed this endurance. The apostles maintained this discipline from the law of the Lord, not to murmur in adversity, but to accept bravely and patiently whatever things happen in the world.

INFRA HEBDOMADAM IV SEPTEMBRIS

Feria Secunda: Jdt 4:1–12

S. Rabanus Maurus, *Expositio in librum Judith* (cap. 4)

"Et miserunt in omnem Samariam per circuitum usque Jericho, et praeoccupaverunt omnes vertices montium, et muris circumdederunt vicos suos et congregaverunt frumenta in prae-

"And they sent into all Samaria round about, as far as Jericho, and seized upon all the tops of the mountains: And they compassed their towns with walls, and gathered together corn for provision for war" (Jdt 4:3–

parationem pugnae" (Jdt 4:3–4). Aestuante persecutore timor et tremor invasit Israelitas, ne hoc faceret Jerusalem et templo Domini, quod fecerat caeteris civitatibus et templis eorum; cum Ecclesia Christi fragilitati compatiens infirmarum animarum, quas sub cura sua susceptas, quae et rudium in fide casum pertimescens, saevitia atque calliditate hostis antiqui praecavere studet, ne per lictores suos, hoc est, paganos, Judaeos et haereticos, corda innocentium decipiat, atque gravem in populo Domini efficiat ruinam. Et propter hoc dicitur, quod mittentes Israelitae circumquaque praeoccupaverint omnes vertices montium, quia sanctae Ecclesiae auctoritas praepositorum suorum commovet strenuitatem, quatenus probos viros, atque virtutum studiis celsos omni intentione et insitam precibus, quam etiam exhortatione confortare et servare studeat illaesos; ut si alicubi hostis per simplicium injuriam in castra Ecclesiae irrumpere tentaverit, per istorum fortitudinem, ac robur fidei ocius repellatur.

4). As the persecutor raged, fear and trembling invaded the Israelites, lest he should do this to Jerusalem and the Temple of the Lord, which he had done to the other cities and their temples, while the Church of Christ, sympathizing with the frailty of the weak souls whom she has received under her care, and fearing the defection from faith of the simple people, endeavors to prevent the cruelty and cunning of the ancient enemy, lest by his licitors, that is, pagans, Jews, and heretics, he should deceive the hearts of the innocent, and he will bring about a ruin in the Lord's People. And for this reason it is said that the Israelites sent forth and occupied all the summits of the mountains in advance, because the authority of the Holy Church stirs up the zeal of her shepherds. With this zeal, imbued with prayers and every good intention, the Church strives even through exhortation to strengthen and preserve unharmed honest men, and those who are exalted in the pursuit of virtues; so that if somewhere the enemy tries to break into the camp of the Church injuring the simple, he is more quickly repulsed by their courage and the strength of faith.

Feria Tertia: Jdt 8:1–11
S. Ambrosius, *De viduis* (cap. 7)

Fortitudinem viduis non deesse in Judith ostenditur: cujus veste ac ieiuniis commemoratis, describitur ejusdem in Holophernem praeparatio. Quanta fuerit ejus castitas, atque in commentanda pia fraude sapientia: quanta etiam temperantia et sobrietas (cf. Jdt 8:4–8). Ad extremum demonstrato non majorem in ipsa fortitudinis quam prudentiae laudem emicare, summa ejus in tanto successu modestia declaratur. Sed nec fortitudo bonae viduae deesse consuevit. Haec enim vera est fortitudo, quae naturae usum, sexus infirmitatem, mentis devotione transgreditur: qualis in illa fuit, cui nomen Judith, quae viros obsidione fractos, perculsos metu, tabidos fame, sola potuit a colluvione revocare, ab hoste defendere. Ea enim, ut legimus, cum Holophernes successu multorum terribilis praeliorum, intra muros innumera virorum millia coegisset, armatis paventibus, et de extrema jam sorte tractantibus, extra murum processit: et illo

That courage is not lacking in widows is shown in Judith: her dress and fasting are mentioned, and her preparation for Holofernes is described. How great was her chastity, and how great was her wisdom in commenting on pious fraud: how great was her temperance and sobriety (cf. Jdt 8:4–8). In the end, it is shown that she does not shine a greater praise on her courage than on her prudence, and her utmost modesty is declared in her great success. Bravery also is usually not wanting to a good widow. For this is true bravery, which surpasses the usual nature and the weakness of the sex by the devotion of the mind, such as was in her who was named Judith, who of herself alone was able to rouse up from utter prostration and defend from the enemy men broken down by the siege, smitten with fear, and pining with hunger. For she, as we read, when Holofernes, dreaded after his success in so many battles, had driven countless thousands of men within the walls; when the armed men were afraid, and were already

praestantior exercitu, quem liberavit; et eo fortior, quem fugavit.

treating about the final surrender, went forth outside the wall, both excelling that army which she delivered, and braver than that which she put to flight.

Feria Quarta: Judith 10:1–4, 11–12, 16–20
S. Ambrosius, *De virginibus* (lib. 2, cap. 24–25)

Nec virginis nomen agnoscitur, ubi virginitatis auctor negatur. Nam quemadmodum virgo, si meretricem colas: quemadmodum virgo, si adulteros diligas, quemadmodum virgo, si amorem petas? Tolerabilius est mentem virginem quam carnem habere. Utrumque bonum, si liceat: si non liceat, saltem non homini castae, sed Deo simus. Et Rahab meretrix fuit, sed postquam Deo credidit, salutem invenit. (cf. Jo 2:9). Et Judith se, ut adultero placeret, ornavit (cf. Jdt 10:1–3); quae tamen quia hoc religione, non amore faciebat, nemo eam adulteram judicavit. Bene successit exemplum. Nam si illa quae se commisit religioni, et pudorem servavit et patriam; fortassis et nos servando religionem, servabimus etiam castitatem. Quod si Judith pudicitiam religioni praeferre voluisset,

The name of virgin is not acknowledged where the Author of virginity is denied. How can one be a virgin who cherishes a harlot? How can one be a virgin who loves adulterers? How a virgin if she seeks for a lover? It is preferable to have a virgin mind than a virgin body. Each is good if each be possible; if it be not possible, let me be chaste, not to man but to God. Rahab, too, was a harlot, but after she believed in God, she found salvation (cf. Jo 2:9). And Judith adorned herself that she might please an adulterer (cf. Jdt 10:1–3), but because she did this for religion and not for love, no one considered her an adulteress. This instance turned out well. For if she who entrusted herself to religion both preserved her chastity and her country, perhaps we, by preserving my religion, shall also preserve chastity. But if Judith had

perdita patria, etiam pudicitiam perdidisset. Itaque talibus informata exemplis, simul animo tenens verba Domini, quibus ait: "Quicumque perdiderit animam suam propter me, inveniet eam" (Mk 10:39); flevit, tacuit, ne eam vel loquentem adulter audiret: nec pudoris elegit injuriam, sed Christi recusavit. Aestimate utrum adulterare potuerit corpus, quae nec vocem adulteravit.

preferred her chastity to her religion, when her country had been lost, she would also have lost her chastity. And so, instructed by such examples, and at the same time bearing in mind the words of the Lord, where He says: "Whosoever shall lose his life for My sake, shall find it" (Mt 10:39), she wept, and was silent, that the adulterer might not even hear her speaking, and she did not choose the wrong done to her modesty, but rejected wrong done to Christ. Consider whether it was possible for her to allow her body to be unchaste, who guarded even her speech.

Feria Quinta: Jdt 12:10–13; 13:1–11
S. Clemens I Papa, *Epistula I ad Corinthios* (cap. 54–55)

Quis ergo inter vos generosus? quis misericors? Quis caritatis plenus? Ut autem etiam gentium exempla proferamus: multi reges et principes, pestifero tempore saeviente, cum oraculo admoniti essent, se ipsos morti tradiderunt, ut cives suo sanguine liberarent. Multi a suis civitatibus, ne seditio amplius duraret, secesserunt. Multos e nostris cognovimus, qui se ipsos in vincula coniecerunt, ut

Who then among you is noble-minded? Who compassionate? Who full of love? To bring forward some examples from among the heathen: Many kings and princes, in times of pestilence, when they had been instructed by an oracle, have given themselves up to death, in order that by their own blood they might deliver their fellow citizens from destruction. Many have gone forth from their own cities, that so

alios redimerent. Multi se ipsi in servitutem dederant, et accepto pretio sui, alios cibarunt. Mulieres complures per gratiam Dei corroboratae, strenua et virilia multa gesserunt. Beata Judith, cum urbs obsideretur, rogavit seniores ut sibi liceret in alienigenarum castra transire: ac se ipsam periculo tradena, propter caritatem patriae populique obsessi egressa est; et Dominus tradidit Olophernem in manu feminae (cf. Jdt 13:3–10).

sedition might be brought to an end within them. We know many among ourselves who have given themselves up to bonds, in order that they might ransom others. Many, too, have surrendered themselves to slavery, that with the price which they received for themselves, they might provide food for others. Many women also, being strengthened by the grace of God, have performed numerous manly exploits. The blessed Judith, when her city was besieged, asked of the elders' permission to go forth into the camp of the strangers; and, exposing herself to danger, she went out for the love which she bare to her country and people then besieged; and the Lord delivered Holofernes into the hands of a woman (cf. Jdt 13:3–10).

Feria Sexta: Jdt 15:1–12
S. Ambrosius, *De officiis ministrorum* (lib. 3, cap. 13)

Ecce tibi Judith se offert mirabilis, quae formidatum populis virum Holophernem adit, Assyriorum triumphali septum caterva. Quem primo formae gratia et vultus decore perculit, deinde sermonis circumscripsit elegantia. Primus triumphus ejus fuit,

See! Judith presents herself to thee as worthy of admiration. She approaches Holophernes, a man feared by the people and surrounded by the victorious troops of the Assyrians. At first, she makes an impression on him by the grace of her form and the beauty of her

quod integrum pudorem de tabernaculo hostis revexit: secundus, quod femina de viro reportavit victoriam, fugavit populos consilio suo. Horruerunt Persae audaciam ejus. Quantum ad molem spectat periculi, moritura processit: quantum ad fidem, dimicatura. Honestatem igitur secuta est Judith, et dum eam sequitur, utilitatem invenit. Honestatis enim fuit prohibere ne populus Dei se profanis dederet, ne ritus patrios et sacramenta proderet; ne sacras virgines, viduas graves, pudicas matronas barbaricae subiiceret impuritati; ne obsidionem deditione solveret: honestatis fuit se malle pro omnibus periclitari, ut omnes eximeret periculo. Quanta honestatis auctoritas, ut consilium de summis rebus femina sibi vindicaret, nec principibus populi committeret! Quanta honestatis auctoritas, ut Deum adjutorem praesumeret: quanta gratia, ut inveniret!

countenance. Then she entraps him by the refinement of her speech. Her first triumph was that she returned from the tent of the enemy with her purity unspotted. Her second, that she gained a victory over a man, and put to flight the people by her counsel. The Persians were terrified at her daring. As one looks at her overwhelming danger, one would say she went out to die; as one looks at her faith, one says she went but out to fight. Judith then followed the call of virtue, and as she follows that, she wins great benefits. It was virtuous to prevent the people of the Lord from giving themselves up to the heathen; to prevent them from betraying their native rites and mysteries, or from yielding up their consecrated virgins, their venerable widows, and modest matrons to barbarian impurity, or from ending the siege by a surrender. It was virtuous for her to be willing to encounter danger on behalf of all, so as to deliver all from danger. How great must have been the power of her virtue, that she, a woman, should claim to give counsel on the chiefest matters and not leave it in the hands

of the leaders of the people! How great, again, the power of her virtue to reckon for certain upon God to help her! How great her grace to find His help!

Sabbato: Jdt 16:22–31
S. Rabanus Maurus, *Expositio in librum Judith* (cap. 16)

"In omni autem spatio vitae ejus non fuit, qui perturbaret Israel, et post mortem ejus annis multis" (Jdt 16:30). Quomodo autem dicitur quod in spatio vitae Judith nullus perturbaret Israel, cum tota humani generis vita tentatio sit super terram. Sed forsitan de clade hostium forinsecus dicit, quod post acceptam per Judith victoriam minus molesti fuerint ad tempus genti Judaeorum. Mysterium autem manifestum est, quod nullus electos Dei in praesenti Ecclesia nocere funditus possit; id est, usque ad animae interitum pertingere. Hinc et Apostolus ait: "Si Deus pro nobis, quis contra nos?" (Rom 8:31). Cunctis ergo diebus, quibus Ecclesia in incolatu istius mundi peregrinatur, electi filii ejus sub umbra alarum Dei usque ad finem proteguntur illaesi. Et si in hoc tempore dolo-

"And all the time of her life there was none that troubled Israel, nor many years after her death" (Jdt 16:30). But how is it said that during the life of Judith no one disturbed Israel, since the whole life of the human race is a temptation on earth. But perhaps he says of the defeat of the enemy, that after the victory received by Judith, they were for a time less troublesome to the nation of the Jews. Now the mystery is manifest, that no one can utterly harm the elect of God in the present Church; that is, to reach even to the destruction of the soul. Hence the apostle says: "If God be for us, who is against us?" (Rom 8:31). During all the days, therefore, during which the Church is on her pilgrimage in the dwellings if this world, her chosen children are sheltered unharmed under the shadow of God's wings until the end. And if in this time

ribus et angustiis plenissimo sine damno salutis suae conservantur, quanto magis post finem istius vitae sine omni angustia, gemitu et periculo custodiuntur, ubi dolor vel gemitus amplius jam non erit ullus. Et hoc est quod dicitur "post mortem ejus annis multis" (Jdt 16:30); quia post obitum praesentis vitae in saeculum saeculi anni ejus sunt, quibus cum Christo feliciter vivit, et regnat in aeternum.

full of pains and distresses they are preserved without harm for their salvation, how much more after the end of that life they are preserved without all distress, groaning, and danger, when there will no longer be any pain or groaning. And this is what is said "many years after her death" (Jdt 16:30); because after the death of the present life into the age of the ages are her years, in which she lives happily with Christ, and reigns forever.

Infra Hebdomadam V Septembris
Feria Secunda: Est 2:5–11, 15–17
S. Rabanus Maurus, *Expositio in librum Esther* (cap. 3)

Quid per Esther, quae interpretatur absconsa, et altero nomine vocabatur Edissa, hoc est misericordia, nisi gentium Ecclesia designatur, quae in abscondito cordis sui propter fidei castitatem placet Deo, et misericordiam ac gratiam coram oculis Dei magis invenit quam Synagoga Judaeorum, quae merito impietatis suae absque misericordia per Oseam prophetam vocatur. Hanc ergo Mardochaeus spiritualis, quia utrumque parentem amiserat, sibi adoptavit in filiam. Et quid per Mardochaeum,

What is meant by Esther, which is interpreted as the hidden, and was called Edissa by another name, this is mercy, unless the Church of the Gentiles is signified, which in the secret of her heart, because of the chastity of her faith, pleases God, and finds mercy and grace in the sight of God more than the synagogue of the Jews, which because of impiety is called by the prophet Osee without mercy. Therefore, the spiritual Mardochai, because he had lost both parents, adopted her as his daughter. And what is meant

nisi doctores gentium significantur? Haec ergo (Synagoga Judaeorum) quondam per Nabuchodonosor regem Babylonis in captivitatem traducta est, cum per diabolum a naturali lege et cultu unius Dei in confusionem idololatriae translata est. Sed eam pietas divina omnino non deseruit, imo per praedicatores suos ad veritatis viam iterum revocavit, qui ejus curam diligentius habentes, educaverant eam in omni pietate, et justitia, et veritate.

by Mardochai, if not the teachers of the nations? This (Jewish synagogue) was once taken into captivity by Nabuchodonosor, king of Babylon, when by the devil it was transferred from the natural law and the worship of one God into the confusion of idolatry. But divine piety did not abandon the synagogue at all, nay, through His preachers, He again recalled her to the way of truth, Who, taking care of her more carefully, had brought her up in all piety, justice, and truth.

Feria Tertia: Est 3:1–7
S. Rabanus Maurus, *Expositio in librum Esther* (cap. 6)

Quid per Aman superbum, nisi fastus potentum hujus saeculi exprimitur, qui beneficiis divina pietate sibi collatis abutentes, proximos suos, quos consortes habent naturae, socios gratiae habere despiciunt. Unde honorem ac reverentiam, quam soli Deo impendere juste debuerant, in se nequiter transferre contendunt; eos autem qui hoc agere atque consentire nolunt, odiis insectantur, cruciatibus persequuntur, atque morti tradere conantur. Sed supernus judex, qui humilia respicit,

What is expressed by Aman the proud, if not the pride of the powerful of this age, who, abusing the favors bestowed upon them by divine piety, despise their neighbors as partners of grace, whom they have as companions of nature. Wherefore they wretchedly strive to transfer to themselves the honor and reverence which they ought justly to have paid to God alone; and those who do not want to do this and consent, they attack with hatred, persecute with tortures, and they try to deliver them to death.

et alta a longe cognoscit, qui novit decipientem et eum qui decipitur, convertit dolorem iniquorum in caput eorum, et in verticem eorum iniquitas eorum descendit. In insidiis suis capientur iniqui: "justus de angustia sua liberabitur, et tradetur impius pro eo" (Prv 11:8).

But the heavenly judge, Who looks down on the lowly and knows the high from afar, Who knows the deceiver and the one who is deceived, returned the pains of the wicked upon their own head, and on their own skull their violence descends. The wicked shall be caught in their snares: "The righteous is delivered from trouble, and the wicked walks into it instead" (Prv 11:8).

Feria Quarta: Est 4:1–17

S. Augustinus, *De gratia christi et de peccato originali* (lib. 1, cap. 25)

Utrum rex ille Assyrius cujus Esther sancta mulier exsecrabatur cubile (cf. Est 14:15), quando considebat in throno regni sui, et omni stola illustrationis suae indutus erat, totus auro variegatus lapidibusque pretiosis, et erat formidolosus valde, et elevata facie sua inflammata in claritate intuitus est eam, tamquam taurus in impetu indignationis suae; et timuit regina, et conversus est color ejus per dissolutionem, et inclinavit se super caput delicatae suae, quae praecedebat eam (cf. Est 15:9–10). Vellem ergo diceret iste nobis, utrum rex ille ad Dominum jam cucurrerat, et

Now I want him to tell us whether that king of Assyria, whose holy wife Esther abhorred his bed (cf. Est 14:15), while sitting upon the throne of his kingdom, and clothed in all his glorious apparel, adorned all over with gold and precious stones, and dreadful in his majesty when he raised his face, which was inflamed with anger, in the midst of his splendor, and beheld her, with the glare of a wild bull in the fierceness of his indignation; and the queen was afraid, and her color changed as she fainted, and she bowed herself upon the head of the maid that went before her (cf. Est 15:9–10)—I want him to tell us whether this king

ab eo se regi cupiverat, suamque voluntatem ex ejus voluntate suspenderat, et ei iugiter inhaerendo unus cum illo spiritus factus erat (cf. 1 Cor 6:17), nonnisi de arbitrii libertate; utrum se totum Deo tradiderat, omnemque suam mortificaverat voluntatem, et cor suum in manu Dei posuerat. Puto non desipere, sed insanire hominem, quisquis de illo rege, qualis tunc erat, haec senserit: et tamen convertit Deus et transtulit indignationem ejus in lenitatem. Quis autem non videat, multo majus esse, indignationem a contrario in lenitatem convertere atque transferre, quam cor neutra affectione praeoccupatum, sed inter utramque medium in aliquid declinare? Legant ergo et intellegant, intueantur atque fateantur, non lege atque doctrina insonante forinsecus, sed interna et occulta, mirabili ac ineffabili potestate operari Deum in cordibus hominum, non solum veras revelationes, sed bonas etiam voluntates.

had yet hastened to the Lord, and had desired to be directed by Him, and had subordinated his own will to His, and had, by cleaving fast to God, become one spirit with Him (cf. 1 Cor 6:17), simply by the force of his own free will. Had he surrendered himself wholly to God, and entirely mortified his own will, and placed his heart in the hand of God? I suppose that anybody who should think this of the king, in the state he was then in, would be not foolish only, but even mad. And yet God converted him and turned his indignation into gentleness. Who, however, can fail to see how much greater a task it is to change and turn wrath completely into gentleness, than to bend the heart to something, when it is not preoccupied with either affection, but is indifferently poised between the two? Let them therefore read and understand, observe and acknowledge, that it is not by law and teaching uttering their lessons from without, but by a secret, wonderful, and ineffable power operating within, that God works in men's hearts not only revelations of the truth, but also good dispositions of the will.

Feria Quinta: Est 5:1–5, 9–14
S. Rabanus Maurus, *Expositio in librum Esther* (cap. 8)

Quid est quod "die tertia induta est Esther regalibus vestimentis" (Est 5:1), nisi quod Ecclesia gentium tertio tempore saeculi, hoc est post incarnationem, passionem et resurrectionem Christi, in sacramenta baptismatis per sanctae Trinitatis confessionem, fide, spe et charitate, omniumque virtutum se induit decore, ut inde regali consortio digna fieret, cum ejus amore praecipuo incessanter ferveret. Quae stat in atrio domus regiae quod erat interius contra basilicam regis, hoc est in praesentis vitae pia operatione quae spectat ad futuram in caelis remunerationem, ubi ipse rex regum solio consedit superno, et precibus pie ad se clamantium annuit. Qui extendit contra hanc reginam virgam quam tenet manu, cum ostendit illi regiminis sui potentiam, vel crucem passionis suae, per quam sibi acquisivit potestatem in caelo, et in terra, et subtus terram; ita ut "in nomine ejus omne genu flectatur caelestium, terrestrium et infernorum" (Phil 2:10). Hanc [virgam] quidem ipsa amabiliter

What is the reason that "on the third day Esther was clothed in royal garments" (Est 5:1), except that the Church of the Gentiles in the third time of the age, that is, after the Incarnation, Passion and Resurrection of Christ, in the sacraments of baptism through the confession of the Holy Trinity, faith, hope and charity, and she clothed herself with the adornment of all the virtues, so that she might thereby become worthy of a royal companionship, burning unceasingly with her chief love. What stands in the court of the royal house, which was on the inside opposite the king's basilica, is in the pious activity of the present life which looks to the future reward in the heavens, where the King of Kings Himself sits on the throne above, and nods to the prayers of those who cry to Him in piety. He stretched out against this queen the staff which He held in His hand, when He showed her the power of His government, or the Cross of His Passion, by which He acquired for Himself power in heaven, and

osculatur, hoc est omni devotione veneratur. Cujus petitioni et ipse rex spondet se assensurum, sicut in Evangelio ait: "Petite et dabitur vobis; quaerite et invenietis; pulsate et aperietur vobis "(Mt 7:7).

on earth, and under the earth; so that "at the name of Jesus every knee should bow, in heaven and on earth and under the earth" (Phil 2:10). She indeed kisses the staff lovingly, that is, she venerates it with all devotion. To whose request the King Himself promises that He will agree, as He says in the Gospel: "Ask, and it will be given to you; seek, and you will find; knock, and it will be opened to you" (Mt 7:7).

Feria Sexta: Est 6:1–13
S. Rabanus Maurus, *Expositio in librum Esther* (cap. 9)

"Haec est immutatio dexterae Excelsi" (Ps 76:11), ut ille qui nuper gloriabatur super alios se esse potentem et prae omnibus gloriosum, subito fieret vilior caeteris et infirmior cunctis. Cujus dispositionis magnitudinem considerans Maria mater Domini in cantico Evangelii ait: "Fecit potentiam in brachio suo, dispersit superbos mente cordis sui. Deposuit potentes de sede, et exaltavit humiles. Esurientes implevit bonis et divites dimisit inanes" (Lk 1:51–53). Hinc videmus Judaeorum Synagogae contumaciam compressam, et humilitatem Ecclesiae

"This is the change of the right hand of the Most High" (Ps 76:11), so that he who had recently boasted that he was powerful above others and glorious above all, should suddenly become inferior to the rest and weaker than all. Considering the greatness of his disposition, Mary, the Mother of the Lord, says in the song of the Gospel: "He has shown strength with His arm; He has scattered the proud in the thoughts of their hearts; He has brought down the mighty from their thrones and exalted those of humble estate; He has filled the hungry with good things, and the

gentium exaltatam. Hinc persecutores Christianae fidei, qui quondam ut leones feroces laceraverunt gregem Christi, modo destructi et ad nihilum sunt redacti: confessores quoque Christi in toto orbe statu sanae fidei erecti et potentia virtutum sunt sublimati. Caput in caudam et cauda in caput versa est, quia "omnis qui se exaltat, humiliabitur; et qui se humiliat, exaltabitur" (Mt 23:12).

rich He has sent away empty" (Lk 1:51–53). Hence, we see the obstinacy of the Jewish synagogue suppressed, and the humility of the Church of the Gentiles exalted. Hence the persecutors of the Christian faith, who once tore the flock of Christ like ferocious lions, were just destroyed and reduced to nothing. The head is turned into the tail and the tail into the head, because "whoever exalts himself will be humbled, and whoever humbles himself will be exalted" (Mt 23:12).

Sabbato: Est 7:1–10

S. Ambrosius, *De officiis ministrorum* (lib. 3, cap. 21)

Esther vitae periculo honestatis decus secutam esse, immo et regem barbarum, illata nece viro amicissimo; amicitiam enim honestati semper conjungendam, ut Jonathae atque Alchimelech exempla probant. Quid Esther regina, nonne ut populum suum periculo exueret, quod erat decorum atque honestum, morti se obtulit, nec immitis regis trepidavit furorem (cf. Est 4:16)? Ipse quoque rex Persarum ferox, atque tumido corde, tamen decorum judicavit indici insidiarum

Esther in danger of her life followed the grace of virtue; nay, even a heathen king did so, when death was threatened to a man most friendly to him. For friendship must ever be combined with virtue, as the examples of Jonathan and Achimelech show. Why did Queen Esther expose herself to death and not fear the wrath of a fierce king (cf. Est 4:16)? Was it not to save her people from death, an act both seemly and virtuous? The king of Persia himself also, though fierce and proud, yet thought it seemly to show honor to

quae sibi paratae forent, gratiam repraesentare, populumque liberum a servitute eripere, eruere neci, nec parcere ei, qui tam indecora suasisset (cf. Est 6:3 et seq.). Denique quem secundum a se, ac praecipuum inter omnes amicos haberet, cruci tradidit, quod dehonestatum se ejus fraudulentis consiliis animadvertisset (cf. Est 7:9). Ea enim amicitia probabilis, quae honestatem tuetur, praeferenda sane opibus, honoribus, potestatibus: honestati vero praeferri non solet, sed honestatem sequi.

the man who had given information about a plot which had been laid against himself, to save a free people from slavery, to snatch them from death, and not to spare him who had pressed on such unseemly plans (cf. Est 6:3ff.). So finally, he handed over to the gallows the man that stood second to himself, and whom he counted chief among all his friends, because he considered that he had dishonored him by his false counsels (cf. Est 7:9). For that commendable friendship which maintains virtue is to be preferred most certainly to wealth, or honors, or power.

INFRA HEBDOMADAM I OCTOBRIS

Feria Secunda: 1 Mc 1:17–29
S. Rabanus Maurus, *Commentaria in libros Machabaeorum* (in librum primum, cap. 1)

Mystice autem Antiochus hic, qui intravit in terram sanctam cum superbia, et devastavit templum, et locum sanctum polluit superstitione gentili (cf. 1 Mc 1:17–24), typum tenet Antichristi, qui contra Ecclesiam Christi bellum crudeliter gerit, et animas credentium, quae vere templum Dei sunt, errore suo polluere contendit.

Mystically, however, this Antiochus, who entered the Holy Land with pride, and devastated the Temple, and polluted the holy place with the superstition of the Gentiles (cf. 1 Mc 1:17–24), holds the type of the antichrist, who cruelly wages war against the Church of Christ, and strives to pollute the souls of believers, who are truly the temple of God,

Nulli dubium est quin haec quae sub Antiocho Epiphane in imagine praecesserunt, hoc est ut rex sceleratissimus persecutus sit populum Dei, saevitiam praefiguret Antichristi, qui Christianum populum persequetur, qui indignabitur contra testamentum Dei, et cogitabit adversus illos quos vult Dei legem relinquere, polluetque sanctuarium Dei, homines videlicet ad imaginem Dei creatos diversis vitiis corrumpendo; auferet iuge sacrificium quando hostiam laudis Christo Dei Filio offerre in Ecclesia prohibebit; abominationem desolationis in loco sancto statuet, quando divinum cultum a Christianis sibi extorquebit exhiberi, ita ut in templo Dei sedens, ostendat se tanquam ipse sit Deus (cf. 2 Thes 2:4).

with his error. There is no doubt that these things that preceded Antiochus Epiphanes in the image, this is that a most wicked king persecuted the People of God, foreshadows the cruelty of the antichrist, who will persecute the Christian people, who will be indignant against the covenant of God and will think against those whom he wants to leave the law of God, and pollute the sanctuary of God, corrupting namely men created in the image of God with different vices; he will take away the continual sacrifice when he will forbid the offering of the sacrifice of praise to Christ the Son of God in the Church; he will establish the abomination of desolation in the holy place, when he will extort divine worship from the Christians to be presented to him, so that sitting in the temple of God, he will show himself as if he were God (cf. 2 Thes 2:4).

Feria Tertia: 1 Mc 2:1–10, 14–16
S. Rabanus Maurus, *Commentaria in libros Machabaeorum* (in librum primum, cap. 2)

Mystice autem Mathathias Dominum salvatorem significat, qui princeps est populi Dei et defensor electorum suorum; cujus filii

Mystically, Mathathias signifies the Lord the Savior, Who is the leader of God's People and the defender of His elect; Whose sons fight for the

pugnant pro domo Israel, defendunt sanctuarium Dei ac legem divinam. Interpretatur autem Mathathias donum Dei, cujus nominis arcanum ipsius incarnationis nobis patefecit sacramentum. Unde et ipse ait in Evangelio: "Sic enim Deus dilexit mundum, ut Filium suum unigenitum daret, ut omnis qui credit in eum non pereat, sed habeat vitam aeternam" (Jn 3:16). Qui enim datus a Deo est, perfectum Dei donum est. Sed haec de incarnatione ipsius tantum dicta sunt. Caeterum de divinitate ipsius, qua aequalis est Patri et Spiritui sancto, simul cum Patre et Spiritu sancto ipsam dispensationem facere credi oportet. Sicut et Spiritus sanctus donum Dei legitur, sed tamen cum Patre et Filio unus Deus creditur atque adoratur: unde in Evangelio et missus legitur, et sponte venisse, ut est illud Dominicum: "Rogabo Patrem, et alium Paracletum dabit vobis" (Jn 14:16).

house of Israel, defend the sanctuary of God and the divine law. But Mathathias interprets the gift of God, the secret meaning of whose name revealed to us the sacrament of His Incarnation. Wherefore He also says in the Gospel: "For God so loved the world, that He gave His only begotten Son, that whosoever believeth in Him should not perish, but have eternal life" (Jn 3:16). For he who is given by God is a perfect gift of God. But these things have only been said about His Incarnation. As for the rest of His divinity, in which He is equal to the Father and the Holy Spirit, we must believe that He does the dispensation itself together with the Father and the Holy Spirit. Just as the Holy Spirit is read as a gift of God, but is believed and worshiped with the Father and the Son as one God: whence it is read in the Gospel that He was sent, and that He came of His own free will, as is said by the Lord's word: "I will ask the Father, and He will give you another Paraclete" (Jn 14:16).

Feria Quarta: 1 Mc 2:19–30
S. Rabanus Maurus, *Commentaria in libros Machabaeorum*
(in librum primum, cap. 2)

"Et respondit Mathathias et dixit magna voce," etc. (1 Mc 2:19). Constantia Mathathiae confortabat animos filiorum suorum; sic et patientia et longanimitas Domini nostri Jesu Christi omnium credentium corroborat fidem. Unde discipulis suis ait: "Nolite mirari si odit vos mundus, scitote quia me priorem vobis odio habuerit" (Jn 15:18): "neque timeatis eos qui occidunt corpus, animam autem occidere non possunt; sed potius eum qui potest et animam et corpus perdere in gehennam" (Mt 10:28). "In patientia vestra possidebitis animas vestras" (Lk 21:19), et erit merces vestra multa in caelo. "Qui autem perseveraverit usque in finem, hic salvus erit" (Mt 24:13). Judaeus hic qui sacrificavit coram oculis omnium idolis, significat malos catholicos, qui pravis operibus et peccatorum nota scandalizant proximos suos. In eo enim idolis sacrificare probantur quod principalibus vitiis captivati esse manifestantur.

"And Mathathias answered and said in a loud voice," etc. (1 Mc 2:19). The constancy of Mathathias strengthened the spirits of his sons; so also the patience and long-suffering of Our Lord Jesus Christ strengthens the faith of all believers. Wherefore He said to His disciples: "Do not be surprised if the world hates you, know that it hated Me before you" (Jn 15:18): "Snd do not fear those who kill the body, but cannot kill the soul; but rather He Who is able to destroy both soul and body in hell" (Mt 10:28). "In your patience you will possess your souls" (Lk 21:19), and your reward will be great in heaven. "But he who perseveres to the end will be saved" (Mt 24:13). This Jew, who sacrificed to the idols before the eyes of all, signifies the bad Catholics, who offend their neighbors by their bad deeds and sins. For in that they are proved to sacrifice to idols, because they are shown to be captive to their principal vices.

Feria Quinta: 1 Mc 2:49–69
S. Cyprianus, *Testimonia adversus Judaeos* (lib. 3, tract. 12, cap. 15)

Ad hoc tentari homines a Deo ut probentur. In Genesi: "Et tentavit Deus Abraham, et dixit ad illum: Accipe filium tuum unicum quem diligis Isaac, et vade in terram altam, imponens illum ibi in holocaustum hostiam in unum ex montibus de quo tibi dixero" (Gn 21:1). De hoc ipso in Deuteronomio: "Tentat Dominus Deus vester vos, ut sciat si diligitis Dominum Deum vestrum ex toto corde vestro et ex tota anima vestra" (Dt 13:3). De hoc ipso in Sapientia Salomonis: "Et si coram hominibus tormenta passi sunt, spes eorum immortalitate plena est; et in paucis vexati, in multis bene disponentur, quoniam Deus tentavit illos et invenit illos dignos se. Tamquam aurum in fornace probavit illos, et quasi holocausta hostiae accepit illos, et in tempore erit respectus illorum. Judicabunt nationes et dominabuntur populis, et regnabit Dominus eorum in perpetuum" (Ws 3:4). De hoc ipso in Machabaeis: "Abraham nonne in tentatione inventus est fidelis, et deputatum est ei ad justitiam?" (1 Mc 2:52).

In Genesis: "And God tempted Abraham, and said to him, take your only son whom you love, Isaac, and go into the high land, and offer him there as a burnt-offering on one of the mountains of which I will tell you" (Gn 21:1). Of this same thing in Deuteronomy: "The Lord your God proves you, that He may know if you love the Lord your God with all your heart, and with all your soul" (Dt 13:3). Of this same thing in the Wisdom of Solomon: "Although in the sight of men they suffered torments, their hope is full of immortality; and having been in few things distressed, yet in many things they shall be happily ordered, because God tried them, and found them worthy of Himself. As gold in the furnace, He proved them, and as a burnt-offering He received them. And in their time, there shall be respect of them; they shall judge the nations and shall rule over the people; and their Lord shall reign forever" (Ws 3:4). Of this same thing in the Machabees: "Was not Abraham found faithful in temptation, and it was accounted unto him for righteousness?" (1 Mc 2:52).

Feria Sexta: 1 Mc 2:70; 3:13, 5–12, 25–28
S. Rabanus Maurus, *Commentaria in libros Machabaeorum*
(in librum primum, cap. 2)

"Et surrexit Judas, qui vocabatur Machabaeus, filius ejus pro eo" (1 Mc 3:1). Mathathia decedente, Judas Machabaeus, filius ejus, successit in locum ipsius, quem adjuvabant omnes fratres ejus, et universi qui se junxerant patri ejus (cf. 1 Mc 3:2). Quid ergo hoc facto nobis innuitur, nisi Redemptor noster postquam passione ac resurrectione sua completa ascendit in caelos, successores sibi in evangelica praedicatione, misso de caelo Spiritu Sancto, apostolos primum ordinavit, qui merito Judae nomine, hoc est confitentes, censentur, quia de ipsis Lucas in Evangelio ait: "Erant semper in templo laudantes et benedicentes Dominum" (Lk 24:53). Hunc ergo omnes fratres sui et universi qui se conjunxerant patri ejus adjuvabant: quia minoris ordinis viri, et omnes credentes qui dogmate Christi ad fidem convenerunt, in attestatione Evangelii pro viribus choro apostolorum collaborabant. "Et praeliabantur praelium Israel cum Laetitia" (1 Mc 3:2), et

"And Judas, who was called Machabeus, his son rose up in his stead" (1 Mc 3:1). When Mattathias died, Judas Machabeus, his son, succeeded in his place, who was supported by all his brothers and all who had joined his father (cf. 1 Mc 3:2). What, then, is hinted at by this fact, except that our Redeemer, after having ascended into heaven after His Passion and Resurrection had been completed, first ordained the apostles as His successors in the preaching of the gospel, being sent from heaven the Holy Spirit, who are considered to be worthy of the name of Judas, that is, confessors, because of them Luke says in the Gospel: "They were always in the temple praising and blessing the Lord" (Lk 24:53). All his brothers, therefore, and all those who had joined his father, helped him: for men of lesser rank, and all believers who had come to the Faith by the dogma of Christ, collaborated in the attestation of the gospel for the strength of the choir of the apostles. "And they fought the battle of

dilatavit gloriam populo suo. Quia ipse apostolicus coetus, Spiritus Sancti gratia repletus, instanter ubique verbum Dei praedicabat, gaudentes in tribulationibus et in pressuris, et in necessitatibus, augendo et multiplicando ubique numerum in Domino credentium.

Israel with joy" (1 Mc 3:2), and he enlarged the glory of his people. Because the company of the apostles itself, filled with the grace of the Holy Spirit, preached urgently everywhere the Word of God, rejoicing in tribulations and pressures and in necessities, increasing and multiplying everywhere the number of believers in the Lord.

Sabbato: 1 Mc 3:42–60
S. Rabanus Maurus, *Commentaria in libros Machabaeorum* (in librum primum, cap. 2)

Jejunaverunt illa die, quia continentiae operam dabant. Induerunt se ciliciis et cinere in capite suo (1 Mc 3:47). Quia paenitentiam pro peccatis suis, quae per carnis fragilitatem contraxerunt agentes, Deo digne deserviunt. "Et sciderunt vestimenta sua" (1 Mc 3:47), cum corpus castigant, et carnalia in se desideria mortificant. Quod autem sequitur quia, "expanderunt libros legis, de quibus scrutabantur gentes similitudinem simulacrorum suorum" (1 Mc 3:48), ostendit quod memoriam divinorum praeceptorum bonis actibus demonstrant, qui digne militare probantur. "Lex enim

They fasted that day, because they paid attention to continence. They clothed themselves in sackcloth and ashes on their heads (1 Mc 3:47). Because by doing penance for their sins, which they contracted through the frailty of the flesh, they serve God worthily. "And they rent their clothes" (1 Mc 3:47), when they chastise the body and mortify the carnal desires in themselves. And what follows is that "They laid open the books of the Law, in which the Gentiles searched for the likeness of their idols" (1 Mc 3:48), shows that they show the memory of the divine teachers by good deeds, who are proved worthy of mili-

Domini irreprehensibilis, convertens animas" (Ps 18:8) electorum, reprobat malefacta perfidorum, et detestatur idolorum culturam, et omnem contradicit impietatis facturam. Attollunt sacerdotalia ornamenta, qui sacerdotii ecclesiastici digne faciunt officia; primitias et decimas donant (cf. 1 Mc 3:49), qui initium et perfectionem boni operis Deo deputant; suscitant Nazaraeos qui impleverunt dies, qui per castitatis munditiam gratam vitam omni tempore Deo exhibere student; "et clamaverunt voce magna in caelum" (1 Mc 3:50), qui Divinitatem piis precibus ac bonis actibus ad misericordiam provocant. Sicut enim clamor impiorum, quem blasphemia et pravis operibus proferunt, Deum irritat; sic confessio et fides sanctorum, quae per dilectionem operatur, majestatem divinam in omni tempore placat.

tary service. "The law of the Lord is unspotted, converting souls" (Ps 18:8), reproves the evil deeds of the unfaithful, and detests the worship of idols, and contradicts every work of impiety. They lift up the priestly ornaments, who perform the duties of the ecclesiastical priesthood worthily; they give first-fruits and tithes (cf. 1 Mc 3:49), who depute the beginning and completion of a good work to God; they raise up the Nazarenes who have fulfilled their days, who strive to present a pleasing life to God at all times through the cleanliness of chastity. "And they cried with a loud voice to heaven" (1 Mc 3:50), who provoke the Divinity to mercy by pious prayers and good deeds. For just as the cry of the wicked, which they utter with blasphemy and wicked works, irritates God; so the confession and faith of the saints, which works through love, appeases the divine majesty at all times.

INFRA HEBDOMADAM II OCTOBRIS
Feria Secunda: 1 Mc 4:52–61
S. Rabanus Maurus, *Commentaria in libros Machabaeorum*
(in librum primum, cap. 4)

Celebravit autem Judas cum civibus suis pro renovatione templi sacrificia per dies octo (cf. 4 Kgs 4:56), nullum genus deliciarum relinquens, pretiosissimis dapibus eos pascens: Deum autem laudibus et psalmis glorificabant, seque mutuo cantibus delectabant. Pro renovatione vero solemnium, post multum tempus instaurata religione, receptores legis posuerunt ut posteri post octo dies hanc renovationem templi celebrarent. Unde et ab illo tempore hactenus hanc festivitatem celebramus; vocantes eam Lumina, eo quod praeter spem hoc nobis splendide lumen colendae religionis apparuit, mystice autem renovatio templi conversio est hominum ad poenitentiam peccatorum, qui aliquibus erroribus atque facinoribus contaminati erant. Tunc enim cantandum, gaudendum, laetandum, jubilandum atque laudandum quibusque fidelibus est, quando viderint proximos suos per correctionem viarum atque meditationem legis Dei in semetip-

Judas and his citizens celebrated sacrifices for the renewal of the Temple for eight days (cf. 4 Kgs 4:56), omitting no kind of delicacy, feeding the people with the most precious food. They glorified God with praises and psalms, and delighted in one another through songs. For the renewal of the solemn feasts, after a long time had passed and religion was restored, the receivers of the Law decreed that posterity should celebrate this renewal of the Temple during eight days. Hence from that time until now we celebrate this festival, calling it the Lights, because beyond expectation this light of the worship of religion appeared to us brilliantly. Mystically, however, the renewal of the Temple means the conversion of men, who had been contaminated by certain errors and misdeeds, to penitence for their sins. For then it is for all the faithful to sing, to rejoice, to be glad, to exult, and to praise, when they see their neighbors, by correcting their ways and meditating on the Law of

sis instaurare, quod ante jam per negligentiam destruxerant. Unde et sacrum Evangelium narrat Salvatorem dixisse in caelis gaudium nasci super uno peccatore poenitentiam agente (cf. Lk 15:7): si de uno, quanto magis de multis exsultatio erit conversis ad verum cultum Dei. Quia sicut scriptum est: "In multitudinem plebis dignitas est principis" (Prv 14:28); illius videlicet principis: "qui vult homines omnes salvos esse et ad agnitionem veritatis pervenire" (1 Tm 2:4).

God in themselves, reestablishing what they had previously destroyed through negligence. Hence the Holy Gospel tells us that the Savior said there is joy in heaven over one sinner doing penance (cf. Lk 15:7): if over one sinner, how much more will there be exultation over many converted to the true worship of God. Because as it is written: "In the multitude of the people is the dignity of the prince" (Prv 14:28); that is, of that prince "Who wants all men to be saved and to come to the knowledge of the truth" (1 Tm 2:4).

Feria Tertia: 1 Mc 5:1–13
S. Rabanus Maurus, *Commentaria in libros Machabaeorum* (in librum primum, cap. 5)

"Et factum est ut audirent gentes in circuitu, quia aedificatum est altare et sanctuarium sicut prius, iratae sunt valde," etc. (1 Mc 5:1). Irritantur gentes cum viderint culturae Dei renovari facturam, quia sive hostes visibiles seu invisibiles, qui invidiae aestibus contra fidei ac virtutum profectum anhelant, irascuntur, cruciantur ac persequuntur servos Dei, ad nihilum eos redigere volentes, quando considerant eos in altari rectae fidei

"And it came to pass that the nations round about heard, because the altar and the sanctuary were built as before, that they were very angry," etc. (1 Mc 5:1). The nations are angry when they see that the worship of God is being renewed, because whether visible or invisible enemies, who in the heat of envy pant against the progress of faith and virtue, are angry, torment and persecute the servants of God, wanting to reduce them to noth-

bonorum operum velle observantiam. Inde dicitur quod cogitarent tollere genus Jacob qui erant inter eos, et coeperunt ejus occidere, quia clarescente in mundo Evangelio Christi, et omnibus fidem Dei recipientibus, torquebantur persecutores, et poenis eos mactantes inde avertere studebant. Similiter et hostes spiritales cum viderint aliquos ex desidia et negligentia se restaurare velle in cultu pietatis, moliuntur eos gladio impietatis occidere, ac pro morte peccatorum trucidare. Sed Judas, fortiter cum scuto fidei hostibus resistens, debellat filios Esau in Idumaea, quia chorus sanctorum doctorum idololatras, qui spinetis vitiorum sunt asperrimi, et funestis sacrificiis atque luxuria mundana fetidissimi, gladio spiritus interimens, de contrariis efficit subjectos ac de hostibus facit amicos.

ing, when they observe how they desire to observe good works on the altar of right faith. From this it is said that they thought to remove the tribe of Jacob who were among them, and began to kill him, because the gospel of Christ was shining in the world, and all who received the Faith of God, were tormented by the persecutors, and by punishing them they sought to turn them away from there. In the same way, when the spiritual enemies see that some of them wish to restore themselves from laziness and negligence to the worship of piety, they plan to kill them with the sword of impiety, and to slaughter them with the death of sinners. But Judas, resisting the enemies of the Faith with a strong shield, defeated the sons of Esau in Idumaea, because the chorus of the holy teachers killing the spirit with the sword the idolaters, who are the sharpest thorns of vice, and the most repulsive with fatal sacrifices and worldly lust, makes subjects of the opposites and makes friends of the enemies.

Feria Quarta: 1 Mc 5:55–67
S. Rabanus Maurus, *Commentaria in libros Machabaeorum* (in librum primum, cap. 5)

"Dixitque Judas Simoni fratri suo," etc. (1 Mc 5:17). Sicut diversae sunt impugnationes Ecclesiae ab hostibus, sic et distincta debent esse praelia spiritualium bellatorum. Id igitur Simon in Galilaeam cum tribus millibus viris, sicut in sequentibus ostenditur, ut liberet fratres suos; Judas autem et Jonathas eunt in Galaaditim cum octo millibus. Et quid per Simonem, qui in Galilaeam, hoc est rotam, mittitur, nisi praedicatores in gentes directi insinuantur; qui cum tribus millibus, hoc est, cum sanctae Trinitatis fide, contra adversarios suos ire parantes, per evangelicam praedicationem hostes dejicere et credentes liberare decertant. Judas autem et Jonathas illos doctores exprimunt qui, in Judaea verbum Dei praedicantes, sive Judaeos, sive et haereticos, Scripturarum testimoniis abutentes, per veritatem sani intellectus debellare student. Et nota quod contra gentiles solum Simon cum suis mittitur, contra Judaeos autem et haereticos duo

"Judas said to Simon his brother," etc. (cf. 1 Mc 5:17). Just as the attacks of the Church by the enemies are different, so must the battles of the spiritual warriors be distinct. Simon therefore went into Galilee with three thousand men, as is shown in what follows, to free his brethren; Now Judas and Jonathan went to Galaad with eight thousand. And what is sent by Simon, who is sent into Galilee, that is, a circle, but preachers directed to the Gentiles? who, with three thousand, that is, with the Faith of the Holy Trinity, preparing to go against their adversaries, strive to cast down the enemies by preaching the gospel, and deliver the believers. But Judas and Jonathan express those teachers who, preaching the Word of God in Judea, both Jews and heretics, abusing the testimonies of the Scriptures, seek to fight with the truth of a sound understanding. And note that against the Gentiles only Simon is sent with his followers, but against the Jews and the heretics the two

pergere cum pluribus moliuntur: quia in gentibus sola idololatria cum errore paganico debellanda erat, in Judaeis vero et haereticis partim veteranus usus, partim nova superstitio, per duorum Testamentorum spiritalem scientiam corrigenda fuerunt.

intend to go on with the majority: because among the Gentiles only idolatry with pagan error was to be overcome, but among the Jews and heretics partly an old practice, partly a new superstition was to be corrected through the spiritual knowledge of the two Testaments.

Feria Quinta: 1 Mc 6:1–13
S. Rabanus Maurus, *Commentaria in libros Machabaeorum* (in librum primum, cap. 6)

De morte Antiochi et successione filii ejus, qui misit exercitum ad debellandum Judam, et vincitur (cf. 1 Mc 6:6): pacem dat ficte quam cito rumpit; hic dicitur in bellis usus elephantis (cf. 1 Mc 6:34–35). Et rex Antiochus perambulavit superiores regiones, etc. (cf. 1 Mc 6:1). Post impietatis opera plurima quae gessit Antiochus in loco sancto et in populo Dei, divino judicio juste peremptus est, sicut ipse in sequentibus testatur, dicens se cognovisse quia propter ea invenissent se mala, et inde periret tristitia in terra aliena (cf. 1 Mc 6:12–13). Quod autem contra Domini omnipotentem superbia intumuit, condignam ultionem recepit: sic et omnes impii;

On the death of Antiochus and the succession of his son, who sent an army to defeat Juda and was defeated (cf. 1 Mc 6:6): he gives a false peace which he quickly breaks; here it is said that he used elephants in wars (cf. 1 Mc 6:34–35). And King Antiochus traveled through the upper regions, etc. (cf. 1 Mc 6:1). After the numerous works of impiety which Antiochus performed in the holy place and among the people of God, he was justly destroyed by divine judgment, as he testifies in what follows, saying that he knew that because of them evils had found themselves, and that he would perish of sadness in a foreign land (cf. 1 Mc 6:12–13). But that which swelled with pride against the Lord

nec non et ipse novissime novus filius perditionis, "qui extollitur super omne quod dicitur Deus aut colitur" (2 Thes 2:4), cujus hic Antiochus typus fuit, propter impietatis opera quae faciet, superno visitantis judicio interibit, quem Dominus Jesus, juxta Pauli vocem "interficiet spiritu oris sui et destruet illustratione adventus sui" (2 Thes 2:8). Unde hic Antiochus typum tenet persecutorum Christi et Ecclesiae.

Almighty, received a worthy vengeance: so also all the wicked; and so also lastly the new son of perdition, "who exalts himself above all that is called God or is worshiped" (2 Thes 2:4), of whom this Antiochus was a type, because of the works of impiety he will do, he will perish by the judgment of the heavenly visitor, whom the Lord Jesus, according to Paul "will kill with the voice with the spirit of His mouth and destroy it with the illumination of His coming" (2 Thes 2:8). Wherefore this Antiochus holds the type of the persecutors of Christ and the Church.

Feria Sexta: 1 Mc 7:1, 4–17
S. Rabanus Maurus, Commentaria in libros Machabaeorum (in librum primum, cap. 7)

Ad hunc ergo principem (Demetrium) veniunt viri iniqui et impii ex Israel, et Alcimus dux eorum (cf. 1 Mc 7:5), cum illi qui post fidem Christi perceptam ad apostasiam redierunt, religionem Christianam blasphemant et ecclesiastico detrahunt cultui; quorum duces sunt haeretici, qui per ambitionem sublimitatis volunt ab omnibus magni videri. Sed proditione hujuscemodi suscepta mit-

Unrighteous and impious men from Israel come to this prince (Demetrius), and Alcimus their leader (cf. 1 Mc 7:5), while those who, after having received the Faith of Christ, returned to apostasy, blaspheme the Christian religion and detract from ecclesiastical worship; whose leaders are heretics, who, through the ambition of exaltation, want to be seen as great by all. But Demetrius, having received

tit Demetrius typice Bacchidem, qui dominabatur trans flumen in regno, ut Alcimum impium constituat in sacerdotem, et ultionem faciat in filios Israel. Cum per paganos quoslibet apud saeculum potentes, qui necdum meruerunt Christi baptismate tingi et in numero fidelium computari, haereticis fastus sui praebebunt adminiculum, et veris confessoribus Christi tormentorum ingerent cruciatum; sed licet tales personae Judae et fratribus ejus verbis pacificis loquantur in dolo, non tamen accedunt sermonibus eorum, quia nullo modo confidunt perfidiae eorum.

this kind of treachery, typically sends Bacchides, who ruled across the river in the kingdom, to appoint the impious Alcimus as priest, and to wreak vengeance on the children of Israel. Since, through the pagans any powerful people of the age, who have not yet deserved to be dipped in Christ's baptism and counted among the number of the faithful, will provide support to heretics with their pride, and inflict torture on the true confessors of Christ. But though such persons as Judas and his brethren speak pacific words in guile, yet they do not come near to their words, because they in no way trust their treachery.

Sabbato: 1 Mc 8:1–4, 17–27
S. Rabanus Maurus, *Commentaria in libros Machabaeorum* (in librum primum, cap. 8)

"Et audivit Judas nomen Romanorum, quia sunt potentes viribus," etc. (1 Mc 8:1). Judas mittit legatos ad Romanos constituere cum illis amicitiam et societatem, (cf. 1 Mc 8:17) significat Redemptorem nostrum per praedicatores suos Evangelium pacis gentibus offerre et convocare eas ad fidem suam. Quibus illi rescripserunt in

"And Judas heard the name of Romans, because they are mighty in strength," etc. (1 Mc 8:1). Judas sends ambassadors to the Romans to establish friendship and partnership with them (cf. 1 Mc 8:17); this means that our Redeemer through his preachers offers the gospel of peace to the nations and calls them to His Faith. To whom they wrote

tabulis aereis, quod postulati fuerunt, et miserunt in Jerusalem, ut esset ibi apud eos memoriale pacis et societatis (cf. 1 Mc 8:22): quia gentes ad credulitatem Christi conversae, firmae fidei suae statuunt pactum, quod significat longo tempore duraturum, et verae confessionis monumentum tradunt in Ecclesia catholica, ut ibi sit memoriale societatis eorum in perpetuum. Unde per prophetam dicitur: Ecce Dominus auditum fecit, "et legatos ad gentes misit" (Jer 49:14). Item: "Et angelus faciei ejus salvabit eos, in dilectione sua et indulgentia sua: ipse redemit eos" (Is 63:9). Et item: "Parvum est, inquit, ut sis mihi servus ad suscitandas tribus Jacob et faeces Israel convertendas, dedi te in lucem gentium, ut sis salus mea usque ad extremum terrae" (Is 49:6). Et iterum: "Dedi te in foedus populi, ut suscitares terram et possideres hereditates dissipatas" (Is 49:8).

back on tablets in bronze what they had been asked for, and sent them to Jerusalem, that there might be with them a memorial of peace and fellowship (cf. 1 Mc 8:22): because the nations, having been converted to the credulity of Christ, establish a covenant of the firmness of their faith, which it means that it will last for a long time, and they deliver a monument of true confession in the Catholic Church, so that there may be a memorial of their association forever. Whence it is said through the prophet: Behold, "The Lord has heard and sent ambassadors to the nations" (Jer 49:14). Also: "And the angel of His face will save them, in His love and His indulgence: He will redeem them" (Is 63:9). And again: "It is a small thing, He says, that you should be My servant to raise up the tribes of Jacob and to convert the dregs of Israel" (Is 49:6). And again: "I gave you to be a covenant of the people, that thou mightest raise up the earth, and possess the inheritances that were destroyed" (Is 49:8).

INFRA HEBDOMADAM III OCTOBRIS

Feria Secunda: 1 Mc 9:28–40
S. Rabanus Maurus, *Commentaria in libros Machabaeorum*
(in librum primum, cap. 9)

"Et congregati sunt omnes amici Judae, et dixerunt Jonathae," etc. (1 Mc 9:28). Quid est quod post obitum Judae legitur Jonathas a populo in sacerdotium eligi ut suppleat locum fratris sui, nisi quod obeuntibus per martyrium primum doctoribus Ecclesiae, successores eorum, administrante Spiritus sancti gratia, in locum ipsorum substituuntur, cujus administrationis efficaciam nominis Jonathae interpretatio demonstrat: interpretatur enim columba eorum, sicut superius demonstratum est, admovens praedicatores verbi quatenus digne ducatus sui officium in plebe Dei gerant, et defensionem congruam contra hostes subditis impendant. Sed sicut prioribus ita et sequentibus populi Dei doctoribus ab infidelibus et haereticis truculenta immittuntur tela, et saeva hostium adversatur inimicitia.

"And all the friends of Judas were gathered together, and Jonathan said," etc. (1 Mc 9:28). What is the meaning of the fact that after the death of Judas it is read that Jonathan was elected to the priesthood by the people to take the place of his brother, except that those who first submitted to the teachers of the Church through martyrdom, their successors, administered by the grace of the Holy Spirit, are substituted in their place, and the interpretation of Jonathan's name shows the effectiveness of this administration: for this interpretation means their dove, as has been shown above, moving the preachers of the word to the extent that they carry out their duty of leadership among the People of God worthily, and mount a suitable defense against the enemies of their subjects. But as before, and so after, the teachers of God's People are hurled by unbelievers and heretics with fierce weapons, and the savage enmity of the enemy is turned against them.

Feria Tertia: 1 Mc 12:1–11
S. Rabanus Maurus, *Commentaria in libros Machabaeorum*
(in librum primum, cap. 12)

Quod mittit Jonathas epistolas ad Romanos et ad Spartiatos, et ad alia loca, ut renovent pactum et amicitiam cum eis (cf. 1 Mc 12:1–3) quae frater suus Judas prior cum illis sponte iniit, demonstrat quod magna sollicitudo sanctis debet esse praedicatoribus ut pacem quam Christus in mundo obtulit, ipsi toto studio innovare atque conservare ubique contendant: quia ipse Dei Filius, qui venit in terram ut pacificaret in carne sua caelestia atque terrestria (cf. Col 1:20); qui statim in exortu nativitatis suae voluit ab angelis decantari: "Gloria in excelsis Deo, et in terra pax hominibus bonae voluntatis" (Lk 2:14); quam utique pacem idem mediator Dei et hominum jam homo factus suis discipulis commendavit dicens: "Habete pacem inter vos" (Mt 9:50); et: pacem meam do vobis; pacem meam relinquo vobis (Jn 14:27); pace etenim et concordantia universum corpus Christi adunatur, regitur ac stabilitur: qui autem cum proximis suis

The fact that Jonathan sends letters to the Romans and the Spartans, and to other places, to renew the pact and friendship (cf. 1 Mc 12:1–3) which his brother Judas had voluntarily entered into with them, shows that sacred preachers must have great concern, that the peace which Christ has offered in the world, they themselves strive everywhere to renew and preserve with all their diligence: because the Son of God Himself, Who came to earth to make peace in His flesh between the heavenly and earthly (cf. Col 1:20); Who at the very beginning of His birth wanted to be sung by the angels: "Glory to God in the highest, and on earth peace to men of good will" (Lk 2:14); which indeed the same mediator of God and men, having already become man, commended to His disciples, saying: "Have peace among yourselves" (Mt 9:50); and: "I give you My peace; I leave My peace with you" (Jn 14:27); for by peace and concord the whole body of Christ is united, governed, and

non vult habere pacem, in corpore Christi nullam habet societatem, nec jam ad aeternam potest pervenire requiem, unde se separavit per contentionem.

established; but he who does not want to have peace with his neighbors has no fellowship in the body of Christ, and can no longer reach eternal rest, from which he has separated himself by strife.

Feria Quarta: 1 Mc 12:39–52
S. Rabanus Maurus, *Commentaria in libros Machabaeorum* (in librum primum, cap. 12)

Quod Tryphon dolo persuasit Jonathae ut remiserit a se exercitum secumque pacifice perceperit (cf. 1 Mc 12:42–44), sicque eum delusum captivavit atque secum commeantes occidit (cf. 1 Mc 12:48), significat eorum ruinam qui legitime se non observant, nec cautelam in circumspectione cordis et conversatione corporis habent. Hi enim quia Evangelii illam doctrinam non attendit ubi Salvator discipulis suis praecepit dicens: "Vigilate et orate, ut non intretis in tentationem" (Mt 26:41); et item: "Attendite," inquit, "vobis a falsis prophetis, qui veniunt ad vos in vestimentis ovium, intrinsecus autem sunt lupi rapaces" (Mt 7:15); merito ergo horum superatur atque interimitur ex-

The fact that Tryphon persuaded Jonathan by trickery to withdraw his army from him after he found himself at peace (cf. 1 Mc 12:42–44), and thus deceived him into captivity and killed those who were traveling with him (cf. 1 Mc 12:48), signifies the downfall of those who do not maintain the legitime vigilance towards themselves, nor are cautious in the examination of the heart and the conduct of the body. For these people do not pay attention to that doctrine of the Gospel where the Savior commanded His disciples, saying: "Watch and pray, that you may not enter into temptation" (Mt 26:41); and again: "Beware," He says, "of false prophets, who come to you in sheep's clothing, but inwardly they are ravenous wolves" (Mt 7:15); therefore,

ercitus, quia magisterii caelestis doctrina ab illis non condigne servatur. Porro loco Jonathae Simon frater ejus sacerdotio fungitur, et populi ducatum gerit (cf. 1 Mc 13:1), cum in praesenti Ecclesia, aliis recedentibus alii substituuntur qui locum regiminis teneant et in castris spiritalibus milites Christi sedulo exerceant, quatenus hostibus universis belli gerendi opportune resistere valeant. Sed Tryphon typicus simili modo sermonum fictionibus talibus ut fratrem ejus deluserat decipere conatur, quia nunquam antiquus hostis per se suosque ministros cultoribus Christi insidias disponere cessat; sed qui Simonis, hoc est, obedientis et divinis praeceptis rite obtemperantis, digne gerit officium, universorum hostium, superno adiutus auxilio, potest devitare scandalum.

the army of these is rightly overcome and destroyed, because the doctrine of the heavenly teaching is not properly observed by them. Furthermore, instead of Jonathan, his brother Simon functions as a priest, and carries the leadership of the people (cf. 1 Mc 13:1), when in the present Church, others who withdraw are replaced by others who hold the place of government and diligently train the soldiers of Christ in the spiritual camps, so that they be able to resist in a timely manner all the enemies of the war. But the typical Tryphon tries to deceive his brother in a similar way with such fictions, because the ancient enemy never ceases to arrange plots for the worshipers of Christ through himself and his ministers. Yet he who is obedient to Simon, that is, who duly obeys the divine precepts, who carries out his duty worthily, is able to avoid the offense of all enemies, aided by help from above.

Feria Quinta: 1 Mc 13:1–19
S. Rabanus Maurus, *Commentaria in libros Machabaeorum*
(in librum primum, cap. 13)

Et audivit Simon quod congregavit Tryphon exercitum copiosum ut veniret in terram Juda, etc. (cf. 1 Mc 13:1). Et aedificavit Simon super sepulcrum patris sui, etc. (cf. 1 Mc 13:27). Simon patri, et matri, et fratribus, ex lapide polito memoriam super sepulcra fabricat, cum sancti praedicatores facta praecedentium patrum ac finem gloriosum, ad exemplum praesentibus commemorando, magna auctoritate ostendunt: hoc enim ante et retro lapidem politum ponere, ut qualiter ante finem vitae pro dogmate et sancta conversatione vixerunt, et quale exemplum patientiae longanimitatis suae post obitum posteris reliquerunt, manifeste auditoribus suis studeant fida narratione declarare. Quod autem sancti viri patris ac matris atque fratrum nomine nuncupentur, ostendit Salvator in Evangelio dicens: "Quicunque fecerit voluntatem Patris mei, qui in caelis est, ipse meus frater, soror et mater est" (Mt 12:50). Hinc apostolus Paulus ad Corin-

And Simon heard that Tryphon had assembled a large army to come into the land of Juda, etc. (cf. 1 Mc 13:1). And Simon built over his father's tomb, etc. (cf. 1 Mc 13:27). Simon builds a memorial for his father, mother, and brothers on the tombs from a polished stone, when the holy preachers show with great authority the deeds of the preceding fathers and their glorious end, by commemorating the example for those present. The placing of the stone, which is polished before and behind, shows how they lived before the end of their lives for the sake of the dogma and holy conduct, and what example of their patience and long-suffering they left to posterity after their death. This they plainly manifest to their hearers by a faithful narration. And the fact that holy men are called by the name of father and mother and brothers is shown by the Savior in the Gospel, saying: "Whoever does the will of My Father Who is in heaven, he is My brother, sister and mother" (Mt 12:50). Hence the apostle Paul, writing to the Cor-

thios scribens ait: "Nam si decem millia paedagogorum habeatis in Christo, sed non multos patres: nam in Christo Jesu per Evangelium ego vos genui" (1 Cor 4:15).

inthians, said: "For if you have ten thousand teachers in Christ, but not many fathers, for in Christ Jesus I have begotten you through the gospel" (1 Cor 4:15).

Feria Sexta: 1 Mc 14:16–26
S. Rabanus Maurus, *Commentaria in libros Machabaeorum* (in librum primum, cap. 14)

In loco ergo celebri atrii interioris domus ponebantur tabulae aereae (cf. 1 Mc 14:26), in quibus confirmatum fuerat per scripturam sacerdotium Simonis et filiorum ejus. Mystice autem Christi sacerdotium et filiorum ejus, hoc est populi Christiani, in atrio domus Domini, hoc est in praesenti Ecclesia, Scriptura testificante, confirmatur, et in omnibus gentibus stabile et perpetuum esse declaratur. "Semel," inquit, "juravi in sancto meo, si David mentiar: semen ejus in aeternum manebit, et sedes ejus sicut sol in conspectu meo, et sicut luna perfecta in aeternum et testis in caelo fidelis" (Ps 88:36–38). Consuetudo est frequenter jurare ut eis possit aliquis credere: Deus autem semel jurat, quia nulla varietate temporis immutatur. Semen Christi

Therefore, in the place of the famous inner court of the house, the bronze tablets were placed (cf. 1 Mc 14:26), in which the priesthood of Simon and his sons had been confirmed by Scripture. Mystically, however, it signifies the priesthood of Christ and His sons, that is, of the Christian people, in the court of the Lord's house, that is, in the present Church, which confirmed by the witness of the Scripture, is declared to be stable and permanent in all nations. "Once," He says, "I swore by My holy one, if David should lie: his seed will remain forever, and his seat will be like the sun in My sight, and like the perfect moon forever and a faithful witness in heaven" (Ps 88:36–38). It is a custom to swear frequently, that one may believe them: but God swears once, because no variety of time

sunt omnes qui ei fideli mente crediderunt, quia in ipsis futurum regnum seminatum est, quod ventura messis ostendit.

changes. The seed of Christ are all those who believed in Him with a faithful mind, because in them the future Kingdom was sown, which shows the coming harvest.

Sabbato: 1 Mc 16:14–24
S. Rabanus Maurus, *Commentaria in libros Machabaeorum* (in librum primum, cap. 16)

"Et Ptolemaeus filius Abobi constitutus erat dux in campo Jericho," etc. (cf. 1 Mc 16:11). Quid per Ptolemaeum nisi hypocritae atque versuti homines figurantur. Hi ergo ficto disciplinatu bonis magistris adhaerentes, simulantesque pietatem, cujus virtutem penitus ignorant, plerumque ad honorem ecclesiasticamque dignitatem, ipsis magistris tribuentibus, perveniunt: hoc est enim summi sacerdotis generum esse, illas utique personas quas boni magistri aqua et verbo regenerabant, in potestatem regiminis sui accipere; sed cum, accepto gradu, propriae potestatis esse coeperunt, singuli cupiditatibus servientes, ipsos sui auctores honoris dolis et mentitionibus supplantare atque subvertere student; occiduntque filios eorum ac pueros pariter, cum

"And Ptolemy the son of Abobi was appointed commander in the field of Jericho," etc. (cf. 1 Mc 16:11). What is signified by Ptolemy, if not hypocritical and cunning men? These men, then, clinging to the good teachers with false discipline and feigning piety, whose virtue of they entirely lack, ofen attain honor and ecclesiastical dignity, granted by those very teachers. This is akin to being the son-in-law of the high priest—that is, taking under their authority those whom good teachers have regenerated through water and the word. However, once they have obtained rank and begun to exercise their own authority, each, serving his own desires, endeavors to supplant and subvert the very authors of their honor by deceit and falsehood. They kill their sons and children alike, sparing no person

nulli personae secum habitanti parcunt, sed pecunias atque adulationes sibi saeculares potestates. Ecclesiam occultis insidiis seu manifestis persecutionibus infestant. Nec mirum talem nequitiam aliquando praevalere in Ecclesia posse, cum legimus Ecclesiae capere dolum Judae proditoris; magus a Philippo baptizatus est, sed non a nequitia mentis purgatus; Julianus, apostata a lectore Ecclesiae excitatus, usque ad finem vitae hostis truculentus in coepta malitia perseveravit: quales et istius temporis aetas nonnullos habet, qui, licet magistros suos non occidunt gladio, tamen invidia atque odiis persequi non cessant.

who dwells with them. They covet wealth and worldly flattery, assailing the Church with hidden plots or open persecutions. Nor is it surprising that such wickedness should sometimes prevail in the Church, when we read that the Church harbored the decit of Judas the betrayer; the magician was baptized by Philip, but not cleansed of the wickedness of his mind; Julian the Apostate, raised as a lector in the Church, persisted in his malevolence as a fierce enemy until the end of his life. Likewise, the present age also has some who, although they do not kill their teachers with the sword, nevertheless persist in persecuting them with envy and hatred.

INFRA HEBDOMADAM IV OCTOBRIS

Feria Secunda: 2 Mc 2:1–9

S. Ambrosius, *De officiis ministrorum* (lib. 3, cap. 17)

Rex Persarum eo loco in quo ignis fuerat absconditus, et postea reperta est aqua, templum fieri mandavit, cui inferebantur dona plurima (cf. 1 Mc 1:34–35). Appellaverunt autem illud qui erant cum sancto Neemia, ephthar, quod interpretationem habet purificationis (cf. 2 Mc 1:36): a plurimis nephthe vocatur. Invenitur

The king of Persia ordered a temple to be built on that spot where the fire had been hidden and the water afterwards found, to which many gifts were made. (cf. 1 Mc 1:34–35). They who were with holy Nehemias called it Nephthar (cf. 2 Mc 1:36)—which means cleansing—by many it is called Nephthe.

autem in descriptionibus Hieremiae prophetae, quod iusserit accipere de igne eos qui postea essent futuri (cf. 2 Mc 2:1 seq.). Hic est ignis qui cecidit super sacrificium Moysi, et consumpsit illud, sicut scriptum est: "Quia exivit ignis a Domino, et consumpsit universa quae erant super altare holocausta" (Lv 9:24). Hoc igne oportebat sanctificari sacrificium; ideoque et in filios Aaron qui alienum ignem inferre voluerunt, exivit iterum ignis a Domino et consumpsit eos, ita ut mortui extra castra projicerentur (cf. Lv 10:2). "Veniens autem Hieremias in locum, invenit domum in modum speluncae, et tabernaculum et arcam, et altare incensi intulit illuc, et obstruxit ostium" (2 Mc 2:5). "Quod cum hi qui simul venerant, curiosius perscrutarentur, ut notarent sibi locum; nequaquam comprehendere atque invenire potuerunt" (2 Mc 2:6). Ut autem cognovit Hieremias quod affectassent, dixit: "Ignotus erit locus, donec congreget Deus congregationem populi, et propitius fiat. Tunc Deus ostendet haec, et apparebit majestas Domini" (2 Mc 2:7–8).

It is to be found also in the history of the prophet Jeremias, that he bade those who should come after him to take of the fire (cf. 2 Mc 2:1ff.). That is the fire which fell on Moses' sacrifice and consumed it, as it is written: "There came a fire out from the Lord and consumed upon the altar all the whole burnt-offering" (Lv 9:24). The sacrifice must be hallowed with this fire only. Therefore, also, fire went out from the Lord upon the sons of Aaron who wished to offer strange fire, and consumed them, so that their dead bodies were cast forth without the camp (cf. Lv 10:2). "Jeremias coming to a spot found there a house like a cave, and brought into it the tabernacle, the ark, and the altar of incense, and closed up the entrance" (2 Mc 2:5). "And when those who had come with him examined it rather closely to mark the spot, they could not discover nor find it" (2 Mc 2:6). When Jeremias understood what they wanted he said: "The spot will remain unknown until God shall gather His People together and be gracious to them. Then God shall reveal these things, and the majesty of the Lord shall appear" (2 Mc 2:7–8).

Feria Tertia: 2 Mc 3:1–12
S. Ambrosius, *De officiis ministrorum* (lib. 2, cap. 29)

Fides enim exhibenda omnibus est, sed major est viduarum causa et pupillorum. Denique hoc solo viduarum nomine, sicut in libris Machabaeorum legimus (cf. 2 Mc 3:10 et seq.), commendatum templo omne servatum est. Nam cum indicium factum esset pecuniarum, quas in templo Hierosolymis maximas reperiri posse Simon nefarius Antiocho regi prodidit (cf. 2 Mc 3:11), missus in rem Heliodorus, ad templum venit, et summo sacerdoti aperuit indicii invidiam, et adventus sui causam. "Tunc sacerdos deposita esse dixit viduarum victualia et pupillorum" (2 Mc 3:10): quaedam autem Hircani Tobiae viri sancti, eaque demonstravit; argenti talenta quadraginta erant, auri vero ducenta (cf. 2 Mc 3:11). Quae cum Heliodorus ereptum ire vellet, et regis vindicare commodis, "sacerdotes ante altare jactaverunt se, induti sacerdotales stolas: et Deum vivum qui de depositis legem dederat" (2 Mc 3:15), flentes invocabant, ut custodem se praeceptorum praestaret

Good faith must be shown to all, though the cause of the widow and orphans comes first. So everything entrusted to the Temple was preserved in the name of the widows alone, as we read in the book of the Machabees (cf. 2 Mc 3:10ff.). For when information was given of the money, which Simon treacherously had told King Antiochus could be found in large quantities in the Temple at Jerusalem (cf. 2 Mc 3:11), Heliodorus was sent to look into the matter. He came to the Temple and made known to the high priest his hateful information and the reason of his coming. "Then the priest said that only means for the maintenance of the widows and orphans was laid up there" (2 Mc 3:10): and certain things belonging to the holy man Hircan Tobias, he pointed them out; there were forty talents of silver, but two hundred of gold (cf. 2 Mc 3:11). And when Heliodorus would have gone to seize it, and to claim it on the king's behalf, the, "priests cast themselves before the altar, after putting on their priestly robes, and with tears called on the living God Who had given

suorum (cf. 2 Mc 3:15). Vultus vero et color summi sacerdotis immutatus declarabat dolorem animi, et mentis intentae sollicitudinem (cf. 2 Mc 3:16). Flebant omnes, quod in contemptum locus venturus foret, si nec in Dei templo tuta fidei servaretur custodia: accinctaeque mulieres pectus, et clausae virgines pulsabant januam: ad muros alii currebant, per fenestras alii prospectabant, omnes ad caelum tendebant manus, orantes ut suis Dominus adesset legibus (cf. 2 Mc 3:19–20).

them the Law" (2 Mc 3:15), weeping, they called upon Him to be the guardian of His commandments (cf. 2 Mc 3:15). The changed look and color of the high priest showed what grief of soul and anxiety, and tension of mind were his (cf. 2 Mc 3:16). All wept, for the spot would fall into contempt, if not even in the Temple of God safe and faithful guardianship could be preserved. Women with breasts girded, and virgins who usually were shut in, knocked at the doors. Some ran to the walls, others looked out of the windows, all raised their hands to heaven in prayer that God would stand by His laws (cf. 2 Mc 3:19–20).

Feria Quarta: 2 Mc 3:23–29, 32–34
S. Rabanus Maurus, *Commentaria in libros Machabaeorum* (in librum secundum, cap. 3)

Sicque fiet ut iste qui ante templum aggressus est superbus, per correptionem disciplinae appareat invalidus (cf. 1 Mc 3:23 et seq.): quia "non est sapientia, non est prudentia, non est consilium contra Dominum" (Prv 21:30); quia "omnia quaecunque voluit, fecit in caelo et in terra, in mari et in omnibus abyssis" (Ps 134:6): et

Thus it will happen that he who attacked the Temple proudly, through the correction of discipline will appear weak (cf. 1 Mc 3:23ff.): because "there is no wisdom, there is no prudence, there is no counsel against the Lord" (Prv 21:30); because "whatever He willed He does in heaven and on earth, in the sea and in all the deeps" (Ps 134:6): and

non est qui possit resistere voluntati ejus; Dominus universorum ipse. Quod autem Onias, offerens hostiam salutarem pro salute viri, salvavit ipsum Heliodorum multa caligine circumfusum (cf. 1 Mc 3:31 et seq.), significat quod misericordia Redemptoris nostri saepe ingratis et immeritis confert beneficium conversionis, quatenus per ejus gratiam qui semetipsum obtulit hostiam salutarem pro mundi peccatis, exuantur ab erroribus suis et liberentur a potestate Satanae, cujus nequitia quondam captivi erant ad ipsius voluntatem, referant gratias Redemptori suo et laudem ejus praedicent in universa terra.

there is no one who can resist His will, He is the Lord of the universe. And the fact that Onias, offering a salutary sacrifice for the man's salvation, saved Heliodus, surrounded by much darkness (cf. 1 Mc 3:31ff.), signifies that the mercy of our Redeemer often confers the benefit of conversion on the ungrateful and undeserving who, by the grace of Him Who offered Himself as a sacrificial offering for the sins of the world, are stripped of their errors and freed from the power of Satan, to whose wickedness they were once captives at his will. They will offer thanks to their Redeemer and will proclaim His praise in all the earth.

Feria Quinta: 2 Mc 4:1–11
S. Rabanus Maurus, *Commentaria in libros Machabaeorum*
(in librum secundum, cap. 4)

Antiochus Epiphanes cum de regione Ptolemaeorum, quam subito invaserat, senatus praecepto recessisset, in Judaeam venit; ibique Iason, qui et fratri Oniae, pontificatum tradidit. Itaque ob sacerdotii dignitatem orta seditione inter principes (cf. 2 Mc 4:1–7), ingentium miseriarum semina

When Antiochus Epiphanes had withdrawn from the country of the Ptolemies, which he had suddenly invaded, by order of the senate, he came into Judea; and there he delivered the pontificate to Jason, the brother of Onias. Therefore, because of the dignity of the priesthood, a rebellion arose among the lead-

pullulaverunt. Haec ergo facta superborum atque transgressorum legis Dei non allegoriam aliquam ad aedificationem utilem nobis ingerit, sed, proh dolor! isto tempore imitatores facinoris sui plures inveniuntur, hi qui in Ecclesia populi Dei et sanguine ejus Filii unigeniti redempta praeponuntur, deserta Evangelii doctrina et vera religione, a cultu unius Dei qui ibi commendatur ac insinuatur, pravis moribus ad occultam convolant idololatriam, cum per ambitionem pecuniarum et divitias praesentis vitae luxuriosam vitam et Deo detestabilem ducendo, adulatorum attendentes favorem, multos secum trahunt ad perditionem. Isti profecto secundum Apostolum confitentur quidem se nosse Deum, factis autem negant (cf. Ti 1:16); namque victu et vestitu moderato non sunt contenti, sed volentes divites fieri, incidunt in tentationem, et in laqueum diaboli, et desideria multa, et inutilia, et nociva, quae ingerunt homines in interitum et perditionem.

ers of the people (cf. 2 Mc 4:1–7), and the seeds of immense miseries sprouted. These acts of the proud and the transgressors of the Law of God do not inculcate any allegory useful for our edification, but alas! At this time many imitators of his wickedness are found, those who are ruling the Church of the People of God, redeemed by the blood of His only begotten Son. They abandon the doctrine of the gospel and from the worship of the one God, Who is there commended and insinuated, through bad manners they drag to secret idolatry, when through the ambition of money and the riches of this present life, by leading an unchaste life and detestable to God, they heed the favor of flatterers drawing many with them to destruction. Indeed, according to the apostle, they confess that they know God, but they deny Him by their deeds (cf. Ti 1:16); for they are not content with moderate food and clothing, but desiring to become rich, they fall into temptation, and into the trap of the devil, and into many desires, both useless and harmful, which plunge men into destruction and perdition.

Feria Sexta: 2 Mc 5:1–10
S. Rabanus Maurus, *Commentaria in libros Machabaeorum*
(in librum secundum, cap. 5)

Spiritaliter autem Judas merito dicitur esse decimus, quia Decalogi praecepta in fide et devotione perfecta invenitur servasse, ipsamque legem zelando ab hostium manibus primus post patrem armis defendisse. Qui vere inter feras scribitur cum suis in montibus vitam duxisse, et feni cibo vesci (cf. 2 Mc 5:27): quia sanctorum exempla secutus (ipsi enim sunt montes Dei), bestiales persecutorum mores contemnendo, vitam Deo placitam elegit, et virtutum semper virenti pabulo se pavisse optimum duxit, quatenus indeficienti animae victu nutritus famem non sentiret perpetuam. Nobis autem lectio actuum Judae ita solummodo proficit, si constantiae ejus ac sobrietatis virtutes imitari voluerimus; nec praeponimus delicias mundi ac pompam hujus saeculi justitiae et veritati Dei, memores semper illius vocis Dominicae quae ait: "Quid enim proderit homini, si universum mundum lucretur, animae vero suae detrimentum patiatur?"

Spiritually, however, Judas is rightly said to be the tenth, because he is found to have kept the precepts of the Decalogue in perfect faith and devotion, and to have zealously defended the Law itself from the hands of the enemy, the first after his father with arms. He who is truly among the beasts is written to have led a life with his own in the mountains, and to have fed on hay (cf. 2 Mc 5:27): he led himself best to feed himself on the ever-green fodder of the virtues, to the extent that, nourished by the insufficient food of his soul, he did not feel perpetual hunger. For us, however, the reading of the acts of Judas is only successful in this way, if we choose to imitate his virtues of constancy and sobriety; nor do we prefer the pleasures of the world and the pomp of this world to the justice and truth of God, always remembering that voice of Sunday which says: "For what doth it profit a man, if he gain the whole world, and suffer the loss of his own soul?" (Mt 16:26). And again: "He that loves

(Mt 16:26). Et iterum: "Qui amat animam suam perdet eam, qui odit animam suam in hunc mundum in vitam aeternam custodit eam" (Jn 12:25).

his life shall lose it; and he that hates his life in this world, keeps it unto life eternal" (Jn 12:25).

Sabbato: 2 Mc 6:1–12
S. Aphraates Sapiens, *Demonstrationes* (de bellis, cap. 20)

Antiochus enim ad regnum provectus "tres reges humiliavit" (Dn 7:24), atque adversum sanctos Altissimi superbivit (cf. Dn 7:25) et adversum Jerusalem; domum Sanctuarii foedavit, sacrificia et oblationes hebdomadem et dimidium hebdomadis cessare fecit, annos scilicet decem et dimidium; scortatores in domum Domini introduxit, observantias legis praepedivit, viros justos interfecit et volucribus caeli bestiisque terrae tradidit (cf. 2 Mc 6:2–9). Sicque in diebus ejus adimpletum est verbum quod dixerat David: "Deus, intraverunt gentes in hereditatem tuam, polluerunt templum sanctum tuum, effecerunt Jerusalem desolatam; cadavera servorum tuorum in escam dederunt volatilibus caeli, carnem sanctorum tuorum bestiis terrae. Effuderunt sanguinem eorum ve-

Antiochus arose in the kingdom, "He humbled three kings" (Dn 7:24), and he exalted himself against the saints of the Most High (cf. Dn 7:25) and against Jerusalem. And he defiled the sanctuary. And he caused the sacrifice and the offerings to cease for a week and half a week, namely, for ten and a half years. And he brought in fornicators into the house of the Lord, and he caused the observances of the Law to cease. And he slew righteous men and gave them to the birds of heaven and to the beasts of the earth (cf. 2 Mc 6:2–9). For in his days was fulfilled the word that David spoke: "O God, the Gentiles have come into Thine inheritance and have defiled Thy holy temple. They have made Jerusalem desolate. They have given the dead bodies of Thy servants as food to the birds of heaven, and the flesh

lut aquam in circuitu Jerusalem, nec fuit qui sepeliret" (Ps 78:1–3). Haec eo tempore completa sunt, quo vir venerabilis diebusque provectus Eleazar, et beatae Samunae filii, qui septem erant numero, occisi sunt (cf. 2 Mc 7:1 seq.); et quando Judas et fratres ejus pro populo suo luctabantur, seque latibulis tegebant (cf. 2 Mc 5:27). Eo tempore "bellum gessit cornu cum sanctis" (Dn 7:21) sed eorum virtus praevaluit. Tum Antiochus, vir iniquus, sermones "adversus Altissimum locutus est; tempora et festa mutavit" (Dn 7:25) foedus Abrahae corrupit, Sabbatum requietis abolevit (cf. 2 Mc 6:6), Judaeis praescribens ne circumciderentur (cf. 2 Mc 6:10).

of Thy righteous ones to the beasts of the earth. They have poured out their blood like water round about Jerusalem, and there is none to bury them" (Ps 78:1–3). For this was accomplished at that time, when the venerable and aged Eleazar was slain, and the sons of the blessed Samuna, seven in number (cf. 2 Mc 7:1ff.), and when Judas Machabeus and his brethren were struggling on behalf of their people, when they were dwelling in hiding places. (cf. 2 Mc 5:27). At that time "the horn made war with the saints" (Dn 7:21), and their power prevailed. And the wicked Antiochus "spake words against the Most High and changed the times and the seasons" (Dn 7:25). And he made to cease the covenant of Abraham and abolished the Sabbath of rest (cf. 2 Mc 6:6). For he commanded the Jews that they should not circumcise (cf. 2 Mc 6:10).

INFRA HEBDOMADAM V OCTOBRIS

Feria Secunda: 2 Mc 6:18–28; 7:1–5
S. Augustinus, *De moribus Ecclesiae catholicae et de moribus Manichaeorum* (lib. 1, cap. 23)

Offerunt enim mihi Scripturae illae stupendae fortitudinis feminam et ad eam jam me transire compellunt. Quae cum septem liberis tyranno atque carnifici prius viscera omnia quam unum verbum sacrilegum impendit, cum ejus hortatione filii roborarentur, in quorum membris ipsa torquebatur, latura tamen etiam proprio munere, quod eos ferre praeceperat (cf. 2 Mc 7:7 et seq.) Quid ad tantam patientiam quaeso addi poterit? Quid tamen mirum si omnibus medullis conceptus Dei amor et tyranno et carnifici et dolori et corpori et sexui et affectui resistebat? An non audierat: "Pretiosa in conspectu Domini mors sanctorum ejus" (Ps 115:15)? Non audierat: "Melior viro patiens fortissimo" (Prv 16:32)? Non audierat: "Omne quod tibi applicitum fuerit, accipe et in dolore sustine et in humilitate tua habe patientiam, quoniam in igne probatur aurum et argentum" (Ecclus 2:4–5)? Non audierat: Vasa figuli

Scriptures present to me a woman of amazing fortitude, and I must at once go on to her case. This woman, along with seven children, allowed the tyrant and executioner to extract her vitals from her body rather than a profane word from her mouth, encouraging her sons by her exhortations, though she suffered in the tortures of their bodies, and was herself to undergo what she called on them to bear (cf. 2 Mc 7:7ff.). What patience could be greater than this? And yet why should we be astonished that the love of God, implanted in her inmost heart, bore up against tyrant, and executioner, and pain, and sex, and natural affection? Had she not heard, "Precious in the sight of the Lord is the death of His saints" (Ps 115:15)? Had she not heard, "A patient man is better than the mightiest" (Prv 16:32)? Had she not heard, "All that is appointed you receive; and in pain bear it; and in abasement keep your patience: for in fire are gold and silver tried"

probat fornax et homines justos temptatio tribulationis (Ecclus 27:6)? Immo vero et haec et alia plura perceperat, quae uno Sancto Dei Spiritu ut in istis Novi Testamenti sic in illis, qui soli adhuc erant, libris divina fortitudinis praecepta conscripta sunt.

(Ecclus 2:4–5)? Had she not heard, "The fire tries the vessels of the potter, and for just men is the trial of tribulation" (Ecclus 27:6)? These she knew, and many other precepts of fortitude written in these books, which alone existed at that time, by the same divine Spirit Who writes those in the New Testament.

Feria Tertia: 2 Mc 7:7–23
S. Cyprianus, *Epistula de exhortatione martyrii* (cap. 11)

Admirabilis quoque mater, quae nec sexus infirmitate fracta, nec multiplici orbitate commota, morientes liberos spectavit libenter, nec poenas illas pignorum, sed glorias computavit, tam grande martyrium Deo praebens virtute oculorum suorum, quam praebuerant filii ejus tormentis et passione membrorum (cf. 2 Mc 7:24 et seq.): cum sex punitis et occisis superesset unus ex fratribus, cui rex divitias et potentatus et multa pollicebatur, ut crudelitas ejus ac feritas vel unius subacti solatio foveretur, et peteret ut ad filium dejiciendum secum deprecaretur et mater; deprecata est illa, sed ut decebat martyrum matrem, ut decebat legis et Dei memorem,

There was the admirable mother, who, neither broken down by the weakness of her sex, nor moved by her manifold bereavement, looked upon her dying children with cheerfulness, and did not reckon those things punishments of her darlings, but glories, giving as great a witness to God by the virtue of her eyes, as her children had given by the tortures and suffering of their limbs (cf. 2 Mc 7:24ff.); when, after the punishment and slaying of six, there remained one of the brethren, to whom the king promised riches, and power, and many things, that his cruelty and ferocity might be soothed by the satisfaction of even one being subdued, and asked that the mother would

ut decebat filios suos non delicate sed fortiter diligentem. Deprecata est enim, sed ut Deum confiteretur: deprecata est ne a fratribus suis frater in consortio laudis et gloriae separaretur: tunc se septem filiorum computans matrem, si sibi contingeret filios septem Deo potius peperisse, non saeculo. Magna laus matris in exhortatione virtutis, sed major in Dei timore et in fidei veritate. Posthaec liberis suis commoritur et mater; neque enim aliud jam decebat, quam ut quae martyres pepererat et fecerat, in consortio illis gloriae jungeretur; et quos ad Deum praemiserat, ipsa quoque sequeretur.

entreat that her son might be cast down with herself; she entreated, but it was as became a mother of martyrs—as became one who was mindful of the Law and of God—as became one who loved her sons not delicately, but bravely. For she entreated, but it was that he would confess God. She entreated that the brother would not be separated from his brothers in the alliance of praise and glory; then only considering herself the mother of seven sons, if it should happen to her to have brought forth seven sons, not to the world, but to God. The mother's praise was great in her exhortation to virtue, but greater in the fear of God and in the truth of faith. After this the mother also dies with her children; for neither was anything else becoming, than that she who had borne and made martyrs, should be joined in the fellowship of glory with them, and that she herself should follow those whom she had sent before to God.

Feria Quarta: 2 Mc 7:24–41
S. Rabanus Maurus, *Commentaria in libros Machabaeorum*
(in librum secundum, cap. 8)

Judas cum septem millibus contra Nicanorem et socios ejus confligit ac vincit (cf. 2 Mc 8:16 et seq.), quia per septiformis gratiam Spiritus populus Ecclesiae cum rectoribus suis vincit hostes universos; nec de eo unquam victoriam capit Judaeus, sive paganus, seu haereticus, vel schismaticus, sive ullus hypocritarum aut nequam: imo ipse cum rege suo vincente tropaeum gloriae possidebit in aeternum. Et cum epicinia agerent in Jerosolymis, eum qui sacras januas incenderat, id est Callisthenem, cum in quoddam domicilium refugisset incenderunt, etc. (cf. 2 Mc 8:33). Superatis ergo hostibus Judas festum celebrat, quia cum sanctis quilibet per gratiam Christi de hoste antiquo triumphat, gaudio spiritali repletus laudes condignas cavere, ac grates multiplices auctori suo debet referre; nec decet fieri ingratum, qui se meminit divino opere esse adiutum.

Judas with seven thousand engages against Nicanor and his allies and wins (cf. 2 Mc 8:16ff.), because by the sevenfold grace of the Spirit the People of the Church with their leaders conquer all enemies; nor does a Jew, a heathen, a heretic, or a schismatic, or any hypocrite or wicked person, ever gain victory over him: nay, the People of the Church himself, together with his conquering king, will possess the trophy of glory forever. And when they were celebrating the victory in their ancestral city in Jerusalem, they set fire to him who had set fire to the sacred doors, that is, Callisthenes, when he had fled to a certain residence, etc. (cf. 2 Mc 8:33). Judas, therefore, having overcome his enemies, celebrates the festival, because whoever triumphs with the saints through the grace of Christ over an ancient enemy, filled with spiritual joy, must beware of worthy praises, and must return manifold thanks to his author; nor should he become ungrateful who remembers that he has been helped by divine operation.

Feria Quinta: 2 Mc 9:1–10
S. Aphraates Sapiens, *Demonstrationes* (De bellis, cap. 20-21)

Antiocho utique judicium occurrit de caelo, acri pessimoque morbo implicitus est (cf. 2 Mc 9:5–12), et prae putore quo fetebat, nemo ei propinquabat, dum vermes de eo scaturiebant, ejusque carnem exedebant, propterea quod "vermiculum Jacob" (Is 41:14) oppresserat; et putruit caro ejus adhuc vivi (cf. 2 Mc 9:9–10), eo quod filiorum Jerusalem cadavera siverat insepulta corrumpi (cf. 2 Mc 9:5–10). Labem habuit in oculis animae suae, quia sanctuarium Dei inquinaverat. Oravit neque exauditus est, eo quod non audierat gemitum justorum quos interfecit (cf. 2 Mc 9:13). Litteras enim scripsit, quas Judaeis misit, eos appellans amicos (cf. 2 Mc 9:18); verum ejus non misertus est Deus, et in cruciatu suo interiit (cf. 2 Mc 9:28). Ait deinde [Antiquus dierum]: "Suscipient regnum sancti [Dei] Altissimi" (Dn 7:27). Quid ad haec dicemus? Num filii Israel regnum Altissimi acceperunt? Absit. Num forte populus ille supra nubes caeli pervenit? Procul ab eis illud transiit.

The judgment came on Antiochus, a judgment from heaven (cf. 2 Mc 9:5–12). He fell sick with an obstinate and evil disease; on account of his ill-smelling odour, no man came near to him, for worms were creeping and falling from him and eating his flesh, because he oppressed "the worm of Jacob" (Is 41:14). His flesh putrefied in his lifetime (cf. 2 Mc 9:9–10), because he caused the corpses of the children of Jerusalem to putrefy, and they were not buried (cf. 2 Mc 9:5–10). He became polluted in his own eyes because he defiled the holy place of God. He prayed but he was not heard because he did not hear the groaning of the righteous ones whom he killed (cf. 2 Mc 9:13). He wrote, however, a letter and sent it to the Jews and called them my friends (cf. 2 Mc 9:18), but God did not have mercy on him, and he died in his torment (cf. 2 Mc 9:28). And [the Ancient of Days] said again, "The saints of the Most High shall receive the Kingdom" (Dn 7:27). What shall we say about this? Did the children of Israel receive the

De eis enim Jeremias ait: "Argentum reprobatum vocate eos, quia projecit eos Dominus" (Jer 6:30). De Sanctis autem Altissimi sic loquitur Daniel: "In saecula saeculorum hereditabunt regnum" (Dn 7:27). Ipsi enim "aliquantulum quieverunt ab onere regum et principum" (Os 8:10), nempe ab Antiocho mortuo donec hebdomades sexaginta duae completae sunt.

Kingdom of the Most High? Far from it. Or did that people come upon the clouds of heaven? This left them behind. For Jeremias said about them, "Call them rejected silver, because the Lord has rejected them" (Jer 6:30). About the saints of the Most High he (the Ancient of Days) said thus, "They shall inherit the Kingdom forever" (Dn 7:27). "For they rested a while from the burden of the kings and of the princes" (Os 8:10), that is after the death of Antiochus till sixty-two weeks were completed.

Feria Sexta: 2 Mc 10:1–5, 24–32
S. Rabanus Maurus, *Commentaria in libros Machabaeorum* (in librum secundum, cap. 10)

"At Timotheus, qui prius fuerat a Judaeis superatus, convocato exercitu peregrinae multitudinis," etc. (2 Mc 10:24). Timotheus iste tenet typum haereticorum, qui tam per se quam per aliorum auxilium et suffragia, fidem Christi ac veritatem Evangelii destruere nituntur semper; sed contra istorum nequitiam doctores sancti a Domino auxilium petunt, ipsique certa spe de caelesti confidentes adjutorio, contra hostes fortiter pug-

"But Timotheus, who had previously been overcome by the Jews, having assembled an army of foreign multitudes," etc. (2 Mc 10:24). This Timotheus holds the type of heretics, who, both by themselves and through the help and votes of others, always strive to destroy the Faith of Christ and the truth of the gospel. but against the wickedness of these the holy teachers ask help from the Lord, and they themselves, confident in the sure hope of the

nant. Equites autem quinque, qui "in equis apparuerunt cum frenis aureis decori, ac Judaeis ducatum praestabant" (2 Mc 10:29), quinque libros legis significant, quibus ad spiritalem scientiam redactis ac de typico velamine litterae ad sensum Evangelii spiritali scientia retractis, opportunum solatium suis praebent exsecutoribus, ac veros confessores Christi per duo praecepta charitatis dextra laevaque tuentes, in adversarios ignita sententiarum tela jactant, e quibus caecitate mentis confusi, repleti perturbatione sensus cadunt. Ex his autem viginti millia et quingenti prosternuntur (cf. 2 Mc 10:31), cum omnes qui catholicae doctrinae, quae in duobus Testamentis est, et Spiritus sancti gratiae contraria sapiunt, veritate vincente, superantur atque dejiciuntur; similiter et equites sexcenti conteruntur, cum superbia mentis eorum, qua saepe praevalere catholicis sperabant, superno nutu perfecte destruuntur.

heavenly help, fight bravely against their enemies. And "the five horsemen, who appeared on horses with golden bridles, and gave leadership to the Jews" (2 Mc 10:29), signify the five books of the Law, which, reduced to spiritual knowledge and withdrawn from the typical covering of the letter to the sense of the gospel with spiritual knowledge, provide a suitable consolation to their executors, and protecting the true confessors of Christ on the right and on the left by the two precepts of charity, they throw at their adversaries fiery weapons of their sentences, from which they fall, confused by the blindness of the mind, filled with confusion of the senses. Of these, twenty thousand and five hundred are prostrated (cf. 2 Mc 10:31), when all who are wise against the Catholic doctrine, which is in the two Testaments, and the Holy Spirit of grace, are overcome and cast down by the conquering truth; in the same way the six hundred horsemen were crushed, when the pride of their minds, by which they often hoped to prevail against the Catholics, was completely destroyed by a nod from above.

Sabbato: 2 Mc 15:7–19
S. Rabanus Maurus, *Commentaria in libros Machabaeorum*
(in librum secundum, cap. 15)

Apparet Onias et Jeremias qui tradit Judae gladium aureum a Deo missum. Manibus Judaei pugnabant, cordibus orabant (cf. 2 Mc 15:12–16). "Oniam, qui fuerat summus sacerdos, virum bonum et benignum, verecundum visu, modestum moribus et eloquio decorum," etc. (2 Mc 15:12). Si quis autem quaesierit utrum haec visio ad ministerium aliquod referri possit, hoc ni fallor ex eo sentiri potest quod Onias sacerdos sacerdotalem significat ordinem; et Jeremias propheta, qui interpretatur excelsus Domini, ipsum Dominum et caput exprimit prophetarum; de quo Moyses dicit: "Prophetam suscitabit Dominus de fratribus vestris, ipsum tanquam me audietis" (Dt 18:15). Ipse sacerdotalis ergo ordo per homines qui in templo Dei sub Veteri Testamento divino officio rite fungebantur, non solum pro populi delictis exorabatur, sed et incarnationem Mediatoris nostri futuram demonstrat, cujus ope mundus salvandus erat. Hic

Onias appears and Jeremias, who delivers to Judas the golden sword sent by God. The Jews fought with their hands, they prayed with their hearts (cf. 2 Mc 15:12–16). "Onias, who had been high priest, was a good and kind man, modest in appearance, modest in manners and decent in speech," etc. (2 Mc 15:12). But if anyone asks whether this vision can be related to any ministry, this can be understood from the fact that Onias the priest signifies a priestly order; and the prophet Jeremias, who is interpreted as the exalted one of the Lord, expresses the Lord Himself and the head of the prophets; of whom Moses says: "The Lord will raise up a prophet from among your brothers, you will listen to him as if to me" (Dt 18:15). The priestly order itself, therefore, through the men who properly performed the divine office in the Temple of God under the Old Testament, not only interceded for the transgressors of the people, but also pointed to the future Incarnation of our Mediator, through Whom the world was to

ergo dedit gladium aureum Judae (cf. 2 Mc 15:15) divinam Scripturam sensu spiritali fulgentem ad munimentum totius Ecclesiae defensionemque populi sui concessit doctoribus, quatenus contra hostes universos armatura uterentur, et hostium prosternerent multitudinem.

be saved. He therefore gave Judas the golden sword (cf. 2 Mc 15:15), which signifies the divine Scripture shining in a spiritual sense for the defense of the whole Church, and he granted to his people teachers, so that they might use weapons against all enemies, and prostrate the multitude of the enemies.

INFRA HEBDOMADAM I NOVEMBRIS

Feria Secunda: Ez 2:2–9
S. Gregorius Magnus Papa, *Homiliarum in Ezechielem Prophetam* (lib. 1, hom. 9, cap. 5–6)

Quid est hoc, quod electi in faciem, et reprobi retrorsum cadunt, nisi quod omnis qui post se cadit ibi procul dubio cadit, ubi non videt; qui vero ante se ceciderit, ibi cecidit, ubi videt? Iniqui ergo quia in invisibilibus cadunt, post se cadere dicuntur, quia ibi corruunt, ubi quid eos tunc sequatur modo videre non possunt. Justi vero, quia in istis visibilibus semetipsos sponte dejiciunt, ut in invisibilibus erigantur, quasi in faciem cadunt, quia, timore compuncti, videntes humiliantur. Notandum vero quod dicitur: "Mitto ego te ad filios Israel, ad gentes apostatrices, quae recesserunt a me" (Ez 2:3).

What is this, that the elect fall upon their faces, and the reprobate fall backwards, if not that everyone who falls backwards undoubtedly falls without a doubt into a place he cannot see; whereas he who falls forward falls into a place he can see? The wicked, therefore, because they fall into unseen things, are said to fall backwards, because they fall into that which they cannot now perceive to follow them. But the righteous, because they voluntarily cast themselves down in these visible things so that they may be raised up in the invisible ones, fall as it were on their faces, because they are contrite out of

Sicut enim duobus modis a Deo receditur, ita duobus modis a Deo apostatae homines fiunt. Nam unusquisque a conditore suo aut fide recedit, aut opere. Sicut ergo qui a fide recedit apostata est, ita qui ad perversum opus quod deseruerat redit, ab omnipotente Deo apostata absque ulla dubietate deputatur, etiamsi fidem tenere videatur. Unum enim sine altero nil prodesse valet, quia nec fides sine operibus, nec opera adjuvant sine fide, nisi fortasse pro fide percipienda fiant.

fear and humbled by what they see. Note also what is said: "I will send thee to the children of Israel, to the apostate nations that have turned away from Me" (Ez 2:3). For just as one departs from God in two ways, so men become apostates from God in two ways. For everyone departs from his Creator either by faith or by works. Thus, just as he who departs from the Faith is an apostate, so also is he who returns to perverse works, which he had abandoned, without any doubt reckoned an apostate by Almighty God, even if he appears to maintiain the Faith. For the one without the other profits nothing, because neither faith without works, nor works without faith, avail, unless perhaps they are performed for the sake of attaining faith.

Feria Tertia: Ez 3:1–13
S. Gregorius Magnus Papa, *Homiliarum in Ezechielem Prophetam* (lib. 1, hom. 10, cap. 5)

"Et aperui os meum et cibavit me volumine illo" (Ez 3:2). Os ergo aperimus, quando sensum ad intelligentiam sacri verbi praeparamus. Itaque ad vocem Domini propheta os aperit, quia ad

"And I opened my mouth, and He fed me with that scroll" (Ez 3:2). We therefore open our mouths when we prepare our mind for the understanding of the sacred Word. And so the prophet opens

spiramentum dominici praecepti cordis nostri desideria inhiant, ut de cibo vitae aliquid sumant. Sed tamen hoc ipsum sumere nostrarum virium non est, nisi ipse cibaverit qui ut comedatur jussit. Ille etenim cibatur, qui per se edere non potest. Et quia ad capienda verba caelestia idonea nostra infirmitas non est, ipse nos cibat, qui nobis "in tempore mensuram tritici" (Lk 12:42) temperat, quatenus in sacro verbo dum hodie intelligimus quod hesterno die nesciebamus, cras quoque comprehendamus quod hodie nescimus, per divinae dispensationis gratiam quotidiano alimento nutriamur. Omnipotens etenim Deus quasi toties ad os cordis nostri manum porrigit, quoties nobis intellectum aperit, et cibum sacri eloquii in nostris sensibus mittit. Cibat ergo nos volumine, cum sensum nobis Scripturae sacrae dispensando aperit, et ejus dulcedine nostras cogitationes replet (cf. Ez 3:3).

his mouth at the voice of the Lord because the desires of our hearts yearn for the inspiration of the Lord's commands, so that they may partake of the food of life. But it is not our power to partake in it, unless He Who commanded that it be eaten also feeds us. For he is fed, who cannot eat on his own. And because our weakness is not suitable for grasping the heavenly Words, He Himself feeds us, adjusting for us the "measure of wheat in due season" (Lk 12:42), in that while we understand today in the sacred Word what we did could not yesterday, and when tomorrow likewise we unsertand what we cannot grasp today, we are through the grace of the divine dispensation nourished with daily food. For Almighty God, as it were, extends His hand to the mouth of our hearts as often as He opens our understanding, and places the food of His sacred Word into our mind. He therefore feeds us with a scroll, when He unveils for us the meaning of Sacred Scripture and fills our thoughts with its sweetness (cf. Ez 3:3).

Feria Quarta: Ez 7:1–13
S. Hieronymus, *Commentaria in Ezechielem* (lib. 2, ad cap. 7, 12)

"Venit tempus, appropinquavit dies" (Ez 7:12). Non solum ad Jerusalem dicitur, quod venerit ei tempus captivitatis, et appropinquaverit dies quo Babylonio sit vallanda exercitu; sed et ei qui exstructis et dilatatis horreis exsultabat, Dominus loquitur: "Stulte, hac nocte auferetur anima tua a te: quae autem praeparasti, cujus erunt?" (Lk 11:20). Unde et Apostolus: "Tempus," ait, "abbreviatum est" (1 Cor 7:29). Et in alio loco: "Praeterit enim figura hujus mundi" (1 Cor 7:31). Notandum quod non in futurum distulerit, sed de praesenti dixerit, praeterit, et quotidie labitur figura mundi. Numquam enim in eodem statu permanet; sed semper crescentium et decrescentium figura praetervolat et mutatur. Unde et Dominus: "Caelum," inquit, "et terra praeteribit" (Mt 24:35). Sin autem haec quibus omnia quae in mundo sunt continentur, praetereunt atque pertranseunt, quid potest in humanis rebus esse perpetuum?

"The time has come, the day is near" (Ez 7:12). It is not only said to Jerusalem that the time of its captivity had come, and the day was near it would be besieged by the army of Babylon; but also to him who exulted in the constructed and enlarged storehouses, the Lord says: "Fool, this night thy soul will be required of thee. But what you hast prepared, whose shall they be?" (Lk 11:20). Hence the apostle also says: "The time is short" (1 Cor 7:29). And in another place: "For the figure of this world is passing away" (1 Cor 7:31). It should be noted that he does not speak of the future, but said of the present that it "is passing away," and that the figure of the world daily slips away. For it never remains in the same state; but the form of things is constantly fleeting and changing as they increase or diminish. Hence the Lord also says: "Heaven and earth shall pass away" (Mt 24:35). If, then, these things that contain all that is in the world pass away and vanish, what can be permanent in human affairs?

Feria Quinta: Ez 13:1–14
S. Gregorius Magnus, *Regula pastoralis* (lib. 2, cap. 4)

Sit rector discretus in silentio, utilis in verbo, ne aut tacenda proferat, aut proferenda reticescat. Nam sicut incauta locutio in errorem pertrahit, ita indiscretum silentium hos qui erudiri poterant, in errore derelinquit. Saepe namque rectores improvidi humanam amittere gratiam formidantes, loqui libere recta pertimescunt; et juxta veritatis vocem (cf. Jn 10:12), nequaquam jam gregis costodiae pastorum studio, sed mercenariorum vice deserviunt, quia veniente lupo fugiunt, dum se sub silentio abscondunt. Hinc namque eos per prophetam Dominus increpat, dicens: "Canes muti non valentes latrare" (Is 56:10). Hinc rursum queritur, dicens: "Non ascendistis ex adverso, nec opposuistis murum pro domo Israel, ut staretis in praelio in die Domini" (Ez 13:5). Ex adverso quippe ascendere, est pro defensione gregis voce libera hujus mundi potestatibus contraire. Et in die Domini in praelio stare, est pravis decertantibus ex justitiae amore resistere. Pastori enim recta timuisse dicere,

The ruler should be discreet in keeping silence, profitable in speech; lest he either utter what ought to be suppressed or suppress what he ought to utter. For, as incautious speaking leads into error, so indiscreet silence leaves in error those who might have been instructed. For often improvident rulers, fearing to lose human favour, shrink timidly from speaking freely the things that are right; and, according to the voice of the Truth (cf. Jn 10:12), serve unto the custody of the flock by no means with the zeal of shepherds, but in the way of hirelings; since they fly when the wolf comes if they hide themselves under silence. For hence it is that the Lord through the prophet upbraids them, saying, "Dumb dogs, that cannot bark" (Is 56:10). Hence again He complains, saying, "You have not gone up against the enemy, neither opposed a wall for the house of Israel, to stand in the battle in the day of the Lord" (Ez 13:5). Now to go up against the enemy is to go with free voice against the powers of this world for defense of the flock; and to stand in the battle in the day of

quid est aliud quam tacendo terga praebuisse? qui nimirum si pro grege se objicit, murum pro domo Israel hostibus opponit.

the Lord is out of love of justice to resist bad men when they contend against us. Because, for a shepherd to have feared to say what is right, what else is it but to have turned his back in keeping silence? But surely, if he puts himself in front for the flock, he opposes a wall against the enemy for the house of Israel.

Feria Sexta: Ez 15:1–8; 16:1–5
S. Augustinus, *In Evangelium Joannis tractatus* (tr. 81, cap. 3)

Ne quisquam putaret saltem parvum aliquem fructum posse a semetipso palmitem ferre, cum Dominus dixisset, hic fert fructum multum, non ait, quia sine me parum potestis facere; sed, "nihil potestis facere" (Jn 15:5). Sive ergo parum, sive multum, sine illo fieri non potest, sine quo nihil fieri potest. Quia etsi parum attulerit palmes, eum purgat agricola ut plus afferat: tamen nisi in vite manserit et vixerit de radice, quantumlibet fructum a semetipso non potest ferre. Quamvis autem Christus vitis non esset, nisi homo esset; tamen istam gratiam palmitibus non praeberet, nisi etiam Deus esset. Verum quia ita sine ista gratia non potest vivi,

For just to keep any from supposing that the branch can bear at least some little fruit of itself, after saying, the same brings forth much fruit, His next words are not without Me you can do but little, but "you can do nothing" (Jn 15:5). Whether then it be little or much, without Him it is impracticable; for without Him nothing can be done. For although, when the branch bears little fruit, the husbandman purges it that it may bring forth more; yet if it abides not in the vine, and draw its life from the root, it can bear no fruit whatever of itself. And although Christ would not have been the vine had He not been man, yet He could not have supplied such grace to the branches had He not also been God. And just

ut et mors in potestate sit liberi arbitrii: "Si quis in me," inquit, "non manserit, mittetur foras sicut palmites: et arescet, et colligent eum, et in ignem mittent, et ardet" (Jn 15:6). Ligna itaque vitis tanto sunt contemptibiliora si in vite non manserint, quanto gloriosiora si manserint: denique, sicut de his etiam per Ezechielem prophetam Dominus dicit, praecisa nullis agricolarum usibus prosunt, nullis fabrilibus operibus deputantur (cf. Ez 15:5). Unum de duobus palmiti congruit, aut vitis, aut ignis; si in vite non est, in igne erit: ut ergo in igne non sit, in vite sit.

because such grace is so essential to life, that even death itself ceases to be at the disposal of free will, He adds, "If anyone abide not in Me, he shall be cast forth as a branch, and wither; and they shall gather him, and cast him into the fire, and he is burned" (Jn 15:6). The wood of the vine, therefore, is in the same proportion the more contemptible if it abide not in the vine, as it is glorious while so abiding; in fine, as the Lord likewise says of them in the prophet Ezechiel, when cut off, they are of no use for any purpose of the husbandman, and can be applied to no labor of the mechanic (cf. Ez 15:5). The branch is suitable only for one of two things, either the vine or the fire: if it is not in the vine, its place will be in the fire; and that it may escape the latter, may it have its place in the vine.

Sabbato: Ez 19:1–14

S. Hieronymus, *Commentaria in Ezechielem* (lib. 6, ad cap. 19, 14)

A planctu enim incipit, et finitur in planctu). "Assume planctum super principes Israel" (Ez 19:1). Hoc est, in principio et nunc in fine, planctus est; et lamentatione, planctuque parabolae stirps regia

For it begins with weeping and ends with weeping. "Take up a lamentation for the princes of Israel" (Ez 19:1). This is, at the beginning and now in the end, there is weeping; and with lamentation and

prosequenda. Porro secundum anagogem, quod alii ad caelestem referunt Jerusalem, ut dicant ex ea in istam vallem lacrimarum plurimos corruisse, et reges esse desisse, et vineam quondam pulcherrimam vento urente siccatam, ita ut nullus in ea virentium palmitum remanserit, quam postea sub urbis figura plangat Jeremias (cf. Jer 4:19), nos intelligimus super Ecclesiam, eo quod in novissimo tempore multiplicata iniquitate, refrigescat, refrigescet caritas multorum (cf. Mt 24:12): ita ut probentur si fieri potest etiam electi Dei. Palmites quoque Ecclesiae qui dudum floribus et rubori sanguinis aequabantur, postea vento siccentur. Quam expositionem et Evangelii quoque parabola sonat, in qua "sole orto, ea quae germinaverant, aestuavevunt, et repente siccata sunt" (Mk 4:6). Unde debemus plangere, et lamentari super principes Israel, quorum vitio et superbia Judaea deserta, et capta est Jerusalem.

weeping the royal line of the parable should be pursued. Moreover, according to the anagogical interpretation—which others refer to the heavenly Jerusalem, saying that many have fallen from it into this valley of tears, and that kings have ceased, and that the once-beautiful vine has been dried up by a burning wind, so that no green branch remains in it—Jeremias later laments this under the figure of the city (cf. Jer. 4:19). We understand this concerning the Church, since in the last days, with iniquity multiplied, the charity of many will grow cold (cf. Mt 24:12): so that even God's elect, if it were possible, might be tested. Even the branches of the Church, which once were equal to flowers and blush of blood, will later be dried up by the wind. This interpretation is also echoed in the parable of the Gospel, where "when the sun was risen, it was scorched; and because it had no root, it withered away" (Mk 4:6). Wherefore we ought to weep and lament for the princes of Israel, by whose fault and pride Judea was deserted, and Jerusalem was captured.

INFRA HEBDOMADAM II NOVEMBRIS

Feria Secunda: Ez 33:1–11
S. Cyprianus, *De lapsis* (cap. 36)

Si precem toto corde quis faciat, si veris paenitentiae lamentationibus et lacrimis ingemiscat, si ad veniam delicti sui Dominum justis et continuis operibus inflectat, misereri talium potest qui et misericordiam suam protulit dicens: "Nolo mortem morientis, dicit Dominus, quantum ut revertatur et vivat" (Ez 33:11). Potest ille indulgentiam dare, sententiam suam potest ille deflectere. Paenitenti, operanti, roganti potest elementer ignoscere, potest in acceptum referre quidquid pro talibus et petierint martyres et fecerint sacerdotes. Vel si quis plus eum suis satisfactionibus moverit, si ejus iram, si indignantis offensam justa deprecatione placaverit, dat ille et arma rursum quibus victus armetur, reparat et corroborat vires quibus fides instaurata vegetetur. Repetet certamen suum miles, iterabit aciem, provocabit hostem, et quidem factus ad praelium fortior per dolorem. Qui sic Deo satisfecerit, qui paenitentia facti sui, qui pudore delicti, plus et virtutis

If anyone make prayer with his whole heart, if he groan with the true lamentations and tears of repentance, if he incline the Lord to pardon of his sin by righteous and continual works, he who expressed His mercy in these words may pity such men: "I have no pleasure in the death of him that dies, says the Lord, but that he should return and live" (Ez 33:11). He can show mercy; He can turn back His judgment. He can mercifully pardon the repenting, the laboring, the beseeching sinner. He can regard as effectual whatever, on behalf of such as these, either martyrs have besought, or priests have done. Or if anyone move Him still more by his own atonement, if he appease His anger, if he appeases the wrath of an indignant God by righteous entreaty, He gives arms again whereby the vanquished may be armed; He restores and confirms the strength whereby the refreshed faith may be invigorated. The soldier will seek his contest anew; he will repeat the fight, he will provoke the enemy, and indeed by his very suffering he

et fidei de ipso lapsus sui dolore conceperit, exauditus et adiutus a Domino, quam contristaverat, nuper laetam faciet Ecclesiam; nec jam solam Dei veniam merebitur, sed et coronam.

is made braver for the battle. He who has thus made atonement to God; he who by repentance for his deed, who by shame for his sin, has conceived more both of virtue and of faith from the very grief of his fall, heard and aided by the Lord, shall make the Church which he had lately saddened glad, and shall now deserve of the Lord not only pardon, but a crown.

Feria Tertia: Ez 34:1–7, 10–12
S. Augustinus, *Sermones* (De pastoribus in Ezechiel 34, 1–16: serm. 46, cap. 2)

"Et factum est verbum Domini ad me, dicens: Fili hominis, propheta super pastores Israel et dic ad pastores Israel" (Ez 34:1–2). Hanc lectionem modo, cum legeretur, audivimus: hinc cum vestra sanctitate aliquid loqui decrevimus. Adjuvabit ipse ut vera dicamus, si non nostra dicamus. Nam si nostra dixerimus, pastores erimus pascentes nos, non oves; si autem illius sunt quae dicimus, per quemlibet ipse vos pascit. Haec dicit Dominus Deus: "O pastores Israel, qui pascunt se solos! Numquid non oves pascunt pastores?" (Ez 34:2). Id est, non se pascunt

"And the Word of the Lord came to me saying, Son of man, prophesy over the shepherds of Israel, and say to the shepherds of Israel" (Ez 34:1–2). We heard this lesson when it was read just now; I have decided to say a few things about it to your holinesses. He Himself will help me to say true things, if I do not just say my own thing. If I do just say my own thing, I shall be a shepherd feeding myself, not the sheep; but if what I say is His thing, then it is He Who is feeding you, whoever may be speaking. Thus says the Lord God: "O shepherds of Israel, who feed themselves alone!

pastores, sed oves. Haec prima causa est, quare arguantur isti pastores, quia se ipsos pascunt, non oves. Qui sunt qui se ipsos pascunt? De quibus Apostolus dicit: "Omnes enim sua quaerunt, non quae Jesu Christi" (Phil 2:21). Nos enim, quos in loco isto, de quo periculosa ratio redditur, Dominus secundum dignationem suam non secundum meritum nostrum constituit, habemus duo quaedam plane distinguenda: unum quod christiani sumus, alterum quod praepositi sumus. Illud quod christiani sumus, propter nos est; quod praepositi sumus, propter vos est. In eo quod christiani sumus, attenditur utilitas nostra; in eo quod praepositi, nonnisi vestra.

Do not shepherds feed sheep?" (Ez 34:2). That is, shepherds do not feed themselves, but sheep. That is the first cause of complaint against these shepherds, that they do feed themselves, and not the sheep. Who are the ones that feed themselves? Those about whom the apostle says, "For all seek their own advantage, not that of Jesus Christ" (Phil 2:21). You see, we whom the Lord has deigned, thanks to no merits of ours, to set in this high station (about which a very strict account indeed must be rendered) have two things about us that must be clearly distinguished: one, that we are Christians, the other, that we are placed in charge. Being Christians is for our sake; being in charge is for yours. It is to our advantage that we are Christians, only to yours that we are in charge.

Feria Quarta: Ez 40:1–6
S. Gregorius Magnus Papa, *Homiliae in Ezechielem* (lib. 2, hom. 2, 15)

Latitudo itaque aedificii (cf. Ez 40:5) ad caritatem pertinet, de qua Psalmista dicit: "Latum mandatum tuum nimis" (Ps 118:96). Nil enim latius quam omnes in sinu amoris recipere, et nullas odii

The breadth of the building (cf. Ez 40:5) pertains to charity, of which the psalmist says: "Thy commandment is exceedingly broad" (Ps 118:96). For there is nothing wider than to receive all in the bosom of

angustias sustinere. Sic quippe lata est caritas, ut in amplitudine dilectionis suae capere etiam inimicos possit. Unde et praecipitur: "Diligite inimicos vestros, benefacite iis qui oderunt vos" (Lk 6:27). Considerandum quoque nobis est quia latitudo in aequalitate, altitudo vero in sublimitate tenditur. Latitudo ergo pertinet ad caritatem proximi, altitudo ad intelligentiam conditoris. Sed latitudo et altitudo aedificii uno calamo mensuratur (cf. Ez 40:5), quia videlicet unaquaeque anima quantum lata fuerit in amore proximi, tantum et alta erit in cognitione Dei. Dum enim se per amorem juxta dilatat, per cognitionem se superius exaltat; et tantum super semetipsam excelsa fit, quantum se juxta se in proximi amorem tendit. Et quia aedificium quod inhabitat Deus ex angelica simul et humana natura perficitur, per hoc quod angelica creatura sursum est, et humana adhuc deorsum, potest per latitudinem atque altitudinem aedificii utraque haec creatura significari, quia ista adhuc in imis degit, illa vero in sublimibus permanet. Sed

love, and to endure no constraints of hatred. Indeed, charity is so wide that in the breadth of its love it can embrace even its enemies. Hence it is commanded: "Love your enemies, do good to those who hate you" (Lk 6:27). We must also consider that breadth tends toward equality, but height toward sublimity. The breadth therefore belongs to the charity of the neighbor, the height to the intelligence of the Creator. But the width and height of a building are measured with a single rod (cf. Ez 40:5), because obviously each soul will be as wide as it is in the love of its neighbor, as much as it will be high in the knowledge of God. For while one expands himself by love, one exalts himself above by knowledge; and one becomes exalted above himself only in so far as one grows in the love of his neighbor. And since the building in which God dwells is completed by angelic and human nature at the same time, by the fact that the angelic creature is above, and the human still below, both of these creatures can be signified by the width and height of the building, because the latter still dwells in

uno calamo mensuratur utraque, quia humilitas hominum quandoque ad aequalitatem perducitur angelorum.

the lowest places, while the latter remains in the sublime. But both are measured with one rod, because the humility of men is sometimes raised to equality with the angels.

Feria Quinta: Ez 41:1–9
S. Hieronymus, *Commentaria in Ezechielem* (lib. 12, ad cap. 41:1)

"Et introduxit me in templum, et mensus est frontes sex cubitos latitudinis hinc, et sex cubitos latitudinis inde, latitudinem tabernaculi. Et latitudo portae decem cubitorum erat, et latera (sive humeri) portae quinque cubitis hinc, et quinque cubitis inde. Et mensus est longitudinem ejus quadraginta cubitorum, et latitudinem viginti cubitorum" (Ez 41:1–2). Post multa mysteria, variosque introitus, et locorum singulorum proprietates, tandem aliquando vir, cujus funiculus caementariorum, et mensurae calamus in manu erat, Ezechielem prophetam introducit in templum, et mensus est frontem templi. Et ex utraque parte latitudo tabernaculi senum cubitorum erat, sacramentum creaturarum omnium continens: in sex enim diebus mundus est consummatus. Per quorum notitiam causasque condi-

"And he brought me into the Temple, and he measured the fronts six cubits broad on this side, and six cubits on that side, the breadth of the tabernacle. And the breadth of the gate was ten cubits: and the sides of the gate five cubits on this side, and five cubits on that side: and he measured the length thereof forty cubits, and the breadth twenty cubits" (Ez 41:1–2). After many mysteries, various entrances, and the peculiarities of each place, at last one day a man, with a mason's cord and a measuring stick in his hand, led the prophet Ezechiel into the Temple, and he measured the front of the Temple. And on each side the width of the tabernacle were six cubits, containing the mysterious meaning of all creatures: for in six days the world was completed. Through the knowledge of their condition and reason we enter the

tionis atque rationem intramus ad templum Dei, et ex creaturarum ordine atque constantia cognoscimus Creatorem. Latitudo autem portae templi erat decem cubitorum, qui sacratus et perfectus est numerus, et in quo mense septimo, die decima mensis, ieiunium et propitiatio est. Decima autem die mensis primi, qui appellatur Nisan, ad immolationem et praeparationem Paschae agnus assumitur.

Temple of God, and from the order and consistency of the creatures we know the Creator. Now the width of the gate of the Temple was ten cubits, which is a sacred and perfect number, and in the seventh month, on the tenth day of the month there is fasting and atonement. On the tenth day of the first month, which is called Nisan, the lamb is taken up for the sacrifice and preparation of the Passover.

Feria Sexta: Ez 43:1–11
S. Hieronymus, *Commentaria in Ezechielem* (lib. 13, ad cap. 43, 1 et seq.)

Majestas Domini ingressa est templum per viam portae, quae respiciebat ad Orientem, statimque me elevavit spiritus, et introduxit me in atrium interitus, foris enim cecideram; et ecce, qui prius conspexeram gloriam Dei Israel venientem per viam Orientalem, vidi repletam gloria Domini domum ejus, et vocem ad me de domo interiori loquentem audivi (cf. Ez 43:4–6). Quae quid sit locuta, Scriptura non narrat, nisi forte illud Apostoli: "Et audivi verba ineffabilia quae non licet homini loqui" (2 Cor 12:4). Vir autem, inquit, qui stabat juxta

The Lord's majesty entered the Temple by the way of the gate, which looked towards the east, and immediately the spirit lifted me up and brought me into the court of destruction, for I had fallen outside. And behold, I saw before the glory of the God of Israel coming by the Eastern road, I saw His house filled with the glory of the Lord, and I heard a voice speaking to me from the inner house (cf. Ez 43:4–6). The Scriptures do not tell us what was spoken, except perhaps that of the apostle: "And I heard unspeakable words which it is not lawful for a man to speak" (2 Cor 12:4). And

prophetam, dixit ad eum: quem perspicue Dominum intelligimus. Cui enim alii poterit convenire quod sequitur: "Fili hominis, locus solii mei, et locus vestigiorum pedum meorum, ubi habito in medio filiorum Israel in aeternum" (Ez 43:7), nisi illi qui habitat in Ecclesia in medio filiorum Israel cernentium Deum, et habitat in perpetuum, non secundum templum Salomonis ad tempus? Et pulchre dixit, steterunt: in Ecclesia enim stant pedes Domini, in synagoga ambulant et praetereunt.

the man, he says, who stood by the prophet, said to him: Whom we clearly understand as the Lord. For to whom others may agree what follows: "Son of man, the place of My throne, and the place of the footsteps of My feet, where I dwell in the midst of the children of Israel forever" (Ez 43:7), except He Who dwells in the Church in the midst of the children of Israel Who see God, and dwells forever, not according to the Temple of Solomon for a time? And he said well, they stood: for the feet of the Lord stand in the Church, they walk in the synagogue and pass by.

Sabbato: Ez 47:1–9

S. Hieronymus, *Commentaria in Ezechielem* (lib. 14, ad cap. 47, 1 et seq.)

"Vir autem," inquit, "ille qui habebat funiculum in manu, cum me duxisset per portam Aquilonis forinsecus ad viam, quae respiciebat Orientem, et ipse quoque esset in eodem loco, mensus est ejusdem aquae mille cubitos" (Ez 47:2–3); et transivit in aquam remissionis: quod intelligere possumus prima hominum significare peccata, quae ingredientibus nobis aquas Domini dimittuntur, et baptismi

"And the man," says he, "who had the line in his hand, when he led me out by the way of the north gate, and caused me to turn to the way without the outward gate to the way that looked toward the east, and he was also in the same place, measured a thousand cubits of the same water" (Ez 47:2–3); and he passed into the water of forgiveness: which we can understand to mean the first sins of men, which

ostendunt gratiam salutarem et initia sunt profectuum, tamen ipsa sublimia. Denique ad talos usque pertingunt, qui plantae calcaneoque vicini sunt, qui patet morsibus colubri, dicente Domino: Tu ejus observabis caput, et ipse observabit tuum calcaneum (cf. Gn 3:15). Post mille autem cubitos qui perveniunt usque ad talum, mensus est alios mille cubitos in aqua, et transduxit me usque ad genua (cf. Ez 47:4). Post remissionem siquidem peccatorum, et iter profectuum, quando paululum de terrenis ad altiora conamur ascendere, flectimus Domino genua. Tertio mensus est mille alios cubitos, et transduxit, inquit, me per aquam usque ad renes. His enim gradibus ad sublimia pervenimus: quae tamen ipsa sublimia usque ad lumbos et renes perveniunt, ut omnis in nobis ignobilis libido truncetur; et possideamus sanctificationem corporis, sine qua nemo videt Deum.

are forgiven when we enter the waters of the Lord, and in baptism they show saving grace and are the beginnings of progress, yet the very sublime. Finally, they reach even to the ankles, which are close to the plant and the heel, which is evident from the bites of the serpent, saying to the Lord: Thou wilt lie in wait of his head, and he will lie in wait of thy heel (cf. Gn 3:15). And after a thousand cubits, which reach up to the ankle, he measured another thousand cubits in the water and brought me up to my knees (cf. Ez 47:4). Indeed, after the remission of sins, and the way of spiritual progress, when we try to ascend a little from the earthly to the higher, we bow our knees to the Lord. The third measured another thousand cubits, and he carried me through the water up to my knees, he said. For by these steps, we reach the sublimity: which sublimity, however, reaches up to the loins and reins, so that every base lust in us is cut off; and let us possess the sanctification of the body, without which no one sees God.

INFRA HEBDOMADAM III NOVEMBRIS

Feria Secunda: Dn 2:31–44

S. Augustinus, *Sermones* (serm. 147A, cap. 4)

Qui offendit in lapidem, ignoscendum est illi; qui offendit in montem, quales oculos habet? Fratres mei, excusabiliores sunt Judaei; Judaei enim in lapidem offenderunt, haeretici in montem offendunt. Quomodo offenderunt Judaei in lapidem? Quia adhuc Christus, quando patiebatur, parvulus erat; et dictum est: Offenderunt in lapidem offensionis (cf. Rom. 9:32). Daniel autem sanctus vidit visum, et scripsit quod vidit, et ait, vidisse se lapidem praecisum de monte sine manibus (cf. Dn 2:34). Christus est, de gente Judaeorum veniens; erat enim et illa mons, quia regnum habet. Quid est: Sine manibus? Sine opere humano lapis praecisus, quia masculinum opus non accessit ad virginem, ut nasceretur sine opere humano. Lapis praecisus de monte sine manibus; et confregit statuam, in qua significabantur regna terrarum. Et quid dictum est? Ipse est lapis, in quem offenderunt Judaei; offenderunt in lapidem offensio-

Anyone can be excused for stumbling over a stone; but if thou stumblest over a mountain—well, what sort of eyes hast thou got? My brothers, the Jews are more excusable; the Jews after all stumbled over a stone, the heretics trip over a mountain. How did the Jews trip over a stone? It was because Christ, during His Passion, was still small; and it was said, They stumbled over the stone of stumbling (cf. Rom 9:32). The holy Daniel, however, saw a vision, and wrote down what he saw, and he said that he had seen a stone hewn out of a mountain without hands (cf. Dn 2:34). It is Christ, coming from the nation of the Jews, which was also a mountain, you see, because it has the Kingdom. What does it mean, without hands? A stone hewn without human activity, because no masculine activity was involved with the virgin, so that He was born without human activity. A stone hewn without hands from the mountain; and it shattered the statue in which all the kingdoms of the earth were

nis. Quis est mons, in quem offenderunt haeretici? Audi ipsum Danielem: "Et crevit lapis ille, ait, et factus est mons magnus, ita ut impleret universam faciem terrae" (Dn 2:35). Merito psalmus Christo Domino resurgenti ait: "Exaltare super caelos, Deus, et super omnem terram gloria tua" (Ps 56:12; 107:6). Quid est: Super omnem terram gloria tua? Super omnem terram Ecclesia tua, super omnem terram sponsa tua.

represented. And what is said? That is the stone over which the Jews stumbled; they stumbled over the stone of stumbling. What is the mountain over which the heretics tripped? Listen to Daniel again: "And that stone grew, he said, and became a great mountain, such that it filled all the face of the earth" (Dn 2:35). How right the psalm is to say to Christ the Lord as He rises again, "Be exalted over the heavens, O God, and over the whole earth Thy glory" (Ps 56:12; 107:6). What is over the whole earth Thy glory? Over the whole earth Thy Church, over the whole earth Thy Bride.

Feria Tertia: Dn 3:14–19, 21–24
S. Joannes Chrysostomus, *Liber Quod nemo laeditur nisi a seipso* (cap. 17)

Verumtamen ego pueros non eo miror, beatosque ac felices aestimo, quod flammam conculcarunt, vim ignis vicerunt; sed quod verorum dogmatum causa vincti, in caminum coniecti et igni traditi sunt. Hic enim eis totum tropaeum absolutum est, et simul atque in caminum coeiecti sunt, imposita corona, et ab illis verbis texi coepta etiam ante re-

Nevertheless, I do not wonder at the children, and I consider them happy, because they have trodden the flame, conquered the power of fire; but because they were bound for the sake of true dogmas, they were thrown into the furnace and delivered to the fire. For here the whole trophy was taken away from them, and they were thrown into the fire at the same time, with

rum eventum, quae magna cum fiducia libertateque loquendi ad regem ducti in medium protulerunt: "Non oportet de hac re respondere tibi. Potest enim Deus noster qui est in caelis, quem nos colimus, eripere nos ex camino ignis ardentis; et de tuis manibus, rex, liberabit nos: sin minus, notum sit tibi rex, quia deos tuos non colimus, et statuam auream, quam erexisti, non adoramus" (Dn 3:16–18). Jam inde ab illis verbis eos victores pronuntio; jam inde ab illis reportato victoriae praemio ad insignem martyrii coronam, confessioni verborum addita confessione rerum, cucurrerunt. Sin ignis reveritus est immissa eorum corpora et vincula solvit, securum descensum praebuit, suae virtutis oblitus, et caminus ignis factus est fons frigidarum aquarum: id jam divinae gratiae, et supernae stupendarum rerum operationis miraculum fuit.

crowns placed upon them, and from these words they started, even before things happened, which they spoke to the king with great confidence and freedom of speech: "We have no need to answer thee in this matter. If this be so, our God Whom we serve is able to deliver us from the burning fiery furnace, and He will deliver us out of thy hand, O king. But if not, be it known to thee, O king, that we will not serve thy gods or worship the golden image that thou hast set up" (Dn 3:16–18). Now from these words I pronounce them conquerors; and having they already received the reward of the victory, they ran to the distinguished crown of martyrdom, adding to the confession of words the confession of things. Indeed, the fire respected their bodies, when they were thrown down and loosened their bonds, it provided for them a safe descent, forgetting its power, and the hearth of the fire became a fountain of cold waters: this was already a miracle of divine grace, and of the operation of astonishing things from above.

Feria Quarta: Dn 4:16–25
S. Hieronymus, *Commentaria in Danielem* (in cap. 4, vers. 24)

Neque enim Deus hominibus, sed vitiis irascitur: quae cum in homine non fuerint, nequaquam punit quod mutatum est. Dicamus et aliter: Fecit quidem Nabuchodonosor juxta Danielis consilium misericordias in pauperes; et idcirco usque ad mensem duodecimum in eum est dilata sententia: sed quia postea ambulans in aula Babylonis, gloriatur et dicit: "Nonne haec est Babylon magna, quam ego aedificavi in domum regni; in robore fortitudinis meae in gloria nominis mei?" (Dn 4:27) bonum misericordiae perdidit malo superbiae. "Forsitan ignoscet Deus delictis tuis" (Dn 4:24). Cum beatus Daniel praescius futurorum de sententia Dei dubitet, rem temerariam faciunt, qui audacter peccatoribus indulgentiam pollicentur. Et tamen sciendum quod si Nabuchodonosor bona opera facienti venia repromittitur; multo magis aliis promittitur qui leviora peccata commiserunt. Arrogans gloriatio statim punitur a Domino. Et ideo non differtur sententia, ne videatur misericor-

For God is not angry with men, but with vices: which, when they were not in man, He in no way would punish that which has been changed (which had been converted from sin). Let us say it in another way: Nabuchodonosor did, in accordance with the counsel of Daniel, show mercy to the poor; and therefore until the twelfth month there is a sentence pronounced against him; but because afterwards he is walking in the court of Babylon, he boasts and says: "Is not this Babylon the great, which I have built for the house of the kingdom? in the strength of my power and in the glory of my name?" (Dn 4:27), and so he lost the good of mercy by the evil of pride. "Perhaps God will forgive thy transgressions" (Dn 4:24). Blessed Daniel, although knowing the future, was doubting God's decision, they are people doing a temerarious thing by recklessly promising forgiveness to sinners. And yet it must be known that if Nabuchodonosor does good works, forgiveness is promised; much more is promised to others

dia in pauperes minime profuisse. Sed statim ut locutus est per superbiam, perdidit regnum quod ob eleemosynas fuerat reservatum.

who have committed lesser sins. Arrogant boasting is immediately punished by the Lord. And therefore, the sentence is not postponed, lest it be seen that mercy has not benefited the poor in the least. But as soon as he spoke through pride, he lost the kingdom which had been reserved due to almsgiving.

Feria Quinta: Dn 5:1–6, 13–17, 25–31
S. Hieronymus, *Commentaria in Danielem* (in cap. 5, vers. 4)

Postquam autem humanis usibus divina contaminant, statim poena sequitur post sacrilegium. Laudant autem deos suos, insultantes Deo Judaeorum (cf. Dn 5:4); quod illis victoriam tribuentibus, bibebant in vasis ejus. Juxta tropologiam, hoc dicendum est: quod omnes haeretici, et doctrina contraria veritati, quae assumit verba prophetarum; et testimoniis divinae Scripturae abutitur ad sensum suum; et dat bibere his quos decipit, et cum quibus fornicata est: tollat vasa templi Dei, et inebrietur in eis: et non Deum cujus vasa sunt, sed deos laudet aureos et argenteos, et aeneos, et ferreos, ligneosque et lapideos. Aurei mihi videntur hi qui saeculari ratione

But after they contaminate the divine things with human uses, punishment immediately follows after the sacrilege. Yet they praise their gods, insulting the God of the Jews (cf. Dn 5:4); that, giving them the victory, they drank from His vessels. According to tropology [the moral meaning], must be said the following: that all are heretics, and a doctrine contrary to the truth, which assumes the words of the prophets; and which abuses the evidences of the divine Scriptures for his own sense; and which gives drink to those whom she (the doctrine) deceives, and with whom she has committed fornication, takes away the vessels of the Temple of God, and gets drunk in them: and praises not

compositi sunt. Argentei, qui habent eloquii venustatem, et rhetorica arte constructi sunt. Qui autem inferunt fabulas poetarum, et vetustis utuntur traditionibus, habentes inter se multam vel elegantiae vel stultitiae differentiam, isti vocantur aenei et ferrei. Qui autem penitus inepta proponunt, lignei appellantur et lapidei. Quos omnes in duas partes Deuteronomium dividit, scribens: "Maledictus qui facit sculptile, et conflatile, opus manuum artificis, et ponit illud in abscondito" (Dt 27:15). Abscondunt enim omnes haeretici, et operiunt mendaciorum suorum dogmata, ut sagittent in obscuro rectos corde.

God Whose vessels they are, but gods of gold and silver, and bronze, and iron, and wood, and stone. They seem to me to be golden vessels, who are composed according to the worldly reason. Silver vessels, who have a charm of speech, and are built with rhetorical skill. But those who import the fables of the poets, and make use of ancient traditions, having among themselves a great difference either in elegance or stupidity, are called bronze and iron. But those who propose to be utterly foolish are called wooden and stone made. Deuteronomy divides all of them into two parts, writing: "Cursed is he who makes carved and molded work of the hands of the craftsman and sets it up in secret" (Dt 27:15). For all heretics are hiding, and covering up the doctrines of their lies, that they may shoot in the darkness those who are upright in their heart.

Feria Sexta: Dn 6:11–24
S. Hieronymus, *Commentaria in Danielem* (in cap. 6, vers. 21)

"Deus meus misit angelum suum, et conclusit ora leonum, et non nocuerunt mihi" (Dn 6:22). Non leonum feritas immutata est: sed rictus eorum, et rabies conclusa

"My God sent His angel and closed the mouths of the lions, and they did not harm me" (Dn 6:22). The ferocity of the lions was not changed: but their roar and rage were shut up by

est ab angelo, et idcirco clausa, quia prophetae bona opera praecesserant: ut non tam gratia liberationis sit, quam justitiae retributio. Has autem voces, omnis sanctus vir proferat qui ereptus est de ore leonum invisibilium, et de lacu inferni: quia credidit in Deum suum (cf. Dn 6:25). "Tunc Darius rex scripsit universis populis, tribubus et linguis habitantibus in universa terra: Pax vobis multiplicetur. A me constitutum est decretum, ut in universo imperio et regno meo, tremiscant et paveant Deum Danielis. Ipse est enim Deus vivens, et aeternus in saecula, et regnum ejus non dissipabitur, et potestas ejus usque in aeternum. Ipse liberator atque salvator, faciens signa, et mirabilia in caelo et in terra, qui liberavit Danielem de lacu leonum" (Dn 6:25–27). Sicut Nabuchodonosor scribentem linguis et gentibus, quidam interpretatus est in contrarias fortitudines, ita et Darium interpretatur, quod omnes ad paenitentiam provocet. Ideo signa fieri per servos Dei apud barbaras nationes, ut unius Dei cultus, et religio praedicetur.

the angel, and therefore shut up, because the good works of the prophet had preceded it: so that it was not so much the grace of deliverance as the retribution of justice. But every holy man utters these words who has been rescued from the mouth of invisible lions and from the lake of hell, because he believed in his God (cf. Dn 6:25). Then King Darius wrote to all the peoples, tribes and languages inhabiting the whole earth: "Peace be multiplied unto you. It is decreed by me, that in all my empire and my kingdom all men dread and fear the God of Daniel. For He is the living and eternal God for ever: and His Kingdom shall not be destroyed, and His power shall be forever. He is the deliverer, and Savior, doing signs and wonders in heaven, and in earth: Who hath delivered Daniel out of the lions' den" (Dn 6:25–27). As Nabuchodonosor, writing to different languages and nations, was interpreted by some into opposite powers, so also is interpreted Darius, who calls all to repentance. Therefore, signs are to be done by the servants of God among the barbarous nations, so that the worship and religion of one God is preached.

Sabbato: Dn 9:1–5, 21–27
S. Athanasius, *Oratio de Incarnatione Verbi* (cap. 39–40)

Daniel et praesens tempus et divinum Salvatoris adventum his verbis praesignificavit: "Septuaginta hebdomadae contractae sunt super populum tuum et super urbem sanctam, et consummetur peccatum, et obsignentur peccata, et deleantur iniquitates, et remittantur injustitiae, et adducatur justitia sempiterna, et obsignetur visio et propheta, et ungatur Sanctus sanctorum, et cognoses et intelliges ab exitu sermonis ut respondeatur et aedificetur Jerusalem utque ad Christum ducem" (Dn 9:24–25). Quid autem ad haec dicere vel opponere habent, ubi nempe et Christus significatur, et is, qui ungitur, non homo simpliciter, sed Sanctus sanctorum esse declaratur, et usque ad ejus adventum stat Jerusalem, ac postea desinit propheta et visio in Israel? Olim quidem David, Salomon, et Ezechias uncti sunt, sed tamen et Jerusalem et locus stetit, prophetaeque vaticinati sunt. Praeterea, ii qui uncti fuerunt, homines quidem sancti vocati sunt, non vero Sancti sanctorum.

Daniel foretells both the actual date, and the divine sojourn of the Savior, saying: "Seventy weeks are cut short upon your people, and upon the holy city, for a full end to be made of sin, and for sins to be sealed up, and to blot out iniquities, and to make atonement for iniquities, and to bring everlasting righteousness, and to seal vision and prophet, and to anoint a Holy of Holies; and you shall know and understand from the going forth of the word to restore and to build Jerusalem unto Christ the Prince" (Dn 9:24–25). But what can they say to this, or can they face it at all? Where not only is the Christ referred to, but He that is to be anointed is declared to be not man simply, but Holy of Holies; and Jerusalem is to stand till His coming, and thenceforth, prophet and vision cease in Israel. David was anointed of old, and Solomon and Ezekias; but then, nevertheless, Jerusalem and the place stood, and prophets were prophesying. And again, the actual men that were anointed were called holy, and not Holy of Holies. For when did prophet and vision

Quando enim propheta vel visio ab Israel defecit, nisi cum Sanctus sanctorum Christus advenit? Magnum siquidem signum est indicium et Dei Verbi adventus, quod nec jam stet Jerusalem, nec propheta exsurgat, nec illis visio appareat. Postquam enim is, qui significabatur, advenit, quid adhuc signorum opus esset? Similiter praesente veritate, quid prodesset umbra? Unde tandiu stetit Jerusalem, ut illic veritatis figuras praemeditarentur. Quapropter praesente Sancto sanctorum, congruenter visio et prophetia obsignatae sunt, ac finem habuit Jerosolymorum regnum.

cease from Israel, save when Christ came, the Holy of Holies? For it is a sign, and an important proof, of the coming of the Word of God, that Jerusalem no longer stands, nor is any prophet raised up nor vision revealed to them. For when He that was signified had come, what need was there any longer of any to signify Him? Similarly, with truth was there, what good would a shadow do? And this was why Jerusalem stood till then—namely, that there they might be exercised in the types as a preparation for the reality. So, when the Holy of Holies had come, naturally vision and prophecy were sealed and the kingdom of Jerusalem ceased.

INFRA HEBDOMADAM IV NOVEMBRIS
Feria Secunda: Os 4:1–10
S. Gregorius Magnus Papa, *Homiliae in Evangelia*
(hom. 17, cap. 14–15)

Considerate ergo quid de gregibus agatur, quando pastores lupi fiunt. Hi enim custodiam gregis suscipiunt, qui insidiari gregi dominico non metuunt, contra quos Dei greges custodiri debuerant. Nulla animarum lucra quaerimus, ad nostra quotidie studia vacamus,

Consider what will become of the flocks, when wolves become shepherds! They undertake to guard the flock and are not afraid to waylay the Lord's flock. We do not seek to gain souls; we devote ourselves daily to our own pursuits, we attend to earthly matters, we strive

terrena concupiscimus, humanam gloriam intenta mente captamus. Et quia eo ipso quo caeteris praelati sumus, ad agenda quaelibet majorem licentiam habemus, susceptae benedictionis ministerium vertimus ad ambitionis argumentum; Dei causam relinquimus, ad terrena negotia vacamus; locum sanctitatis accipimus, et terrenis actibus implicamur. Impletum est in nobis profecto quod scriptum est: "Et erit sicut populus, sic sacerdos" (Os 4:9). Sacerdos enim non distat a populo, quando nullo merito suae vulgi transcendit actionem. Imploremus Jeremiae lacrimas; consideret mortem nostram, et deplorans dicat: "Quomodo obscuratum est aurum, mutatus est color optimus, dispersi sunt lapides sanctuarii in capite omnium platearum?" (Lam 4:1). Aurum quippe obscuratum est, quia sacerdotum vita quondam per gloriam virtutum clara, nunc per actiones infimas ostenditur reproba.

for human praise with all our will. From being set over others we have greater freedom to do anything we like, and so we turn the ministry we have received into an occasion for display. We abandon God's cause, and we devote ourselves to earthly business; we accept a place of holiness and involve ourselves in earthly deeds. What is written in Osee is truly fulfilled in us: "And so it will be, like people, like priest" (Os 4:9). A priest does not differ from the people when he does not surpass their deeds by any merit of his own. Let us invoke the tears of Jeremias. Let him look at our death and say with tears: "How the gold has become tarnished, its color been changed; the precious stones of the sanctuary lie scattered at the head of every street" (Lam 4:1). The gold has tarnished because the life of priests once made illustrious by the glory of its virtues, is now shown to be depraved because of its base actions. Its color has been changed, because that holy state has come into disgrace and contempt through worldly and despicable deeds.

Feria Tertia: Jl 1:1–11
S. Gregorius Magnus, *Moralia in Job* (lib. 8, cap. 48)

O miseri, qui affectantes laudes hominum, in semetipsis dissipant fructus laborum; cumque se ostendere alienis oculis appetunt, damnant quod agunt! Quos nimirum maligni spiritus cum adjactantiam provocant, eorum sicut diximus, opera captivantes denudant. Unde sub cujusdam gentis specie antiquorum hostium malitiam signans per prophetam Veritas dicit: "Posuit vineam meam in desertum, decorticavit ficum meam, nudans exspoliavit ficum eam, albi facti sunt rami ejus" (Jl 1:7). Insidiantibus quippe spiritibus, Dei vinea in desertum ponitur cum plena fructibus anima humanae laudis cupiditate dissipatur. Ficum Dei gens ista decorticat, quia seductam mentem in favoris appetitum rapiens, quo hanc ad ostentationem pertrahit, tegmen ei humilitatis tollit; eamque nudans exspoliat quia quousque in bonis suis absconditur, quasi proprii tegminis cortice vestitur. Cum vero mens hoc quod egerit videri ab aliis concupiscit, quasi spoliata ficus, eum qui se texerat

O wretched beings, who by going after the praises of men, waste to themselves all the fruits of their labors, and whilst they aim to shew themselves to the eyes of others, blast all that they do. Which same when the evil spirits prompt to boastfulness, taking them for a prey they strip bare their works, as we have said. Whence Truth in setting forth by the prophet the rancor of our old enemies, under the form of a particular people, saith, "He has laid my vineyard waste and barked my fig tree: he has made it clean bare, and despoiled it; the branches thereof are made white" (Jl 1:7). For by spirits lying in wait the vineyard of God is made a desert, when the soul that is replenished with fruits is wasted with the longing after the praise of men. That people barks the fig-tree of God, in that carrying away the misguided soul in the appetite for applause, in the degree that it draws her on to ostentation, it strips her of the covering of humility, and "making it clean bare despoils it," in that so long as it is withdrawn from sight in its good-

corticem amisit. Ubi apte subditur: "Albi facti sunt rami ejus" (Jl 1:7), quia ostensa humanis oculis ejus opera candescunt, de sanctitate nomen sumitur, cum recta actio divulgatur. Sed quoniam, subducto cortice, rami fici huis arefiunt, solerter intuendum est quia facta arrogantium homanis oculis ostensa, unde placere appetunt inde siccantur.

ness, it is as it were clothed with the bark of its own covering. But when the mind longs for that it has done to be seen by others, it is as though "the fig-tree despoiled" had lost the bark that covered it. And it is properly added there, "The branches thereof are made white" (Jl 1:7); in that his works being displayed to the eyes of men, turn white; a name for sanctity is gotten, when right practice is made appear, but whereas upon the bark being removed, the branches of this fig-tree wither, it is to be observed with due discrimination that the deeds of presumptuous men, when they are paraded before human eyes, by the same act whereby they aim to win favour, are rendered dry and sapless.

Feria Quarta: Jl 3:1–12
S. Hieronymus, *Commentaria in Joelem* (cap. 3)

Si autem ad diem judicii, quae scripta sunt, voluerimus referre, dicimus omnem qui salvatur, salvari in Ecclesia, sive in caelesti Jerusalem. Et postquam Judae fuerit et Jerusalem conversa captivitas, tunc congregandos et deducendos omnes in vallem Josaphat: et ibi disceptaturum

But if we wish to refer to the Day of Judgment what is written, we say that everyone who is saved must be saved in the Church, or in the heavenly Jerusalem. And after the captivity of Juda and Jerusalem had been turned, then they were to be gathered together and brought down to the valley of Jehoshaphat:

Dominum cum eis qui suum populum persecuti sunt, et diviserunt sibi hereditatem Domini, et disperserunt eos in nationibus (cf. Jl 3:1–2), et super terram illius miserunt sortem (cf. Jl 3:3): quae non solum super haereticis debemus accipere, qui sibi Dei populum diviserunt, et eos faciunt esse gentiles, sed ad omnem rigidum superbumque doctorem, qui sub nomine doctrinae et sacerdotii dominantur cleris, et opprimunt eos qui subjecti sunt. Haereticus quoscumque deceperit, et sua fecerit adorare simulacra, filios Juda et filios Jerusalem vendit Graecis (cf. Jl 3:6), sive gentilibus, et eos de Christianis ethnicos facit: ut exterminet de finibus suis, in quibus in Christo fuerant procreati, et nequaquam in Judaea, et veritatis confessione, sed in gentium errore versentur. Nos autem dicamus, quod et suscitavit Dominus post adventum suum (cf. Jl 3:7), et quotidie suscitat, et suscitaturus est eos, quos varius error eduxerat de finibus suis. Pulchreque suscitabo, ait, quasi jacentes et corruentes, ut qui iacebant in haeresi, stent in Ecclesia, reddens

and there the Lord would reason with those who persecuted His People, and divided the inheritance of the Lord among themselves, and scattered them among the nations, (cf. Jl 3:1–2) and over that land they cast lots (cf. Jl 3:3): which we must refer not only to the heretics, who have divided the People of God for themselves, and make them to be Gentiles, but to every rigid and proud teacher, who under the name of doctrine and priesthood dominate the clergy, and oppress those who are subject. Whomever the heretic has deceived and made people worship his own idols, sells the children of Juda and the children of Jerusalem to the Greeks (cf. Jl 3:6), or to the Gentiles, and makes of Christians pagans. The heretic exterminates them from their lands, in which they were begotten in Christ, and they live by no means in Juda and in the confession of the truth (i.e., in the Church), but in the error of the Gentiles. We affirm that the Lord also raises up after His coming (cf. Jl 3:7), and He raises up every day, and is about to raise up those whom various errors had led away from their borders. And I will raise

haereticis quod fecerant: Ut filios eorum et filias, quos et in mysticis et in carnalibus erudierant, tradat in manibus filiorum Juda (cf. Jl 3:8), in manibus eorum, qui Ecclesiarum principes exstiterunt; et instructi sunt armatura Apostoli, et habent scutum et lanceam veteris et novi Testamenti.

up beautifully, He says, so that those were lying and falling down, as those who were lying in heresy, stand again up in the Church, paying back to the heretics what they had done: that the Lord would deliver their sons and daughters, whom the heretics had trained both in the mystical and in the carnal, into the hands of the sons of Juda (cf. Jl 3:8), in the hands of those who are the leaders of the Churches; and they are furnished with the armor of the apostle, and have the shield and lance of the Old and New Testament.

Feria Quinta: Am 1:1–8
S. Hieronymus, *Epistulae* (Ad Sabinianum Lapsum, ep. 147, cap. 3)

Et in tribus et in quatuor impietatibus, nonne aversabor eum, dicit Dominus? (cf. Am 1:3). Dominus causas justissimas profert, dicens: In tribus et quatuor impietatibus nonne aversabor eos? (cf. Am 1:3). Sceleratum est, inquit, mala cogitare: concessi. Nequius est male cogitata velle perficere, et hoc pro mea misericordia benignus indulsi. Numquid et opere implendum peccatum fuit? et mea superbe calcanda clementia? Tamen et post factum, quia malo paeni-

Thus says the Lord, For three transgressions and for four shall I not oppose him? (cf. Am 1:3). The Lord wishing to show that He had most just cause for the wrath that He was going to bring upon them used the words already quoted, For three transgressions and for four shall I not oppose them? (cf. Am 1:3). It is wicked, God says, to harbor evil thoughts; yet I have allowed them to do so. It is still more wicked to carry them out; yet in My mercy and kindness I have pardoned. Has

tentiam peccatoris, quam mortem: "Non enim sani opus habent medico, sed male habentes" (Lk 5:31), jacenti manum porrigo, et conspersum in sanguine suo (cf. Ez 16:6), ut propriis fletibus lavetur, exhortor. Quod si nec sic paenitentiam vult agere, et fracto navigio tabulam, per quam salvari poterat, non retentat, cogor dicere: Super tribus et quatuor impietatibus, nonne aversabor eum, dicit Dominus? (cf. Am 1:3). Aversionem aestimans esse pro poena, dum suae peccator relinquitur voluntati. Inde est quod peccata patrum in tertiam et quartam generationem restituit (cf. Ex. 20:5), dum non vult statim punire peccantes, sed ignoscens primis, postrema condemnat. Alioqui si protinus scelerum ultor existeret: et multos alios, et certe Paulum Apostolum Ecclesiae non haberent.

not the sinful thought have become the sinful deed? "It is not they that are whole who need a physician but they that are sick" (Lk 5:31), even after his sin I hold out a hand to the prostrate sinner and exhort him, polluted as he is in his own blood (cf. Ez 16:6), to wash away his stains with tears of penitence. But if even then he shows himself unwilling to repent, and if, after he has suffered shipwreck, he refuses to clutch the plank which alone can save him, I am compelled at last to say: Thus says the Lord, For three transgressions and for four shall I not oppose him? (cf. Am 1:3). For this turning away God accounts a punishment, inasmuch as the sinner is left to his own devices. It is thus that He visits the sins of the fathers upon the children unto the third and fourth generation (cf. Ex 20:5), not punishing those who sin immediately but pardoning their first offenses and only passing sentence on them for their last. For if it were otherwise and if God were to stand forth on the moment as the avenger of iniquity, the Church would lose many of its saints, and certainly would be deprived of the apostle Paul.

Feria Sexta: Abd 1–11
S. Hieronymus, *Commentaria in Abdiam* (ad vers. 1)

Terram Idumaeorum adversariam esse terrae repromissionis, et Esau inimicum legimus Jacob, et populum esse cui iratus est Dominus in sempiternum (cf. Abd 18 et seq.), nosse debemus secundum leges tropologiae, aut contra Judaeos factum esse sermonem (qui sunt aemuli Christianis, et persequuntur fratrem suum Jacob, populum supplantatorem, qui illis primogenita praeripuit), aut certe adversus omnes haereses et contraria dogmata veritati, quae videntur quidem nobis esse vicina; sed magis adversaria sunt, et de paterna hereditate simplicem, et habitatorem domus Jacob nituntur expellere. Porro quia Idumaea et terrena interpretatur, et propter colorem rubrum cruenta quoque intelligi potest. Et in Isaia stupentes interrogabant: "Quis est iste qui ascendit de Edom, fulvida veste de Bosor, sic formosus in stola candida?" (Is 63:1). Et ad ipsum comminus loquebantur: "Quare rubrum est indumentum tuum: et vestimenta tua sicut calcantium in torculari?" (Is 63:2).

We read that the land of the Idumeans was the adversary of the land of promise, and that Esau was the enemy of Jacob, and that they were a people with whom the Lord was angry forever (cf. Abd 8ff.), we must know according to the laws of tropology [the moral meaning], or that the discourse was made against the Jews (who are the enemies of the Christians, and they persecute their brother Jacob, a people who supplanted them, who snatched away their firstborn), and certainly the discourse was against all the heresies and dogmas contrary to the truth, which indeed seem to be close to us; but they are more adversaries, and endeavor to drive out of the paternal inheritance the simple, and the inhabitant of the house of Jacob. Furthermore, because Idumaea is interpreted as earthly, and because of its red color it can also be understood as bloody. And in Isaias they asked in astonishment: "Who is this who came up from Edom, in a golden garment from Bosor, so beautiful in a white robe?" (Is 63:1). And they

Ipse loquitur in triumpho, exponens palmas crucis suae: "Torcular calcavi solus, et de gentibus non est vir mecum" (Is 63:3). Sunt qui Idumaeam ad carnem referant, et adversus illius pugnam animam aestimant provocari, ut mortificantes membra nostra super terram, fornicationem, immunditiam, passionem, aeternam in Christo victoriam consequamur.

said unto Him directly, "Why is thy raiment red, and thy garments like those trodden in a press?" (Is 63:2). He speaks in triumph, exposing the palms of His Cross: "I have trodden the press alone, and there is no man with Me of the nations" (Is 63:3). There are those who relate Idumaea to the flesh and consider the soul to be provoked to fight against it (flesh), so that by mortifying our members on earth, as they are fornication, impurity, passions, we may obtain eternal victory in Christ.

Sabbato: Jon 1:1–12
S. Gregorius Nazianzenus, *Orationes* (or. 2, cap. 106, 108)

Fugiebat quoque Jonas a facie Domini, vel potius fugere putabat; verum a mari, et tempestate, ac sorte, cetique ventre, atque triduana sepultura, majoris mysterii figuram gerente, comprehensus est (cf. Jon 1:3 et seq). Haec porro ineundae fugae causa ipsi erat, quod vereretur, ne cum tristem et praeposterum Ninivitis nuntium tulisset, periculo postea per paenitentiam liberata civitate, mendax inveniretur. Non enim improborum hominum salutem aegre ferebat, sed mendacii ministerium

Jonah also was fleeing from the face of God, or rather, thought that he was fleeing: but he was overtaken by the sea, and the storm, and the lot, and the whale's belly, and the three days' entombment, the type of a greater mystery (cf. Jon 1:3ff.). He fled from having to announce the dread and awful message to the Ninevites, and from being subsequently, if the city was saved by repentance, convicted of falsehood: not that he was displeased at the salvation of the wicked, but he was ashamed of being made an instru-

obire prae pudore non sustinebat, ac prophetiae fidem et auctoritatem velut zelotypia quadam
prosequebatur, quae quidem, ne
in ipso exstingueretur, periculum
erat, nimirum pericula multitudine
quae divini in hujusmodi rebus
consilii alttiudinem perspicere non
valet. Solus quippe ex omnibus rebus Deus est, qui nec fuga vitari,
nec superari potest, cum aliquem
arripere, ac sub manum et potestatem redigere voluerit. Celeres
antevertit, prudentes decipit, fortes
subvertit, sublimes contrahit, audaciam mitigat, potentiam premit.

ment of falsehood, and exceedingly
zealous for the credit of prophecy,
which was in danger of being destroyed in his person, since most
men are unable to penetrate the
depth of the divine dispensation
in such cases. For God alone of all
things cannot be escaped from or
contended with; if He wills to seize
and bring them under His hand,
He outstrips the swift, He outwits
the wise, He overthrows the strong,
He abases the lofty, He subdues
rashness, He represses power.

INFRA HEBDOMADAM V. NOVEMBRIS

Feria Secunda: Na 1:1–10

S. Hieronymus, *Commentaria in Naum* (ad vers. 9)

"Non consurget duplex tribulation"
(Na 1:9): falsa est ergo et crudelitas ejus quae in Lege descripta
est. Quod si verum est, ut negare
non poterunt, dicente propheta:
Non vindicabit Dominus bis in
idipsum in tribulatione: ergo qui
puniti sunt, postea non punientur. Si autem illi postea punientur,
Scriptura mentitur, quod dicere
nefas est. Receperunt ergo et qui
in diluvio perierunt, et Sodomitae,

"A double tribulation will not arise"
(Na 1:9): therefore, the cruelty described in the Law is false. And if
it is true, as they cannot deny, as
the prophet says: the Lord will not
avenge twice in the same tribulation, therefore, those who have been
punished will not be punished again.
But if they are punished again,
Scripture is lying, which is blas-
phemous to claim. Therefore, those
who perished in the flood, the Sod-

et Aegyptii, et Israelitae in solitudine, mala sua in vita sua. Quaerat hic aliquis, si fidelis deprehensus in adulterio decolletur, quid de eo postea fiat. Aut enim punietur, et falsum est hoc quod dicitur: Non vindicabit Dominus bis in idipsum in tribulatione. Aut non punietur, et optandum est adulteris, ut in praesentiarum brevi et cita poena cruciatus frustrentur aeternos. Ad quod respondebimus, Deum ut omnium rerum, ita et suppliciorum quoque scire mensuras, et non praeveniri sententia judicis, nec illi in peccatorem exercendae dehinc poenae auferri potestatem, et magnum peccatum magnis diuturnisque elui cruciatibus. Si quis autem punitus sit, tales postea non puniri, quia culpa levis praesenti supplicio compensata sit.

omites, the Egyptians, and the Israelites in the wilderness, all received their misfortunes in this life. Here someone might ask, if a believer is caught in adultery and is beheaded, what happens to him afterwards? For either he will be punished, and thus what is said: The Lord will not avenge twice in the same tribulation, is false, or he will not be punished, and it would be better for adulterers that they quickly and briefly suffer in this life rather than face eternal torment. To this, we answer that God, like He knows all things, also knows the measures of punishments, and the judgment of the judge will not be preempted. If anyone is punished, such a person shall not be punished again, because the slight fault has been compensated by the present punishment.

Feria Tertia: Hb 1:1–10
S. Hieronymus, *Commentaria in Naum* (lib. 1, ad cap. 1, vers. 1–2)

"Usquequo, Domine, clamabo, et non exaudies? vociferabor ad te vim patiens, et non salvabis? Quare ostendisti mihi iniquitatem et dolorem, videre praedam et injustitiam contra me?" (Hb 1:2–3). Et quomodo si aegrotus et

"How long, O Lord, shall I cry, and Thou wilt not hear? shall I cry out to thee suffering violence, and Thou wilt not save? Why hast Thou shewn me iniquity and grievance, to see rapine and injustice before me?" (Hb 1:2–3). And what if a

aestuans febribus aquam frigidam postulet, et dicat ad medicum: Vim patior, crucior, uror, exanimor: usquequo, medice, clamabo, et non exaudies? Et respondeat ei sapientissimus et clementissimus medicus: Scio quo tempore debeam dare quod postulas: non misereor modo, quia misericordia ista crudelitas est, et voluntas tua contra te petit. Ita et Dominus Deus noster sciens clementiae suae pondera atque mensuras, interdum non exaudit clamantem, ut eum probet, et magis provocet ad rogandum, et quasi igne excoctum justiorem et puriorem faciat. Quod intelligens apostolus secundum id quod misericordiam est consecutus a Domino, ait: "Non deficiamus in tribulationibus" (Eph 3:13). Et cum Jeremia dicit: Tribulationem, et miseriam invocabo (cf. Jer 20:8). Ut quomodo alius invocat Deum: sic sanctus vir et bellator invictus, ad exercendum se et probandum, tribulationem et miseriam venire desideret.

sick person, with fever, asks for cold water, and says to the physician: I am suffering from violence, I am suffering, I am burning, I am fainting: How long, physician, will I cry, and thou wilt not listen? And let the wisest and most merciful physician answer him: I know at what time I must give what thou askest: I will not be merciful, because that mercy is cruelty, and thy will demands against thee. Even so Our Lord God, knowing the weights and measures of His clemency, sometimes does not hear the one who cries, in order to test him, and to provoke him more to beg, and to make him more righteous and purer as if he had been cooked by fire. What the apostle understands according to the fact that he obtained mercy from the Lord, he says: "Let us not fail in tribulations" (Eph 3:13). And when Jeremias says: I will invoke tribulation and misery (cf. Jer 20:8). As another invokes God, so a holy man and an invincible warrior longed to come to tribulation and misery in order to exercise and prove himself.

Feria Quarta: Soph 1:1–9
S. Hieronymus, *Commentaria in Sophoniam* (ad cap. 1, vers. 8–9)

"Et visitabo super omnes qui arroganter ingrediuntur super limen in die illa" (Soph 1:9) hoc est, adversum superbos, qui cum quodam fastu et dignitatis supercilio, gradus templi et sanctuarii limen ascendunt. Visitabit Dominus in adventu et passione Salvatoris, id est, in die hostiae Filii sui super Pontifices et Sacerdotes populi Judaici, et super domum regiam. Usque ad illud enim tempus perseveraverunt reges Judae de stirpe David, secundum prophetiam Jacob: "Non deficiet princeps ex Juda, neque dux de femoribus ejus, donec veniat cui repositum est, et ipse erit exspectatio gentium" (Gn 49:10). Post hostiam enim Domini ablatum est regnum a Judaeis. "Et super omnes," inquit, "qui induti sunt vestimentis alienis" (Soph 1:8), qui recesserunt a protectione et indumento Dei, et suo errore cooperti sunt. Et ulciscar super omnes manifeste qui sunt in vestibulis, hoc est, qui egressi sunt de templo Dei: et cum deberent esse intrinsecus, propter peccata sua egressi sunt foras, et de Ecclesia Dei recesse-

"And I will visit in that day upon every one that enter arrogantly over the threshold" (Soph 1:9), that is, against the proud, who ascend the steps of the Temple and the threshold of the sanctuary with a certain boasting and prideful dignity. The Lord will visit in the coming and suffering of the Savior, that is, on the day of the sacrifice of His Son the pontiffs and priests of the Jewish people, and the royal house. For up to that time the kings of Juda continued to be of the line of David, according to Jacob's prophecy: "A prince shall not fail from Juda, nor a leader from his loins, until He comes to Whom he is appointed, and He shall be the hope of the nations" (Gn 49:10). For after the sacrifice of the Lord the Kingdom was taken away from the Jews. "And above all," he says, "who are clothed themselves in foreign attire" (Soph 1:8), who have withdrawn from the protection and clothing of God and are covered by their own error. And I will take vengeance on all those who are in the vestibules, that is, those who have gone out of the

runt, adimplentes templum ejus impietate et dolo. Hoc intellectum sit in primo Salvatoris advent.

Temple of God. Let this be understood referring to the first coming of the Savior.

Feria Quinta: Agg 1:1–10
S. Augustinus, *Enarrationes in Psalmos* (in Ps 111:1)

Ut fiat quisque lapis vivus ad talem fabricam idoneus, spiritaliter intellegat templi renovationem ex ruina vetere quae in Adam facta est, reparationem novi populi secundum novum hominem atque caelestem: ut sicut portavimus imaginem terreni, portemus et imaginem ejus qui de caelo est (cf. 1 Cor 15:49), quo possimus post omnes saeculi hujus aetates tamquam post septuaginta annos, qui mystico perfectionis numero praesignantur, et tamquam post captivitatem longinquae peregrinationis, non ruitura mole construi, sed aeterna immortalitate solidari. Hoc est templum Dei, ad quod pertinet sacramentum prophetationis Aggaei (cf. Agg 1:8–9) et Zachariae (cf. Zac 1:16): cui rursus idem apostolus dicit: "Templum enim Dei sanctum est, quod estis vos" (1 Cor 3:17). Quisquis igitur se ad opus hujus coaedificationis, et ad spem

That each man may become a living stone fit for such a building, let him understand spiritually the restoration of the temple from the ancient ruin which was made in Adam, as the renovation of a new people, according to the new and heavenly man: that as we have borne the image of the earthly, we may also bear the image of Him Who is from heaven, (cf. 1 Cor 15:49) that we may after all the ages of this world, the seventy years, as it were, which are fixed beforehand in the mystic number of perfection, and, as it were, after the bondage of a long pilgrimage, not be built together in a framework that shall fall, but be made firm by an immortality that shall last for evermore. This is the temple of God, unto which pertains the mystery of the prophecy of Aggaeus (cf. Agg 1:8–9) and Zacharias (Zac 1:16): to which again the same Apostle saith, "For the temple of God is holy, which temple you

sanctae firmaeque compaginis, tamquam lapidem vivum ab hujus mundi ruinosa labe convertit; intellegit titulum Psalmi ("Beatus enim vir qui timet Dominum, in mandatis ejus volet nimis," Ps 111:1), intellegit conversionem Aggaei et Zachariae. Cantet ergo quae sequuntur, non tam linguae voce, quam vitae. Erit enim aedificii perfectio, ineffabilis pax illa sapientiae, cujus initium est timor Domini (cf. Prv 1:7): inde ergo incipiat, quem coaedificat ista conversio.

are" (1 Cor 3:17). Whoever therefore converts himself to the work of this building together, and to the hope of a firm and holy edifice, like a living stone from the miserable ruin of this world, understands the title of the psalm ("Blessed the man who fears the Lord, who greatly delights in His commands," Ps 111:1), understands the conversion of Aggaeus and Zacharias. Let him therefore chant the following verses, not so much with the voice of his tongue as of his life. For the completion of the building will be that ineffable peace of wisdom, the beginning of which is the fear of the Lord (cf. Prv 1:7): let him therefore, whom this conversion builds together, begin thence.

Feria Sexta: Zac 1:1–6
S. Augustinus, *De gratia et libero arbitrio* (cap. 5)

"Convertimini ad me, et convertar ad vos" (Zac 1:3), unum horum videtur esse nostrae voluntatis, id est, ut convertamur ad eum; alterum vero ipsius gratiae, id est, ut etiam ipse convertatur ad nos. Ubi possunt putare Pelagiani suam obtinere sententiam, qua dicunt gratiam Dei secundum merita nostra

When God says, "Turn ye unto Me, and I will turn unto you" (Zac 1:3), one of these clauses—that which invites our return to God—evidently belongs to our will; while the other, which promises His return to us, belongs to His grace. Here, possibly, the Pelagians think they have a justification for their opinion which

dari. Talia ergo de Scripturis colligunt, quale est hoc unum quod paulo ante dixi: "Convertimini ad me, et convertar ad vos," ut secundum meritum conversionis nostrae ad Deum, detur gratia ejus, in qua ad nos et ipse convertitur. Nec attendunt qui hoc sentiunt, quia nisi donum Dei esset etiam ipsa ad Deum nostra conversio, non ei diceretur: "Deus virtutum, converte nos" (Ps 79:8); et: "Deus, tu convertens vivificabis nos"; et: "Converte nos, Deus sanitatum nostrarum" (Ps 84:7, 5). Nam et venire ad Christum, quid est aliud nisi ad eum credendo converti? Et tamen ait: "Nemo potest venire ad me, nisi datum fuerit ei a Patre meo" (Jn 6:65).

they so prominently advance, that God's grace is given according to our merits. Such passages do they collect out of the Scriptures—like the one which I just now quoted, "Turn ye unto Me, and I will turn unto you"—as if it were owing to the merit of our turning to God that His grace were given us, wherein He Himself even turns unto us. Now the persons who hold this opinion fail to observe that, unless our turning to God were itself God's gift, it would not be said to Him in prayer, "Turn us again, O God of hosts" (Ps 79:8); and, "Thou, O God, wilt turn and quicken us"; and again, "Turn us, O God of our salvation" (Ps 84:7, 5). For, with respect to our coming unto Christ, what else does it mean than our being turned to Him by believing? And yet He says: "No man can come unto Me, except it were given unto him of My Father" (Jn 6:65).

Sabbato: Mal. 1:1–11
S. Irenaeus Lugdunensis, *Adversus haereses* (lib. 4, cap. 17, 5)

Suis discipulis dans consilium, primitias Deo offerre ex suis creaturis, non quasi indigenti, sed ut ipsi nec infructuosi, nec ingrati sint, eum qui ex creatura panis est,

Giving directions to His disciples to offer to God the first-fruits of His own, created things—not as if He stood in need of them, but that they might be themselves neither

accepit, gratias egit, dicens: "Hoc est meum corpus" (Mt 26:26). Et calicem similiter, qui est ex ea creatura, qua secundum nos, suum sanguinem confessus est, Novi Testamenti novam docuit oblationem; quam Ecclesia ab apostolis accipiens, in universo mundo offert Deo, et qui alimenta nobis praestat, primitias suorom munerum in Novo Testamento, de quo in duodecim prophetis Malachias sic praesignificavit: "Non est mihi voluntas in vobis, dicit Dominus omnipotens, sacrificium non accipiam de manibus vestris. Quoniam ab orto solis usque ad occasum nomen meum clarificatur inter gentes, ut in omni loco incensum offertur nomini meo et sacrificium purum" (Mal 1:10–11). Manifestissime significans per haec, quoniam prior quidem populus cessabit offerre Deo, omni autem loco sacrificium offeretur ei, et hoc purum.

unfruitful nor ungrateful—He took that created thing, bread, and gave thanks, and said, "This is My Body" (Mt 26:26). And the cup likewise, which is part of that creation to which we belong, He confessed to be His Blood, and taught the new oblation of the New Covenant; which the Church receiving from the apostles, offers to God throughout all the world, to Him Who gives us as the means of subsistence the first-fruits of His own gifts in the New Testament, concerning which Malachi, among the twelve prophets, thus spoke beforehand: "I have no pleasure in you, says the Lord Omnipotent, and I will not accept sacrifice at your hands. For from the rising of the sun, unto the going down of the same, My name is glorified among the Gentiles, and in every place incense is offered to My name, and a pure sacrifice" (Mal 1:10–11)—indicating in the plainest manner, by these words, that the former people [the Jews] shall indeed cease to make offerings to God, but that in every place sacrifice shall be offered to Him, and that a pure one; and His name is glorified among the Gentiles.

ADNOTATIONES BIOGRAPHICAE AUCTORUM

BIOGRAPHICAL NOTES OF THE AUTHORS

S. Alexander Alexandrinus, Episcopus

Natus Alexandriae in Aegypto, qui, jam senex gloriosus ac fidei zelo succensus, post sanctum Petrum Alexandrinae Ecclesiae factus antistes, Arium presbyterum suum haeretica impietate depravatum et divina veritate infirmatum de communione Ecclesiae ejecit, quem mox inter trecentos decem et octo Patres annumeratus in Concilio Niceno Primo damnavit. Mortuus die 26 februarii anni 328.

St. Alexander of Alexandria, Bishop

Born in Alexandria in Egypt, by the time he was already a glorious old man with a burning with zeal for the Faith he became, after St. Peter, bishop of the Church of Alexandria. He expelled the priest Arius, corrupted by heretical impiety and deprived of divine truth, from the communion of the Church, whom he soon condemned at the First Nicene Council, being numbered among the three hundred and eighteen Fathers of the same Council. He died on February 26, 328.

S. Ambrosius, Episcopus et Ecclesiae doctor

Natus Treviris circa annum 340 e familia romana, studiis Romae incubuit et Sirmii cursum honorum coepit. Anno 374, dum Mediolani degebat, extemplo episcopus civitatis electus, die 7 decembris ordinatus est. Munere adamussim fungens, caritatem maxime exercuit in omnes, verus pastor et doctor fidelium factus. Jura Ecclesiae strenue tutatus est; rectae fidei doctrinam, scriptis et opere contra Arianos defendit. Mortuus est Sabbato sancto die 4 aprilis anni 397.

St. Ambrose, Bishop and Doctor of the Church

Born in Trier about the year 340 of a Roman family, he devoted himself to his studies in Rome and began the course of honors in Sirmium. In the year 374, while he was living in Milan, he was surprisingly elected bishop of the city and was ordained on December 7. Performing his duties diligently, he exercised the greatest charity towards all, becoming a true shepherd and teacher of the faithful. He vigorously defended the rights of the Church; he defended the doctrine of the right faith against the Arians by his writings and works. He died on Holy Saturday, April 4, 397.

S. Amphilochius Iconiensis, Episcopus

Natus est in Cappadocia circa annum 340, qui, sanctorum Basilii et Gregorii Nazianzeni in eremo socius et anno 373 episcopus Iconiensis in Lycaonia factus est, sanctitate et doctrina clarus, multa suscepit pro catholica fide certamina. Mortuus est circa annum 403.

St. Amphilochius of Iconium, Bishop

He was born in Cappadocia about the year 340. He was an associate of Sts. Basil and Gregory of Nazianzus in the desert, and in 373 became bishop of Iconium in Lycaonia. Famous for his sanctity and doctrine, he undertook many battles for the Catholic Faith. He died around the year 403.

S. Aphraates Sapiens, Monachus

Natus est circa annum 300 in Persia. Anachoreta, qui, apud Persas natus atque institutus, magorum vestigia persequens in Bethlehem ad Dominum se convertit et Edessam petens in domunculam extra moenia se recepit, Antiochiae demum catholicam fidem adversus arianos praedicatione et scriptis defendit. Mortuus prope Antiochiam in Syria circa annum 378.

S. Athanasius, Episcopus et Ecclesiae doctor

Natus Alexandriae anno 295, episcopo Alexandro in concilio Nicaeno astitit eique successit. Egregia scripsit opera pro fidei orthodoxae illustratione et defensione. Alexandriae in Aegypto orthodoxam fidem a Constantini temporibus usque ad Valentem imperatorem strenue propugnavit. Contra Arianos strenue dimicavit, propter quod multa perpessus est et pluries exsilio mulctatus. Mortuus est anno 373.

St. Aphraates the Wise, Monk

He was born around the year 300 in Persia. He was an anchoret who, having been born and educated among the Persians, followed in the footsteps of the Magi who came to the Lord in Bethlehem, and reaching Edessa, he lived in a little house outside the walls. He finally defended the Catholic Faith of Antioch against the Arians by his preaching and writings. He died near Antioch in Syria about the year 378.

St. Athanasius, Bishop and Doctor of the Church

Born in Alexandria in the year 295, he assisted Bishop Alexander in the Council of Nicaea and succeeded him. He wrote excellent works for the enlightenment and defense of the right Faith. In Alexandria in Egypt, he vigorously fought for the right Faith from the time of Constantine until the emperor Valens. He fought strenuously against the Arians, for which he suffered much and was punished several times with exile. He died in 373.

S. Augustinus, Episcopus et Ecclesiae doctor

Natus est Tagaste in Africa anno 354, adulescentiam doctrinis et moribus inquietam transegit, donec Mediolani, ad fidem conversus, anno 387 ab episcopo Ambrosio baptizatus est. In patriam reversus vitam asceticam professus est, et episcopus Hipponensis electus, per triginta quattuor annos forma gregis factus, illum erudivit sermonibus et scriptis copiosis, quibus etiam strenue contra errores sui temporis dimicavit vel fidem erudite illustravit. Mortuus est anno 430.

Epistula Barnabae

Epistula Barnabae est liber ecclesiae antiquae ad collectionem Patrum Apostolicorum pertinens. Etsi epistula vocatur, tamen potius tractatus theologicus est. Nomina neque auctoris neque accipientis dantur. Saepe modo allegorico argumenta confirmat. Cum prima epistulae mentio Alexandriae facta sit et ibidem praeterea allegoria floruerit, librum ibi conscriptum esse conjectura colligitur.

St. Augustine, Bishop and Doctor of the Church

Born in Tagaste in Africa in the year 354, he spent his youth turbulently regarding doctrine and the moral life, until in Milan, he converted to the Faith and was baptized by bishop Ambrose in the year 387. Returning to his country, he professed an ascetic life, and being elected bishop of Hippo, he became the form and model for his flock over thirty-four years, educating it with copious speeches and writings, with which he also vigorously fought against the errors of his time or eruditely illustrated the Faith. He died in 430.

Epistle of Barnabas

The *Epistle of Barnabas* is a book of the ancient Church belonging to the collection of the Apostolic Fathers. Although it is called an epistle, it is more of a theological treatise. Neither the names of the author nor the recipient are given. The author often reinforces his arguments in an allegorical manner. Since the first mention of the epistle was made in Alexandria, and there, moreover, allegories

Nonnulli Patres Ecclesiae (Clemens Alexandrinus, Origenes, Hieronymus) epistulam inter libros canonicos numerabantur; etiam in Codice Sinaitico inclusa est ab libris canonicis Novi Testamenti minime saepta.

flourished, it is inferred that the book was written there. Some of the Fathers of the Church (Clement of Alexandria, Origen, Jerome) counted the *Epistle* among the canonical books; it is also included in the *Codex Sinaiticus* but is not included among the canonical books of the New Testament.

S. Basilius Magnus, Episcopus et Ecclesiae doctor

St. Basil the Great, Bishop and Doctor of the Church

Basilius natus est Caesareae in Cappadocia anno 330 ex familia christiana; litteris eruditus et virtutibus micans, vitam eremiticam agere coepit, sed anno 370 episcopus suae civitatis factus est. Contra Arianos pugnavit; multa egregie scripsit, et praecipue monasticas regulas, quibus plurimi orientales monachi étiam nunc astringuntur; egenos magnopere iuvit. Mortuus est anno 379, die 1 januarii.

Basil was born in Caesarea in Cappadocia in the year 330 from a Christian family; educated in literature and shining with virtues, he began to lead a hermit's life, but in 370 he became the bishop of his city. He fought against the Arians. He published many excellent writings, and especially the monastic rules, by which most Eastern monks are bound to live even now; he greatly helped the needy. He died in the year 379, on January 1.

S. Beda Venerabilis, Presbyter et Ecclesiae doctor

St. Bede the Venerable, Priest and Doctor of the Church

Natus est circa annum 673 in Anglia, qui, famulus Christi ab anno aetatis octavo cunctum vitae tempus Girvi in Northumbria

He was born about the year 673 in England. Being a follower of Christ from the eighth year of his age, he spent the whole period of

Angliae in eodem monasterio peragens, omnem meditandis et exponendis Scripturis operam dedit atque inter observantiam disciplinae regularis et cotidianam cantandi in ecclesia curam semper aut discere aut docere aut scribere dulce habuit. Mortuus est die 25 maii anni 735.

his life at Jarrow in Northumbria, England, in the same monastery. He gave all his labor to meditating and expounding the Scriptures, and between the observance of regular discipline and the daily singing in the church it was sweet for him either to learn, to teach, or to sing. He died on May 25, 735.

S. Bernardus, Presbyter et Ecclesiae doctor

Natus est anno 1090 prope Divionem in Gallia. Pie educatus anno 1111 monachis Cistercensibus se adiunxit, et paulo post abbas monasterii Claraevallis electus, sodales actione et exemplo ad virtutes excolendas egregie direxit. Propter schismata in Ecclesia exorta, Europam peragravit ad pacem restituendam et unitatem. Multa scripsit ad theologiam et rem asceticam pertinentia. Mortuus est anno 1153.

St. Bernard, Priest and Doctor of the Church

He was born in 1090 near Dijon in France. Piously educated, he joined the Cistercian monks in 1111, and shortly after was elected abbot of the monastery of Clairvaux and led its members by action and example to cultivate the virtues. Because of the schisms that arose in the Church, he traveled through Europe to restore peace and unity. He wrote many things related to theology and asceticism. He died in 1153.

S. Caesarius Arelatensis, Episcopus

Natus est anno 470 in Gallia meridionali. Post vitam monasticam in insula Lirinensi ductam, circa annum 496 episcopus Arelaten-

St. Caesarius of Arles, Bishop

He was born in 470 in southern France. After leading a monastic life on the island of Lérins, around the year 496 he became, albeit unwillingly, the bishop of Arles in

sis in Provincia licet invitus factus est. Sermones festivitatibus congruos ad catechizandum populum presbyteris legendos paravit collegitque et regulas quoque tam pro viris quam pro virginibus conscripsit ad monasticam moderandam conversationem. Mortuus est Arelatae die 27 augusti anni 542.

Provence. He prepared sermons suitable for the festivals to be read by the priests to catechize the people and collected and composed rules both for men and for virgins to regulate monastic conversation. He died in Arles on August 27, 542.

S. Chromatius Aquilejensis, Episcopus

Natus est circa annum 350. Anno 387 electus est episcopus Aquilejae in Venetia, qui, verus artifex pacis, Italiae claustris ab Alarico dirutis ac populorum luctibus remedia comparavit et, Divini verbi mysteriorum exquisitus explanator, ad altiora mentes extulit. Mortuus est anno 407.

St. Chromatius of Aquileia, Bishop

He was born about the year 350. In 387 he was elected bishop of Aquileia in Veneto. A true architect of peace, he procured remedies for the regions of Italy destroyed by Alaric and for its mourning people, and an exquisite expounder of the mysteries of the Divine Word, he raised them to a higher understanding. He died in 407.

S. Clemens I, Papa et martyr

Natus est Romae. Tertius post beatum Petrum Apostolum, Romanam rexit Ecclesiam et ad Corinthios praclaram scripsit epistulam ad pacem et concordiam inter illos firmandam. Martyrio coronatus est exeunte saeculo I. Die 23 novembris depositio corporis ejus Romae colitur.

St. Clement I, Pope and Martyr

He was born in Rome. Third, after the blessed Peter the apostle, he ruled the Roman Church and wrote a letter to the Corinthians in order to establish peace and harmony among them. He was martyred at the end of the first century. On November 23, the deposition of his body is celebrated in Rome.

Constitutiones Apostolicae

Constitutiones apostolicae nomen est operis inde a saeculo IV, velut ab apostolis scriptum et per Clementem Romanum transmissum. Constat ex octo libris diversi propositi, inter quos sunt Didascalia Apostolorum et Didache. Magni interest aspectus disciplinaris vel liturgicus primaevae christianitatis ejusque evolutionis. Septimus liber, praeter nonnullas Didachei partes, seriem precationum et rituum in caeremoniis liturgicis ac pro catechumenorum usu praebet. Octavus liber continet textum *Traditionis Apostolicae*.

Apostolic Constitutions

Apostolic Constitutions is the name of a work from the fourth century, supposedly written by the apostles and transmitted by Clement of Rome. It consists of eight books of different purposes, among which are the *Didascalia of the Apostles* and the *Didache*. The disciplinary or liturgical aspects of early Christianity and its development are of great interest. The seventh book, in addition to some parts of the *Didache*, provides a series of prayers and rites in liturgical ceremonies and for the use of catechumens. The eighth book contains the text of the *Apostolic Tradition*.

S. Cyprianus, Episcopus et martyr

Natus est Carthagine circa annum 210. Ad fidem conversus et sacerdotio initiatus, anno 249 Episcopus Carthaginensis factus est, qui fuit sanctitate et doctrina clarissimus. Ecclesiam optime exit operibus et scriptis. Sub Valeriano et Gallieno Principibus, post durum exsilium, capitis detruncatione martyrium consummavit, sexto milliario a Carthagine, juxta mare. Mortuus est die 14 septembris anno 258.

St. Cyprian, Bishop and Martyr

He was born in Carthage around the year 210. Converted to the Faith and initiated into the priesthood, in 249 he became bishop of Carthage, and was most famous for his sanctity and doctrine. He served the Church meritoriously by his works and writings. After a hard exile under the emperors Valerian and Gallienus, he completed his martyrdom being beheaded six miles from Carthage, on the shore of the sea. He died on September 14, 258.

S. Cyrillus Alexandrinus, Episcopus et Ecclesiae doctor

Natus est Alexandriae. Ad sedem Alexandrinam in Egypto anno 412 electus, singulari pro catholicae fidei integritate studio in Concilio Ephesino dogmata de una in Christo eademque persona ac divina Virginis Mariae maternitate disseruit. Mortuus est die 27 iunii anno 444.

S. Cyrillus Hierosolymitanus, Episcopus et Ecclesiae doctor

Natus est circa annum 315 in Palestiona. Anno 350 Episcopus Hierosolymitanus factus est; qui, ab arianis multas fidei causa perpessus injurias et e sede saepe pulsus, orationibus et catechesi orthodoxam doctrinam, Scripturas et sacra mysteria fidelibus mire exposuit. Mortuus est anno 386.

S. Ephraem, Diaconus et Ecclesiae doctor

Natus est circa annum 306. Primum Nisibi in patria sua munus praedicandi et sacram doctrinam tradendi exercuit, deinde, cum

St. Cyril of Alexandria, Bishop and Doctor of the Church

He was born in Alexandria. Elected to the see of Alexandria in Egypt in the year 412, he argued for the integrity of the Catholic Faith, in the Council of Ephesus, the dogmas of the one and the same Person in Christ and the divine motherhood of the Virgin Mary. He died on June 27, 444.

St. Cyril of Jerusalem, Bishop and Doctor of the Church

He was born about the year 315 in Palestine. In 350 he became bishop of Jerusalem. Having suffered many injuries from the Arians in the cause of the Faith, and being often driven from his seat, through prayers and catechesis, he wonderfully expounded the right doctrine, the Scriptures, and the sacred mysteries to the faithful. He died in 386.

St. Ephraem, Deacon and Doctor of the Church

He was born about the year 306. First, in his own country, in Nisibi, he exercised the office of preaching and handing down the sacred

Persae Nisiben invasissent, Edessee in Osrhoene, quo cum discipulis confugerat, fundamenta posuit schola theoligicae, verbis ac scriptis ministerium suum adimplens atque austeritate vitae et doctrina adeo conspicuus, ut ob exquisitos hymnos compositos cithara Spiritus Sancti mereretur appellari. Mortuus est die 9 iunii anno 373.

doctrine, then, when the Persians invaded Nisibi, he established a theological school in Osrhoene, where he had settled with his disciples, fulfilling his ministry in words and writings, and was so conspicuous by the austerity of his life and teaching that he deserved to be called "the harp of the Holy Spirit" for the exquisite hymns he composed. He died on June 9, 373.

S. Fulgentius Ruspensis, Episcopus

Natus est circa annum 468 in provincia Byzacenae in Africa, qui, munere procuratoris Byzacenae functus, monachus evasit; deinde episcopus Ruspensis effectus, tempore vandalicae persecutionis, ab Arianis multa perpessus est et in Sardiniam a rege Thrasamundo bis relegatus. Tandem populo suo restitutus, eum per reliquos vitae annos veritatis et gratiae verbo fideliter nutrivit. Mortuus est die 1 januarii anni 533.

St. Fulgentius of Ruspe, Bishop

He was born about the year 468 in the province of Byzacena in Africa. Having served as the procurator of Byzacena, he became a monk; then was made bishop of Ruspe; during the vandalic persecution he suffered much from the Arians, and was twice banished to Sardinia by King Thrasamund. Finally, being restored to his people, he faithfully nourished them during the remaining years of his life with the word of truth and grace. He died on January 1, 533.

S. Gregorius Magnus, Papa et Ecclesiae doctor

Natus est Romae circa annum 540. Cursum honorum ingressus, praefectus Urbis renuntiatus est. Vita monastica inita, diaconus ordinatus et munere legati Constantinopoli functus est. Anno 590, die 3 septembris, ad Petri cathedram evectus, verum pastorem se exhibuit in rebus gerendis, in pauperibus juvandis, in fide propaganda vel firmanda. Multa etiam scripsit de re morali et theologica. Mortuus est anno 604, die 12 martii.

St. Gregory the Great, Pope and Doctor of the Church

He was born in Rome about the year 540. Entering the course of honors, he resigned the prefecture of the city of Rome. Entering the monastic life, he was ordained a deacon and served as ambassador to Constantinople. In the year 590, on September 3, upon being raised to the chair of Peter, he showed himself to be a true pastor in administration, in helping the poor, in propagating and strengthening the Faith. He also wrote much on moral and theological matters. He died in 604, on March 12.

S. Gregorius Nazianzenus, Episcopus et Ecclesiae doctor

Gregorius anno 330 prope Nazianzum natus, multas peregrinationes suscepit ad scientiam acquirendam. Amicum Basilium in solitudine secutus est, sed presbyter et episcopus ordinatus est. Anno 381 episcopus Constantinopolitanus electus est; attamen, propter factiones Ecclésiam suam dividentes, Nazianzum recessit, ubi mortuus est die 25 januarii anni 389 vel 390. Eximiae doctri-

St. Gregory of Nazianzus, Bishop and Doctor of the Church

Gregory was born in the same year 330 near Nazianzus and undertook many pilgrimages to acquire knowledge. He followed his friend Basil in solitude but was ordained a priest and bishop. In 381 he was elected bishop of Constantinople; however, because of factions dividing his Church, he retired to Nazianzus, where he died on January 25 in the year 389 or 390. Thanks to his exceptional doctrine and el-

nae et eloquentiae gratia, theologus vocatus est.

S. Hieronymus, Presbyter et Ecclesiae doctor

Stridone, in Dalmatia, natus est circa annum 340; Romae litteris studuit ibique baptizatus est. Vitam asceticam amplexus, in Orientem perrexit et presbyter ordinatus est. Romam reversus, a secretis fuit Damasi papae, ibique cœpit vertere sacros Libros in linguam latinam et vitam monasticam promovit. Bethlehem constitutus, mirum in modum Ecclesiae necessitatibus particeps fuit. Multa conscripsit opera, praesertim commentaria in sacram Scripturam. Mortuus est Bethlehem anno 420.

S. Hilarius Pictaviensis, Episcopus et Ecclesiae doctor

Natus est circa annum 315 Pictavii in Aquitania. Circa annum 350 ad sedem Pictaviensem evectus, sub Constantio imperatore Arianae haeresi addicto scriptis fidem Nicaenam de Trinitáte ac de Christi divinitate strenue propug-

oquence, he was called "the Theologian."

St. Jerome, Priest and Doctor of the Church

He was born in Stridon, in Dalmatia, about the year 340. He studied literature in Rome and was baptized there. Embracing an ascetic life, he went to the East and was ordained a priest. Returning to Rome, he was among the secretaries of Pope Damasus, and there he began to translate the books of the Holy Scripture into the Latin language and promoted the monastic life. Settled at Bethlehem, he shared in a wonderful way the needs of the Church. He wrote many works, especially commentaries on the Holy Scripture. He died in Bethlehem in 420.

St. Hilary of Poitiers, Bishop and Doctor of the Church

He was born around the year 315 in Poitiers in Aquitaine. About the year 350 he was raised to the see of Poitiers, and under the emperor Constantius, adherent of the Arian heresy, he vigorously fought for the Nicaean faith concerning the

navit, quapropter quadriennium in Phrygiam relegatus est. Commentaria quoque celeberrima in Psalmos necnon in Matthaei Evangelium confecit. Mortuus est circam annum 368.

S. Joannes Cassianus, Presbyter

Natus est circa annum 360 in Dalmatia. Massiliae in Provincia Galliae condidit duo monasteria, alterum pro viris, alterum pro mulieribus, et, longo rerum monasticarum usu peritus, de Coenobiticis Institutis et Collationes Patrum scripsit ad aedificationem monachorum. Mortuus est circa annum 435.

S. Joannes Chrysostomus, Episcopus et Ecclesiae doctor

Antiochiae natus est circa annum 349; optime educatus, vitam asceticam coepit, et sacerdotio initiatus, magno cum fructu munere praedicationis functus est. Episcopus Constantinopolitanus anno 397 electus, optimum se praebuit pastorem, mores cleri et fidelium ad amussim redigere satagens. Odio aulae imperialis et invidorum obrutus, semel et

Trinity and the divinity of Christ, after which he was exiled to Phrygia for four years. He also wrote the most famous commentaries on the Psalms and on the Gospel of Matthew. He died about the year 368.

St. John Cassian, Priest

He was born around the year 360 in Dalmatia. At Marseille in Provence of Gaul he founded two monasteries, one for men, the other for women; being for a long time an expert in monastic matters, he wrote about the Cenobitic Institutes and the Collations of the Fathers for the edification of the monks. He died about the year 435.

St. John Chrysostom, Bishop and Doctor of the Church

He was born in Antioch about the year 349; well educated, he began an ascetic life, and being initiated into the priesthood, he served with great success in the ministry of preaching. Elected bishop of Constantinople in 397, he proved himself to be an excellent shepherd, endeavoring to reform the morals of the clergy and the faithful. Opposed by the hatred of the imperial court and the envi-

bis exsulare coactus est; aerumnis confectus, mortuus est apud Comanam in Ponto, die 14 septembris anni 407. Multa dixit et scripsit ad doctrinam catholicam explicandam et vitam christianam recte informandam, ita ut nomine Chrysostomi appellari meruerit.

ous, he was forced to exile once, and then again; He died at Comana in Pontus, on the fourteenth of September in the year 407. He said and wrote much to explain the Catholic doctrine and provide a correct understanding of the Christian life, so that he deserved to be called by the name of *Chrysostom*, "the golden-mouthed."

S. Joannes Damascenus, Presbyter et Ecclesiae doctor

Natus est Damasci anno 675. Sanctitate et doctrina celebris, qui pro cultu sacrarum Imaginum verbo et scriptis adversus Leonem Isauricum imperatorem strenue decertavit et, monachus effectus in laura Sancti Sabae prope Hierosolymam, sacros hymnos composuit. Mortuus est circa annum 749.

St. John Damascene, Priest and Doctor of the Church

He was born in Damascus in the year 675. He was famous for his sanctity and doctrine, and vigorously contended with the emperor Leo the Isaurian for the worship of sacred images by word and writing, and, having been made a monk in the Laura of St. Sabbas near Jerusalem, he composed sacred hymns. He died about the year 749.

S. Irenaeus Lugdunensis, Episcopus, Ecclesiae doctor et martyr

Natus est circa annum 130 et Smyrnae educatus; discipulus fuit sancti Polycarpi, illius civitatis episcopi. Anno 177 presbyter erat Lugduni in Gallia, et paulo post

St. Irenaeus of Lyons, Bishop, Doctor of the Church, and Martyr

He was born about the year 130 and brought up in Smyrna. He was a disciple of St. Polycarp, bishop of that city. In 177 he was priest of Lyon in Gaul, and a little later

ejusdem urbis episcopus factus est. Opera composuit ad fidem catholicam contra Gnosticorum errores tuendam. Martyrio, ut fertur, coronatus est circa annum 200.

he became bishop of the same city. He composed works to defend the Catholic Faith against the errors of the Gnostics. He is held to have been martyred about the year 200.

S. Justinus, Martyr

Justinus, philosophus et martyr, Flavia Neapoli (Nablus) in Samaria, initio saeculi II natus est ex familia ethnica. Ad fidem conversus, multa conscripsit pro religionis defensione; exstant vero tantum duae Apologiae, Dialogus cum Tryphone et Demonstratio Apostolicae Praedicationis. Romae scholam aperuit publicasque habuit disputationes. Cum sociis martyrium subiit tempore Marci Aurelii, circa annum 165.

St. Justin, Martyr

Justin, philosopher and martyr, was born in the beginning of the second century from a pagan family in Flavia Neapoli (Nablus) in Samaria. Converted to the Faith, he wrote many works for the defense of religion; but there remain only two *Apologies*, the *Dialogue with Tryphon*, and the *Demonstration of the Apostolic Preaching*. He opened a school in Rome and held public debates. He was martyred with his companions in the time of Marcus Aurelius, about the year 165.

S. Leandrus Hispalensis, Episcopus.

Natus est Carthagenae in Hispania circa annum 549. Anno 584 episcopus Hispalensis electus est. Frater sanctórum Isidori, Fulgentii ac Florentinae, praedicatione et industria sua gentem Visigothorum, Reccaredo rege eorum adjuvante, ab ariana impietate ad catholicam fidem convertit. Mortuus est die 13 martii anni 600.

St. Leander of Spain, Bishop

He was born in Carthagena in Spain around the year 549. In 584 he was elected bishop of Sevilla. Brother of Sts. Isidore, Fulgentius, and Florentine, by his preaching and energy, he converted the nation of the Visigoths, assisted by Reccared, their king, from Arian impiety to the Catholic Faith. He died on March 13, 600.

S. Leo Magnus Papa et Ecclesiae doctor

In Etruria natus et ad Petri cathedram anno 440 evectus, verus pastor et pater animarum fuit. Fidei integritatem omnimode firmare satagens, Ecclesiae unitatem strenue defendens, incursus barbarorum pro viribus repellens vel mitigans, jure meritoque Magnus meruit appellari. Mortuus est anno 461.

S. Maximus Taurinensis, Episcopus

Natus est circa annum 380. Anno 390 primus episcopus Augustae Taurinórum in Liguria factus est, qui gentilium turbas paterno eloquio ad Christi fidem vocavit et caelesti doctrina ad praemium salutis direxit. Mortuus est circa annum 465.

S. Melito Sardianus, Episcopus

Natus est saeculo II in Asia Minore. Vixit in virginitate, et episcopus Sardianus in Lydia factus est; ut propheta Ecclesiae Asiae Minoris veneratus, qui Spiritu Sancto affatus cuncta gessit. Melito Palaestinam peragravisse

St. Leo the Great, Pope and Doctor of the Church

Born in Etruria and raised to the chair of Peter in 440, he was a true shepherd and father of souls. Endeavoring to strengthen the integrity of the Faith in every way, vigorously defending the unity of the Church, repelling or mitigating the incursions of the barbarians by force, he deserved to be called Great by right and merit. He died in 461.

St. Maximus of Turin, Bishop

He was born about the year 380. In 390 he became the first bishop of Turin in Liguria, who called the pagan crowds to the Faith of Christ with fatherly speech and directed them with heavenly doctrine to the reward of salvation. He died about the year 465.

St. Melito of Sardis, Bishop

He was born in the second century in Asia Minor. He lived in virginity and became bishop of Sardis in Lydia; as a venerated prophet of the Church of Asia Minor, who performed all things moved by the Holy Spirit. Melito asserts that he traveled through Pal-

affirmat, ut libros Veteris Testamenti probaret indicemque eorum faceret. Scripsit apologiam ad Imperatorem Marcum Aurelium pro defensione christianorum; confecitque alia scripta ad explanandum Sacras Scripturas, nota est ejus homilia "De Pascha." Mortuus est exeunte saeculo II.

estine in order to prove the books of the Old Testament and make a list of them. He wrote an apology to the emperor Marcus Aurelius for the defense of the Christians, and composed other writings to explain the Holy Scriptures. His homily "On the Passover" is well known. He died at the end of the second century.

S. Methodius Olympius, Episcopus et marrtyr

Natus saeculo II in Asia Minore. Episcopus Olympensis in Lycia, qui nitidi et compositi sermonis libros confecit et ad extremum persecutionis Diocletiani imperatoris martyrio coronatus est circa annum 312.

St. Methodius of Olympus, Bishop and Martyr

Born in the second century in Asia Minor. The bishop of Olympus in Lycia, he composed books of sermons in a clear and orderly arrangement, and was crowned with martyrdom at the end of the persecution of the emperor Diocletian about the year 312.

S. Rabanus Maurus, Episcopus

Natus est in Germania circa annum 780. Prius abbas monasterii Fuldensis, anno 847 ad sedem Moguntinam electus, quidquid ad honorem Dei facere posset numquam praetermisit, scientia vere peritus, eloquio disertus et acceptus Deo pontifex, appelatus est "Praeceptor Germaniae." Mortuus est die 4 februarii anni 856.

St. Rabanus Maurus, Bishop

He was born in Germany around the year 780. First abbot of the monastery of Fulda, he elected then to the see of Mainz in 847, he never neglected whatever he could do for the honor of God; truly expert in science and versed in speech, a bishop pleasing to God, he was called "Teacher of Germany." He died on February 4, 856.

S. Victorinus Petavionensis, Episcopus et martyr

Natus est in Pannonia. Episcopus Petavionensis exeunte saeculo III factus, ad explanandos Sacrorum Bibliorum libros multa edidit scripta et in persecutione Diocletiani imperatoris martyrio coronatus est circa annum 306.

S. Vincentius Lerinensis, Presbyter

Natus est exeunte saeculo IV in Gallia. Presbyter et monachus doctrina christiana et sanctitate vitae valde conspícuus et attente in profectum fidei animarum enixus. Mortuus est circa annum 450 in monasterio Lirinensi in Provincia.

St. Victorinus of Petau, Bishop and Martyr

He was born in Pannonia. At the end of the third century, he became bishop of Petau, published many works to explain the books of the Holy Bible, and was martyred in the persecution of the emperor Diocletian around the year 306.

St. Vincent of Lérins, Priest

He was born at the end of the fourth century in France. A priest and a monk, he was distinguished by Christian doctrine and sanctity of life and was attentive to the advancement of the faith of souls. He died around the year 450 in the monastery of Lérins in Provence.

Our mission is to publish authentically Catholic books that are traditional, accessible, and beautiful.

Benedictus Books takes its name from the opening Latin phrase of the Canticle of Zechariah, prayed daily in the Catholic Church since the earliest centuries. Our logo evokes the antiquity of Gregorian chant and the illuminated manuscript tradition, emphasizing continuity with the faith and worship of the past and the continuing relevance of our sacred patrimony today.

Benedictus Books was established in 2021 with the launch of our acclaimed periodical *Benedictus*, the "Traditional Catholic Companion"—a daily devotional drawing on the theological riches and customs of the ancient Roman Rite, and allowing for a deeper experience of the traditional Latin Mass, liturgical calendar, and writings of countless saints and theologians. This periodical reflects the three core values of Benedictus Books:

Traditional. We are committed to preserving and handing on the Faith of our forefathers without diminution or change, publishing works that are both inspired by and conformable to traditional Catholic doctrine, liturgy, and spirituality. Our primary focus is on republishing reliably orthodox works that help to promote the interior life and sanctification of the domestic church through classical forms of prayer and worship.

Accessible. Recognizing that many aspects of Catholic doctrine, liturgy, and custom have become obscured in recent decades, we place an emphasis on texts that explain and assist readers in mining the vast theological wealth that is contained and expressed in the traditional Roman Rite, as well as those writings of saints and scholars that have been profoundly shaped by the same.

Beautiful. Rooted in the perennial tradition of Western sacred art, we believe that texts treating such exalted subjects deserve a truly beautiful and durable presentation. We invest extensive time and meticulous care to create inspiring new typesettings with rich ornament and illustration, crisp typography, clean layouts, and classic bindings to make every book as pleasing to hold and look at as it is to read.

In order to be worthy of the noble content they contain, all of our books are crafted to the most exacting standards, allowing these priceless treasures from our Catholic tradition to be cherished for years to come.